The Education of Nations

The Education of Nations

A Comparison in Historical Perspective

Robert Ulich

Revised Edition

Harvard University Press
Cambridge, Massachusetts

© COPYRIGHT, 1961, 1967, BY THE PRESIDENT AND FELLOWS OF HARVARD COLLEGE

ALL RIGHTS RESERVED

SECOND PRINTING, 1972

DISTRIBUTED IN GREAT BRITAIN BY OXFORD UNIVERSITY PRESS, LONDON

LIBRARY OF CONGRESS CATALOG CARD NUMBER 67–27094

SBN 674–23900–8

PRINTED IN THE UNITED STATES OF AMERICA

Prefatory Note

When I recently reread the final chapters of this book, I approached them with the feeling that they would need to be brought up to date. But I was pleasantly surprised to find that there was not much reason for change. "The 'New' and 'Old' Nations and the Persistent Problems of Education" (Chapter X), as well as the "Concluding Remarks" (Chapter XI), seemed essentially as pertinent today as they were at the beginning of the decade. Again and again it appears that the large undercurrents in the ocean of human culture move more slowly than the waves we observe on the surface.

So I decided to leave these chapters as they are — testimony to how the world looked to an educational observer seven years ago. Some individual facts, of course, now belong to the past. But I would like to believe that every reader of such a book knows that Nehru died, that Sukarno lost the confidence of his nation (at least temporarily), and that the number of independent African states increased (from twenty-nine in 1961 to forty-three in the spring of 1967).

However, it does seem necessary that I add a chapter on new developments in the educational policies of the major nations described in this book. Even here, it appears, recent events have not been so decisive as we might have expected in our "era of change." Some countries have prudently advanced already existing trends; elsewhere, aimless floundering and lack of decision have prevented urgent reforms; and all have understandably hesitated to act radically in cultural areas, of which education is one, which are deeply rooted in a long social tradition. Good or bad, the tradition exists; and to tear the schools out of it, even against the wishes of parents and teachers, is a risk which every wise government will have to consider carefully.

Nevertheless, some new events should be recorded and some critical remarks are therefore desirable. Because a number of pub-

PREFATORY NOTE

lications have appeared about which the reader may wish information, a short bibliography has been added.

I can only hope that this revised edition will receive the same favorable reception as the first.

R. U.

Cambridge, Massachusetts
April 1967

NOTES TO THE READER

This book is intended to contribute to an understanding of the forces that have molded the educational ideals and systems of a number of nations. It is historical, because the author is convinced that one cannot comprehend the nature of the educational process without seeing it in its historical context. But this book is also comparative, because only by means of comparison will those features come clearly to light which distinguish the educational evolution in one country from that in others.

The combination of the historical and the comparative approach will reveal that despite all differences the so-called Western nations — to speak of them first — have much in common. If this were not so, they could only be described side by side, and not meaningfully compared. All true comparison needs a *tertium comparationis*. Our Western nations possess a unifying heritage that reaches through the Middle Ages deep into antiquity, and they all have participated in modern cultural movements that, ascending vertically with the evolution of modern culture, have also spread horizontally — movements like the Renaissance, the Enlightenment, nationalism, and the rise of science and technology.

Those nations that for lack of a better term are called in this book the "new nations" (though they often rest on old and venerable traditions, India and China, for example) distinguish themselves from the countries with a primarily European background by the fact that they have not gone through the renaissances that have formed our modern Western culture. But whether they like it or not, they are now confronted with the task of absorbing within a few generations movements such as rationalism, nationalism, and industrialism, which the Western nations were allowed to develop within centuries — though often even then with doubtful success. Here lies the cause of the gigantic world revolution which we now experience and with which the educator must be concerned just as much as the statesman, for it is mainly through education that these new nations try to diminish the distance between their efforts and ours.

While trying to understand the role of education in human history, one is driven from one stage of methodological contemplation to another. What are — this question emerges first — the really educative agents in man's development? If education means the forming of minds for constructive purposes, or the turning of passive into productively active human beings, almost every significant and wholesome event in a person's life educates: the political system as well as the physical environment within which he lives, his work, his community, his family, his religious and social affiliations, and perhaps his hobbies. To describe and evaluate completely all these educative streams that flow through each person and his group is beyond the capacity of any human mind.

Somewhere the line must be drawn. All we can do is to be aware of the limitations under which we labor when by "education" we understand primarily a conscious and institutionalized enterprise of humanity, in contrast to the vast variety of unconscious, environmental, cultural, and anticultural forces that may affect a person, a nation, and a civilization.[1]

However, this restriction cannot mean that in a comparative and historical study of education we merely describe schools and school systems from outside. If we wish to understand them we have to relate them to the surrounding political, cultural, and economic forces. It is, to give only some examples, highly relevant to the spirit and content of formal education to consider whether it operates within a hierarchical, monarchical, totalitarian, or democratic society, under a religious or mainly secular aspect of life, or under a primitive or technological form of production. But, unless the study of education is to turn into a study of civilization in the widest sense of the term, the analysis of political, economic, spiritual, and other influences must here be considered subsidiary, not as an end in itself.

Second, though for a treatise on education, especially in its

---

[1] See in this connection a most valuable essay by I. L. Kandel, "The Methodology of Comparative Education," *International Review of Education*, No. 3 (1959). Reprinted in *Thoughts on Comparative Education*. Festschrift for Pedro Rossello. (The Hague: Martinus Nighoff, 1959). This publication also contains other valuable contributions on the methodology of comparative education.

modern phases, the concept of nations recommends itself as the organizing category (for it is within them that school systems and their ideals develop), this concept is nevertheless deceptive. For history has not merely divided humanity into separate units; it has also created the world community of civilized men. The greatest in the past of every great nation continues to live in every other nation that participates in the cultural enterprise of the race. Thank heaven, there are the embracing qualities of intellectual and spiritual comradeship, sympathy, and empathy. Many a soldier remembers hours when, perhaps even with the gun in his hand, he felt nearer to a member of the enemy country than to a man in his own battalion. And every people, unless it forgets its obligations to humanity and thus degrades itself, is proud of its personalities who through their universality have enriched and bound together the cultural evolution of humanity. Certainly, men of this quality are nearer to each other, however far away in space and time, than to the Philistines within their own nations who may celebrate their birthdays with patriotic speeches.

At the very present, overshadowed by the cold war, our hope rests with the comprehensive minds who help us to understand that, despite all national wars and suspicions, humanity is a whole and that, whereas evil divides, there is also the good that unites. It is, therefore, the obligation of education, rightly conceived, to think of itself not only in terms of national cultures with their specific histories, boundaries, and competitions, but in terms of a universal tradition that leads man from narrowness and self-isolation toward the great and profound ideas that have emerged from the endless endeavors of humanity.

Third, the quantitative as well as qualitative problems increase when one thinks of the number of nations that should be included in a book like this. Switzerland, the home of Rousseau, Pestalozzi, Fellenberg, and Father Girard, or the Netherlands with its school reforms of the early nineteenth century, or the Scandinavian countries with their exemplary school system and their adult education deserve a prominent place in any comparative study of education. Yet I have not been able to include them. Nor can the few selections in any more than a general fashion adequately deal with the nations of the Orient. There is only one comfort — namely, that the principles of approach developed in this book are of a certain universality and can therefore be applied to varying situations even if these situations are not explicitly described. There must be a master motif to which the various national means and goals of education are subordinate. It is the desire inherent in every vital people to educate a younger generation of which the older can be proud and which, while reverent toward the tradition, will nevertheless contribute courageously toward constructive development. Such a goal, of course, needs physically and mentally sound leaders, parents, teachers, and pupils who possess a sense of the best that can be found not only in their own national environment, but in humanity as a whole. In this way individual, national, and international progress would fall into one. Even if there were not vested interests that militate against such a comprehensive concept of education, this goal would never be achieved. Yet, unless there were the unattainable as a constant voice and guardian in the conscience of man, he would still live in barbarism.

Finally, I was also tempted to deal more extensively than I have done with the development of higher education, especially since for many years I have given a course on this subject in the Harvard Department of History of Science and Learning. But this would have added too many pages to the size of this book. The reader who wants to know how I would have done it may be referred to my essays "On the Rise and Decline of Higher Education" in *Goals for American Education*, Ninth Symposium of the Conference on Science, Philosophy, and Religion (New York: Harper, 1950), and "The American University and Changing Philosophies of Education" in *Issues in University Education*, ed. Charles Frankel (New York: Harper, 1959).

ROBERT ULICH

Cambridge, Massachusetts
May 1960

ACKNOWLEDGMENTS

I am indebted to the Rockefeller Foundation for giving me a grant that made it possible for me to teach and travel abroad. My sincere thanks are due to Dr. Hedwig Schleiffer for her assistance in the research for this book, and to my wife for the patient interest she has shown during its preparation.

Pantheon Books, Inc., New York, has kindly permitted me to quote at some length from Jakob Burckhardt's *Force and Freedom: Reflections on History* (1943). I am also indebted to The Open Court Publishing Company for permission to reprint some paragraphs from Ockham: *Studies and Selections* (1938) and to the University of Chicago Press to quote from *The Renaissance Philosophy of Man* (1948).

Contents

CONTENTS

CONTENTS

PART ONE

HISTORICAL AND CULTURAL FOUNDATIONS

I

The Middle Ages

THE common origin of the earth's civilizations, hence also of education, is still hidden from us in the mist of prehistoric times. The establishment of the year "one" in the different chronologies of the Jews, the Christians, the Mohammedans, and other religious groups is due to mythical preferences, just as it is due to a specific system of values that the history textbooks of the older classical schools identified the beginning of our Western culture with the rise of Greece and Rome. Thus it can be questioned whether this treatise should begin with a description of the cultural forces of the Middle Ages. As a matter of fact, the first version of this book began with the contributions of the ancient Asiatic nations. Yet, the later decision is not arbitrary. For it is in the period of the Middle Ages that the Western nations and certain cultural constellations formed themselves, which, in spite of all transformations, still determine to a large degree our social and educational life.

Medieval man began his career with a bewildering heritage. Through the Bible and the writings of the Church Fathers he received the message of the Judaeo-Christian revelation; through encyclopedias and anthologies, also through a number of original works, he knew enough of Greco-Roman literature to see there the summit of secular wisdom; and through his own birthright the Teutonic warrior heritage was also in his blood.

But how reconcile these various forces? Christian theology emphasized, on the one hand, the difference between divine revelation and heathen philosophy; on the other hand, it tried to prove that the Greek Logos and the Christian God meet in the depth of meaning. The Gospel According to St. John says: "In the beginning was the Word" (Logos). Also, Plato has his heaven for the excellent, as Christianity produced a heaven for the saints. Those, he says, who have survived the most difficult tests in war and peace and "approved themselves altogether the best in every task and form of knowledge . . . shall depart to the Islands of the Blest and there dwell. And the State shall establish public memorials and sacrifices for them as to divinities if the Pythian oracle approves or, if not, as to divine and godlike men." [1]

Only a profoundly religious man could have conceived of such types of heroes and their apotheosis, but there is no Father, no grace, no revelation, and no semblance of Christian humility.

> And he opened his mouth, and taught them, saying,
> Blessed are the poor in spirit: for theirs is the kingdom of heaven.
> Blessed are they that mourn: for they shall be comforted.
> Blessed are the meek: for they shall inherit the earth . . .
> Blessed are ye, when men shall revile you, and persecute you, and shall say all manner of evil against you falsely, for my sake. [2]

In the Greek anthropocentric or autonomous tradition, man reaches up to the Divine, perhaps becoming divine himself; in the Christian tradition, God reaches down to save the sinner who surrenders to his judgment. There is a world of difference between the two.

Yet, the philosophy of the classical secondary schools of Europe was based on the idea of the compatibility between Christian and Greco-Roman wisdom. In the older humanistic institutions many teachers belonged to the clergy and the day began with chapel and prayer. Nevertheless, most of the day's work was spent with the interpretation of the pagan classics because for the future administrators of kingdoms and empires Caesar and Plutarch were supposed to be of more practical importance than Christ. To be sure, the difference was sometimes bridged by comprehensive minds, especially by those, like Erasmus of Rotterdam, for whom the Church Fathers represented the real consummation of antiquity. But the conflict increased by necessity when later generations were no

[1] *The Republic*, Bk. VII, 18.   [2] Matthew 5:2–5, 11.

longer able to consider the great pagans merely as "forerunners" of Christianity, but saw them in their own right and spirit. Thus many a sensitive man felt deeply troubled by his continual wavering between the Christian ideal of self-negation and the humanist ideal of self-realization. And the conflict is still with us in the endless discussion between the humanist and rationalist philosophies, on the one hand, and the Christian schools of thought, on the other. The split goes through our whole Western culture. And it certainly was the most hypocritical of all possible solutions — one that still exercises its influence in many countries today — that one centered the curriculum of the elementary schools designed for the poor around Christianity and that of the schools for the privileged around the classics. The first had to learn patience; the second, how to rule.

Just as in the realm of thought and learning, so also in the realm of practical ideas a real synthesis was never achieved. Examine the often-mentioned ideal of Christian chivalry, which, to a degree, is the original of the modern gentleman ideal. The Anglo-Saxon *Beowulf*, the German *Nibelungenlied*, the French *Roman de Roland* may be considered the earliest expressions of the knightly spirit. In the latter we read of the brilliant combat between Roland and D'Olivier, and then of the generosity that compels Roland to grant Olivier a respite and a new weapon. Or take the grandiose scene of the *Nibelungenlied* where the Margrave Rüdeger gives his shield to Hagen, the strongest among the enemies, knowing well that thus he prepares his own defeat:

"I am in grievous trouble," yet Hagen said, "The shield
That Lady Gotelinda gave me as mine to wield,
The Huns for me have batter'd and hack'd it out of hand:
In Friendliness I brought it unto King Etzel's land.

"If so be God in heaven would grant me of His grace
To hold as good a buckler once more before my face,
As that which thou dost handle, right noble Rüdeger,
No longer in the combat need I a hauberk wear."

"Right gladly would I serve thee as touching this my shield,
Durst I make thee the offer in spite of Dame Kriemhild.
But do thou take it, Hagen, and bear it on thine hand;
Ay! what if thou shouldst bring it to thy Burgundian land!" [3]

[3] *The Lay of the Nibelungs*, ed. Edward Bell, trans. Alice Horton (London, George Bell, 1898), Adventure XXXVII, "How the Margrave Rudeger Was Slain," p. 374.

Though the authors of these epics were under Christian influence, the noble heroes were anything but Christian. Their code of honor has a superb dignity, but it does not come from the Bible; it comes from the battlefield, and it survives as a powerful force in later military ideas. It is the forerunner of the duel, often fought by men who first went to church to pray before they tried to kill a man because of a delicate point of honor. All the later ideals of chivalry are, in the best case, hybrid adaptions of Christian influences to essentially glory-seeking ambitions. Wherever we look, only a good dose of superficiality (which is probably necessary for healthy living) can deceive us as to the essential duality in our civilization and our educational ideals.

But are these conflicts merely negative? Sometimes, if too polar and extreme, they were so. Often, however, tensions may lead the human mind into productive depths of existence it might otherwise miss. Furthermore, though they appear in our Western culture within a sequence of historical events — Greece, Rome, Christianity, the Teutonic conquest — these conflicts could not have had such a profound and lasting spiritual effect if they were not reflections of polarities potentially inherent in every human person. The Greek, the Roman, the Christian, and the warrior, the sense of love and the instinct of power, are in each of us, and they emerge with increased force the more sensitive and the more exposed we are to the allurement of life.

Tensions similar to those we observe in our Western history have been working in every great civilization. For certain periods one particular trend may dominate, especially if we look at it from afar. For example, up to some decades ago India represented to most of us a country of mystic transcendentalism — hence, so we thought, its passivity, its doctrine of nonviolence, its calmness despite all its sufferings. Yet, the upper caste of India descended from warring Indo-Germanic horsemen, and shortly after the liberation from English rule the most cruel slaughter began between Pakistan and Hindustan. Today the country is seething with political and industrial fervor. Similar contrasts have shaken Japan and China and emerge all over Africa. Obviously, we in the West are not alone.

Yet as, despite all inner contrasts, conflicts, and warfare, there are an India, China, and Japan, perhaps even an "Asia," so there is also a "Europe," not only geographically, but culturally. This Europe, looking on the globe like a small part of an enormous continent, has spread that hardly definable phenomenon we call Western culture over areas much larger than itself, over wide parts of Asia and Africa and over almost all the American and Australian continents.

How did this become possible?

The prodigious wildness, confusion, and energy that was Europe's after the Teutonic tribesmen had destroyed Rome and somehow settled within new and uncertain boundaries was gradually channeled politically into the feudal monarchical system of more or less hereditary lords and princes, ecclesiastically into the episcopal system, and educationally into a slowly emerging system of schools. Dependent as they were on each other, all three constantly overlapped. And in connection with this pattern of living there developed three great universal ideas, or ideals, each of which had its origin in classical times — the Holy Roman Empire (*Imperium*), which was the highest symbol of the political order; the Church (*Sacerdotium*), the system of the spiritual order; and education (*Studium*), which attempted to provide the theoretical foundation for both the divine and the secular order of the world. None of these ideals was ever fully materialized — which is in the nature of every ideal. Yet, each of them worked as an inspiring force within the European mind and helped it to persist even after the original impulses from which they had grown had faded.

THE THREE UNIVERSAL IDEAS

Imperium *and* Sacerdotium

The idea of a political unity of civilized nations goes back to Alexander the Great of Macedonia, who led his troops from Greece into India. His empire broke into pieces immediately after his death in 323 B.C., but it nevertheless formed the foundation for the Hellenistic world, particularly for the political ideas of the Stoic philosophers. They knew not only of nations, but also of internationalism, not only of men, but also of mankind. Thus, when about the beginning of our modern chronology the Roman Caesars organized large parts of Europe, Asia, and Africa into a political whole, they could refer to two great and then still-living memories: one of political nature, namely, the great, almost mythical, empire of Alexander, the whole Hellenistic world; the other of spiritual nature, the idea of "humanity." Despite the destruction of the ancient world the reminiscence of the great past was never completely extinguished. It was revived when in A.D. 800 Charlemagne accepted, though not without hesitation, the imperial crown from Pope Leo III, whom he had helped to return to his rebellious capital. Against the Eastern emperor in Constantinople, who had always claimed to be the real successor of the Roman Caesars, there now appeared a rival of Germanic, or more or less barbarian, origin, with his seat at Aachen. But, whatever the contemptuous sentiments of the Byzantine monarchy may have been, a great vision was reconstructed. The West had now its *imperator* (the title of the Roman emperor in his capacity as political sovereign). His mission was to unite the princes of Europe under a supreme monarchy and to protect the Church, ruled by the *pontifex maximus* (the title of the Roman emperor in his capacity as the highest priest of the realm). Both pope and emperor hoped to form a unity of transcendent sanction guaranteeing Christian morality within a world of conflict.

During the tenth to the twelfth century Europe had sometimes good reason to cherish the hope that there would be a European power strong enough to guarantee some degree of authority in a troubled world. But in the course of time the original companionship between empire and papacy dissolved into bitter hatred. When Charles entered Rome in 800, the papacy had been suffering from a gradual shrinkage of power. Even from the ninth until the middle of the eleventh century it was a tool in the hands of the Roman aristocracy and other political factions. But then began the reform. The Order of the Cluniac Benedictines, with its seat at Cluny, had become the source of the moral revival of French monasteries; for about two hundred years, from 910–1157, it had had a succession of seven great abbots whose authority spread over all Europe. St. Bernard of Clairvaux, of the Cistercian Order (1090–1153), a strange mixture of ruthless radicalism and charity, kindled new fires of religious transcendentalism; for a while he was the actual ruler of Christendom. The crusades (1096–1291) gave, at least in their beginning, a goal to Christian enthusiasm and knightly energy. In 1059 the papal election was removed from the influence of the great families of Rome (though not entirely, as the Borgia's and Medici's proved later in the Renaissance). And there followed the appointment of one of the strongest men to ever occupy the Papal See, Hildebrand of the Cluniac Order, who reigned as Pope Gregory VII from 1073 to 1085.

This priest's work can be understood only in view of the decisive fact in the history of the medieval papacy, namely, that more often than a spiritual source, it was a feudal power, rivaling with the other princes of the world in the conquest and defense of territory, in the widening and preservation of political influence, and in the mastery of ruthless diplomatic conspiracies.

If the claims of Gregory VII and his successors, based on the spurious donation of Constantine, had become reality, then, according to feudal law, all monarchs of Europe except the Greek would have been vassals of the pope. At the same time, according to Gregory's intention, all the holders of abbeys and bishoprics, of which there were many hundreds, would have been directly dependent on the Church, with no interference possible on the part of the government in which these ecclesiastical territories were situated. With such enormous might to wield and administer, the papacy would soon have completely succumbed to the sins and devices of power politics; it would have become an idolatrous and demonic power, and for some centuries it actually was. The clash between secular and ecclesiastical forces was bound to occur, and the Holy Roman Empire, thus far the protecting and even the judging authority over the popes, was naturally the first to be forced into battle. This battle was the end of the dreams not only of the emperors, but also of Pope Gregory and his successors.

The mental and moral derangement that issued from the confusion of values in an age so often praised for its spiritual unity is most strikingly reflected in the correspondence between the Emperor Frederick II (1215–1250) of the German House of Hohenstaufen and the Papal See. As King of Germany and ruler over Sicily and southern Italy, Frederick threatened to encircle the papal states, while, as one of the first free minds influenced by Arabic philosophy and art, he threatened to undermine the ecclesiastical claim for absolute authority in matters religious. In his southern realm he developed the pattern of bureaucratic absolutism that later was taken over by France and other nations. He also dreamed of the salvation of European society by a universal monarchy raised above the strife of nations by its synthesis of political power and spiritual purity. In his younger years a man of unusual vision, of the kind that sometimes results when genius and power unite in one person, he became one of the most ruthless despots in the raging battle with the Church, a battle in which his enemies did not refrain from bribing, waylaying, and even poisoning. But, in order to let the actors speak themselves, let us read parts of an exchange of documents of the year 1239 between Frederick and Gregory IX, connected with the second excommunication of the Emperor because of his refusal to support a new crusade.

The papal message with its redundant style and symbolic language is hard to translate into modern English. As in all solemn medieval documents, frequent reference is made to the Bible; both the Pope and the Emperor allude especially to the Revelation of St. John, which because of its obscure content permitted any sort of allegorical abuse. The Pope, in comparing the Emperor with "the beast that rises up out of the sea," refers to chapter 13, while the Emperor, in comparing the Pope with the great dragon, quotes chapter 12 of the same book.

A beast rises up out of the sea full of names of profanity. Raging with the claws of a bear and the mouth of a lion, it has the limbs of a panther. When it opens its mouth it utters blasphemy. Nor does it cease to throw spears against the tabernacle of God. This monster tries to crush everything. With its feet it would like to trample the whole earth to pieces. Secretly it has built battering rams against our faith, and now, in plain light, it directs against us the power of the Saracens (*nunc apertas machinas instruit Israelitarum*). This beast prepares the arenas of spiritual corruption and stands up, so rumor goes, against Christ, the Savior of mankind, whose gospel it tries to destroy with heretical ideas. Hence, you all who may hear of the calumnies thrown against me by this monster cease to be astounded that we who attempt to live in the servitude of the Lord are attacked by his arrows — even the Lord himself has not remained immune from his onslaught. Cease to be astounded that this sort of defamation is directed against us by a man who girds himself to wipe the name of the Lord from this earth.

Nay, that you may be able to resist its lies in the spirit of truth and to refute its fallacies with the argument of purity, look carefully at the head, the body, and the tail of this beast, this so-called Emperor Frederick. Then, discovering the abomination and sinfulness of his words, arm yourselves against his guile with the shield of verity and observe how Frederick, this arrogant potter of falsity, attempts to defile the Apostolic See and my sincerity through polluted letters and rumors, which he sends over the world.[4]

In the following sentences the Pope, distorting facts for the mere purpose of conjuring up before the Christian world the image of a world-destroying monster, heaps calumny after calumny on the Emperor. He, so the letter says, betrayed the crusaders at Brindisi, poisoned the Margrave of Thuringia (his main German rival supported by the Pope). He entered into a plot with the Sultan of the Holy Land, and he has made Sicily a hell of injustice, enslavement, and impoverishment.

In contrast, what a picture of humility, he, the Pope himself! He confesses himself unworthy of being the vicar of Christ; what human being could carry such burden without divine help? Nevertheless, not as a person, but as Christ's delegate and successor to St. Peter, he has the right to bind and to loose, or to ban and to absolve; he holds the key by which to open and close the doors to the Church, and through them the doors to salvation.

At the end of the letter the Pope uses the sharpest weapon he can think of in order to defame the Emperor in the eyes of the Christian world. Frederick, so he says, "iste rex pestilentiae," has asserted that by

three imposters, namely, Jesus Christ, Moses, and Mohammed, the whole world has been deceived. And, while two of them died in glory, this same Christ was suspended from a tree. Furthermore, Frederick has spread the damnable lie that all those are simpletons who believe that a God, Creator of nature and all that is, could have been born from a virgin. This heresy he even tried to corroborate with the error that no one can be borne whose conception has not been preceded by the intercourse between man and woman, and that man should believe nothing that he cannot prove by the

[4] Encyclica of Pope Gregory against Frederick II (1239), in *Historia Diplomatica Frederici Secundi*, ed. J. L. A. Huillard-Bréholles (Paris, 1857), Vol. V, Part I, p. 327f. Freely translated by the author.

force and law of nature (*et homo nihil debet aliud credere nisi quod potest vi et ratione nature probare*).

To this letter *Fridericus, Romanorum imperator*, responds as follows:

At the beginning of the world divine and ineffable Providence, free from all alien influence, has set two luminaries into the firmament of heaven, a larger and a smaller, the larger that it reign over the day, the smaller that it reign over the night. These two luminaries fulfill their duties in the constellation of the zodiac so that — though sometimes looking obliquely at each other — they avoid mutual offense. Rather the superior star gives its light to the inferior. Similarly, eternal Providence wished to have two dominions set up on the earthly firmament, the *sacerdotium* and the *imperium*, the one for the guidance of the souls, the other for their protection, so that man who for long was split in his two components might be restrained by two bridles. Thus all excesses should be limited and peace should be on earth.

But the man who now sits on the seat of perverted dogma, this pharisee anointed with the oil of iniquity, this highest Roman priest, wishes even more than his companions to annihilate that which has its reason in the emulation of divine order.

And thus he believes to be in agreement with the superior powers that are dependent on nature, but not on will; he intends to eclipse our majesty's splendor when he changes truth into lie and sends to different parts of the world papal letters full of falsehood and concoctions by which to accuse the purity of our faith. This Pope — pope only according to the word — has written that a beast rises out of the sea, full of names of profanity, and looking like a panther in every fashion. But now it is us who declare that he himself is the monster of which it is said that there emerged another horse from the sea, a red one, and its rider took away peace from the earth so that the living killed each other.

For since his appointment this father, not of pity, but of discord, this provider of desolation rather than of consolation, has filled the whole world with scandal. And, if we interpret his words correctly, he himself is the great dragon who has seduced the whole world; he is the Antichrist whose forerunner, so he said, we were. He is the other Balaam, hired for money to excommunicate us; he is the prince of the princes of darkness who have abused the prophecies. He is the angel emerging from the abyss, holding the cup of bitterness to do harm to the sea and the land.

This false vicar of Christ has mixed into his lies the statement that we do not justly adhere to the Christian religion and that we have spoken of three deceitful seducers of the world, a word that, be sure, could never have come from our lips. For we profess openly that there is one only Son of God, coeternal and coequal to the Father and the Holy Ghost, our Lord

Jesus Christ, created from the beginning and before all days, sent to earth in the process of time for the succor of mankind, not from potency he received, but from his own potency (*non de potentia ordinata, sed de potentia ordinante*), who was borne from the glorious Virgin mother, who has then suffered, and who died according to the flesh and his second nature, which he assumed in the womb of his mother, but by the power of deity he rose from his grave after three days.

In contrast, about Mohammed we have learned that his body lies suspended in the air, besieged by demons, with his soul thrown into the tortures of hell, for his works were of darkness and against the will of the Highest. And from Moses we hold that he was the friend and confident of God, that he spoke with him on Mount Sinai, that God appeared to him in a flame of fire out of a bush and caused him to do signs and miracles in Egypt. The tradition says that later he was called to the glory of the elect . . .

And because the injuries that the Pope inflicts to our majesty persist, and because we cannot tolerate them nor relax our power, we are forced to revenge ourselves. But you who should assist him with wise council and possess the excellence of insight and judgment, recall this howling enemy of ours from the action that was detestable from its beginning and pay attention to the consequences that must come from the preceding causes. Otherwise here and there the earth will feel how the Augustus will proceed against his persecutor and the princes and patrons who follow him. With his sword he will bring upon them the punishment of a Caesar.[5]

I have quoted from these letters at some length because they are of extreme interest to the historian of culture and education. Rather than using our modern logical principles, thinking is still involved in symbols and allegories. The sun-moon metaphor is accepted even by the chancellery of the assumedly heretical Emperor. Furthermore, in public debate both of the two "antichrists" accept the Christian framework of thought. The very fact that they call each other by apocalyptic names is proof of it. On the other hand, the powerful vocabulary has lost its meaning through abuse. One no longer believes in it. In actuality, Frederick entered as a crusader into Jerusalem under ban of excommunication; secular as well as earthly princes took sides for or against him according to the constellation of interests, not according to faith. For the popes themselves, banning and absolving had become a matter of expediency.

In spite of mythical thinking a certain empiricism begins to

[5] *Ibid.*, Vol. V, Part I, p. 348f.

assert itself. Though the Pope declares as heresy any doubt in the virgin birth of Christ, the doubt had nevertheless been expressed. "And . . . man should believe nothing that he cannot prove by the force of law and nature."

Comparison between cultures and religions, as was inevitable in the Sicilian realm of Frederick's empire, bred partly tolerance, partly cynicism. Tolerance appeared in the parable of the "Three Rings," used later by Boccaccio and Lessing, according to which Judaism, Christianity, and Islam are like three indistinguishable rings given by a kind father to his equally loved three sons. Cynicism emerges in the story according to which Moses, Christ, and Mohammed were not representatives of the divine principle, but "three impostors."

On the whole, the world around the Mediterranean entered from a narrow and secluded Europe into a new atmosphere of international contact. The crusades themselves prepared for what they intended to prevent. The whole medieval structure began to crack as a result of the conduct of those who felt the mission to defend it. The Holy Roman Empire was defeated by the popes and their allies, and the popes were led into the Captivity of Avignon by a France that had profited from the strife of the two great rivals.

Yet, the edifice of medievalism stood for about two more centuries, mainly because the new system of absolutism that was to replace the feudal order had not yet ripened. And, as we will see later in the discussion of the *studium*, it would be incorrect to speak of an end of the Middle Ages. In spite of bitterness, corruption, and disillusion, there was no exhaustion, but a change of ideas. Everywhere there began "a dozen little renaissances" during which "men learned to doubt, to think, and to criticize, until at last the more energetic and venturesome spirits became weary of their bargain of lifelong dependence on the Church in return for effective religious control." [6]

Thus, in time, Gregory VII's doctrine of papal supremacy over earthly governments was systematically scrutinized by Churchmen themselves. Among the heralds of a new period, besides the more passionate Marsilius of Padua, William of Occam (*c.* 1300–

[6] *De Imperatorum et Pontificum Potestate* (of William of Occam), ed. C. Kenneth Brampton (Oxford: Clarendon Press, 1927).

c. 1349) impressed his contemporaries by his steadfast courage. Despite all persecution, with Ludwig of Bavaria often his only protector, he assailed the papal abuse of excommunication, the alienation of subjects from their princes, the expulsion of men from their property, and the condemnation of thinking men as heretics. The spirit of the Protestant Reformation, even more, a spirit of free and empirical research such as that advocated by neither Luther nor Calvin, appeared in Occam, the disciple of Roger Bacon. The seeds planted during the era of Frederick II began to burst their shells and appear in more and more places above the ground of the earth. But let us hear the voice of Occam himself.

In matters of faith and of science I am more impressed by one evident reason or by one authoritative passage of the Holy Writ correctly understood than by the common chorus of mankind. I am not ashamed to be convinced by truth. In fact, to have truth victorious over me I estimate the most useful thing for me, but I never want to be defeated by the multitude.

In appointing Saint Peter to be the head and sovereign of all the faithful, Christ assigned to his power certain limits which he was not to overstep. That Christ did not give him a plenitude of power in temporal matters can be proved by authority and reason. But not even in spiritual matters is he endowed with such plenitude of power, because, then, the law of the Gospel, which Saint James, in his canonical letter, chapter 1, calls a "law of perfect liberty," would impose a greater servitude than the law of Moses . . . Whenever, therefore, the pope, in case of necessity, meddles in temporal affairs, he is thrusting his sickle in alien crops, unless he be entrusted with power to do so by the emperor or by some other person . . .

In the same spirit, scientific assertions, especially those of the realm of natural philosophy which are not related to theology, are not to be condemned by anybody in a solemn way nor to be forbidden. In such things everybody ought to be free to say freely whatever he pleases . . .

The church of Avignon tries to rule over all Christians tyrannically, inflicting upon the faithful of Christ serious and enormous injustices. To do this more freely and without any fear, she persecutes tyrannically all those who dare to start an argument about her powers, even though they do it with the best of motives . . .

The church of Avignon does an especial wrong to the Roman Empire by claiming greater temporal right over it than over other kingdoms. This church does not possess such prerogative over the Roman Empire either by divine or human right. The Roman Empire was earlier than the papacy. Its inceptions did not spring from the pope and, consequently, it cannot be subjected to the pope after the institution of the papacy.

The church of Avignon, further, does injustice not only to the Roman

Empire but, as regards ecclesiastical affairs, to all Christians too, in a very material way. They usurp a power which they do not possess, depriving the faithful, clergy and laity, of their possessions, rights and liberties. They impose upon their shoulders unsupportable burdens. They instigate warfare among the Christians, sedition and discord and foment them after instigation. They impose wicked sentences and unjust procedures, trapping the simple minded. They materially impede the progress of science and coerce the more learned and intelligent to submit their intellect to them in captivity, against reason and against the holy scriptures. Innumerable other injustices and excesses could be adduced, whereby they afflict the Christian people, disturb them, seduce them and try to force them into servitude against the liberty of the law of Gospel.

It is my conviction that peace will never be confirmed between the occupants of the apostolic seat and the rest of the Christians, until the clergy and laity settle irrefragably, and sanction what powers the pope possesses by divine right. As long as the multitude of the faithful is ignorant of this, the stubborn strife between the pope and the people will not cease.[7]

William of Occam, though thrown into jail for his defense of freedom, expressed what intelligent men already felt. The power of the papacy to extend its absolutist claims from the religious over into the political and intellectual realm was declining rapidly. There were still cases when a pope was called to influence the policy of governments. In 1493, for example, the newly arisen colonial powers asked Pope Alexander VI for help in settling their territorial claims in foreign continents. But they did so not out of respect for a pope who was one of the most corrupt ecclesiastics the Church has ever had, but because there was need for a court that was Catholic and had no immediate interest in colonial expansion On the whole, the decades before and during the Renaissance were decades of reckless exploitation of the faithful and the local churches, of shameless nepotism, crime, and luxury.

Probably recognizing the end of an era, the popes of the Renaissance turned their interest toward art and the new learning. There were still the papal states with their political affiliations, but the Donation of Constantine, which once had caused endless harm, could no longer remain a point of principle after the humanist Lorenzo Valla (1407–1457) had proved it a forgery.

[7] Taken from Stephen Chak Tornay, *Ockham: Studies and Selections* (LaSalle: Open Court Publishing Co., 1938), pp. 196–201, "Political Philosophy." (Quotations taken from *De Imperatorum et Pontificum Potestate* and from *Dialogus inter Magistrum et Discipulum de Imperatorum et Pontificum Potestate*.)

THE MIDDLE AGES

Studium

The Rise. By the third universal idea, the *studium*, I understand not any one particular institution, but the totality of the intellectual endeavor of the Middle Ages, though I will have to speak primarily of the universities.

The *imperium* and the *sacerdotium*, at their best, were not only attempts at political and ecclesiastical unification; they were also attempts at cultural continuity. Without the claim of the emperor to be the successor of the Caesars, and of the pope to be the successor of Christ, or at least of St. Peter, the hope of unification would have been idle. For medieval man had little respect for his own culture; his own achievements, great though they were, counted little in comparison with the *one* period of revelation — antiquity with both its pagan and Christian legacies. Perhaps one could sometimes live up to it, but never without or beyond it.[8] There was, in addition, even in a man such as Dante, the expectation of the end of the world taken over from the early Christians. The idea of historical evolution was unknown.

Yet, whereas up to the beginning of the second millennium the relation to antiquity was mainly one of reverential imitation, from the eleventh century onwards it became more and more one of adaptation, absorption, and transmutation, often unconscious and even against intention. As a matter of fact, in manner of thinking, in the free use of Latin for changing purposes of expression, and in the often naive and unhistorical exploitation of ancient authorities, a Dante or a Thomas Aquinas was less orthodox than the humanist writers and schoolmasters during and after the Renaissance. Yet the shadow of Greco-Roman and Christian antiquity hovered over all that happened in the learned world. This lack of originality, as modern individualistic man would call it, was one of the greatest blessings for European civilization, for it preserved a heritage far more unifying than that any individual nation would have been able to produce.

[8] This attitude is not only medieval. We find it to a high degree, also, in later periods of classicism up to the nineteenth century. Even the older Goethe lived in this climate of thought. The pupils of the old humanist schools of Europe were educated in it. In some places they still are. Catholic philosophers proudly consider themselves as "interpreters," not as innovators.

There were schools at princely courts; the merits of the Englishman Alcuin as the educational and literary adviser of Charlemagne can hardly be overestimated. There were also schools at the great monasteries. But the diluted seven liberal arts they taught from the encyclopedias or summaries of a Boethius, Cassiodorus, Martianus Capella, or Isidore of Seville were all they could afford. These seven liberal arts, which would be unthinkable without the vast work of Aristotle, were systematically developed in great ancient schools, such as the University of Alexandria, and transmitted to the Middle Ages through Roman education.[9] They were divided into the trivium of grammar, dialectic, and rhetoric and the more advanced quadrivium of geometry, arithmetic, music, and astronomy. The names are somewhat misleading for the modern reader. Grammar, at its best, was the study of literature, at its worst, the memorizing of dull rules; dialectic was formal logic; rhetoric was composition and perhaps an introduction into Roman law as a legacy from the old Roman schools of oratory; geometry was largely geography; arithmetic was taught mainly for calendar computation and performed in cumbersome Roman notation, for the Hindu-Arabic system did not become known in Arabic Spain before the tenth century or put in common use before the fifteenth; music, required for choral singing, was combined with metaphysical speculations about the terrestrial and heavenly spheres; finally, astronomy was often connected with astrology. Yet, though the content of the liberal arts as taught in the Middle Ages is obsolete today, they provided the framework for later developments, the traces of which we can still observe in the classification of the modern scholarly disciplines and the departmental structure of our universities.

Within a world shrunken by the conquests of Islam there developed a shrunken outlook. At the end of the first and beginning of the second millennium it was actually the Arabic culture that continued the ancient tradition of learning. Granada, Toledo, and Cordova in Spain by far excelled the Christian cities as centers of science, art, and luxury; Averroes (Ibn Rushd, 1126–1198) developed a relatively free and pantheistic Aristotelian system that

[9] See Paul Abelson, *The Seven Liberal Arts* (New York: Columbia University, 1906).

attracted some of the best minds at the Universities of Padua and Oxford. Even the University of Paris felt the impact of his heretical ideas, until they were refuted by Thomas Aquinas (*c.* 1225–1274). The institutions of higher learning in Moorish Spain influenced the medieval universities. In the eastern Arabic world Bagdad and Cairo aroused the admiration of the traveler. In that region the philosopher Avicenna (Ibn Sina, 980–1037), through his famous *Canon of Medicine*, revised the tradition of Galen, Hippocrates, and Aristotle. Pharmacy was developed into a scientific discipline. In spite of the prevailing speculative, often profoundly mystical, character of Arabic knowledge there was more empirical observation among the Arabians than the Christians. Even when, in consequence of military defeats, religious orthodoxy, and the suppression of an internal "renaissance" similar to that of the European world, the cultural superiority of Islam had declined, the historian Ibn Khaldun (1332–1406) wrote his universal history. It represents the first attempt to explain the growth of nations in reference to intellectual, social, and climatic conditions, thus anticipating by four and five centuries the later works of Vico, Montesquieu, Herder, and Taine.[10]

Because of the development of the monarchical and feudal system medieval man won in the beginning of the second millennium the brutal battle of physical existence against his natural and human enemies. The economic system changed from primitive barter to money exchange, which meant that people could travel more freely and trade their goods over wider distances. Governments of some stability could protect the roads; and the cities, the sources and centers of modern culture, could provide the chance for meeting interesting men and ideas within safe walls. At the French city of Chartres, John of Salisbury (*c.* 1115–1180), a man of international fame and contact, interested his students in the study of classical literature for its own value. In Paris and other places where he sought refuge from his many enemies Peter Abelard (1079–1142) developed before enthusiastic students the method of discourse that set the pattern for the form of teaching used at the scholastic

[10] For extracts from Ibn Khaldun, see Robert Ulich, *Three Thousand Years of Educational Wisdom* (Harvard University Press, 1959), p. 199f. Complete edition: Ibn Haldun al-Mugrabi, *The Muguaddimah*, trans. F. Rosenthal (New York: Pantheon Books, 1958).

universities. Abelard's method was no longer one of dull memorizing, but consisted in rational interpretation.

In his *Sic et Non* (Yea and Nay) he juxtaposes contradictory opinions on doctrinal questions taken from the Bible and the writings of the Church Fathers. Here are some of his 158 questions:[11]

> Whether faith should be built on human reason, or not. (No. 1)
> Whether God is threefold, or not. (No. 6)
> Whether the Son is without beginning, or not. (No. 14)
> Whether Christ after his Resurrection appeared first to Mary Magdalene, or not. (No. 86)
> Whether it is permitted to lie, or not. (No. 154)
> Whether the punishment of nonbaptized children may be very mild with respect to the sins of the other damned, or not. (No. 158)

The whole method was still primitive indeed. There is no attempt at a logical reconciliation of the contrasts. But, if we may believe the prologue, in which he introduces his bold work with several pious excuses and safeguards, the collection of questions in his *Sic et Non* was intended to be the mere material for animated debate. For at the end of the prologue, referring to Aristotle and the words in the Bible, "Seek and ye shall find," he explains that his quotations "should excite the reader and stimulate him to inquire about truth."

Abelard taught around 1100. About one hundred and fifty years later there existed one of the most impressive schools of thought in Western theological and philosophical history. Albertus Magnus of Cologne, the *Doctor Universalis* (c. 1192–1280), equally interested in natural as in divine knowledge, utilized without prejudice Arabic, Jewish, Neoplatonic, and Aristotelian elements of thought for his attempted synthesis of human and superhuman reason. His great mind transcended the geographical isolation of the Middle Ages. At almost the same time Thomas Aquinas, the *Doctor Angelicus* (c. 1225–1274), worked on his *Summa Theologica*, in which he intended to summarize all available learning under the three divisions, God, Man, and Christ, and on his *Summa contra Gentiles*. In the latter he discussed not only the common aims of, but also the distinctions between faith and reason, or revelation

[11] Pierre Abailard, *Sic et Non*, ed. E. L. T. Henke and G. S. Lindenkohl (Marburg, 1851).

and natural knowledge, in order to give his contemporaries the necessary criteria for differentiating non-Christian from Christian ideas. Today St. Thomas is still the canonic philosopher of the Catholic Church. Only one generation after Thomas, Master Eckhart (1260–1327), writing both in Latin and in a German never surpasssed by any German philosophical writer, developed the first great speculative-mystical system of the West. God was for him the undefinable yet all-permeating Essence in the unity of which all individual existences are embedded. The human soul, understanding that it is nothing in isolation, can thus discover in itself the divine spark and accomplish its union with the Eternal without need of special ecclesiastical institutions. Master Eckhart's contemporary, Duns Scotus (1265–1308), who was rightly named the *Doctor Subtilis* and who probably possessed the keenest philosophical mind of the period, became the Franciscan critic of the Dominican Thomas Aquinas. His emphasis on the importance of will and activity as conditions of knowledge and salvation, and on the inductive method as against the idea of the receiving passivity of the soul, place him close to modern voluntaristic schools of thought. His theory of categories and logical relations has influenced the thinking of some of our most reputed modern philosophers, for example, Franz Brentano, Edmund Husserl, and Martin Heidegger.

There is finally William of Occam (*c.* 1300–*c.* 1349), the *Doctor Invincibilis*, of whose part in the controversy between empire and papacy we have already heard. He had the courage to express his skepticism concerning proofs of the existence of God and his attributes. Against Thomas' faith in the inner connection between the human mind and the divine essence (realism) he set his nominalism, the belief that ideas are only in our minds, mere *nomina* without any guarantee of their inherence in reality itself. This "new way" of thinking, or *via nova*, was actually old and pre-Thomistic (Abelard had already been persecuted for this doctrine). It was merely another form of distrust in abstractions and another invitation to concrete observation, as pursued a few generations after William of Occam by the great pioneers of science.

While these learned scholars courageously applied Aristotelian thought to Christian theology, the vernacular also burst into flower. Dante (1265–1321), a man of immense erudition, wrote his *Divine*

Comedy in order "to put into verse things difficult" and to form man's character by showing him what rewards he has to expect here and hereafter from his deeds. And in Germany Wolfram von Eschenbach (*c.* 1170–*c.* 1220) transformed the Perceval saga, transmitted to him through translations from French, into a philosophical epic, in order to illustrate the work of God in the working of the world. His purpose was to satisfy the soul's longing for transcendental salvation, but at the same time to do justice to man's desire for full and productive participation in the joys and labors of earthly life. In other words, through poetry he attempted the same task as did Albert of Cologne and Thomas Aquinas, namely, a synthesis between the two worlds in which, according to the medieval view, man is embedded: the world of *natura* and the world of *supernatura*.[12]

What are the reasons for this amazing development in thought and poetic insight from crude beginnings to the highest degree of refinement in a period of profound political and spiritual unrest? In the last analysis, the attempt to explain the genesis of great periods of mental creativity ends in a mystery. "The wind bloweth where it listeth" (John 3:8). Yet, four interacting factors can be clearly discriminated.

The first was the rediscovery of Aristotle. All that Abelard had available was a part of the logical writings of the great Greek in misleading translations. During his lifetime scholars learned to know the whole *Organon*; in 1175 the *Metaphysics* had been translated, and at the end of the twelfth century the *Physics* and *De Caelo*.[13] Very soon there developed a most elaborate technique of fitting Aristotle's works into the medieval form of studies. Commentaries were written; abbreviations, compendia, summulae, lexica, anthologies, collections of quotations under the characteristic name of "Auctoritates" appeared in all great centers of learning.[14]

[12] See in this connection Gottfried Weber, *Der Gottesbegriff des Parzival* (Frankfurt-au-Main: M. Diesterweg, 1935) and *Parzival, Ringen und Vollendung* (Oberursel: Kompass-Verlag, 1948).

[13] H. Rashdall, *The Universities of Europe in the Middle Ages*, ed. F. M. Powicke and A. B. Emden (Oxford: Clarendon Press, 1936).

[14] Martin Grabmann, "Methoden und Hilfsmittel des Aristotelesstudiums im Mittelalter," *Sitzungberichte der phil. hist. Abteilung der Bayrischen Akademie der Wissenschaften* (Munich, 1939), Heft. 5.

THE MIDDLE AGES

The Church looked first with suspicion at the pagan intruder: it forbade the use of his *Metaphysics* and his *Natural Philosophy* to the students of the University of Paris.[15] Thomas Aquinas was opposed as an innovator and destroyer of the old religious metaphysics, by, among others, the Franciscan William of Mara, who, probably assisted by Roger Bacon, wrote in 1284 a *Summa contra Thomam*. But the wave of enthusiasm was too great to be resisted. For Aristotle's works meant more than a new source of information; they contained a new method of thinking. One no longer needed to accept the Christian heritage on mere faith; perhaps one could try to explain it rationally. If not completely, one could at least try to find out how far the boundaries of reason could be extended into the realm of faith.

Most of us may see little rationality in many of St. Thomas' arguments, in his discussion of the nature of angels, for example. We may wonder why even a more empirical scholar like Duns Scotus spends his time with deliberations on the hylomorphic composition, the development, and the intelligence of these suprahuman beings.[16] But still today some people are concerned with the same problems. And, if Thomas Aquinas and Duns Scotus, with their inquisitive minds, lived today, they would read Newton, Kant, and Einstein. The mere fact that they tried to buttress a magic and supernatural world with a rational framework was in itself an enormous step forward — a revolution of no lesser intellectual consequence than that which began with Copernicus and Galileo.

The second reason for the rapid ascension of thought in the thirteenth century was the opportunity for exchanging ideas. How uniform must have been the life in one of the old isolated monasteries, despite a sometimes precious library, in comparison with the intellectual striving at the University of Paris. There we find the famous Englishmen, Bonaventura, Roger Bacon, William of Occam, the Italian Thomas Aquinas, the Belgian Siger of Brabant,

[15] Statutes of Cardinal Robert of Courçon for Paris, 1215, *Chartularium Univ. Parisiensis*, I, No. 20, 78, 79. English trans. in D. C. Monroe, *The Medieval Student* (Philadelphia, 1895). Translations and reprints from The *Original Sources of European History*, II, 3.
[16] St. Thomas Aquinas, *Summa Theologica* (London and New York: Benziger, 1912), Part I. Second Number Questions L–LXIV: "Treatise on the Angels," pp. 285–459; Joannes Scotus Duns, *Opera Omnia*, ed. Wadding (Paris, L. Vivès, 1891–95), V, 11–12. *Distinctio*, 1–11.

the Scotch Duns Scotus, but not a single Frenchman,[17] among the *doctores* who made the university so great that for the French it was as much an object of pride as the papacy for the Italians or the empire for the Germans.

But—and this is the third reason—all this bubbling intellectual life was not mere effervescence; it was caught and directed into an organization. If a profession is a social institution accruing from the possession of a definable body of knowledge, a method of thought and research, and a well-regarded ritual of selection, examination, and honor, the Universities of Paris, Bologna, Oxford, and Cambridge must be credited with the creation of such an institution. For these universities determined the literature to be read, organized methods of logical discourse and dispute, developed their selective system often against the resistance of their own ecclesiastical superiors, and did not hesitate to strike, or to cause riot, when they felt that their honor and independence were violated. They were not merely a peaceful cluster of saints and speculating monks, but an extremely lively and realistic crowd. In fact, their devotion to the arts was not at all airy and disinterested; rather it existed for a definite, if one wants to say so, vocational purpose. The broad base of the faculty of the *artes liberales* trained the average clergyman and clerk, the latter increasingly needed by the developing system of government, while the "graduate schools" of theology, law, and medicine, attended by relatively few students, educated the professional élite.[18] Whereas too rigid an organization can be stifling, and in the course of time this proved to be a danger in the universities, the lack of organization creates chaos. It seems that the higher schools of the thirteenth century found the right balance. They stimulated and also disciplined the mind.

The fourth, and probably most essential, reason for the rise of thought was the state of inner disquietude. As we saw, during the thirteenth century empire and papacy, while in some respects de-

---

[17] See Alexander Budinszky, *Die Universität Paris und die Fremden an derselben im Mittelalter* (Berlin, 1876); Étienne Gilson, *Medieval Universalism and Its Present Value* (New York and London: Sheed and Ward, 1937).

[18] Theology flowered especially at Paris; Bologna was famous for its law school, Salerno was the great center of medical studies. Originally, civil law and medicine were not favored by the Church, but increased in importance during the following centuries.

veloping their greatest ambitions, were also engaged in the struggle of mutual destruction. Against this turmoil, the steady building up of a great and subtle system of thought in scholarly campuses, protected by papal and imperial decrees, looks like the tilling of peaceful valleys by industrious farmers. But this analogy would be misleading. The use of Aristotle for explaining the teaching of Christ was just as much a source of conflict as it was an attempt at a solution, as the Church felt distinctly at the beginning of the thirteenth century, and Luther at the beginning of the sixteenth. And why all the arguing? Not because the believers were merely obsessed by an abstract desire for system, but because heretics such as pantheists and free thinkers appeared all over the world, first among the Jews and the Arabs, and then within the walls of Christianity itself. Even the great masters of theology and the popes were not free from the suspicion of heresy.

The Decline. The mention of heresy leads us over to the second part of this discussion of the *studium*, the reasons for its decay. Hegel once formulated the significant statement that the owls of Athena begin their flight at sunset, meaning that the urge toward rationalization begins when a culture has reached its last and highest stage of ripeness. Is this perhaps true also of the great scholastic systems?

As a matter of fact, the germ of disintegration was mixed into the very composition of the scholastic *Weltanschauung*. The conflict between the two authorities of Christ and Aristotle is merely a sequel to the conflicts between the Greek and the Judaeo-Christian strands of our civilization mentioned before. Philosophical inquiry cannot be stopped arbitrarily. It has its own inner momentum. Initially used for enlivening the Christian faith, it undermined it; the medicine became too strong.

One group of the scholastics speculated according to the *ratio divina*, the other according to the *ratio humana*, and sometimes the two aspects were struggling against each other in the same mind. The split that since the seventeenth century has divided science from theology was already prepared.

In reality, there was much more at stake than philosophical abstractions. For the medieval thinker up to the fourteenth century, the constituent components of human life, such as ideas, nature,

Church and dogma, state, the corporate system of society, and the feudal and ecclesiastical hierarchies, were conceived as self-manifestations of a divine reality. The sacraments, the holiness of emperor or king and his power to heal, rich ritual (as we still observe it in the coronation of an English monarch) — all this was not mere symbolism, but the true and solemn language of God.

Consequently, when critical nominalism lifted human concepts out of the supposedly divine and all-embracing order, it shattered, though without foreknowledge, not only medieval theory, but also — as we have seen in William of Occam's attacks against papal supremacy — the medieval social structure. Both belonged together; when they were separated, the modern world slowly arose with all its change, doubt, lack of respect, and endless inquiry. And it came long before the rise of modern science, which is merely a product of the changed situation.

The disintegration of the old order inevitably aggravated the predicament of the universities and the learned world. Using phrases from the Revelation in the accusations popes and emperors hurled against each other gave this strange work an eerie reality. People saw the apocalyptic woman (Revelation 17: 3ff):

> and I saw a woman sit upon a scarlet coloured beast, full of names of blasphemy, having seven heads and ten horns . . .
> And upon her forehead was a name written, MYSTERY, BABYLON THE GREAT, THE MOTHER OF HARLOTS AND ABOMINATIONS OF THE EARTH.

And they thought (Revelation 20: 7, 8):

> And when the thousand years are expired, Satan shall be loosed out of his prison,
> And shall go out to deceive the nations which are in the four quarters of the earth, Gog and Magog, to gather them together to battle . . .

Among those who had gone through the universities,. there circulated songs and stories full of satire and cynicism.

> Here beginneth the Holy Gospel according to Marks of silver. At that time the Pope said unto the Romans, "When the Son of Man shall have come to the throne of our Majesty, say unto him first, 'Friend, wherefore art thou come?' But if he shall continue knocking without giving you any

present, thrust him out into outer darkness." And it came to pass that a certain poor clergyman came to the court of our lord, the Pope, and cried out, saying, "Have pity upon me, doorkeepers of the Pope, because the hand of poverty has been laid upon me. I am poor and needy and beseech you to turn away my misfortune and my misery." But when they heard him they were exceedingly wroth and said, "Friend, thy poverty perish with thee! Get thee behind me, Satan, because thou knowest not what the pieces of money know. Amen! Amen! I say unto thee, thou shalt not enter into the joy of the Lord until thou shalt have given the uttermost farthing."

So the poor man departed and sold his cloak and his tunic and all that he had, and gave unto the cardinals and the doorkeepers and the chamberlain. But they said, "What is this among so many?" and they cast him out, and he, without the doors, wept bitterly and would not be comforted.

Then there came unto the court a certain clergyman, who was rich, fat, sleek and puffed up, and had killed a man in a riot. He gave, first to the doorkeeper, then to the chamberlain, then to the cardinals. But they thought among themselves that they ought to get more. Then the Lord Pope, hearing that the cardinals and servants had received many gifts from the clergyman, fell sick, even unto death; but the rich man sent him a medicine of gold and silver, and straightway he was healed. Then the Lord Pope called unto him the cardinals and the servants and said to them, "Brethren see to it that no one seduce you with empty words; for lo! I give you an example that just as I receive, so ye receive also." [19]

Soon the corruption entered also into the halls of the universities themselves; as a matter of fact, they had never been free from it. The medieval guild system — the universities also were guilds like those of the craftsmen or knights — suffered at the end of the Middle Ages from inbreeding. Not the best became the masters, but those who had influential relatives, or the means to bribe. The standards, the code of honor, and the system of selection all degenerated. If one may draw conclusions from the apparent necessity of continual admonitions, the proper conduct of students during examinations and the incorruptibility of the examiners must have been a delicate problem. [20] Certainly, the lust for money was not less virulent under medieval transcendentalism than under modern secularism. If we may believe only a small part of the satires appearing around 1500, the reputation of the university professors was lamentable,

[19] Ephraim Emerton, *Mediaeval Europe, 814–1300* (Boston: Ginn & Co., 1909), p. 475. For Latin text, see *Parodistische Texte. Beispiele zur lateinischen Parodie im Mittelalter*, ed. Paul Lehmann (Munich, 1923), pp. 7–8.
[20] See H. Rashdall, *The Universities in the Middle Ages*, I, 466.

and so was that of the mendicant friars who up to the fourteenth century had been the venerated teachers and preachers of the poor. But we do not need the doubtful witness of the satirist. One of the later great scholastics, Juan Luis Vives (1492–1540), not of a rebellious mind like the Renaissance humanists or the Protestant reformers, but a defender of the Catholic Church and its tradition, writes in his book *On the Causes of the Decline of Scholarship*:

> One may show me any candidate whom they have rejected during the past two hundred years, provided he had been long enough in school and paid the necessary amount of money whatever were his age, his estate, his talent, his experience, and his mores. If one does not believe it, he may, throughout France, inspect all kinds of craftsmen, sausage makers, cooks, carters, sailors, smiths, and worse than these, loafers and bandits, who are masters and bachelors of arts. Nor are this type of people missing in Germany, or in Italy, and, if one cannot find them otherwise, he may inquire for them in Rome.[21]

This picture of disintegration suggests, however, a deeper question. To what degree were the majority of people — even those who attended the great universities — mature enough for a real understanding of the nature of the *studium* and its metaphysical background? There is a charming story in the *Historia Naturalis* of the English scholastic Alexander Neckam, who was born in 1157 in St. Albans, taught from 1180 to 1186 at the University of Paris, and then returned to England. Master Neckam tells of a student at the University of Paris who has doubts about the resurrection of the body. This is the way his fellows lead him toward the path of faith:

> If you believe in the resurrection and it is true, you will be rewarded for your faith. If you believe in the resurrection and it is not true, it does you no harm. If you do not believe in the resurrection and it is true, you will be punished for your heresy. Therefore, since you run a certain risk in not believing, and no risk in believing, why not believe? By this argument [so Neckam continues] the student became convinced, and hence he lived and died as a faithful member of the Church.[22]

If one analyzes this story, which is somewhat similar to Pascal's

---

[21] *De Causis Corruptarum Artium*, in his *Opera Omnia* (Valencia, 1782), VI, 73.

[22] *De Naturis Rerum Libri Duo*, ed. Thomas Wright (London: Longmans, Green, 1863), Chap. CLXXIII, p. 297. "De Septem Artibus."

famous "wager," [23] one finds in the same minds a remarkable mixture of refinement in logic (they manage to produce a complicated syllogism) and, at the same time, a primitive attitude of bargaining with the Divine. Apparently, a thin layer of dialectical skill was placed over an essentially crude outlook toward life. This discrepancy prevented the disciples from truly understanding the spirit of the masters, as so often is the case in the history of intellectual and religious institutions. We have many documents that prove the lack of literacy even in the clergy. Probably the universities were a few islands in an ocean of ignorance. But even on the islands themselves the differences in maturity must have been enormous; otherwise we would not have so many testimonies to the vice and crime of the students in their crowded quarters.[24]

The same inbreeding we discover in the institution, we discover in its thought. In the statute book of the University of Paris [25] we find a list of errors rejected by the chancellor and the masters in 1241 as "contrary to true theology." The condemned opinions deal, among others, with such problems as whether the divine essence in itself will be seen or not be seen by any man or angel, whether the Trinity is one in the Father and Son, but not one in three with the Holy Ghost, whether the Holy Ghost does not proceed from the Son, but only from the Father, or from both, whether the Bad Angel was not bad from his creation or was always bad, whether an angel can or cannot be at the same time in different places, and whether the Bad Angel had some ground on which to stand, and so on. Inevitably, with certain groups within the universities providing their self-caricature, the number of mockers from outside grew from decade to decade.

THE CLIMATE OF DISINTEGRATION

In his interesting book, *The Waning of the Middle Ages*, J. Huizinga gives us a vivid description of the decline of medieval

---

[23] *Pascal's Pensées*, trans. H. F. Stewart (London: Routledge, 1950), p. 119.
[24] See *Chartularium Universitatis Parisiensis*, ed. Denifle, I, Nos. 60, 197, 425, *passim* and the description of the life of the students of Paris by Jacobus de Vitriaco (Jacques de Vitry), trans. D. C. Munro, in *The Medieval Student* (Philadelphia, 1895). See also Jacobus de Vitriaco, *Historia Occidentalis*, ed. Dubois (Douai, 1597), Bk. II, Chap. VII.
[25] *Chartularium Universitatis Parisiensis*, I, No. 128.

society in France and the Netherlands.[26] Though France had gone farthest in *raffinement*, the picture he paints reflects also the cultural scene of the other European countries.

We find a pessimism in the privileged classes that is more the result of fatigue, spleen, self-defeating luxury, and boredom than of piety. The idea of death exercises a kind of macabre attraction. In Germany, for instance, illustrations of the dance of death abound: a putrefying figure with grinning face and scythe in his hand stops the pope or king in solemn procession, the knight on his way to battle, the rich merchant before his money bags, the lover during his courtship, the prostitute flaunting her seductive looks. Often one has the feeling that this is not Death in the Christian sense, man's curse but also man's savior, but a cynical reminder of life's meaninglessness: *vanitas, vanitatum vanitas!* Some take refuge in the *Imitatio Christi*; most throw themselves the more passionately into the excitement of life, the less they believe in its meaning. Religion, of course, still plays a great role, especially in pageantry; but the struggle for power and the favor of the mighty seem to be more important — at least until the days when one begins to think of the Last Judgment. Then one donates money to the Church. Even the Orders of the Temple, of Saint John, and of the Teutonic Knights, originally based on a mixture of genuinely Christian and feudal motives, soon give way to political interests.

Despite all preaching about the equality before God, there are monumental differences between various classes. In the conventional sense of the word, only the nobility, to which the city aristocracy of the rich merchants may also belong, has "honor." The peasant is often of less worth than cattle. A slave in antiquity was generally better off. And treachery and corruptibility seem to be no great offense to a noble's honor.

At the end of the Middle Ages, the clergy has lost the inquiring spirit of the great scholastics. There remain their dogmatic statements and their superstitions, no longer their sacrificial sense of devotion to the great cause of truth, however dependent on the knowledge of the time. Even Gerson (1363–1429), the famous

---

[26] Johann Huizinga, *The Waning of the Middle Ages. A Study of the Form of Life, Thought and Art in France and the Netherlands in the XIVth and XVth Centuries* (London: E. Arnold, 1927).

chancellor of the University of Paris and in many respects an admirable priest,[27] writes "contra vanam curiositatem," [28] which we would translate today "against the vain spirit of research."

Thomas Aquinas had also asked for humble reverence before the mysteries of Godhood; yet in their context his words have another ring. Instead of feeling the spur of intellectual excitement, the scholastic now preferred to quote authorities. Worship became increasingly polytheistic and magical. Apparently, many no longer took it seriously. Otherwise, the whole elaborate system of indulgences and of the worship of the Blessed Virgin and the saints could not have disappeared overnight with the spread of the Reformation. On the other hand, those who took the gospel seriously expected the Lord to come down with fire and sword.

A state of extreme fear and radical despair overcame not only isolated individuals, but whole towns. One could speak of anxiety epidemics. Processions of flagellants were seen in the cities of Italy and other countries.[29] A monk of Padua gives the following account of one of these outbreaks of desperate penitence.

In the course of these centuries, when many crimes and vices brought disgrace to Italy, first the inhabitants of Perugia, then those of Rome, then all the people of Italy were hit by a mood of extreme penitence. The fear of Christ befell them to such a degree that noble and ignoble, old and young, even five-year-old children marched almost naked and without a sense of shame in solemn procession through the cities. They all held in their hands scourges with straps with which they scourged themselves, weeping and sighing until blood ran from their shoulders. Under floods of tears, as if they had seen the suffering of Christ with their own eyes, they cried for mercy to the God of mercifulness, and for help to the Mother of Christ. They prayed that he who had pardoned so many sinners might have pity also on them. Day and night, even in the coldest winter, hundreds, thousands, even tens of thousands under the guidance of priests marched to the churches with burning candles, crosses, and banners and

[27] Compare his "On Leading Children to Christ," partly translated in *Three Thousand Years of Educational Wisdom*, ed. Robert Ulich (Cambridge: Harvard University Press, 1954), pp. 181–190.

[28] Huizinga, *The Waning of the Middle Ages*, p. 139.

[29] See Jacques Boileau, *Histoire des Flagellans, où l'on fait voir le Bon et le Mauvais Usage des Flagellations parmi les Chrétians. . . .*, 2nd ed. (Amsterdam, 1732), and Jean L. de Lolme, *Memorials of Human Superstition; Being a Paraphrase and Commentary on the* Historia Flagellantium *of the Abbé Boileau . . .* , 2nd ed. (London, 1784). Also, Ernst G. Förstemann, *Die Christlichen Geisslergesellschaften* (Halle, 1828).

prostrated themselves before the altars. The same they did in villages and hamlets so that the fields and mountains echoed the voices of those who cried to the Lord.[30]

Since in periods of inner uncertainty scapegoats are needed — just as in our own day — men finally concentrated on witches. From the end of the Middle Ages to the seventeenth century, men of otherwise high intellectual quality specialized in demonology. The official theory was laid down in the *Malleus Maleficarum*, or *The Witch Hammer*, written by two Dominicans in 1487, and in the bull *Summis Desiderantes Affectibus* (1484) of Pope Innocent VIII.[31]

SUMMARY

If now, in an evaluative mood, we look at the struggles of medieval man, we may be inclined to ask: "Was it all failure?" In the attempt to create political and cultural unity, the *imperium* did not succeed politically, the *sacerdotium* failed spiritually, the *studium* left at its end more questions and fewer answers than had existed before it. In all three institutions there was corruption. The guardians of the temporal and the supratemporal concerns of man crossed swords, rather than defending their common ground, while the alliance between the philosophy of Greece and the gospel of Judaea, between human reason and supernatural faith, was full of tension.

These facts are hard to doubt. With respect to its greatest and most admirable scheme, namely, to reconcile in a higher unity its various cultural components, the Middle Ages ended in disillusion. But have the greatest dreams and schemes of man ever been fully realized? Were they not all utopias? — yet, not useless. Only minor minds can think that the unattainable has no function in human history. It provides inspiration and focus, and, even when no longer serving its original purpose, it does not completely fade out of memory; rather it remains as a testimony to mankind's eternal imperfection as well as to its eternal greatness.

---

[30] Translated by the author from Förstemann, p. 28.
[31] See Huizinga, *The Waning of the Middle Ages*, p. 220f; *Malleus Maleficarum*, ed. Jacob Sprenger and Heinrich Kramer, trans. Montague Summers (London: Pushkin Press, 1948).

THE MIDDLE AGES

The historical period we call the Middle Ages began at a time when violent changes in power, organization, population, and religious beliefs had destroyed the ancient world. In every respect, physically as well as mentally, there reigned insecurity and confusion. Now, if one compares the life of the still-untamed Merovingian nobles, as St. Gregory of Tours (538–594) describes it in his *Historia Francorum*,[32] with the life of the mighty at the end of the Middle Ages, then one may discover the disappointing truth that the struggle for power easily makes beasts out of men, whether they live in a more primitive or a more refined environment. Certainly, murder as a means of achieving one's goals was used in both periods, as in both periods there appeared also heroic and saintly figures. Generally speaking, the historian may doubt whether external advancement is accompanied by moral progress. But the life of the average man had certainly become more safe during the Middle Ages; proud cities and splendid houses had been built; there were laws in countries and communities which, though not always followed, still served as standards. Profound systems of thought had been developed; eloquent discussions had sharpened man's logic and widened his mental outlook. There were universities, and there were schools for the children of freemen in every large town. To be sure, there was a great and suffering peasantry. Yet, a church was near, and even an ignorant or vicious priest could not totally spoil its blessings. There were the songs of knightly deeds and self-discipline which had their measure of truth and greatness despite an exploiting lord in the castle. If we may believe the sources of the time, some small farmers and townsmen managed to send a son to a university.[33] And where is there a civilization without serfs, even though the name may have disappeared?

The plastic arts had developed from the primitive, though often profoundly touching, sculptures of the early Middle Ages to the

[32] *Monumenta Germaniae Historica, Scriptores Rerum Merovingiarum*, Vol. I, Part I, pp. 1–450.
[33] "To give his son a chance to stay
In Paris, growing wise each day,
Is some old peasant's one ambition,
To pay his bills and his tuition
The poor hard-working father slaves."
From "The Song of the University of Paris," in *Legends and Satires from Medieval Literature*, ed. Martha H. Shackford (Boston: Ginn & Co., 1913), p. 125.

spiritual figures in the Gothic cathedrals; poetry had grown from the *Hildebrandlied* to the *Divine Comedy*; the epics of Tristan and Perceval are still the great symbols of tragical love and of man's desire for purity. The illuminated manuscripts of the time enchant our eyes; the human portrait, new colors, dimensions, and perspectives were discovered in painting. Many of us today anxiously wait for a pilgrimage to the medieval towns of Europe with their cathedrals, their libraries, and their works of art.

These achievements not only resulted from the success of medieval man in achieving greater security and material welfare; they resulted from his mastery of the relationship between individual and community. It is simply not true that the feudal system of the Middle Ages was devoid of any freedom, that it was merely collectivistic and oppressive. There were many democratic features and individual responsibilities in the social hierarchy of the medieval guild system — more, perhaps, than in our mechanized society. Those theologians who wrote about education, such as Vincent of Beauvais (d. 1264), Hugh of St. Victor (1096–1141), and St. Bonaventura (1221–1274), were not at all neglectful of the learner's individuality. In comparison to the scarcity of literate men and books (or perhaps for this very reason) original thinkers appeared at many places, and there were more great rebels and offenders of convention than society could master. Wills of kings and nobles, the various attempts to regulate feudal warfare (*treuga dei*, or "truce of God"), treaties between former enemies — true, many of these were disobeyed and hypocritical, but they nevertheless reveal the improvement of Western man's conscience. While emperors and popes called each other "Antichrist," the people, in all their simplicity, seem to have been penetrated by religious feelings. These feelings were shot through with superstition and magic — even as they are today — but let us not forget that the time of pagan cults was not yet far away. As often, the simple of heart were more pious than the mighty, many of whom used their power without any admixture of conscience.

In concluding, we may understand the spiritual situation of the Middle Ages, as well as its inevitable disintegration, in the following framework of thought and attitude. On the earthly part of the cosmos lives sinful man, driven from Paradise into the valleys of misery by the disobedience of the first pair. In the heavenly abode dwells God, the Creator, the severe Judge, but also the benign Father because he has sent his Son as the Redeemer and founded the Church as the mediator between him and the human race. As his representative, the Church has available all the means of punishment, but also all the means of grace and indulgence. In addition, the Church possesses the consummate wisdom and is the universal educator of mankind. There is an answer to every question, a punishment for every sinner, and remission for every contrite heart. In between Church and heaven a host of saints and angels work as untiring messengers for the Lord and the faithful. A pessimistic view of the nature of man, in many respects justifiable, combines with the optimistic hope of final salvation. Here is the explanation of the profound influence the Catholic Church exercises not only in the Middle Ages, but still today.

But the conflict was bound to begin when medieval man began to doubt that the clergy, whose corruption he observed, could still be the medium of God's grace and forgivingness. How could a disintegrating Church, fighting a disintegrating empire, represent the divine order on earth? The chasm between the human and the divine, which is characteristic of every dualistic system, became unbridgeable.

Besides the Christians who still found comfort in their Church, and those in the grip of anxiety, there emerged, as we have already seen, a third group, the cynical and materialistic, those who whispered into their neighbors' ears their suspicion that all might be a big swindle. When the so-called *Archipoeta*, a vagrant scholar of unusual talent, was required to do public penitence for his frivolous life before the emperor and the clergy, he aimed the spear of scrutiny not at himself, but at his judges. Have you the right to judge other sinners? What do we know about life hereafter? As long as I live on earth, my body is closer to me than heaven.

> Down the broad road do I run,
> As the way of youth is;
> Snare myself in sin, and ne'er
> Think where faith and truth is,
> Eager far for pleasure more
> Than soul's health, the sooth is,

For this flesh of mine I care,
Seek no futh where ruth is.[34]

And beyond these groups of Christians a fourth, the introvert
and sublime type, withdrew into a highly individualistic and mystical form of symbolism. Great was its nearness to the essence of religion. Yet, the Church was suspicious of it. For the mystical spirit,
when expressing itself systematically and not merely in the reverie
of nuns who feel themselves the spouses of Christ, undermined
the dualistic theology of the Church and, consequently, the belief
in the necessity of its mediatorship; it harbored the danger of mo-
nistic idealism or pantheism. Master Eckhart preached in a sermon:

> I have said that there is one agent alone in the soul that is free. Sometimes
> I have called it the tabernacle of the Spirit. Other times I have called it the
> Light of the Spirit and again, a spark. Now I say that it is neither this nor
> that. It is something higher than this or that, as the sky is higher than the
> earth . . . It is free of all names and unconscious of any kind of forms.
> It is at once pure and free, as God himself is, and like him is perfect unity
> and uniformity, so that there is no possible way to spy it out.[35]

Partly under the mystical, partly under the philosophical, influences of men such as William of Occam, Duns Scotus, Wycliff,
and Hus, the German Martin Luther revived the Augustinian
interpretation of Christianity, especially of the Epistles of St. Paul.
Zwingli soon appeared in Switzerland, and Calvin in France. According to these men, it is not only the mystical longing of the
soul, but the grace of God, that drives us near to him. And it is not
Aristotle but the Bible man must know in order to be a Christian.
But in mentioning these men we already are in a new period,
though much of the medieval mentality survived in them. In some
respects, they were even more medieval than the scholastic philosophers, and certainly much more so than the Renaissance popes
with their entourage of critical scholars and daring artists.

[34] From *Wine, Women and Song. Mediaeval Latin Student's Songs*, trans.
John Addington Symonds (London: Chatto and Windus, 1925), p. 67. There is
also a translation by Helen Waddell, *Mediaeval Latin Lyrics* (London: Constable,
1929), p. 171f. For a Latin edition with German poetic rendering, see Robert
Ulich and Max Manitius, *Vagantenlieder* (Jena: E. Diederichs, 1927).

[35] See Raymond Bernard Blakney, *Meister Eckhart. A Modern Translation*
(New York: Harper, 1941), Sermon 24, pp. 210–211.

Finally, still without scientific method and a full consciousness of the implications, some medieval Christians tried to find a way to the mysteries of the universe by observation and experiment, inductively, not deductively. The groping of these men points even beyond the Renaissance into the seventeenth century; yet the beginning of their attitude, as we saw, lies deep in the period of Frederick II, Roger Bacon, William of Occam, and Duns Scotus.

II

Renaissance and Reformation

SINCE the Swiss historian Jakob Burckhardt published his famous work in 1860 on the *Civilization of the Renaissance in Italy*, there has been an uninterrupted debate about the line of demarcation between the Renaissance and the Middle Ages. For every phenomenon that Burckhardt considered uniquely characteristic of the Renaissance we now find in some form in medieval civilization.[1]

Nevertheless, medieval men did not cross the equator (1481), did not discover America (1492), did not reach the Cape of Good Hope (1498) or circumnavigate the earth (1522). The explorations that led to all these discoveries had a more systematic and scientific character than the adventures of previous explorers. They would have been impossible without the magnetic needle. Also, these new explorations were systematically exploited; the old were not. Though, ideologically, the conquests that followed the discoveries were still considered as crusades of a sort, expeditions for the conversion of the many pagans God had kindly left on earth for the stimulation of Christian endeavor, they grew mainly out of the expansionist, imperialist, and mercantilist tendencies of the new absolutist kingdoms. Even a new Bernard of Clairvaux could not have excited the knights of sixteenth-century Europe with a

---

[1] For a summary and analysis of the controversy, see J. Huizinga, *Das Problem der Renaissance* (Tübingen: Wissenschaftliche Buchgemeinschaft, 1953).

new excursion to the Holy Sepulcher. This kind of interest had gone.

It was during the Renaissance that the Medici, of Florence, or the Welsers and Fuggers, of Augsburg, developed a new art of trade, banking, and international investment. They financed emperors, kings, and popes to such a degree that the old ecclesiastical laws against the lending of money for interest became hypocrisy. Leo X, himself of the House of Medici, had to abolish them. By the middle of the sixteenth century the popes had to spend one half and more of their income to pay interest to the great financiers, whose demands would be illegal today.

Also, the artistic and intellectual life of the Renaissance is different from that of the Middle Ages. Certainly, in the Middle Ages there were great patrons of the arts among kings, noblemen, and proud citizens. But now a new generation of lovers of the fine and the intellectual arts grew up who flattered themselves by discussing the depth and measure of beauty with a Leonardo da Vinci or a Michelangelo. And the artists themselves were no longer anonymous craftsmen and guildsmen, but kings in their domain. Some of them were stubborn giants who lived precariously between sensual passions and supernatural visions. Like the nobility and the higher clergy, artists were more or less exempt from the customary sanctions in regard to sexual love. Others were full of inner grace and harmony and the beloved of the town. The funeral of the young Raphael was a day of mourning for all of Rome.

The circles of the artists and their friends were joined by the literati of the time, the humanists. They also were not a completely new crop. In the twelfth century John of Salisbury had taught his disciples at Chartres the appreciation of classical authors for their own wisdom and beauty. And, when we speak of the Renaissance humanists as the heralds of a freer, more critical and empirical spirit of search, let us remember William of Occam and his precursor, the Franciscan friar Roger Bacon (*c.* 1212–1292). Roger Bacon spoke of the "four chief obstacles in grasping truth . . . namely, submission to faulty and unworthy authority, influence of custom, popular prejudice, and concealment of our own ignorance accompanied by an ostentatious display of our knowledge." He also wished to unfold the principles of experimental science, since "without experience nothing can be sufficiently known." [2] He attempted this about three hundred and fifty years before Francis Bacon (1561–1626) wrote in his *Novum Organon* about the four species of idols that beset the human mind (idols of the tribe, of the den, of the market, of the theater).

Some of the ideas we generally connect with Galileo and his time, such as the law of falling bodies and the analysis of projectile motion, were discussed two hundred years before him by professors at the Universities of Oxford and Paris. These men, though using an extremely abstract scholastic terminology, nevertheless developed the science of kinematics, explored the problems of the mathematical nature of infinity, and, in general, fostered the quantitative method of modern science in contrast to the qualitative approach we connect with medieval scholarship.[3]

We generally consider Petrarch the first humanist. In his essay *On His Own Ignorance and That of Many Others* (1358) he not only cautiously indicated that he preferred Cicero to Aristotle in terms of eloquence — *eloquentia* was the supreme virtue especially for the minor humanists who were extremely proud to say the little they had to say in Ciceronian Latin — but he also asked himself "how on earth Aristotle could have known something for which there is no reason and which cannot be proved by experience." [4] At Petrarch's time this little sentence needed courage, because Aristotle was, so to speak, the other part of the gospel.

By the fifteenth and especially the sixteenth centuries, this was no longer the case. Scholars from Constantinople brought with them the original writings of the Greek philosophers. Men learned their language and used the newly discovered art of printing — one of the most powerful factors in the change of civilization — to edit admirable editions that are still the pride of our famous libraries.

[2] *Opus Majus*, trans. R. B. Burke (Philadelphia: University of Pennsylvania Press, 1928), I, 4–5; II, 583f. See also, *Main Currents of Western Thought*, ed. Franklin Le Van Baumer (New York: Knopf, 1952) pp. 62, 63.
[3] See Herbert Butterfield, *The Origins of Modern Science, 1300–1800* (London: G. Bell, 1950); René Dugas, Histoire de la Mechanique (Neuchâtel: Griffon, 1950); Alexandre Koyré, Études Galiléénnes (Paris: Hermann, 1939); Lynn Thorndike, *History of Magic and Experimental Science*. 6 vols. (New York: Macmillan, 1923–1941).
[4] *The Renaissance Philosophy of Man*, ed. E. Cassirer, P. O. Kristeller, and J. H. Randall, Jr. (University of Chicago Press, 1948), p. 74.

More important, they discovered that under the influence of Aristotle they had not sufficiently seen how deeply Western thought was indebted to, and still could learn from, the visions of Aristotle's teacher, Plato. The new Platonism combined with cosmic speculations. Despite all its mysticism, it encouraged systematic curiosity about the wonders of the natural universe, for a majority, though not all, of the Neoplatonists conceived of the universe as working according to definable laws, to be admired for its infinite beauty, rather than despised as the realm of sin and temptation.

Especially Cardinal Nicholas, from the German town of Kues (Nicholas of Cusa, 1401–1464), the most representative genius of this epoch of transition, treaded new paths to approach the mysteries of the cosmos, though many of his ideas were anticipated by Master Eckhart. Aristotelian scholasticism, mystical Neoplatonism, mathematics, and an intense interest in human society combined in this great theologian and ecclesiastical statesman. It is not skepticism, nor agnosticism, he advocates, but pious reverence, or reverential piety. We have to acquire, he says, *docta ignorantia*, the conscious ignorance of the truly learned. No quantity of rational knowledge — here is the further development of the thought of Duns Scotus and William of Occam — will help us to penetrate the divine mystery, for it is qualitatively different from all things and thoughts of human and material nature. It is the *coincidentia oppositorum*, the coincidence of opposites, to be grasped only by the *amor intellectualis dei*, the love that understands through humility.[5]

Despite its deductive nature, Nicholas' thought is at the threshold of a new era. The Aristotelian-Thomistic confidence in the full circle between rational thinking and the supranatural is broken. Nicholas knows of the gap between human reason and the mysterious Whole. All we may comprehend is an image of it, not its Self. "Consequently it is evident that all affirmative names which we attribute to God, are attributable to Him only in infinitely small measure, for such names are given to Him from the aspect of the world of creature." [6] Hence, "negative theology" (or "holy

[5] See Ernst Cassirer, *Individuum und Kosmos in der Philosophie der Renaissance* (Leipzig and Berlin: Studien der Bibliothek Warburg, 1927); Nicolaus Cusanus, *The Learned Ignorance*, trans. Father G. Heron, with Introduction by D. J. B. Hawkins (New Haven: Yale University Press, 1954).
[6] Nicolaus Cusanus, *The Learned Ignorance*, Chap. 24.

ignorance," as he also says) must complement affirmative theology, for without it there would be danger that we venerate God not as the Infinite but as a finite creature. And it is idolatry to give to the image that which should be given only to Truth.[7]

But the infinite distance of the Divine is no reason to despair. In the *Vision of God* the soul speaks to God:

> How can I have Thee, Lord, who am not worthy to appear in Thy sight?

But God answers.

> When I thus rest in silence of contemplation, Thou, Lord, makest reply within my heart, saying: Be thou thine and I too will be thine.[8]

This statement, in all its paradoxicalness, is not only profound, but of enormous historical significance. Rather than indicating the ego-centered, conceited, and somehow juvenile individualism of some Renaissance humanists — so inferior to the self-forgetful anonymity of the great masters of medieval art and thought — it reveals a new understanding of the self. The self needs the courage of selfhood but cannot thrive in isolation. Only to the degree that it opens itself to the influx of eternal creation, which, nevertheless, will always remain a mystery, only to this degree will it receive its supreme dignity and value and enter into the great cosmic rhythm of dying and becoming.

The modernity of Nicholas of Cusa shows in the fact that in all his aprioristic speculation he anticipates modern science in his appreciation of mathematics "for the rational exploration of things." [9] Mathematics, so he says in an argument not unlike Plato's, has the advantage that it abstracts to a large extent from material contingency and thus better understands the symbols by which the Absolute expresses itself in the sphere of being. Through this mixture of metaphysics and mathematics he arrives at the conclusion that "the earth is not the world's center just as the sphere of the fixed stars is not its circumference," [10] that "the earth is in

[7] *Ibid.,* Chap. 26.
[8] Nicolaus Cusanus, *The Vision of God,* trans. Emma Gurney Salter, with an Introduction by Evelyn Underhill (New York: E. P. Dutton, 1928), p. 32.
[9] *The Learned Ignorance,* Chap. 11.
[10] *Ibid.*

constant motion," that the motion is circular, and that our impression of the earth's fixity is a delusion resulting from the fact that we live in a universe of interrelated and movable objects.[11] Finally, in his writings [12] the medieval concept of catholicity receives a new meaning. For medieval Christianity, there was no salvation outside the Church. Most Catholic children learn this still today. For Nicholas of Cusa, the content and language of human beliefs are conditioned by the fact that the symbols through which we can express the Absolute, or the Holy Other, are inseparable from the variety of human environments. Hence we should not condemn each other for differences of faith. In other words, the ideas of tolerance and of internationalism emerge in a man whose gift of genius was enhanced by the fact that, as the leader of a delegation from the Council of Basel to Greece, he came in contact with great men of different cultures.

Neither Petrarch nor Nicholas of Cusa was a typical Renaissance figure; both were harbingers. The first heralded the humanism of eloquence, of aestheticism, of self-concern to the degree of vanity, and of an admiration for the greatness of antiquity which strangely contrasted with the Christian faith still adhered to by most humanists, however sincerely. The second anticipated, on the one hand, the cosmological mysticism of a Giordano Bruno (1548–1600) or a Jakob Boehme (1575–1624) and, on the other hand, the modern systematic philosophies of Descartes (1596–1650) and Leibniz (1646–1716), both also mathematicians.

The document that rightly has been regarded as one of the finest expressions of the Renaissance spirit is the *Oration on the Dignity of Man* by Count Pico della Mirandola (1463–1494). In this oration, written as the introduction to a public disputation in Rome which the Church suspended because of suspicion of heresy, God speaks to man:

> Thou, constrained by no limits, in accordance with thine free will, in whose hand We have placed thee, shall ordain for thyself the limits of thy nature. We have set thee at the world's center that thou mayest from thence more easily observe whatever is in the world. We have made thee neither of heaven nor of earth, neither mortal nor immortal, so that with

[11] *Ibid.*, Chap. 12.
[12] See *De Conjecturis* and *De Pace Fidei*; see also Cassirer, *Individuum und Kosmos*, p. 30f.

freedom of choice and with honor, as though the maker and molder of thyself, thou mayest fashion thyself in whatever shape thou shalt prefer. Thou
shalt have the power to degenerate into the lower forms of life, which are
brutish. Thou shall have the power, out of thy soul's judgment, to be reborn into the higher forms, which are divine.[13]

There is more secularism in Pico's humanist understanding of the
self, its dignity and its freedom, than in Nicholas of Cusa's; yet in
one aspect they are equal: God speaks differently to these men
than to men of the periods before.

When we take all together the trends discussed so far, the
change in world outlook and ways of life made by discoveries of
new continents, new economic methods, and new horizons of art
and thought, we cannot wonder that the political attitudes of men
also changed their character. Here again it is impossible to separate
clearly the new from the old. We observed in Sicily and France
the beginnings of the new absolutism that absorbed the old feudal
system and the criticism of papal claims by William of Occam and
Marsilius of Padua. During the Renaissance, however, these trends
assume full momentum. The old chivalry is in complete decay;
many earn their living as glorified waylayers. Only the really great
vassals are still powerful, and, except in Germany and Italy, they
are gradually subjected by centralizing governments. The rich
bourgeois is often more important to kings and emperors than the
old aristocracy. In consequence of the devaluation of landed property and the use of firearms, the political system outgrows more and
more the old feudal order and enters into the state of modern
nationalism that has so decisively influenced the spirit of our
modern schools. The emperor, as we already saw, loses more and
more of his authority, and so does the pope. The myth of the two
heavenly bodies, the pope representing the sun and the emperor
the moon, no longer corresponds with the temper of the time.
After the learned humanist Lorenzo Valla, with the help of philological methods, had disclosed the Constantinian forgery, the whole
mythology could no longer be upheld.[14]

[13] Giovanni Pico della Mirandola, "Oration on the Dignity of Man," trans.
Elizabeth Livermoore Forbes, in *The Renaissance Philosophy*, ed. E. Cassirer,
P. O. Kristeller, J. H. Randall, Jr. (University of Chicago Press, 1948), p. 225.
[14] *De falso credita et emendita Constantini donatione declamatio*. Written in
1440 and first published in 1517 by Ulrich von Hutten.

But, whereas Valla still saw human life and society embedded in a divine matrix, there now arose the idea of the absolute autonomy of politics in the mind of another Italian, Nicolo Machiavelli (1469–1527). If science is defined as the passion for dispassionateness in observing, interpreting, and establishing causal relationships, then it first reached consummation not among the natural scientists of the seventeenth century, as we mostly hear, but in the mind of the historian and political scientist Machiavelli. What an extraordinary person! At a time when, despite some remarkable theoretical and practical prophecies of the empirical method, the thinking about man and nature deduced the values and modes of living from first causes, Machiavelli shook off all traditions that he considered prejudice. He proceeded to show the true character of that admirable beast called man. He could do so because he was not overfed with erudition when as a young man he was thrown into the arena of human affairs. In that same arena Cesare Borgia and the larger and smaller tyrants of Italy played their game of intrigue and murder. When the fall of Machiavelli's Florentine government forced him into retreat, he had the courage to see what was and to write about it without hypocrisy and pious phrases. As his letters and his comedy *Mandragola* show, he delighted in frivolity; yet at the same time he possessed a genuine sense of greatness.

He admires without restriction the heroes of antiquity, but this reverential attitude gives him no illusions about the fact that a combination of cunning, fraud, and force has generally led the way toward power. Those who wish to rule must be capable of great vision, but — as modern psychologists would say — they must also be without inhibitions. In a strange contrast, he advocates equality, hates the parasitical aristocracy, and, instead of the socially inferior form of tyrannical monarchy, wishes to have free republics. However, the concept of human dignity, on which all free societies must be based, is alien to him.

This limitation also explains Machiavelli's relation to religion. "Our religion," he asserts, "teaches us the truth and the true way of life" in that it "places the supreme happiness in humility, lowliness, and a contempt for worldly objects." But he also makes the point that "the baseness of men who have interpreted our religion according to the promptings of indolence rather than those of virtue" has made Christianity an impediment to true human virtue.[15] Religion for him is the opium that holds the masses in stupidity. But, in contrast to some philosophical skeptics of the eighteenth century, this for him is the very reason to recommend it, for in this way the crowd can be kept quiet. In other words, he is more interested in control than in progress.

It is easy to understand what all this means in terms of statecraft. The highest value for Machiavelli is the reunification of his country, then scattered into small and internationally powerless territories by petty, warring tyrants. Consequently, the latter are to be eliminated by the same cruel means they use themselves in dealing with their enemies. At the end there appears to the ardent patriot and the student of Roman history the image of a great republic and of an *imperium romanum* as they had been in the glory of the past. Needless to say, only a superman, a leader, a *principe*, can achieve this goal — a man whose morality exists in the immorality of putting the great end over the means.

Machiavelli has become one of the most controversial figures in the history of European thought, and this not only for the extremity of his ideas. Extremity without some foundation of truth quickly loses its attraction. Rather it is the ruthless honesty with which he has exposed the demoniac character of the political game which has made him a sting in the conscience of man. After all, how was the unity of the great nations in times of inner stress and conflict achieved?

In the thought of Machiavelli, Europe, where so far even the rebels had lived under some world-transcendent aspect, reached for the first time the state of complete autonomy and world immanence. Nietzsche's *Transvaluation of All Values*, to a large degree inspired by the study of antiquity and of the Renaissance, announces itself. And the curse of modern chauvinist nationalism with its motto, "My country, right or wrong," emerges.

With the isolation of one value (however great) from the total cosmos of human values there necessarily disappears the sense of the unity of life (irrespective of whether one explains it in tran-

---

[15] Niccolo Machiavelli, *Discourses.* 2 vols. (New Haven: Yale University Press, 1950) "Discourses on the First Ten Books of Titus Livy," Bk. I, pp. xii, 5, 6, 7.

scendentalist or naturalist terms). Hence anything, if only passionately conceived and believed in, can be made the idol on the altar of which one is allowed to sacrifice human happiness, freedom, and dignity. And the more man progresses in knowledge, organization, and technological achievement, the nearer is the danger of his becoming blind to the comprehensiveness of human ends and a slave to his means. No one who looks realistically at the role our schools have played in the rise of the modern state will deny the momentous importance of this problem.

With the change from transcendental authority to a high degree of personal autonomy and discovery, man's total relation to reality assumes new directions. If he believes that through skillful maneuvering he can capture the wind of the future into his sails, he will by necessity become a planner and an observer. Hence, modern enterprise, the scientific spirit, and the idea of progress begin. Medieval man was also an adventurer, a curious observer, and an experimenter of a sort, but he did not intend to change the world. The world was static. With the Renaissance, life becomes dynamic; it becomes an enterprise. This is the central fact. Science, capitalism, and technology rather than being the causes are the consequences of this fact. Man is no longer the humble worker employed in God's vineyard; he now becomes the bold entrepreneur.

THE RELIGIOUS REFORMERS

The difficulty in finding the line of demarcation between medievalism and modernity increases when we turn our attention toward the religious reformers of the sixteenth century, who together with the humanists have so decisively influenced our modern civilization and its schools. Some historians tend to see in Luther and Calvin the beginning of a new era; others believe they signify a relapse from more advanced into medieval modes of mind. But what, again, in religion is modern, and what is medieval?

Certainly, Luther's religiosity does not contain Nicholas of Cusa's courage of selfhood, though Luther owes much to him, nor is his concept of human dignity of Pico's lofty humanism. The heroic phase in Luther's life lies between 1517, when he affixed his ninety-five theses against ecclesiastical abuses to the door of the Cathedral of Wittenberg, and the middle of the following decade, when he had become one of Europe's most important figures. So often, a great man's fundamental intuitions may, like an opening seed, lie at first under the visible surface. This is the case with the comments the young professor at the University of Wittenberg wrote down in preparation for his lectures on St. Paul's Epistle to the Romans.

> To Romans 8, 19: I believe to owe it to the Lord to fight philosophy and to exhort people to read the Scripture. If someone else who had not studied the philosophers tried to do so, he would become afraid and people would not believe him. But I have consumed myself with this study for many years and deeply experienced that it is a study of vanity and disaster.
>
> Hence it is time that we devote ourselves to other studies and learn to know Jesus Christ, namely, "The Crucified"!
>
> You will then be the best philosophers and scientists when you will learn from the apostle to understand the creation as one that waits, groans, and suffers in childbirth, that is, as one that abhors that which is and asks for that which will be and, for this reason, is not yet. Then people will soon despise the science of the nature of things, of their accidents and differences.[16]

This was, essentially, also the attitude of John Calvin who shared with other bigoted judges of Geneva the responsibility for the burning of Michel Serveto, one of the great scientists of the time (though it was not his science, but his religion, that aroused Calvin's anger).[17]

There are, however, religious differences between Luther and Calvin. The latter is more of an Aristotelian, an astute and radically logical thinker, the author of the only great systematic work that the Reformation can set beside the *Summa Theologica* of Thomas Aquinas, namely, the *Institutes of the Christian Religion*. It was this very logic that drove him to theological assumptions about free will, original sin, and predestination that, though hard to understand for modern man, have nevertheless the quality of immanent consistency. They aroused in Calvin's followers the stern decision to live with the God whose iron justice the master had revealed so well. These followers suffered martyrdom and emigration, in-

---

[16] Martin Luther, *Vorlesung über den Römerbrief, 1515–1516*, trans. Eduard Ellwein. 2 vols. (Munich, Chr. Kaiser, 1928).

[17] See Roland H. Bainton, *Hunted Heretic: The Life and Death of Michael Servetus* (Boston: Beacon Press, 1953).

deed, did not hesitate to impose martyrdom on others, rather than arouse in themselves the suspicion that they did not belong to the elect of the Lord.

But for the education of nations the political significance of his work was just as important as Calvin's theology. He knew about the inseparability between the religious, the ethical, and the political areas of man's responsibility. "Civil Government," he says,

is designed . . . to cherish and support the external worship of God, to preserve the pure doctrine of religion, to defend the constitution of the Church, to regulate our lives in a manner requisite for the society of men, to form our manners to Civil Justice, to promote our concord with each other and to establish general peace and tranquility.[18]

Luther's attitude toward political government — which is, after all, one of the greatest educational or noneducational factors in human society — is ambiguous, in some respects near to, in other respects different from, that of Calvin. This is the reason why some historians have blamed him for degrading and others for overemphasizing the importance of the state. In his early writings, only God's regiment is important. Essentially, he never left this position. This religiously conditioned devaluation of politics made it possible for the German Lutherans to allow earthly government more and more independence and authority. Their souls were not really in it, and they delegated to it more and more power. Calvinists, on the other hand, were interested to do as much as possible themselves. Thus the countries where they were of influence, namely, Switzerland, England, Scotland, the Netherlands, and North America, developed toward democracy, whereas Germany remained autocratic up to the nineteenth century. Luther himself invited the government's intervention in social, religious, and educational affairs when he realized that his work would break down without the help of the princes. He was terrified when he saw that the cruelties of the Peasants' War of 1524 were connected with his work.[19]

---

[18] John Calvin, *Institutes of the Christian Religion*. Translated from the Original Latin by John Allen, 6th Amer. ed. (Philadelphia: Presbyterian Board of Publication, n.d.), II, 634.

[19] Richard Henry Tawney, *Religion and the Rise of Capitalism* (New York: Harcourt, Brace, 1952), p. 82: "Above all, the Peasants' War . . . not only terrified Luther into his outburst 'Whoso can strike, smite, strangle, or stab, secretly, or publicly . . . such wonderful times are these that a prince can better merit

But it may be wrong to attribute this diverging development of Calvinism and Lutheranism to theological differences. Its origin can be sufficiently explained with reference to the fact that Calvin, a refugee from absolutist France, entered into Geneva, which, however aristocratic a kind of republic, was nevertheless a commonwealth where he could hope to build his "City of God" with the help of the people. Luther, in contrast, started and had to carry through his reform in a realm of absolutist governments where the citizen was supposed to obey. The "City of God" was there a transcendental and otherworldly idea, not a religious-political vision to be realized on earth.

Calvin, influenced by Scripture and by Aristotle, could write:

Indeed, if these three forms of government [monarchy, aristocracy, democracy] . . . be considered in themselves, I shall by no means deny, that either aristocracy, or the mixture of aristocracy and democracy, far excels all others; and that indeed not of itself, but because it very rarely happens that kings regulate themselves so that their will is never at variance with justice and rectitude." [20]

If Luther had written in this vein, he would have spoiled not only his own work, but that of the whole Reformation, for the German Protestant princes did not intend to sacrifice their autocratic position to a religious cause, however genuinely some of them were interested in it. But, though Calvin recommended, so to speak, the more modern and constitutional forms of government, with "magistrates" as the appointed representatives of the people, he was, just as Luther, in no way a friend of revolutionary action, not even against unjust princes.

But if those, to whom the will of God has assigned another form of government, transfer this to themselves so as to be tempted to desire a revolution, the very thought will be not only foolish and useless, but altogether criminal.

This is exactly what Luther thought. Their agreement confirms

---

Heaven with bloodshed, than another with prayer,' it also helped to stamp on Lutheranism an almost servile reliance on the secular authorities." See Luther's "Against the Robbing and Murdering Peasants" in *Works* (Philadelphia: Muhlenberg Press, 1931), Vol. IV.
[20] *Institutes*, II, 640.

the opinion that not theory, but environment, made one group more democratic, the other more autocratic.

In evaluating the cultural effect of the Reformation one should not forget that great events often take directions different from those foreseen by the originators. The genuine character of every great movement, including Christianity, has been changed by the momentum of the motion. Whatever the Reformation under the guidance of a Luther, Calvin, or Zwingli was, whether more or less medieval, individualistic, or magical, whether "the last great flowering of the piety of the Middle Ages" or "the recovery of uncorrupted Christianity," [21] a simplification of religion,[22] or a complication, it stirred up both its followers and its enemies. By breaking down the sacramental forms of the Catholic Church and the wall erected by the priesthood between man and God, it created endless disturbances (Germany has never recovered from harboring both the empire and the Lutheran reform). Yet, it also made man a thinking, and in the course of time a critical, participant in the continual discourse between humanity and the Divine. Certainly, the Protestant craftsman or farmer who at night read the Bible with his family and servants interpreted Holy Writ not more competently than did the scholastics. But, if there was much subjectivity in his supernatural imagination, at least, it was his. In addition, these explorers of the divine word corrected and contradicted each other. And, most of all, they exercised their minds on a great and profound subject that offered an infinite variety of suggestions. Thus, on the one hand, there arose a rich sectarianism that constantly renewed the genuineness of religious experience; on the other hand, there grew doubt and with it the search for new ways of inquiry. Hence, whereas the hierarchy of the Catholic Church kept their faithful firm within the sanctified tradition and even strengthened it by increasing centralization, Bible-centered Protes-

[21] Roland H. Bainton, *The Reformation of the 16th Century* (Boston: Beacon Press, 1952), p. 35.

[22] Adolf Harnack, *What is Christianity?*, trans. Thomas Bailey Saunders, 2nd ed. (New York: Putnam's, 1901), p. 288. "In the first place, religion was here [in Protestantism] brought back again to itself, in so far as the Gospel and the corresponding religious experience were put into the foreground and freed of all alien accretions."

tantism — truly against its initial intention — opened the way for innumerable critics and heretics. Here is the reason for the great intellectual vitality of Protestantism or, in Catholic nations, of the dissenting groups. But here is also the danger that under the weight of so many differences, and finally under the influence of secularism, both Protestant and Catholic dissensions dissolve into such an ocean of difference about anything religious that the end may be indifference.

THE EFFECTS OF THE TIME ON EDUCATION

Great are the changes the Renaissance and Reformation have wrought on the European schools. Yet, here I can describe them briefly because with the sixteenth century we have already entered the period when education loses its universal aspect and becomes increasingly a national responsibility.

There exists a strange discrepancy in the education of the period. On the one hand, books and pamphlets increase by leaps and bounds. The humanists write on the breeding of young noblemen or scholars; the religious reformers, on the upbringing of a Christian youth.[23] Schools also increase rapidly; every major city in northern Italy, central Europe, and England gives the son of a citizen who is willing to pay an opportunity to learn "the three R's" and even Latin. Older historians liked to refer to the fifteenth and sixteenth centuries as the era of learning. Apparently civilization had become too complex to be transmitted to the younger generation without the intermediary role of the teacher. The family, the guildmaster's workshop, and the church no longer suffice.

The new climate is exemplified in the change of the vocabulary concerning the aims of man and education, for one no longer speaks of Christian humility, of man's wandering through this valley of misery toward either heaven or hell, of asceticism and detachment from earthly goods. The goal is the *uomo universale*, the well-rounded, educated person, who is interested in his and his family's

---

[23] For a detailed description of the educational ideas of the humanists and reformers, see Robert Ulich, *History of Educational Thought* (New York: American Book Co., 1950) and *Three Thousand Years of Educational Wisdom.*

glory, honor, and power, who has an elegant style of writing, speaking, and living, and who excels in serving his country, or to be more exact, its prince (the "courtier" appears).

On the other hand, humanist education is below the greatness of the time. There is in these treatises little of the fascination of Renaissance Rome and Florence. In spite of appeals to piety and greatness, humanist instruction seems to be most concerned with the proper imitation of Cicero's Latin. Indeed, in 1528 the most prominent and freest of the humanists, Erasmus of Rotterdam, writes a satirical *Ciceronianus*,[24] admonishing his learned friends that with their insistence on pure and unadulterated Latin they may lead men toward formality rather than independent thinking. Cicero's Latin, after all, could not even interpret the gospel of Christ, for he knew nothing about it. In France, England, and especially in Germany the best of the humanists are men of high moral standards, and good scholars to whom we owe the beginning of the sciences of philology and, to a degree, of historical research. But, when they speak of the education of youth, most of them tend toward the pedantic. Again however, Erasmus in his *Education of a Christian Prince*[25] by far transcends the typical pedagogical literature of the time by painting the picture of a monarch who, in essence, could be the ruler of a modern democracy; and in England Sir Thomas More[26] and Sir Thomas Elyot[27] reveal the sense of responsibility for public affairs typical of English men of letters.

In contrast to the Renaissance educators, especially those of Italy, the Protestant reformers are not humanists; their main concern is the purity of the faith and the salvation of the human soul. Of course, more than the medieval schools of divinity they cultivate the ancient languages, including Hebrew; yet, they do so not because these languages inspire genteelness — Luther was certainly not genteel — but because the Lord has chosen them as the instru-

---

[24] *Ciceronianus, or a Dialogue on the Best Style of Speaking*, trans. Izora Scott (New York, Columbia University Teachers College, 1908).

[25] *Institutio Principis Christiani* (1516), trans. Lester K. Born under the title, *The Education of a Christian Prince* (New York: Columbia University Press, 1936).

[26] *Utopia*, publ. in Latin, 1516; Eng. trans., 1551. Many editions.

[27] *The Boke Named the Governour*.

ment of his revelation. Truly, there may also be beauty and secular wisdom in them, but these are secondary values.

However, the charm of antiquity cannot be pushed aside so easily. Just as with the Church Fathers, it asserts itself again against the zeal of the Protestants. In addition, their worship is based on the sermon. Thus the minister needs eloquence, and where can he find it better than in the ancient orators, especially in Quintilian's *Institutio Oratoria*, which is not only a guide for the speaker, but also a kind of outline for liberal education? Needless to say, the Catholic clergy also appreciated the flower of oratory, especially the Jesuits, who were soon to become the leaders of the Counter Reformation. So the end was again the compromise between pagan antiquity and Christian teaching, a compromise that since early Christianity has so largely determined the course of our moral and intellectual education.

With the sixteenth century there begins, in a sense, the history of the modern national systems of education. However, they all are influenced by two cultural movements, which, like the ancient and Christian heritage and the Renaissance cut horizontally through all Western history. They will be described in the next two chapters.

III

The Age of Reason

INTRODUCTION

Wᴴᴱɴ we progress from the time of the Renaissance
and the Reformation toward the period often named the Age of
Reason or the Age of Rationalism or the Enlightenment, we enter
into stages of cultural development which even more than the
previous ones defy brief and simple definitions. For the more we
advance toward our own age, the more the affairs and interests
of men become specialized and diversified. In the field of art, for
example, styles begin to abound and to live side by side. And,
whether they like it or not, humanists and theologians have to
admit that there are also scientists. Gradually, though not without
heavy convulsions, Catholics become, perhaps not reconciled to,
but at least acquainted with, the fact that there will be Protestants,
and vice versa. There begins the age of pluralistic, and there ends
the age of monolithic, societies.[1] Finally, monarchs learn to adapt
to the phenomenon of democracy, which in the beginning at least
they honestly hate and despise.

Hence, in giving the new era the name Age of Reason, we
know the limitations of such a label. There was much unreason
as well as reason — otherwise it would not have been human —
and much superstition as well as enlightenment.

[1] Carl J. Friedrich, *The Age of Baroque, 1610–1660* (New York: Harper, 1952),
Chap. 5.

INTELLECTUAL CHARACTERISTICS

By the Age of Reason I understand the period between Descartes, who was born in 1596 and died in 1650, and Hegel, who was born in 1770 and died in 1831. Descartes is significant because the only undeniable fact he could think of in his struggle for certainty was his self-consciousness as a thinking being. Scholastic philosophy still lived in him, for together with his emphasis on individual thinking went the similarly emphatic conviction of the deductibility of God and the divine order. Hegel's significance lies in his interpretation of history as the evolution of the Mind toward its absolute self-fulfillment. For him also, as for Descartes, the way of reason was the way of God. After Hegel, needless to say, men were still passionately interested in thinking, but they were no longer so sure about the validity of aprioristic reasoning.

The great Swiss naturalist Louis Agassiz (1807–1873), who, after studying in Germany became a teacher at Harvard University, describes his impression of the speculative school in the following terms:

The temptation to impose one's own ideas upon nature, to explain her mysteries by brilliant theories rather than by patient study of the facts as we find them, still leads us away. With the school of the physio-philosophers began (at least in our day and generation) that overbearing confidence in the abstract conceptions of the human mind as applied to the study of nature, which still impairs the fairness of our classifications and prevents them from interpreting truly the natural relations binding together all living beings. And yet, the young naturalist of that day who did not share, in some degree, the intellectual stimulus given to scientific pursuits by physio-philosophy would have missed a part of his training. There is a great distance between the man who, like Oken [Lorenz Oken, 1770–1851], attempts to construct the whole system of nature from general premises and the one who, while subordinating his conceptions to the facts, is yet capable of generalizing the facts, of recognizing their most comprehensive relations. No thoughtful naturalist can silence the suggestions, continually arising in the course of his investigations, respecting the origin and deeper connection of all living beings; but he is the truest student of nature who, while seeking the solution of these great problems, admits that the only true scientific system must be one in which the thought, the intellectual structure, rises out of and is based upon facts. The great merit of the physio-philosophers consisted in their suggestiveness. They did much in freeing our age from the low estimation of natural history as a science which prevailed in the last century. They stimulated a spirit of independence among observers; but they also instilled a spirit of daring, which from its extravagance, has been fatal to the whole school.[2]

As is evident, the protest of Agassiz and his naturalist friends was not against the use of reason itself, but against its speculative abuses. They insisted that the great German idealists and system-makers, who, in a sense, could be described as secularized scholastics of a sort, and who, in addition, constantly contradicted each other, not be permitted to befuddle their students with profound intuitions about the innermost nature of the universe. Those who worked in the tradition of Galileo, Huygens, Kepler, Newton, and Lavoisier felt that the doors to the workshop of life could not be so easily opened. Even philosophers like Francis Bacon, Locke, Hume, and Kant had looked with suspicion on aprioristic manifestos and transsensual insights. And so had the French *philosophes*, such as Voltaire and Diderot, who opposed a trained "common sense" to all kinds of glorified, and for this very reason dangerous, supernatural insights. Who knew that they were not mere prejudices?

But, despite the variety of trends, there is a certain unity in the period under discussion which permits us to call it the Age of Reason. All the men just mentioned, whether philosophers, scientists, or mystics, whether directly influenced by Descartes or not, live nevertheless under his motto, *cogito, ergo sum* (I think, therefore I am). In addition, like Descartes, they all cultivate, or at least pay homage to, mathematics, irrespective of whether they admire it as the most marvelous achievement of the deductive mind or as the great medium of the empirical disciplines. Of the mystics, who, in a way, already belonged to the scientific-rational era, Comenius (1592–1670) laid the foundation of a systematic understanding of the teaching and learning process by applying Bacon's inductive method to education; Pascal's name ranks high in the history of mathematics; Swedenborg not only professed to know what was going on in heaven, but also knew, better than anyone of his time, what was going on in metals and mines.

[2] *Louis Agassiz. His Life and Correspondence*, ed. Elizabeth Cary Agassiz (Boston: Houghton Mifflin, 1885), I, 152f.

One great idea inspired the leading minds of that period: the idea of order. For by far the largest number of these men, this idea did not exclude a personal God; in this respect a Galileo, Newton, Bacon, or Locke did not greatly differ from the mystics, except that the latter believed themselves to have a more intimate relation to the divine ground than most of their contemporaries. It was only later, toward the end of the eighteenth century, that there appeared, especially in France, a group of thinkers — both of the speculative and the empirical types — for whom the cosmos and man in it were a merely materialistic affair, and religion just another of the many superstitions into which mankind had been led by priests and canny rulers.

Now, if there is a divine order or reason in reality, or if it expresses itself in man in the form of systematic human reason, why not rely on one's intelligence rather than on supernatural faith and traditions? The main requisite, of course, is that one has the right method (from the Greek *meta ton odon*, "according to the right road") for understanding the sequences of cause and effect, or the laws by which the universe is regulated. "Method," in other words, is the logical counterpart of the ontological concept of "world order."

Therefore, whether in the great minds of the period thinking proceeded deductively — *more mathematico*, as Spinoza phrased it — or inductively and experimentally, as with the great scientists, there always was the critical search for the right method. With its help — this was the hope — man would learn how to advance not only theoretically but also morally and practically in the affairs of life; he would master not only himself, but also his natural and social environment.

Thus the Abbé de Condillac could write:

The most recent progress in the arts [arts to be understood in the widest sense of the word] is intimately connected with their beginning. The laws that determine the effect of the lever determine the laws of all machines. The same rules we apply in building up a philosophical system we apply in ordinary sound judgment; we apply them in writing a whole discourse and in formulating a sentence. Finally a savage nation begins to civilize itself by the same rules by which a civilized nation puts the last touch on its legislation. In order to perfect the arts nothing more was necessary than to do on a grand scale what first was done on a small. The method is one and the same everywhere.[3]

Even in the field of art the desire for method reveals itself. The great French drama of Racine and Corneille is built on the Aristotelian science of aesthetics; the aesthetic philosophers of the time were convinced that beauty in art and rectitude in thought were identical virtues.[4]

The effect of this attitude shows strikingly in education. Parents do not easily offer their children for other people's experimental desires, nor do they want their offspring to be exposed to spiritual influences contrary to good convention. Therefore during the Age of Reason a strictly religious interpretation of the aims and ends of human life prevailed in schools, even more than under the Italian humanists. But this Christian philosophy, so Comenius thought, should by no means prevent a methodical and empirical observation of the operations of the human mind, just as four hundred years before him Thomas Aquinas felt no contradiction between the Christian revelation and the logic of Aristotle. The goal of education was to be derived deductively from Christian destiny; the process was to be analyzed and improved according to science. So deeply were Comenius and his friends convinced of the omnipotence of method that they were sure it would equalize all differences of talent and help everyone to learn as easily and as much as everybody else. Paradoxically enough, a mystic transferred Newton's mechanical universe to the realm of mind; the great scientist himself was more careful.

The long and descriptive titles by which authors of earlier times liked to introduce their books are often most revealing. I reproduce here for illustration the title page of Comenius' famous *Great Didactic* of the year 1632.[5]

[3] Translated from the article, "Art," in "Dictionaire des Synonymes" by Condillac in *Oeuvres Philosophiques* (Paris: Presses Universitaires de France, 1951), XXXIII, 57, 58. The idea of the sameness of method in all purposeful human activities occurs in many writings of Condorcet and his friends among the *philosophes*.

[4] Condillac, *Oeuvres Complètes* (Paris, 1798), xx, p. 427f.

[5] *The Great Didactic*, trans. M. W. Keatinge (London: Adam and Charles Black, 1896).

EDUCATION OF NATIONS

The Great Didactic

Setting forth the whole art of teaching all things to all men or a certain inducement to found such schools in all the parishes, towns, and villages of every Christian kingdom, that the entire youth of both sexes, none being excepted, shall *Quickly, Pleasantly* & *Thoroughly* become learned in the sciences, pure in morals, trained to piety, and in this manner instructed in all things necessary for the present and for the future life, in which, with respect to everything that is suggested, its FUNDAMENTAL PRINCIPLES are set forth from the essential nature of the matter, its TRUTH is proved by examples from the several mechanical arts, its ORDER is clearly set forth in years, months, days and hours, and, finally, AN EASY AND SURE METHOD is shown, by which it can be pleasantly brought into existence.

SOCIAL CHARACTERISTICS

We have already seen that whenever the self-interpretation of man and his relation to the universe change, then man's relation to society also changes. It is remarkable that the rationalist era was enclosed by revolutions that began through religious motivation and became increasingly political in the course of the period.

Luther, as we saw, was conservative in social matters; also, he needed the protection of the German princes. Calvin too taught obedience to earthly government. And for both the word of God, not man's reasoning, was absolute authority. But against their own intentions the Protestant reformers prepared for the rational attitude. They were against sacramentalism and the cult of the saints; they taught people to read and interpret the Bible on their own; they made them individualistic; and they proved that old authorities could be overthrown.

In addition, under the impact of the Reformation there appeared in many countries religious minorities, persecuted not only by the dominant church for reasons of religious, but also by the central government for reasons of political, unity. Besides the Germanic countries, France especially suffered from a religious division that assumed the character of civil war. After the massacre of the Protestants on St. Bartholomew's Day (1572), there appeared rebellious pamphlets that searched radically into the problems of political authority. In the anonymous treatise entitled *Vindiciae contra*

Tyrannos, published in 1579 and based largely on biblical history, the contractual basis of royal authority was established and the laws of nature were appealed to as sufficient reason to take arms against tyrants.

About a hundred years after the *Vindiciae* Spinoza published, also anonymously, his *Tractatus Theologico-Politicus* (1670). In it he attempted to prove "that not only is perfect liberty to philosophize" (which meant for the author also perfect liberty to decide about religious matters) "compatible with devout piety and with the peace of the State, but that to take away such liberty is to destroy the public peace and even piety itself." [6]

About the same time John Locke wrote his *Letters on Toleration*, based on his philosophical views concerning the limits of human understanding. The *Letters* were more compromising and of less intellectual honesty than Spinoza's *Tractatus* (Locke had, for example, no objection to the suppression of the Catholic Church in the interest of national sovereignty). Yet they exerted the same great influence on later generations in England and America as his *Two Treatises on Government*, which recommended parliamentary representation on the basis of the theories of the law of nature, universal reason, and common equity. [7]

Locke wrote his *Treatises on Government* in connection with the Glorious Revolution of 1688, which led to the flight of James II, and the Declaration of Rights offered by Parliament to the new monarchs William and Mary. While the change of monarchs in 1689 was relatively peaceful, a few decades before this event the judges of the Commonwealth under Cromwell had ordered the execution of King Charles I (1649). Thus, within a hundred years the Protestant mind had changed from Luther's and Calvin's recommendation of the obedience of the subjects to the concept of the revolutionary right of the people. The American War of Independence (1775–1783) is but one link in this chain of rationalist upheavals, brought to full circle by the French Revolution of 1789.

All this made a tremendous impression on Europe. Until the

[6] *Tractatus Theologico-Politicus: A Critical Inquiry into the History, Purpose, and Authenticity of the Hebrew Scriptures. . . .* , Eng. trans. (London: Trübner, 1862).

[7] *Two Treatises of Government*, in *Works of John Locke* (London, 1823), Vol. IV, Bk. II, Chap. 2.

seventeenth century the common man may have heard that kings and princes had sometimes poisoned and assassinated each other, but he probably believed that this was a privilege of the nobility. Together with absolute religious power, now also absolute political power was shaken in its foundations. God was no longer in institutions as such, but only in the minds and actions of conscientious men. Earthly governments were "social contracts" and could be changed when those entrusted with their execution abused the privilege.

The earth no longer the center of the world, the realms of matter, mind, and society accessible to rational investigation because of their own rational nature, scientific discoveries changing the aspect of the universe, religious tolerance rather than persecution, monarchies and other venerated traditions no longer by the grace of God but by agreement of the people, the old feudal nobility gradually becoming the shadow of the past, the new class of the self-conscious bourgeois feeling its economic power and asking for adequate participation in politics and culture — take all this together, and there emerges the picture of a revolutionary era of unusual depth and genius. One can still today discern an open-minded from a reactionary individual by asking his opinion about the seventeenth and eighteenth centuries. The first admires them; the second does not.

Yet — so one may say — the very same period saw also the expansion of the Jesuit Order, the consolidation of the Catholic Church, the height of absolutism under the Bourbon and the Hapsburg monarchies, and at many places a total absence of reason and morality in politics, comparable only to that of the twentieth century. This objection is true, but it confirms only the facts already stated that human affairs do not change simultaneously and that institutions tend to stiffen when they are threatened.

And was monarchical absolutism really ever so mighty as we read in our history textbooks? In our admiration, or perhaps also our dislike, for the splendor and power of absolutist courts we easily forget that many of these monarchs lived highly precarious lives, always in the grip of cliques when they were weak, and dangerously exposed when they were strong. Henry IV, the founder of French absolutism, was assassinated only thirty-three years before

Louis XIV, *le roi soleil*, ascended the throne to become the symbol of monarchical glory. But Louis XIV himself never forgot that during a rebellion in his childhood the royal family had had to escape from Paris and the mob had invaded the palace, forcing his mother to show them the little king in his bed. Even before the Revolution, which brought them to the guillotine, Louis XVI and his wife Marie Antoinette of Austria were surrounded by "liberals" they did not like and were the targets of public slander they could not control. Nothing connected with man is "absolute"; man always depends.

One could even maintain that absolutism itself was a kind of revolutionary force. In Germany and England monarchs had supported the sedition against the Catholic Church, and Henry IV of France was still a Protestant when he became king. He converted merely for political reasons. (*Paris vaut bien une messe.*) Conservative in regard to royal decorum and the divine right of monarchs, the absolutist rulers nevertheless did not hesitate to punish great feudal vassals like ordinary criminals; and, since they needed money and consequently industry, they protected the newly rising capitalist and rationalist middle classes and thus prepared for democracy.

The monarch centralized the country's administration; he put at his disposal mechanically equipped regiments that defeated the old chivalry in one battle after the other. By the middle of the seventeenth century the various alliances of the big lords against the monarch, who resided in the nation's capital, had proved to be ineffectual. A staff of specialized functionaries worked in the chancelleries. The loyalty of the subject to his immediate master changed into loyalty to king and country; in other words, modern patriotism began to replace old-fashioned allegiances. Even where, as in the Austrian and German domains, monarchy prevailed without serious danger, it took on a rationalist coloring. It assumed and expanded in secular fashion many obligations discharged in earlier times by the Church, especially education and social welfare. Finally, only where, as in England and the Scandinavian countries, liberal monarchs understood the signs of the time and put themselves in the service of democratic developments, could the balance be achieved between continuity and change so desirable in the life of nations.

If one allows analogies between fields seemingly so far apart as politics and philosophy, then the absolutist system of government resembles much more a rational structure built *more geometrico* like Spinoza's system than does the medieval structure of voluntary loyalty and cooperation. But by no means did this planned structure within prevent mobility and aggressiveness. Even during the nineteenth century, when absolutism had already ceded to constitutionalism, monarchs and their councillors rather than the people were the most powerful factors in violent changes of the status quo. Wilhelm I with Bismarck in Germany and Victor Emmanuel with Cavour in Italy succeeded in overthrowing the old order of independent principalities within their countries and in establishing national unity after popular revolutions had failed. They were the real revolutionaries.

SUMMARY

Each period of mankind pays the price for its virtues. The new ideas for which the pioneers fought and died became gradually accepted; with the withdrawal of the opposition they lose their heroic character and may turn into platitudes. In addition, strong development in one area of culture generally engenders weakness in others, or a lack of balance.

No wonder, therefore, that the men of the seventeenth and eighteenth centuries, in so far as they adhered to the gospel of reason, were relatively unproductive in the fields where intelligence by itself is weak, especially in the field of aesthetic imagination. I have said that the period was enclosed by great revolutions and by great philosophers; it was also enclosed by two of the great poetic figures of mankind. Shakespeare was born in the same year as Galileo (1564), and Descartes only five years later. Goethe died in 1832, one year after Hegel. Both Shakespeare and Goethe could by no effort be pressed into the pattern of rationalism — the first completed the Renaissance (as Bach completed the Reformation); the second, in his youth, led the great rebellion against the German *Aufklärer* (rationalists). Among the great French triad of Corneille, Racine, and Molière, all three living during the seventeenth century, only Molière thinks in the patterns of the Age of Reason; the rational and the satirical are somehow of the same kin. The other two were classicists, not untouched, however, by the rational-geo-metrical spirit of the time. Generally, where rationalism prevails too one-sidedly, the Muses go into exile; they leave the place to moralists, critics, and satirical and epigrammatic writers, in whom, indeed, the seventeenth and eighteenth centuries are rich. We still admire Swift, Defoe, and La Rochefoucauld, and perhaps certain works of Pope. But they are not great writers.

Religion suffers also. There are some eminent theologians and orators in France, among them Bossuet. But official Protestant-ism, especially in Germany, becomes drowned in repulsive argu-mentation. The theologians of the leading Lutheran University of Wittenberg are as busy in censuring "errors" as are their Catholic colleagues of the Sorbonne. Everywhere there emerges a second-hand scholasticism. Only Pietists and other mystics offer edification to a longing soul. And most of them are persecuted or at least suspected by orthodox theologians, who with stupendous perti-nacity apply logical method to the elaboration of irrational dogma.

One has but to turn the leaves of some of their bulky volumes in order to understand the sigh of relief of those who escaped from these crossbreeds of superstition and intellectualism into the air of free reason. Indeed, the conception of a scientifically under-standable universe, already dawning in the Renaissance, became now one of the great forces in the liberation of mankind. It created the beautiful enthusiasm of the Enlightenment. Man felt that with some expectation of reward he could direct his curiosity into every corner of the cosmos, even into the premises of religion and mo-rality. Pierre Bayle's *Dictionaire* and the *Encyclopédie Française*, compiled under Diderot's direction, though forbidden by the Church, were avidly read by the educated men all over the world; they were smuggled even into the Spanish colonies. There was hope that man might free himself from the bondage of magic, fear, and prejudice, as well as from the serfdom to natural powers.

A new conception of history began because through compari-son men discovered that other cultures besides the Christian had profound values. Instead of explaining human events with reference to divine dispensation, they tried to find the real causes of human behavior and of the rise and decline of nations. The pragmatic form of historical writing, as first taken up by Macchiavelli, was now cultivated. It created, on the one hand, classic masterpieces (for example, Gibbon's *The Decline and Fall of the Roman Empire*), but, on the other hand, highly subjective speculations. The divine plan was denied; instead there appeared all sorts of human designs to explain the course of mankind.

Humanity, which so far had believed in salvation as coming only from supernatural powers, refused now to suffer any longer from the sins of the first couple. It began to gain confidence in itself. The writers of Greece and Rome were read in a spirit of true emulation, not only in regard to their aesthetic and philosophic values, but also in regard to their political ideas and ideals. The classical studies, which today so often generate a spirit of conservative aloofness, then engendered the temper of political action. Montesquieu, Jefferson, and the Adamses derived much of their inspiration from the ancient heritage. Everywhere the oratory of the time revealed the style of Cicero. Mirabeau and Robespierre had read Seneca and Plutarch, and Camille Desmoulins displayed his knowledge of Homeric and, of course, of Latin eloquence in his addresses to the revolutionary masses of Paris.

But in naming men such as Robespierre and Desmoulins we have trespassed the boundary between prudence and political demagoguery. The wise man consults history for advice; the minor man consults it to confirm his personal prejudices. Furthermore, the latter cannot wait. By confusing his own personal reasoning for the deep reason that may prevail in human events, he finally throws the whole past overboard and begins to make history according to his own pleasure. Just abolish superstition, cut the present off from the past, and a new world will be born. Out of such an attitude arose the mistakes of the French Revolution. Its leaders wanted action; they thought that the main work in constructing a new house would be to pull down the old. The result was first the dictatorship of the masses of Paris, then the dictatorship of Napoleon, and finally a war-ridden Europe.

Yet, whereas we think only with horror of the Thirty Years' War (1618–1648), that symbol of dying feudal and religious hatreds still raging in the time when Galileo and Descartes were creating a new world picture, we connect a different feeling with the French Revolution. Here the constructive and the destructive meet each other. Liberty errs; liberty becomes superstitious about herself; she puts herself into chains; she stands in blood up to her ankles. Yet, at the end there is more liberty than there ever was before; and since that time, whenever liberty is offended, the conscience of mankind rebels. This, despite all errors and contradictions, is the great achievement of the Age of Reason.

In addition, it would be one-sided to consider the Age of Reason an epoch vanishing in the fog of disappointment which the last years of the French Revolution brought over Europe. The tragedy of France was caused not so much by the rationalism of the *philosophes* and their followers as by the irrationalism of their enemies. For all attempts at enlightenment and at improving the life and mind of man were blocked by the unholy alliance between absolutism and clericalism supported by the schools, from the Jesuit colleges up to the Sorbonne. By necessity, this led to the hostility of liberal men against the society in which they lived, to the romantic despair of a Rousseau in the re-creational power of his age, and to the violent interruption of the French educational tradition. On the other hand, in England, where government, Church, and the empirical and critical minds managed to live in peace or at least in some sort of truce with each other, enlightened ideas were gradually absorbed and became a formative element in the gentleman ideal and in the advanced schools. In Germany, whose many little principalities provided no outlet for political development, rationalism helped to create the last great speculative philosophies of Europe and a new type of higher education that influenced the universities of all Western countries. Finally, one cannot understand the history of the American Constitution apart from the great minds whose aim it was to see respected the natural (which meant the rationally conceived) rights of man, not only as regards the individual soul and its transcendental hopes, but also as regards the political and educational aspirations of humanity as a whole.

IV

The Era of Technology

INDUSTRIALIZATION, MECHANIZATION, AND POLITICS

J UST as for the seventeenth and eighteenth centuries the driving force is reason, so for the nineteenth and twentieth centuries it is application, or technology. Yet, here also the observation that an historical era cannot be characterized by one element alone applies.

The main facts are so well known and so near to us that only some cues are needed. On the *positive* side we find in the industrialized countries better living standards and, consequently, better health and lower mortality rates. England's population has increased by five times since 1800; the population of North America, by more than twenty-eight times.[1] The life expectancy of an American was fifty-one around 1920; today it is sixty-seven. Still greater than the mastery over his own physique is modern man's mastery over the forces in his environment. His bridges span the widest rivers, his railways transgress whole continents, his modern ships (in comparison to which most of the princely palaces of the eighteenth century were modestly equipped, though perhaps with better taste) cross the Atlantic in four days, his passenger planes do it in one night and will soon do it in a few hours. The time of atomic energy is rapidly approaching for industrial production. The common man of today has a much wider access to sources of enlightenment and recreation than his ancestors.

[1] One has, of course, to take into account the fact that the United States increased its territory at the same time, and had an enormous influx of immigrants.

On the *negative* side there is the increasing mechanization of man's occupation. The number of people who can throw their whole personality into their daily work will shrink more and more: a few selected will do the creative thinking and planning; the others, though in echelons of different size and importance, will carry out the orders. The frightening term, "human engineering," is already widely used by certain psychologists who offer themselves as experts in the gigantic business of conditioning their fellow men according to any desirable scheme. George Orwell's *1984* and Aldous Huxley's *Brave New World* contain, as every good satiric utopia, sufficient truth to conjure up the image of a frightful reality. Since in the industrially advanced countries the problem is no longer production, but overproduction, and since (is this not the most terrible indictment?) there has been circling over Western societies of the past decades either the vulture of war or the vulture of unemployment, a feeling of insecurity has gripped the seemingly most secure man who ever lived on earth. And, if one of the big nations is driven to despair or becomes insane with power, it may even start the mutual destruction of mankind.

When we look at the economic effects of the rise of technology, we find increasing separation of wealth from the land and, consequently, new possibilities of investment. This allows for the accumulation of enormous fortunes as well as for the most irresponsible financial maneuvers, for artificial crises, for enormous cooperative enterprises as well as for ruthless forms of exploitation. During the first decades of the American democracy 90 per cent of the population lived and worked on their own farms; by 1950, 88.4 per cent were industrial workers with a relatively high living standard but few savings, exposed to the cycles of big business, which in turn is dependent on the vicissitudes of the great world market.

Whether with or against Marx, the industrial masses have protected, or sometimes even overprotected, themselves by unionization. Mainly by this means, they have entered into political life. The "fourth estate" of the worker has arisen beside the "third estate" of the bourgeois. While this means an inestimable gain in terms of welfare and justice, it brings about the problem of the maturity of the masses in regard to decisions of cultural and political importance. It would, however, be totally wrong to look at this modern dilemma with a snobbish prejudice and quote the title of Ortega y Gasset's famous *The Revolt of the Masses* without having read the book. As a matter of fact, in several countries the unionized worker has been a better guardian of peace and steady progress than large groups of a disinherited nobility, a greedy bourgeoisie, and a sophisticated but inexperienced intelligentsia. The split between wise and unwise, the immunity from, or the susceptibility to, irresponsible propaganda, goes through all social classes.

Nor can one say that the appearance of the worker as a political force has caused the modern menace of totalitarianism. Totalitarian ideologies were invented by thinkers often of considerable intellectual acumen, transferred into reality by professional revolutionaries or outright, though cleverly disguised, enemies of mankind. These enemies were supported by reactionaries, businessmen, and militarists alike who even knew that the men they wanted to use for their purposes were scoundrels. This is no denial of the fact that, once the necessary climate of political persuasion and the necessary power were secured, the masses offered themselves as easy prey to the slogans and the martial music of the tyrants. Among the fighting Social Democratic workers of old imperial Germany one could hear the somewhat cruel slogan: "Nur die allergroessten Kaelber waehlen ihre Schlaechter selber." If for the purpose of rhyme one were allowed to change "Kaelber" (calves) into "goats," the English translation would be: "But the most stupendous goats give their slaughterers their votes." Unfortunately, the warning was not heeded in the latter days of the German Republic, nor in several other countries proud of their cultural achievements. There is, of course, the sad explanation of despair, hunger, inflation, unemployment, national defeat, and humiliation. The fact, nevertheless, remains that man's dignity lies in his choice to react to calamity either as *homo sapiens* or as a fool.

And now there is before us perhaps the greatest of all tasks in human history since its change from tribal to national organization, namely, the task of building the existing nation-states into a supernational order, or of combining the citizen's loyalty to his country with his role as a citizen of the world. We all feel that it must be done, but old hatreds, old habits, and even old loves stand in the way. If we succeed in changing and directing these various sentiments toward constructive attitudes, the twentieth century will be praised as one of, if not the, greatest of all centuries; if we fail, it will open the darkest chapter of human civilization.

THE SPIRITUAL SITUATION

The judgment on our modern art, also, will depend on our solving or missing the paramount problem of our social future. If we solve it, the bewildering variety of styles, the seeking of the artist for new forms of expression, the battles of schools of thought, will be valued as we value the wandering years of a great personality who in order to come to himself needs many trials and attempts at self-expression. If we miss, the groping will be judged as but another sign of disintegration and impending chaos.

And achievement or failure in the political and aesthetic realms will go hand in hand with our religious and philosophical meanderings. It is high time that our period discovers the wisdom in Pascal and Kirkegaard, but this should not be done at the expense of the bold criticism and wonderful laughter of a Voltaire, of the grand conception of man's involvement in a cosmic enterprise of the idealists, or of the intellectual depth and honesty of a Renan. There is still upon us the necessity to fight witch hunters and obscurantists, to tell uprooted people that conversions to medievalism, though fashionable, will but aggravate the personal and social evils of the time. A person or a period that speaks only of failure and anxiety and smiles at anyone who still believes in the possibility of human freedom and progress prepares its own downfall.

But we can no longer speak of our spiritual, moral, and social future without asking the question as to whether we will succeed in integrating science into the totality of human interests. So much has been written about this problem, for nothing today excites the world as intensely as a new scientific discovery (especially when it contains new means of wholesale destruction), that a few sentences can suffice in the context of this book.

Science is at the same time our greatest hope and our greatest fear. It is our greatest hope because on its development depend the life and happiness of the ever-growing millions of humanity; our greatest fear because every step forward it takes may also be a step into holocaust. Whatever we would try, this progress of science cannot be stopped for two reasons. First, the human mind is of insatiable curiosity. When and wherever it sees the chance of a new discovery, it goes after it like an animal that scents its prey. Second, since the beginning of time man has known that scientific insight transferred into technology may give him an advantage over his neighbors and enemies. The Russian-American race over satellites and missiles is only the most recent and momentous phase of this oldest and most gruesome competition. Hence the question just raised, namely, whether we will be capable of fitting science into the totality of human concerns, physical as well as mental, has to be embedded in a still greater one, probably the greatest man can ask: whether we will finally become mature enough to direct our competitive instinct toward the universal good of humanity, instead of allowing it to create ever new and widening hostilities.

EDUCATION

At a period when every adult is invited to participate responsibly in the decisions of his nation, education is of utmost importance for the whole of mankind. But people tend to attribute to it a role that it cannot fulfill. For even the best school cannot avert the dangers emerging from modern nationalist competition, mechanization, propaganda, from passive amusements and the hunger for artificial excitement that goes with unnatural forms of living. The battle for better education has to be fought in the whole area of national and international life. It is the duty of those entrusted with the practical or theoretical responsibilities of educational policy to make people conscious of and conscientious in regard to the conditions that must prevail if our schools are to transmit the best in our tradition to the younger generation. These conditions, of which I will speak at the end of this book in more detail, are threefold.

First, there must be a way to protect the individual against the encroachment of the powers of collectivization, especially of the chauvinist tendencies inherent in the modern state. Under the pretext of democracy, or even religion, politicians help today consciously and unconsciously to suppress the individual's freedom of thought, conscience, and expression. Unless democracies revive in themselves the principles on which a free life is built, they will suddenly wake up and recognize that they have been led into dull uniformity or totalitarian tyranny.

Second, how can this revival take place? Only by a new, or, better, an old, self-understanding of the individual. There is no escape from totalitarianism if the person feels himself merely a member of the society in which he happens to live, or if he understands his duty as a citizen merely in terms of loyalty to the government that exists, whether good or evil. In other words, man must not be devoured by his society. Rather he must stand within and before it as a critical person, unwilling to waste the greatest gift he has to spend, namely, his devotion, to humanly unworthy purposes. The pressures of technology, industrialization, political management, and propaganda have made it more difficult than ever to produce in oneself the creative solitude and perspective of the critical mind. People, highly efficient in their specialty, professors, executives, businessmen, and engineers, often display a frightening form of proud and eloquent ignorance outside their offices. We must gain, or regain, the power of transcendence that puts a glimmer of eternity into the frailty of human existences and institutions. The vertical line of height and depth must be added to the horizontal line of socialization.[2]

Third, though seemingly an issue of a different kind, there is nevertheless closely connected with the problems of individual independence and self-transcendence the present concern of thoughtful men with the relation between quality and equality (often glibly identified with democracy). Everywhere the present trend is toward the latter. To be sure, much injustice stemming from old privileges and prejudices has to be removed. On the other hand, there is danger that this is being done at the expense of the precious value of quality.

Many authors establish an inevitable contradiction between the two. But this is false. For, paradoxical though it may appear, equality without quality leads to a struggle of power in which the victory will be won not by the finest but by the roughest com-

[2] See here the various books by Pitirim Sorokin, especially *The Crisis of Our Age; the Social and Cultural Outlook* (New York: Dutton, 1944).

petitor, not by the independent mind, but by the person with the greatest ambition, protection, and connection. On the other hand, the defense of quality without respect for the available quantity of applicants for admission to a natural élite, from whatever social stratification they may emerge, leads to undeserved privilege. While democracy of mass instincts produces the despotism of mediocrity, caste systems cripple a nation's vitality. The future of free societies is secured only if those responsible for our public schools learn the great art of challenging the best qualities in the best of the people, while also giving the lesser talent adequate incentive and guidance.

Today the human person stands before the vast impersonality of his environment. In a way, that has always been so. But whereas in earlier times the impersonality lay in the inscrutable powers of nature that surrounded man, today it lies in man's own man-made world. He is constantly involved in societal changes the value of which he can no longer determine. Sometimes one may have the feeling that he acts like a swimmer who believes his strokes carry him forward, while he is actually driven away by the ocean's undercurrent. He is in danger of losing the zest for freedom and initiative on which a progressive society depends. The economic and political problems of the day, though affecting every little household, are so gigantic and so dependent on international constellations that they can no longer be met by individuals alone, but only by governmental action and interference. Thus the responsibility of political bureaucracy increases. All advanced countries move along a small boundary line between liberty and collectivism, and so do the less developed nations because of the impact of world industrialism on their relatively primitive social order.

Here lies the central issue. Will our educational agents — not only schools, but also churches, political parties, family, and friends — sufficiently strengthen our moral, intellectual, and emotional life to counteract the power of mechanization? Civilization is balance, and every period has to poise its particular weights of responsibility or to perish under the uneven burden. Our mission is to direct into new channels of productivity the tension between individual rights and organization, and to do this not only at home but on a world-wide scale.

PART TWO

INDIVIDUAL COUNTRIES
OF EUROPE

V

England

As every period in history is full of contrasts, so is every country. England makes no exception, but in distinction from the large majority of other European countries it has, at least, retained its monarchy and with it a quality of continuity, not only politically, but also educationally.

In view of the feudal wars that plagued the country at the end of the Middle Ages and the humiliations of its government by external enemies, one wonders that the main symbol of a medieval nation's power, namely, the crown, could hold its influence over the people. The country did not split into political fragments, as did Germany, and as France was in danger of doing. Historians explain this fact by referring to the prestige the institution of monarchy had received from the Norman invader William the Conqueror, who in 1066 landed in England. Many countries, the most notable example being Spain, suffered from foreign invasion and rule. England, the nation that by the grace of destiny emerged with new strength from every crisis, profited from the alien dynasty, just as Sweden did at the beginning of the nineteenth century. Sir Winston Churchill says in his *History of the English-Speaking Peoples* that the conquest of England by the Normans "linked the history of England anew to Europe, and prevented forever a drift into the narrower orbit of a Scandinavian Empire." [1] He describes

[1] Winston S. Churchill, *A History of the English-Speaking Peoples* (London: Cassel, 1956), I, 139, 147.

· 7 5 ·

how William the Conqueror's ecclesiastical adviser Lanfranc infused new life into the English Church and how William's son Henry I introduced the idea and practice of king's justice.

"We see therefore the beginning of an attachment to the King or central Government on the part of the people, which invested the Crown with a new source of strength, sometimes forthcoming and sometimes estranged, but always to be gathered, especially after periods of weakness and disorder, by a strong and righteous ruler." Apparently, the decisive factor is not so much whether the monarch is a foreigner, but whether he is able to abolish inner discord, promote welfare, and impress the people by his and his entourage's standards. In old Britain the impression was so strong that during the twelfth and thirteenth centuries the indigenous Anglo-Saxon culture was in danger of succumbing to French-Norman influence. The power of this influence shows still today in the wealth of the English language.[2]

In spite of the uniting power of the monarchical principle the English, in contrast to most Continental nations, avoided the danger of dynastical absolutism. In 1215 the estates forced the Magna Charta on John Lackland, and twice during the fourteenth century the aristocracy dethroned a king (Edward II, 1327; Richard II, 1399). Only the Tudor Henry VIII may be called an absolutist monarch, and, when the Stuarts dared to restrict the power of Parliament, the effect was the Civil War of 1642, with the decapitation of Charles I in 1649, and the deposition of James II in 1689. Since then the influence of Parliament has been guaranteed. By wisely abstaining from violation of the people's rights, the crown could become a symbol not only of the empire's unity, but also of English freedom — even under weak monarchs — an achievement that neither Hapsburg, nor Bourbon, nor Hohenzollern was prudent enough to secure.

The transition from a still primarily medieval to a modern England occurs in the reign of Henry VIII (1509–1547), himself a representative of the conflict of two eras, for he is at the same time the pre-Renaissance gluttonous ruffian and the refined, though im-

---

[2] See Richard Foster Jones, *The Triumph of the English Language* (Palo Alto: Stanford University Press, 1953) and Otto Jesperson, *Growth and Structure of the English Language* (New York: Doubleday Anchor Book, 1956).

moral, Renaissance prince. Ruthless in the pursuit of his aims, he beheaded two of his six wives.

He was a humanist of a sort who read and spoke Latin, Italian, French, and Spanish, who liked good books, who was a protector of the arts and an accomplished musician besides being a great statesman. To be sure, as a ruler of his nation he was favored by such events as the discovery of new continents and sea routes which directed the trade away from the Mediterranean toward the northern shores. However, he understood how to use these new events to English advantage.

Under Henry VIII the English severed their ties with the Roman Church in a way that has left its permanent traces in the religious life of England. On the one hand, the English Reformation, carried out from the top, was a political act that could be risked because the anti-Roman movement had already swept Germany and other Continental countries. On the other hand, since the times of William of Occam (*c.* 1300–*c.* 1349) and Wycliffe (1328–1384) many of the most brilliant Englishmen had protested against papal corruption and suffered for their convictions. From their genuinely religious concern stems the true Protestantism of the English people, which, successfully resisting all encroachments of the Episcopal hierarchy, has been creative of ever-new religious movements, from Robert Browne's Congregationalism (*c.* 1580), to George Fox's Quakerism (*c.* 1650), to John Wesley's Methodism (*c.* 1750) and modern sectarianism. It is this sectarian life that even in times of exploitation has kept the English worker away from the atheist movements and made it possible that in our time the English could adopt large elements of economic socialism without, as in Russia, Italy, and Germany, running into the traps of totalitarianism.

Politically, England at the time of Henry VIII had recovered from the War of the Roses, which in the fifteenth century had wiped out large parts of the nobility and thus eliminated the most powerful rivals of the monarchy. Moreover, the big landowners needed a strong government for protection against rebellious peasants, whose lot, as in most of Europe, had constantly deteriorated. At the same time, just as in Germany and France, the cities welcomed a central power because it freed their trade from continual disturbance by feudal lords.

The vitality of England at the time of Henry VIII is reflected also in the field of education. Even before his period there existed such schools as Winchester (founded in 1384), Eton (1440), and King's School at Canterbury, which claims to have originated at the time of Alfred the Great. In the English towns city companies and private individuals competed with religious organizations and established nonecclesiastical schools such as we find also in northern Italy, Flanders, and the Hanse cities of the northern Continent. But the figure of Henry VIII, the new humanism, the pride in the new national unity and prosperity with its secularizing influence, together with the liberation of religious life from the retarding authority of Rome: all created a new interest in education. The Chantries Act of 1547 provided for the "erecting of Gramer Scoles to the educacion of Youthe in vertewe and godlinesse" and for "the further augmenting of the Universities." [3] At the same time the humanistic movement, which had spread from Italy to France and Germany, entered the English realm. Good Latin schoolmasters taught the ancient tongue in a modernized fashion. Henry VIII himself wrote the preface to William Lilly's *An introduction of the eyght partes of speche, and the Construction of the same*, compiled and sette forthe by the commandement of our most gracious souerayne lorde the king. London, Anno MD.XLII.

Emong the manyfolde busines and moste weyghty affayres, appertaynying to our regall auctorities and offyce, we forgette not the tendre babes, and the youth of our realme, whose good education and godly bryngying up, is a great furniture to the same and cause of moche goodnesse. And to the intent that hereafter they may the more readily and easily attain the rudymentes of the latyne toung, without the great hynderaunce, which heretofore hath been, through the diuersitie of grammers and teachynges: we will and commounde, and streightly charge al you schoolemaisters and teachers of grāmer within this our realme, and other our dominions as ye intend to auoyde our displeasure and haue our fauor, to teache and learne your scholars this englysshe introduction here ensuing, and the latyne gramme annexed to the same, and non other, which we haue caused for your case, and your scholars spedy preferment bryefely and playnely to be compyled and set forth. Fayle not to apply your scholars in lernynge and godly education.

[3] A. F. Leach, *Educational Charters and Documents, 598 to 1909* (Cambridge University Press, 1911), p. 472f.

After Lilly, Roger Ascham's *The Schoolmaster* (1571) and Richard Mulcaster's *Postitions* (1581) and *Elementarie* (1582) acquired national fame. Whereas for many humanists on the Continent the mother tongue was too vulgar to be a subject of learning, and only that kind of Latin was respectable which could be found in Cicero and Pliny, the English revealed their common sense and patriotic pride by honoring also their native language. In his *Elementarie* Richard Mulcaster writes:

> The question is not to disgrace the Latin, but to grace our own [language] . . . I do not think that anie language, be it whatsoeuer, is better able to utter all arguments, either with more pith, or greater planesse, then our *English* tung is . . .

One may also compare Sir Thomas Elyot's *Boke Named the Governour* (1531) with the Italian Count Castiglione's *Libro del Cortigiano* (1528), translated in 1561 by Sir Thomas Hobby under the title *The Book of the Courtyer*. Castiglione's treatise, which describes conversation of humanist courtiers at the court of the duke of Urbino, was the European nobleman's guide to perfect conduct. Rightly praised by historians of literature as one of the masterpieces of fifteenth-century prose, it is nevertheless from the modern point of view stilted and semierudite. Elyot's *Governour* also displays a sort of erudition by using most dubious examples from history for moral elevation, and it is hard to read for the impatient citizen of our century. Yet, while the Italian's paragons of gentility forebode the uprooted parasitism that went as polite behavior at the courts of Europe, Elyot's ideal nobleman has a social purpose; he prepares himself for responsible governorship. Of course, for Elyot governorship is still a privilege of a few, and noble birth is the indispensable prerequisite.

THE COMMONWEALTH

But the time soon changed. During the reign of Elizabeth (1558–1603) the mercantile middle class installed itself firmly in the religious and economic life of the country. The Puritan part of the gentry felt closer to it than to the Anglican nobility, especially

⁴E. T. Campagnac, ed. (London: Clarendon Press, 1925), pp. 273, 274.

when the latter was suspect of Catholic leanings. In 1649 Charles I was sentenced to death by a revolutionary tribunal of Cromwell's followers.

The king's appeal to supernatural legality had become obsolete in the eyes of a society that no longer listened to the doctrines of Thomas Aquinas or Thomas Hobbes. Monarchy was neither divine nor the necessity of a society living in a natural state of depravity and driven solely by egoistic instincts. Social life is a unity, and what starts in one important area must sooner or later influence all the others. Thus, as we have seen, the new society transplanted the spiritual independence of the Reformation into the political realm, and, despite all its monarchical and aristocratic aspects, England became the seeding ground of democracy. Naturally, it added to the spirit of independence that in 1588 the English had defeated the invincible Spanish Armada. The English had also witnessed the cruel suppression of the Huguenots (1562–1598) by the alliance of the Catholic Church and the French monarchy, and the successful wars of liberation of the Netherlanders (1568–1648) against the powerful monarchy of Spain. If a monarch, supported by ecclesiastical absolutism, could use his power for the willful destruction of human lives, the people had the duty to protect themselves, not, of course, as a disorganized mass, but through their elected magistrates and through parliamentary procedures. Pamphlets and books were published that, a hundred years before John Locke and two hundred years before Jean Jacques Rousseau, advocated the basic ideas of modern constitutional government.

The *Vindiciae contra Tyrannos* (first Latin edition, Basel, 1579) by the anonymous Brutus (supposed by some to be Herbert Languet, by others, Duplessis-Mornay) was widely read not only in France, but also in England. In the century after its appearance, the *Vindiciae* was reprinted in Latin or in English eight times. Boldly, it stated that:

Princes are chosen by God, and established by the people. As all particulars considered one by one, are inferior to the prince; so the whole body of the people and officers of state, who represent that body, are the princes' superiors. In the receiving and inauguration of a prince, there are covenants and contracts passed between him and the people, which are tacit and expressed, natural or civil, . . . The officers of the kingdom are the guardians and protectors of these covenants and contracts. He who maliciously or wilfully violates these conditions, is questionless a tyrant by practice. And therefore the officers of state may judge him according to the laws. And if he support his tyranny by strong hands, their duty binds them, when by no other means it can be effected by force of arms to suppress them.[5]

The men who read the *Vindiciae* also read the Bible. And, just as their ecclesiastical predecessors, they read out of it what *they* thought was right. While the conservatives found in Scripture, "Render unto Caesar the things that are Caesar's," Milton found, "As a roaring lion and a raging bear, so is a wicked ruler over the poor people . . . A man that doeth violence to the blood of *any* person, shall flee to the pit; let no men stay him." [6] Divine authority was no longer thought to recommend autocracy. There was the "covenant" between the people of Israel and the Lord; men spoke now of the freedom and equality of all human beings before God.

> When Adam dolve and Eva span,
> Who was then the gentleman? [7]

However, the poverty with which Adam and Eve had to be content appealed to the middle class of the seventeenth century just as little as the poverty of a Francis of Assisi appealed to the Roman cardinals and the Anglican bishops. In the Middle Ages begging (though not every beggar) had the same aura of holiness as it does among the pious Hindus. For the industrious Puritans, it was a shame. Christian piety still demanded prayer, contemplation, and continual self-examination, perhaps even more than in a sacramental church, where the observance of the ritual can so easily be mistaken for truly Christian conduct. But humbleness was for the strictly personal dialogue between man and God. In the realm of society it was not only man's right but his duty to assert himself. And how could a man belong to the elect of the Lord if he ran around idle? If Adam ploughed the field, why should an Englishman not plough the sea? If Eve span, why should he not

[5] See *A Defense of Liberty against Tyrants*, a translation of *Vinciciae contra Tyrannos* by Junius Brutus, with an Historical Introduction by Harold J. Laski (London: J. Bell, 1924), p. 212.
[6] Luke 20:25; Proverbs XXVIII, 15, 17 (Motto of Milton's *Eikonoklastes*).
[7] W. C. Hazlitt, *English Proverbs* (London: Reaves & Turner, 1907), p. 523.

manufacture man's garment by more efficient means, or sell the fine wool to the cities of Flanders? Also, if the prince expanded the frontiers of the country with the help of his soldiers, he accomplished a good act, for he gave the clergy a chance to convert pagans, and he procured new opportunities for men of business. But, in spite of the same ruthless exploitation of subjected populations, there is a difference between the colonialism of a Fernando Cortez of Spain and that of the English merchant adventurers who soon set out to conquer the world. (The incorporation of the East India Company of London dates to 1600.) In a Cortez and his companions one senses the romanticism of the Christian knight, mixed with greed for power, glory, and treasure. These qualities exist also in the English colonizers, but their enterprise is capitalist, in the modern sense. The overseas possessions of Spain made the country poor; those of England made it rich.

No literary source better reveals the greatness and complexity of English Puritanism of the seventeenth century than the work of John Milton. In a sense, all the works of Milton are educational in that they wish to raise mankind to a higher level of morality, whether they deal with the religious problem poetically, as in *Paradise Lost*, or theoretically, as in the *Treatise on Christian Doctrine*; whether they advocate a new ethics of conjugal relations, as in *The Doctrine and Discipline of Divorce*, or castigate tyrannical power, as in *Eikonoklastes*; or whether, as in *Areopagitica*, they defend "the liberty of unlicensed printing."

And how can a man teach with authority, which is the life of teaching, how can he be a Doctor in his book, as he ought to be, or else had better be silent, when as all he teaches, all he delivers, is but under the tuition, under the correction of his patriarchal licenser, to blot or alter what precisely accords not with the hidebound humor which he calls his judgement? [8]

There is, however, one essay called *Of Education* (1644) in which he deals with teaching and learning in a more specific sense. The academy he there proposes contains much of Renaissance spirit. The author goes even beyond some sixteenth-century humanists in suggesting that young men — he thinks probably of the ages between twelve and twenty-one — not only should become masters in grammar and eloquence, learn Latin, Greek,

[8] "Areopagitica. . . ," *The Works* (London, 1851), IV, 424.

Italian, and probably French, but also should learn Hebrew and possibly add the Chaldean and the Syrian dialect.

For Milton all this learning was not merely ornamental; it was also practical. The classical authors were, from his point of view, most fitted to inspire youth with the great ideals of mankind and also to teach them agriculture, mathematics, and the sciences. Milton's mind and the mind of antiquity were not yet separated by the rise of modern empiricism. Indeed, the classics were also the teachers of politics, or "the beginning, end and reasons of Political Societies" including the "grounds of Law" and legal justice. At the end of their careers Milton hoped to read with the pupils logic, or "those organic arts which enable men to discourse and write per- spicuously, elegantly, and according to the fitted style, or lofty, mean, or lowly." All this will form them "to be able Writers and Composers in every excellent matter, when they shall be thus fraught with an universal insight into things." [9]

But "studies" are only one part of Milton's program. The other part includes "exercise" and "diet" — the latter, "plain, healthful, and moderate"; the first reminiscent of the training in the knightly academies flowering on the Continent. Milton, the militant Chris- tian, was unafraid of teaching the "exact use of Weapon" and "all the Locks and Gripes of Wrastling." [10]

The end then of Learning is to repair the ruines of our first Parents by regaining to know God aright, and out of that knowledge to love him, to imitate him, to be like him, as we may the neerest by possessing our souls of true virtue, which being united to the heavenly grace of faith makes up the highest perfection.

But a young English gentleman should also enjoy

a compleat and generous Education that which fits a man to perform justly, skilfully, and magnanimously all the offices, both private and public, of Peace and War. [11]

These self-manifestations of a great man have made a lasting impression on the English mind, and his classicism was not for- gotten by the masters of Eton, Harrow, and similar schools. Yet, in spite of splendid formulations in regard to the aims of education, Milton's essay is pedantic. The recommendation of the ancient

[9] "Of Education," *The Works*, IV, 388, 389.
[10] *Ibid.*, pp. 391, 393. [11] *Ibid.*, pp. 381, 384.

authors as scientific authorities came too late. Kepler had been dead twenty-four years, Bacon eighteen, and Galileo two when Milton published his program of studies. Harvey had revealed his discovery on the circulation of the blood in 1628, and at the same time that Milton wrote his treatise some of his neighbors may already have planned the meetings of those interested in the new or experimental philosophy. These meetings started in 1645 and led finally, in 1660, to the foundation of the Royal Society, the English center of scientific research. The greatest revolution of the time escaped the revolutionary, as it escaped another of his revolutionary contemporaries in the field of pure thought, the author of the *Ethics* and the *Tractatus Theologico-Politicus*, Baruch Spinoza.

In view of this attitude it is not astounding that Milton had little understanding of the utilitarian trends that appeared among his close friends of the Commonwealth era. While Milton made England great as the harbinger of democratic freedom, and while the scientists prepared for the world of Newton, these utilitarian friends turned the English mind toward a systematic understanding of business and economics. After all, all Europe had begun to tire of the endless and murderous conflicts about divine mysteries going on in the name of religion.

The essay *Of Education* is dedicated to Samuel Hartlib, a man who combined idealism with a strong sense for the useful. To the degree of neglecting his financial interests, he was devoted to all sorts of social, agricultural, and economic experimentation. He published a book on ecclesiastical peace, edited works on husbandry in foreign countries, wrote a utopia of a model state (*A Description of the Famous Kingdom of Macaria*), and was especially interested in educational reforms. As he planned a school for young gentlemen according to the principles of Comenius, he was influential in inviting this educational reformer to London and published, with a zeal not to the author's likings, three of his works. More than Milton's outline of an academy he may have appreciated another pamphlet with his name on the dedication page, namely, Sir William Petty's *Advice for the Advancement of Some Particular Parts of Learning.*[12]

[12] *The Advice of W. P. to Samuel Hartlib for the Advancement of Some Particular Parts of Learning* (London, 1647).

ENGLAND

Sir William Petty (1623–1687) is famous among the historians of economics for his *Political Arithmetic* (1690). Through it he became, together with several Dutchmen, a pioneer in the field of social statistics. Besides such men as the famous diarist John Evelyn (1620–1706) — all of them interested in practical reforms in industry and agriculture — he was one of the many friends of Samuel Hartlib who represented the spirit of the rising mercantile empire. Just as Cromwell and Milton, these men were not democrats in the modern sense of the word. However, they changed the English social structure from the Renaissance aristocracy of a Henry VIII or an Elizabeth, with Anglican ecclesiasticism as the spiritual guide, over into the England that, in broad outline, still exists today. With all its social injustices, about which we will hear later, this England invited the political cooperation of an upper middle class that, though conservative in outlook, dared also to be nonconformist religiously as well as politically. Mixing constantly with the older aristocracy, but later, if necessary, cooperating also with the working class, shrewd in the pursuit of business and profit, and often hypocritical in its religious attitude, this class nevertheless has been a bulwark of decency and good common sense.

Here is the main content of William Petty's *Advice*. To destroy the formalistic separation of education from the life of a busy nation, connect it with its main practical interests. That means, establish a central "Office of Common Addresse," or an advisory agency in all matters of useful knowledge. Link it with *Ergastula Literaria*, or literary workhouses, where such subjects are taught as are of use to the future merchant, manufacturer, and craftsman; also foreign languages. In order to keep all this teaching and advising up to date, appoint a research staff to work in laboratories, clinics, and museums and to form the advanced group in applied science, medicine, and public hygiene. Finally, have a department of education and scientific planning to interest people in all that helps them to be efficient, prosperous, and culturally alive.

This grand scheme, reminding the reader of modern progressive attempts to place the school at the center of the community, was far ahead of the time [13] and was almost completely forgotten.

[13] The practical spirit within this group of "Commonwealth Educators," as one might rightly call them, can be seen from the following list of selected titles:

THE GROWTH OF THE NATION

In 1660 the Cromwellian republic, or the Cromwellian military dictatorship, as some historians call it, was defeated. The victory of the monarchists was thorough. It had been brought about because the more and more organized royalist gentry and the Anglican ministry allied themselves with the increasing part of the population that desired tradition and stability, and perhaps also a little more merriment than the Puritans permitted. Yet, if someone asks the question whether the defeat was complete, he must be answered with "yes" and "no" on all three levels, the political, the religious, and the educational.

Politically, there was an outburst of loyalist feelings. The regicides were punished, and it is a wonder that Milton escaped. Yet, the idea of the covenant, or the social contract between the king and the people, remained in spite of all acts, oaths, and abjurations; and, when Charles II's successor, James II (1685–1688), surpassed his father both in his absolutist and in his Catholic tendencies, the Commons declared "that King James II, having endeavored to subvert the constitution of the Kingdom by breaking the original contract between king and people, and, by the advice of Jesuits and other wicked persons, having violated the fundamental laws and having withdrawn himself out of the kingdom, has abdicated the government, and that the throne has thereby become vacant." [14]

Sir William Petty (1623–1687), *Political Arithmetic* (London, 1690); *Observations upon the Dublin-Bills of Mortality* (London, 1683); *Observations upon the Cities of London and Rome* (London, 1687).

John Evelyn (1620–1706), *The Case Stated Touching the Sovereign's Prerogatives and the People's Liberty, According to Scriptures, Reason and the Consent of our Ancestors* (London, 1660); *Fumifugium: Or the Inconvenience of the Aer and Smoak of London Dissipated* (London, 1661); *Diary* (A famous description of the social conditions of the time), 2 vols. (London, J. M. Dent, 1911–1912).

Jean de La Quintinie (1626–1688), *The Compleate Gard'ner, or, Directions for Cultivating and Right Ordering of Fruit-Gardens and Kitchen-Gardens. . .* Eng. trans. by John Evelyn (London, 1693).

John Graunt (1620–1674), *Natural and Political Observations . . . Made Upon the Bills of Mortality* (London, 1662).

John Drury, a Protestant minister (1596–1680), *The Reformed Schoole*, ed. S. Hartlib (London, 1649). See also Robert H. Quick, *Essays on Educational Reformers* (New York and London: D. Appleton, 1924), p. 203f.

[14] See Lord Macauley, *The History of England from the Accession of James the Second* (New York, 1866), IV, 93.

Shortly after, in 1690, John Locke, a political exile who had returned from the Continent together with his protector, the Earl of
Shaftesbury, published his *Two Treatises on Government.*

> Man being born, as has been proved, with a title to perfect freedom,
> and uncontrolled enjoyment of all the rights and privileges of the law of
> nature, equally with any other man, or number of men in the world, hath
> by nature a power, not only to preserve his property, that is, his life, liberty
> and estate, against the injuries and attempts of other men; but to judge of
> and punish the breaches of that law in others.[15]

On the religious level, the bishops were reinstalled, and the
Episcopalian hierarchy, in alliance with the royal court, imposed a
number of loyalty oaths on all who took some public office. But
the dissenters did not yield so easily. The same Locke who wrote
the *Treatises on Government* wrote also the *Letters on Toleration,*
prefaced with the words: "Absolute liberty, just and true liberty,
equal and impartial liberty, is the thing that we stand in need of." [16]
For his countrymen and the whole European world he provided
the classical formulation of the separation of church and state into
which the Protestant principle must logically issue, though the
English, threatened for a long time by Catholic authoritarianism,
had also seen Protestant Presbyterianism ready to impose its establishment upon the nation.

> The care of souls cannot belong to the civil magistrate, because his
> power consists only in outward force; but true and saving religion consists
> in the inward persuasion of the mind, without which nothing can be ac-
> ceptable to God . . . Confiscation of estate, imprisonment, torments, noth-
> ing of that nature can have any such efficacy as to make men change the
> inward judgment that they have framed of things.[17]

"Yes" and "no" will also be the answer to the question whether
the defeat of the Commonwealth was complete in matters educational. As we have seen and will see more often, the climate of
revolution creates a quick flowering of bold educational schemes,
but they rarely ripen into fruit. Everyone is busy with the most
immediate results; moreover, the political weather may change
suddenly and destroy the hopes for this harvest. After the collapse
of the Commonwealth in 1660 both the court of Charles II and the

---

[15] See *Works* (London, 1823), V, 387.
[16] *Ibid.*, VI, 4.   [17] *Ibid.*, VI, 11.

restored Episcopalian hierarchy sensed the danger of permitting republicans and dissenters to influence the minds of the young. Several acts, initiated by the Act of Uniformity of 1662, according to which no dissenting preacher or teacher was allowed to remain in office, drove all nonconformist education into expensive private academies outside the towns and left the education of the poor to mostly nonexisting charity. Even when under William of Orange the Declaration of Rights (1689) guaranteed a constitutional parliamentary system and thus allowed the Whigs and the Tories the control of government, the injustice in the field of education was not abolished. The consequences, as we will see, were felt up to the end of the nineteenth century, if not up to the First World War. So successful was the Restoration in throwing the ideas of the Commonwealth educators into obscurity that little mention was made of them in English educational literature before 1905, when J. W. Adamson published his book *Pioneers of Modern Education, 1600–1700.*[18]

Nevertheless, even here not everything was lost. While under Charles II and James II the Cavaliers used the last and flickering years of English absolutism for frivolity and cabal, there remained in the people as a whole a good mixture of religious moralism with empiricism and proficiency in practical affairs. It showed not only in politics and ecclesiastical matters, but also in science, philosophy, and education. Newton (1642–1727) laid the foundation of modern physics, and Locke of modern philosophical empiricism. And, like Milton, in fact, even more systematically, Locke also expressed himself on education. In his *Some Thoughts Concerning Education* (1693) he criticized the custom of learning through memorizing rather than through participation; he recommended — all under the care of a private tutor — the study of science and all kinds of handicraft, such as "painting, turning, gardening, tempering, and working in iron"; and he tried to persuade parents "frightened with the disgraceful names of mechanic and trade" to teach accounting. For "though a science not likely to help a gentleman to get an estate, yet possibly there is not any thing of more use and efficacy to make him preserve the estate he has." [19]

[18] Cambridge University Press, 1905.
[19] Paragraphs 202, 210.

But while Locke had little or no influence on the old public schools — how could he, since, what a sacrilege! he recommended that French, as a living language, be taught before Latin — he made a decisive impression on the realistically minded educators of the eighteenth century. In prefaces to textbooks we find references to "the admirable Mr. Locke"; the English dissenting academies as well as the American academy movement learned from him; so did Rousseau and the German educational reformers. Thus, through Locke, the empirical and utilitarian spirit of Hartlib and Petty survived, though in a conservative transformation.

In consequence of the suppressive actions of the political and ecclesiastical Restoration after 1660 historians generally consider the eighteenth century a period of decline in English education. As regards privately supported education, this opinion has been partly corrected by Nicholas Hans in his book *New Trends in Education in the Eighteenth Century*.[20] He shows that the three basic motives, religious, intellectual, and utilitarian, which inspired the era of revolution, affected also the following century.

Religion, in eighteenth-century England, tried to live in peace with science. The Anglican Church was wise enough to avoid quarreling with Newton, especially since he himself knew that science was not able to tear the veil from the mysterious face of the universe.[21] Thus intellectual life flowered in a kind of compromise — sometimes a cold war — between the divines on the one side and the philosophers and scientists on the other. Both camps felt that insistence on logical radicalism might endanger cultural peace. Furthermore, when the hidden tensions in English society grew almost to the point of bursting, there were such men as Jonathan Swift (1667–1745), Dean of St. Patrick's at Dublin, to turn the tragic into the ridiculous and tears into laughter. And there were journals like the *Tatler*, the *Spectator*, the *Guardian*, the *Examiner*, and the *Intelligencer*. They not only served as outlets for angry souls and made statesmen and politicians afraid of public criticism, but also raised the general level of taste and discussion; they caused the other European peoples to look with envy at a nation whose

[20] London: Routlege and Kegan Paul, 1951.
[21] Sir Isaac Newton, *Mathematical Principles*, Bk. III, "General Scholium." Eng. trans., Andrew Molle, 1729. (Mod. ed., Berkeley: University of California Press, 1934.)

affairs were decided not from the top downwards, but by the consensus of a widening group of citizens. Whereas France had been the leading cultural power up to the seventeenth century, England now came to the fore.[22]

Political and religious clubs mixed the pleasure of a glass of ale at the tavern with the excitement of debate in which theists and deists, conservatives and liberals crossed arms. Masonic organizations discussed the same topics that in France kindled the passions of the Revolution,[23] such as the corruption in government and administration, the relation between church and state, and the rights of the citizen.

This vitality could not fail to influence education. The dissenting academies,[24] with the exception of those under Baptist control, continued the utilitarian interests of the Commonwealth educators. Particularly the technical schools and the beginning enterprises in adult education, which catered mainly, though not exclusively, to a middle-class constituency, favored learning for a useful trade more than the "ornamental studies." Even the primarily humanist Anglican schools could not prevent a minority from introducing mathematics, navigation, and astronomy. Oxford established a readership in chemistry in 1704; its students could attend courses in natural and experimental philosophy and in botany. Cambridge, where Newton had lived and taught most of his life, founded in 1704 the Plumian Chair of Astronomy and Natural Philosophy and provided opportunities in other fields of science; according to the *Advice to a Young Student* by Daniel Waterland (written in 1706, published in 1730), a student who preferred the philosophical to the theological and classical courses had to read not only such strictly philosophical works as Locke's *Of Human Understanding* and some less famous books on ethics and metaphysics, but the great works on political theory by Samuel Pufendorf and Hugo Grotius as well as Newton's *Optics* and several

[22] See Paul Hazard, *La Crise de la Conscience Européenne (1680–1715)*. 3 vols. (Paris: Boivin, 1935); Eng. trans., *The European Mind: The Critical Years (1680–1715)* (New Haven: Yale University Press, 1953).

[23] See N. A. Hans, *New Trends in Education in the Eighteenth Century* (London: Routledge, 1951), p. 178f.

[24] *Ibid.*, p. 54f; see also Irene Parker, *Dissenting Academies* (England: Cambridge University Press, 1914) and Herbert McLachlan, *English Education under the Test Acts* (England: Manchester University Press, 1931).

other scientific volumes. Though we may conclude from the many records at the two time-honored universities that a large number of the young gentlemen by-passed the hurdles of academic learning, those who wished to do serious work had the chance.

Nevertheless, some of the most famous Englishmen of the time had very unfavorable opinions of the old places of learning. Among others, Chesterfield writes in 1749 that Cambridge is "sunk into the lowest obscurity; and the existence of Oxford would not be known, if it were not for the treasonable spirit publicly avowed, and often excited there." [25] And the great historian Edward Gibbon says:

> To the University of Oxford I acknowledge no obligation, and she will as cheerfully renounce me for a son, as I am willing to disclaim her for a mother. I spent fourteen months at Magdalen College; they proved the fourteen months the most idle and unprofitable of my whole life.[26]

According to him, the faculty (Society of Fellows) had absolved their consciences "from the toil of reading, or thinking, or writing," and "their conversation stagnated in a round of college business, Tory politics, personal anecdotes and private scandal." [27]

Nor can one deny that, far into the second half of the nineteenth century, the education of the people as a whole was shamefully neglected. There continued the same dual spirit that despite his political liberalism we can discover in Locke: the division of the nation into the gentlemen, who should be well educated, and the rest, who should be kept in order. The appeal to noble sentiments goes side by side with an appalling lack of sympathy for the suffering part of mankind. In Locke's proposals for the bringing up of the children of paupers, intended to "improve" the lot of the poor, he says:

> What they have at home from their parents is seldom more than bread and water, and that, many of them, very scantily too. If therefore care be taken that they have each of them their belly-full of bread daily at school,

[25] See "Lord Chesterfield's Letter to the Rev. Dr. Madden," London, April 15, 1749 (Letter CXCI), in *The Letters of P. D. S. Earl of Chesterfield*, ed. John Bradshaw (London, 1893), II, 924.
[26] *The Memoirs of the Life of Edward Gibbon. . . by Himself*, ed. George Birkbeck Hill (London, 1800), p. 50.
[27] *Ibid.*, p. 58.

they will be in no danger of famishing, but, on the contrary, they will be healthier and stronger than those who are bred otherwise.[28]

We know from Dickens and other writers that these schools (finally established by Parliament in 1722) really were workhouses where the little ones were beaten if they did not earn their bread and were much worse than a prison is today in terms of food and health. Thus, when a great American democrat, Horace Mann, visited England in 1843, he wrote:

England is the only one among the nations of Europe, conspicuous for its civilization and resources, which has not, and never had, any system for the education of its people. And it is the country where, incomparably beyond any other, the greatest and appalling social contrasts exist, — where, in comparison with the intelligence, wealth, and refinement of what are called the higher classes, there is the most ignorance, poverty, and crime among the lower. And yet in no country in the world have there been men who have formed nobler conceptions of the power, and elevation, and blessedness that come on the train of mental cultivation; and in no country have there been bequests, donations, and funds so numerous and munificent as in England. Still, owing to the inherent vice and selfishness of their system, or their no-system, there is no country in which so little is effected, compared with their expenditure of means; and what *is* done only tends to separate the different classes of society more and more widely from each other.[29]

As a matter of fact, in the first decades of the nineteenth century, the lot of the poor was even worse than in the eighteenth century.

Despite the recognition by Parliament of the workers' right of contract, their attempts at coalition were forbidden. In 1799 the prohibitive laws were even intensified. A perverted, ruthlessly capitalist interpretation of liberalism considered self-protective association of the employed to be an offense against the natural laws of society; the employers, however, were not prevented from entering into collective negotiations with the purpose of reducing the workman's pay. The results were desperate and unorganized outbreaks of violence, all revealing the lack of clear insight into the real causes of exploitation during the pre-Marxian era. After

[28] John Locke, *Some Thoughts Concerning Education*, with Introduction and Notes by R. H. Quick (Cambridge University Press, 1899), Appendix A, p. 189f.
[29] Horace Mann, "Seventh Annual Report of the Secretary of the Board of Education to the Board of Education," *The Common School Journal* VI (1844), 84f.

much maneuvering, a parliamentary commission, originally intended to bring to light the abuses of workers' unions (which had emerged despite all persecution), proved that forcible acts had been very rare and that, on the contrary, these associations had been most instrumental in the gradual elevation of the working class. The law of 1871 (five years before the final introduction of obligatory elementary education) acknowledged the full legal status of the trade unions.

Every social abuse somehow succeeds in finding ideological support; so also early capitalism found its doctrine of *laissez faire* and *laissez aller* supported by the economic-sociological theories of Adam Smith and Jeremy Bentham. As so often in the history of religions, divine dispensation was linked with the existing social order. Those whom the Lord has destined to be born into the humbler walks of life should not rebel against him and their masters. As a matter of fact, the old landowners had been generally more sympathetic to their peasants than the capitalist bourgeoisie was to its workers. And this was true not because the latter was morally inferior — if anything, it was at least better educated — but because the impersonal form of technical mass production removed the employer from the employee and the slums from the eyes of the respectable people.

The same society that started the so-called Opium War against China (1840–1842) also used unjust political measures at home. The office of the sheriff, the administrative and judicial duties of which enjoyed high prominence in the rural districts, was by all practical means restricted to the well-to-do. It required landownership and, as all other public duties of some importance, carried no recompense. The *nobile officium* of political leadership — this was the philosophy — should not be spoiled by mercenary considerations. In actuality, it was a class privilege. Also, the old distribution of electoral districts was carefully preserved, so that the rapidly growing industrial cities such as Leeds, Manchester, Sheffield, and Birmingham had no right to send deputies to Parliament, whereas a handful of farmers in old and deserted rural districts had.[30]

[30] See Spencer Walpole, *The Electorate and the Legislature* (London and New York: Macmillan, 1892), p. 56f.

No wonder that the National Petition, or People's Charter, drawn up in 1838 at a workers' meeting near Birmingham, demanded annual parliaments and universal suffrage, vote by ballot, abolition of the property qualification for members of parliament, and payment for their services. The demand for equal electoral districts was added afterwards. The petition was rejected by the Commons, and the Chartist movement decried as a heinous violation of human law. The ensuing riots were quickly broken up. But the ferment remained.

Here, however, an interesting question emerges. Why did England with all its social injustices not only surpass all other nations as an international power, but steadily and without upsetting revolutions develop into a nation of growing democratic stability? Of course, there were military setbacks, commercial crises, and internal divisions bordering on the verge of irreparable conflicts, but there was no civil war and no break of continuity as in the France of 1789, and in later decades as in almost every European country from Spain to Russia. In other words, there must have been fortunate historical conditions that, combined with a high degree of political wisdom, allowed a measure of national self-education without schools, unachieved on the Continent.

Since today we are inclined to forget that the classroom is only one among several factors in the education of a nation, we may give some attention to these extra-curricular factors in the molding of the English nation. First, the growing pride and confidence gave the nation the feeling of participating in a great enterprise in which, even during bad times, defeatism had no place. On the contrary, the greater the crisis, the greater the recuperative courage — up to the last war.

Second, the expanding empire not only brought into the country riches effectively used by a practically minded upper group; it also provided more experience and, consequently, a better training ground for statesmanship. One has only to compare the range of the administrative apprenticeship of a young Englishman, selected for some executive function, with that of a typical government official in the small principalities of Germany, in order to understand the difference in the political maturity of the two countries. The first had his radius of activity over the whole globe; the second, over a few hundred miles, often not even that.

Third, England enjoyed more social mobility than the Continental countries. Despite terrific social contrasts between the upper and middle classes on the one hand and the poor on the other, there was no exclusive ruling caste as in France up to 1789 and again in the later periods of reaction, and as in Germany up to the twentieth century. Greater mobility was also secured by the English custom of succession, or primogeniture, according to which the title of the parent is transmitted only to the eldest son of a noble family, while the other children become commoners. In contrast, in France and Germany every descendant of a nobleman, whether male or female, inherits the title. Until the modern democratic revolutions the mere name made the bearer a privileged person. Intermarriage with commoners meant degradation; even scholarship could only be a hobby. Only through some middlemen could the nobleman go into business. In combination with the increasing destruction of the older feudalism by monarchical centralization and the decreasing income from agricultural property, this aloofness from modern occupations involved a kind of glorified poverty. There remained nothing but to fight desperately for the monopoly of officers' positions in the army and the higher offices of the civil and diplomatic service [31] with the effect that the commoner was prevented from using his talent in important affairs of the state and was often driven out of the country. This does not mean that the privileged always pampered their children. On the contrary, the armies and old classical schools of the Continent were not only places of lordship, but also places of hardship. Even Eton and Harrow accepted the advice that J. Gailhard gave to the English in his *Compleat Gentleman*:

It is not only convenient, but also necessary to use Children to hardship, if their strength and constitution can bear it; for thereby not only they will take exercise, which is necessary to disipate bad humors, and to use

[31] Karl Biedermann, *Deutsche Bildungszustände in der zweiten Hälfte des Achtzehnten Jahrhunderts*, ed. with notes by John A. Waltz (New York: Henry Holt, 1905). Though this work is written from a one-sidedly "liberal" point of view, it nevertheless contains so many undoubted proofs of the division of the German classes that it can still serve as a valuable source. See also Max Weber, "National Character and the Junkers," in *From Max Weber: Essays in Sociology*, trans. H. H. Gerth and C. Wright Mills (New York: Oxford, 1946).

their joynts . . . but also they will use themselves to labor, and make it natural to them. . . .[32]

The English aristocracy excelled in the finest achievements of culture and, without condescension, laid value on the friendship of great men of whatever social origin. It would be difficult to write the history of Britain's artistic and intellectual achievements without mentioning the names of Steele, Bolingbroke, Shaftesbury, Chesterfield, Fielding, and Walpole and their friendships with men such as Addison, Pope, Swift, and Young.[33]

Nor was it, in contrast to Germany, considered a sort of high treason — at least after the middle of the nineteenth century — if a member of the privileged group joined the masses in their struggle for better conditions. Leftists have come from all groups of English society including graduates from Eton; they have provided an organic exchange of ideas, however controversial; and they have supplied labor with men whose background and experience gave them that sense of social security, grace, and freedom that political leaders in other countries, having come from the working class, so often lacked.

Fourth, the combination of experience and mobility taught the English to reckon wisely with reality rather than to exaggerate mere theory and principle against the possibilities inherent in the environment. Certainly, the English had their share of fanaticism. Yet, there was the counterbalance of practical wisdom. In contrast to so many German thinkers, the English have not been obsessed by the desire for logical consistency at the expense of common sense. Thus in his *Letter Concerning Enthusiasm* Anthony, Earl of Shaftesbury, proposes to meet the disturbing "enthusiasm" of the mystical sectarians who, after the revocation of the Edict of Nantes by Louis XIV, had come from France to England, not by new persecution but by the best "antidote" against exaggerated beliefs, namely, "good-humour" and "ridicule." [34]

[32] J. Gailhard, *The Compleat Gentlemen; or Directions for the Education of Youth as to their Breeding at Home and Travelling Abroad*. Two treatises (The Savoy, 1678), Part I, p. 79.

[33] Wilhelm Dibelius, *England*, trans. Mary Agnes Hamilton, with Introduction by A. D. Lindsay (New York and London: Harper, 1930), p. 22.

[34] Anthony, Earl of Shaftesbury, "A Letter Concerning Enthusiasm to My Lord" (Lord Somers). Printed first in the year 1708 in *Characteristics of Man, Manners, Opinions, Times, etc.*, ed. by John M. Robertson with Introduc-

Finally, with all their empiricism and matter-of-factness, the English are a nation with a sincere concern for religion. It is one of England's fortunes that in the period of most ruthless exploitation the English workers did not lose their contact with the Christian religion. For the Established Church was unable to prevent a rich sectarian life, with its simple conventicles where the workman could, as it were, re-establish himself through his dialogue with God and through friendly discussions with his fellow men. In contrast, in France and Germany Catholicism and Protestantism represented official Christianity without allowing a large sectarian development. Consequently, the proletarian fighter, finding no support from the conservative clergy, identified religion with reaction and took recourse in anti-Christian philosophies, especially a materialistically interpreted socialism. Thus the difference in caste and wealth became intensified by the split in the religious tradition.

THE GENTLEMAN IDEAL

It is one of the many paradoxes in history that while one group of English people used its financial capital for exploitation, another group (often even the same) used it to produce the gentleman ideal. Though stemming from a minority, this principle has in the course of time united not only a nation, but cultured men all over the world. A large literature in England as well as in other countries has been devoted to it.[35]

According to George R. Sitwell "there were no 'gentlemen' in

---

tion and Notes (New York: Dutton, 1900), I, 3–39. In the seventeenth and eighteenth centuries the term "enthusiasm" normally carried the implication of "fanaticism."

[35] James Cleland, *The Instruction of a Young Nobleman* (Oxford, 1612); Daniel Defoe, *The True-Born English-man. A Satyr* (London, 1701); J. Gailhard, *The Compleat Gentleman* (Savoy, 1678); August Hoyler, *Gentleman-Ideal und Gentleman-Erziehung mit besonderer Berücksichtigung der Renaissance* (Leipzig: F. Meiner, 1933); Ruth Kelso, "Sixteenth Century Definitions of the Gentleman in England," *Journal of English and German Philology* XXIV (1932) and *The Doctrine of the English Gentleman in the Sixteenth Century* (Urbana: University of Illinois Studies in Language and Literature, 1929): Jonathan Swift, "A Treatise on Good Manners and Good Breeding," in *The Choice Works . . .* (New York: Adam, Wesson, n. d.); *Peacham's Compleat Gentleman* (1634), with an Introduction by G. S. Gordon (Oxford: Clarendon Press, 1906); A. Smyth-Palmer, *The Ideal of a Gentleman, or A Mirror for Gentlefolks. A Portrayal in Literature from the Earliest Times* (London: Routledge, 1908).

the middle ages . . . No one ever described himself, or was described by others, as such before the year 1413 — to be precise before September 29 in that year — and no class of gentlemen can be traced before the third decade of the fifteenth century." [36] However, this is more or less a question of terminology, for in every European country the Middle Ages had already developed the ideal of chivalry with its mixture of Christian service and personal honor, and there is an historical connection between the medieval knight and the later gentleman. Yet, with the social changes occurring during the Renaissance, the standard of a leader of society underwent a process of urbane and humanist refinement. One could no longer be illiterate or an armored ruffian and at the same time an esteemed person. However, the Renaissance did little or nothing to change the caste character of the gentleman position; all it did was to introduce an intellectual and aesthetic component, which, of course, transcended to a degree the limitations of noble birth. During the Puritan period the aristocratic interpretation of genteel behavior had to give room to Christian moralism. However, under the reign of Charles II and James II there appeared the Cavaliers, who, like many of their forebears, cared less about heaven and hell than about a life of cultivated luxury and graceful appearance. Nevertheless, the interest in creating a desirable type of Englishman independent of the accident of birth has never ceased since the seventeenth century. And it would be hard to find an English writer of social importance who has not given it some attention.

Besides John Locke's *Some Thoughts Concerning Education* [37] the best examples of the gradually crystallizing gentleman ideal are Lord Chesterfield's letters to his son [38] and Shaftesbury's *Characteristics of Men, Manners, Opinions, Times.*[39]

Three qualities characterize the attitude of these and other writers. The first is a superior form of detachment. In regard to its

---

[36] Paul Nash, *The English Public-School Gentleman; An Examination of His Nature, Training, and Influence, with Special Reference to the 19th and 20th Centuries.* (Thesis, Harvard University Graduate School of Education, 1959); George R. Sitwell, "English Gentleman," *The Ancestor, A Quarterly Review,* No. 1 (April 1902), pp. 58–103.

[37] First edition, 1693.

[38] *Letters and other Pieces,* selected and edited by Richmond P. Bond. (New York: Doubleday, 1935).

[39] Anthony, Earl of Shaftesbury, *Characteristics of Men, Manners, Opinions, Times,* ed. John M. Robertson (New York: Dutton, 1900).

moral component this attitude stems from Greco-Roman literature and especially Stoic philosophy. It is the *humanitas* of Cicero
and Horace, the inner discipline of Seneca, Epictetus, and Marcus
Aurelius, as well as the fortitude of Plutarch's heroes. Villainy or
dishonesty is not even worthy of deliberation because "stooping
to it" deprives a man of "freedom of mind"; he is no longer "truly
possessor of himself." [40] There is amazingly little, if any, reference
to the Bible. One takes Christianity for granted; or one may also
assume, unconsciously perhaps, that the Beatitudes of the Sermon
on the Mount fit a humble man better than the élite of a growing
empire.

In regard to its social and educational aspects this detachment
results from the wide experience of men of the world. One has
learned from Aristotle that one should cultivate learning and virtue but should not, so to speak, be eaten up by them. Only the
"banausic" man (this Greek word still existed in the eighteenth
century) allows himself to lose his balance and freedom by absorption into a one-sided activity, however worthwhile. The sensitive
and cultured amateur and the "virtuous" and "wise" are of higher
quality than a mere professional man. (With us, this distinction
exists only in sports, and is soon to disappear even there.) And, just
as for Locke "*Learning* must be had, but in the second place, as
subservient only to greater qualities," [41] so also for Chesterfield
"learning (I mean Greek and Roman learning) is a most useful and
necessary ornament, which it is shameful not to be master of."
But it is an "ornament," and if severed from other accomplishments
learning is despicable. Indeed, despite all veneration for the wisdom
of the ancients — so Chesterfield writes to his son — "great modern
knowledge is still more necessary than ancient; and . . . you had
better know perfectly the present, than the old state of Europe;
though I would have you well acquainted with both." The educated
man, irrespective of whether he has specialized in the study of
philosophic systems, should be a "philosopher" who deeply reflects
on the problems of life and "who covets as well to be wise and good,
as agreeable and polite . . . The sum of philosophy is, to learn
what is just in society, and beautiful in Nature, and the order of
the world." [42]

[40] *Ibid.*, I, 86.　　　　　　　　　　　　　　[41] Locke, *Thoughts*, p. 129.
[42] Chesterfield, *Letters*, p. 48; Shaftesbury, *Characteristics*, II, 255.

The second requirement is respect for order and good behavior. One dresses well not because "one values himself upon his dress," as does "the fop," but because a well-dressed man is more pleasant to look at than one who neglects himself. In addition, "there are a thousand foolish customs of this kind, which, not being criminal, must be complied with, and even cheerfully, by men of sense." One does not contradict and insist on being right, for one has a feeling for the climate of a good conversation. One does not attack "a corps collectively." Men, women, lawyers, soldiers, parsons, courtiers, and citizens are "all men, subject to the same passions and sentiments, differing only in the manner, according to their several educations: and it would be as imprudent as unjust to attack any of them by the lump. Individuals forgive sometimes; but bodies and societies never do." [43] One reveres the greater and tries to emulate it rather than indulging in the inferiority of envy. And one respects women. "The greatest man in England would justly be reckoned a brute, if he was not civil to the meanest woman. It is due to their sex, and it is the only protection they have against the superior strength of ours." [44]

Third, a gentleman has confidence in man and nature. Just as there is little reference to the Bible, so there is also little or no reference to the Christian concept of man. The ideas of original sin and human depravity, so central in the thinking of the Puritans, are gone. Morality needs no supernatural foundation; it follows from common sense, the observation of human behavior and the establishment of rules in civilized societies. A good man also "acts from his nature, in a manner necessarily, and without reflection; and if he did not, it were impossible for him to answer his character, or be found that truly well-bred man, on every occasion." [45] In other words, as in every refined culture, the value of a person lies not only in what he does and confesses, but in what he is. Every single value receives its justification from its contribution to the balance, grace, and character of personality.

In every period with the capacity for a self-conscious formation of values, we can learn from the vocabulary used by the

[43] Chesterfield, *Letters*, pp. 17, 19.
[44] Lord Chesterfield, *The Man of Education. . .* (Boston, 1801), Letter XVII, p. 37.
[45] Shaftesbury, "Freedom of Wit and Humour," in *Characteristics*, I, 86.

leaders of opinion. Here the influence of the ancients reveals itself in such terms as "civility" and "humanitas," the Platonic concepts of "philosopher," "justice," "order," and "discipline," and the Stoic-Ciceronian interpretation of "nature." The Renaissance and French influences appear in such terms as "politeness," "gracefulness," and "taste." The English mind makes its contribution by its emphasis on "observation," "common sense," "convenience," and "character." And out of all these qualities there emerges *tolerance*.

But in spite of the intended universality of these values up to the nineteenth century they were related to only a small group of the English people: to the person who had been lucky in the selection of his parents, who could enjoy the advantages of good breeding, including the opportunity for noble sports, and who had the wealth to become a man of the world and to go on the *grand tour* (though there were some misgivings about the vices the young nobleman might pick up in such distant and Catholic cities as Rome and Paris). As in the times of Plato and the Middle Ages, men accepted without much questioning that divine Providence had divided the human world into those who are riding in the saddle and those who may be glad to hold the stirrups.

Nevertheless, despite the ethical odium we feel is in all inherited social monopolies, there still remains the distinction between an aristocracy of mere prerogative and an aristocracy or an élite based on real merit. This same distinction is made in asking the question whether a leading group has developed and preserved qualities that, granted the initial exclusiveness, are sufficiently universal to survive under changing circumstances, to spread over larger groups of the population, and to give direction to future aspirations. The gentleman ideal as it developed in the privileged groups of England from the sixteenth to the nineteenth century had these qualities. It freed itself increasingly from title, from a special kind of erudition, from wealth or the carrying of arms, and became essentially humane. Thus, when Cardinal Newman in the 1850's formulated the modern definition of the gentleman, he not only addressed the students of Dublin, or of Oxford, but gave words to an ideal of international character.

Hence it is that it is almost a definition of a gentleman to say he is one who never inflicts pain . . . He has his eyes on all his company; he is tender towards the bashful, gentle towards the distant, and merciful towards the absurd; . . . he is seldom prominent in conversation, and never wearisome . . . He is never mean or little in his disputes, never takes unfair advantage, never mistakes personalities or sharp sayings for arguments, or insinuates evil which he dare not say out. From a longsighted prudence, he observes the maxim of the ancient sage, that we should ever conduct ourselves towards our enemy, as if he were one day to be our friend . . . He is patient, forbearing, and resigned, on philosophical principles; he submits to pain, because it is inevitable, to bereavement, because it is irreparable, and to death, because it is his destiny . . . He may be right or wrong in his opinion, but he is too clear-headed to be unjust; he is as simple as he is forcible, and as brief as he is decisive . . . If he be an unbeliever, he will be too profound and large-minded to ridicule religion or to act against it; he is too wise to be a dogmatist or fanatic in his infidelity.

Not that he may not hold a religion too, in his own way, even when he is not a Christian. In that case his religion is one of imagination and sentiment; it is the embodiment of those ideas of the sublime, majestic and beautiful, without which there can be no large philosophy.[46]

The universality of the gentleman ideal could also be illustrated by reference to the fact that one of the greatest educators of Asia, Confucius, expressed very similar ideas about those who should rule a nation. When speaking of the *Chün Tzû* (literally, the ruler's son), he refers no longer, as had been the case in earlier times, to an hereditary caste, but to noble qualities in general, a development similar to that of the English gentleman ideal. Confucius' aim was to make gentlemen out of students, and "he never refused to teach anyone, even though he might be so poor that he came with nothing more than a bundle of meat as a present." [47]

DEMOCRATIZATION AND THE DEVELOPMENT
OF THE MODERN SCHOOL SYSTEM

Let me now describe the steps that led English society from the social injustice inherent in the mixture of late feudalism and early capitalism toward conditions that made possible public education and the expansion of the gentleman ideal over the whole nation.

[46] John Henry Newman, *The Idea of a University* (London and New York: Longmans, Green, 1923), p. 208f.
[47] H. G. Creel, *Confucius, the Man and the Myth* (London: Routledge and Kegan Paul, 1951), p. 87.

First, the situation of the worker gradually improved because of the awakening of the social conscience by men of high public responsibility. In 1831 Michael Thomas Sadler delivered a powerful speech in Parliament to disprove the employers' arguments against governmental interference and to expose the misery of his working countrymen to the civilized world.[48] He referred to "a medical gentleman of great intelligence, Mr. Thackrah of Leeds," who had stated "in his work 'On the Effects of Arts and Trades on Health and Longevity' that 'a large proportion of men in' the heckling departments of the flax mills 'die young . . . On inquiry at one of the largest establishments in this neighbourhood, we found that of 1079 persons employed, there are only nine who had attained the age of fifty; and besides these only twenty-two who have reached forty.' " Another "gentleman in this branch of business" (worsted mills) who sympathized with the lot of his workers reports according to Mr. Sadler:

When trade is particularly brisk, the elder children work from six in the morning till seven in the evening, two hours being allowed for meals, etc., and every other night they work all night.

Accidents are frequent; there is also a high degree of sexual promiscuity among the young. Discipline is rigidly and cruelly enforced. Says Mr. Sadler:

It may be thought almost impossible that children should be assembled so early, and dismissed so late, and still kept through the whole period in a state of active exertion. I will attempt to explain this. First, then, their early and punctual attendance is enforced by fines, as are many other regulations of a very severe character; so that a child may lose a considerable part of its wages by being a few minutes too late in the morning: that they should not leave too soon is very sufficiently provided against. Now, this extreme punctuality is no slight aggravation of the sufferings of the child. It is not in one case out of ten perhaps that the parent has a clock; and as nature is not very wakeful in a short night's rest, after a long day's labour, the child, to ensure punctuality, must be often roused much too early. Whoever has lived in a manufacturing town, must have heard, if he happened to be awake many hours before light on a winter's morning, the patter of little pattens on the pavement, continuing perhaps for half an hour together, though the time appointed for assembling was the same. Even then the child

[48] *Memoirs of the Life and Writings of Michael Thomas Sadler* (London, 1842), p. 353f.

is not always safe, however punctual; for, in some mills, two descriptions of clocks are kept, and it is easy to guess how they are occasionally managed. So much for the system of fines, by which, I am told, some mill-owners have boasted that they have made large sums annually.

Then, in order to keep the children awake, and to stimulate their exertions, means are made use of, to which I shall now advert, as a last instance of the degradation to which the system has reduced the manufacturing operatives of this country. Sir, children are beaten with thongs prepared for the purpose. Yes, the females of this country, no matter whether children or grown up, — I hardly know which is the more disgusting outrage, — are beaten upon the face, arms and bosom, — beaten in your "free market of labour," as you term it, like slaves! These are the instruments. — (Here the honourable member exhibited some black, heavy leathern thongs, — one of them fixed in a sort of handle, the smack of which, when struck upon the table, resounded through the House,) — they are quite equal to breaking an arm, but that the bones of the young are, as I have before said, pliant. The marks, however, of the thong are long visible; and the poor wretch is flogged before its companions; flogged, I say, like a dog, by the tyrant overlooker. We speak with execration of the cat-whip of the West Indies — but let us see this night an equal feeling rise against the factory-thong of England. Is it necessary that we should inquire, by means of a select committee, whether this practice is to be put down; and whether females in England shall be still flogged to their labour? Sir, I should wish to propose an additional clause in this Bill, enacting, that the overseer who dares to lay the lash on the almost naked body of the child, shall be sentenced to the tread-wheel for a month; and it would be but right if the master who knowingly tolerates the infliction of this cruelty on abused infancy, this insult upon parental feeling, this disgrace upon the national character, should bear him company, though he roll to the house of correction in his chariot!

Michael Sadler was joined by Dickens,[49] John Ruskin, and Thomas Carlyle. Ruskin protested against the degeneration of human labor through the modern industrial process.

We have much studied and much perfected, of late, the great civilized invention of the division of labour; only we give it a false name. It is not, truly speaking, the labour that is divided; but the men: — Divided into mere segments of men — broken into small fragments and crumbs of life; so that all the little pieces of intelligence that is left in a man is not enough to make a pin or the head of nail. Now it is a good and desirable thing, truly, to make many pins in a day; but if we could only see with what crystal

[49] Charles Dickens, *The Life and Adventures of Martin Chuzzlewit* (London, 1844); *Bleak House* (London, 1853); *The Personal History of David Copperfield* (London, 1850).

sand their points were polished, — sand of human soul, much to be magnified before it can be discerned for what it is — we should think there might be some loss in it also.[50]

And after the defeat of Chartism in 1839 Thomas Carlyle wrote:

The distracted incoherent embodiment of Chartism, whereby in late months it took shape and became visible, this has been put down . . . but the living essence of Chartism has not been put down. Chartism means the bitter discontent grown fierce and mad, the wrong condition therefore or the wrong disposition, of the Working Classes of England. It is a new name for a thing which has had many names, which will yet have many. The matter of Chartism is weighty, deep-rooted, far-extending; did not begin yesterday; will by no means end this day or tomorrow.[51]

But the main factor in the improvement of labor conditions was not charity and sympathy from outside, but the self-help on the part of the workers, who discovered that organized trade unions were more contributive to their welfare than riots and the destruction of machines. It took, however, a long time before the oppressive legislation could be changed. As late as 1867 the court decided that trade unions were illegal associations so that they could not even sue embezzlers within their own ranks. But a few years later the law was changed. Two bills, passed in 1871 and 1875, provided for the recognition of trade unions and permitted "peaceful picketing." In 1874 out of fifteen workingmen candidates two were elected to Parliament; in 1889, as a result of the successful dock strike, trade unionism, so far a privilege of the skilled workman (as for a long time also in the United States), was extended to the unskilled laborer; in 1889 an Independent Labour Party was founded with Ramsay MacDonald as its first secretary; in 1905 John Burns, originally a worker, became a Cabinet minister; in 1911 the absolute veto of the House of Lords was abolished, and with it the superiority of the conservative over the progressive elements; in 1918, as the result of the sacrifices of the English proletariat during the First World War, the electoral system was reformed; and in 1924 England had its first Labour government. The final merging of the nation into a democratic commonwealth occurred dur-

[50] John Ruskin, *The Stones of Venice* in Vol. X of *Works* (London, George Allen, 1904), p. 196.
[51] Thomas Carlyle, "Chartism" (1839), in *Critical and Miscellaneous Essays* (New York: Scribner's, 1901) IV, 119.

ing and after the Second World War. In the middle of that crisis England, the old fortress of free enterprise, surprised the world with the fact that a nation, even in the foremost battle against totalitarianism, could introduce the most advanced social legislation without losing its democratic freedom. Sir William Beveridge submitted to Parliament the so-called Beveridge Plan for Social Security, which he characterized as "a scheme of social insurance against interruption and destruction of earning power and for special expenditure arising at birth, marriage or death." It will be described later in more detail.[52]

England has now one of the most comprehensive systems of socialized medicine, and even the battle over the socialization of certain industries, as it has gone on between the socialist and the conservative parties, will not change the general social-democratic aspect of the country.

The emergence of the political and economic freedom of the English masses was paralleled by the rise of educational democracy. In 1779 the dissenting academies received official recognition, and Protestant nonconformists were no longer excluded from the teaching profession, except in schools under Anglican control.

Even Adam Smith, generally described as the theoretical advocate of modern capitalism, concedes in his famous *Inquiry into the Nature and Causes of the Wealth of Nations* [53] that in certain cases the state of the society places "the greater part of the individuals" in situations where "some attention of government is necessary in order to prevent the almost entire corruption and degeneracy of the great body of the people." This, he says, occurs "in the progress of the division of labour," which forces the far greater part of those who live by the work of their hands into a form of life in which they lose all incentive of exerting their intelligence and generally become "as stupid and ignorant as it is possible for a human creature to become." The torpor of mind resulting in a human person from this situation is dangerous for the nation, for

[52] *Social Insurance and Allied Services. Report Presented to Parliament by Command of His Majesty, November, 1942.* (London: H. M.'s Stationery Office, 1942), p. 9.
[53] First published in 1776. The quotations cited are taken from the 1880 edition (Oxford, Clarendon Press), II, pp. 365, 368.

he is not only incapable of sharing the great and extensive interests of his country, he will also be "equally incapable of defending his country in war . . . The uniformity of his stationary life . . . corrupts even the activity of his body . . ." Consequently, the masses must be educated. They should at least learn how "to read, write, and account . . . at so early a period of life, that the greater part even of those who are to be bred to the lowest occupations, have time to acquire them before they can be employed in those occupations."

And after Adam Smith, Carlyle said:

Heavier wrong [than denying education to the masses] is not done under the sun. It lasts from year to year, from century to century; the blinded sire slaves himself out, and leaves a blinded son; and men, made in the image of God, continue as two-legged beasts of labour; — and in the largest empire of the world, it is a debate whether a small fraction of the Revenue of one Day (30,000 £. is but that) shall, after Thirteen Centuries, be laid out on it, or not laid out on it. Have we Governors, have we Teachers; have we had a Church these thirteen hundred years? What is an Overseer of souls, an Archoverseer, Archiepiscopus? Is he something? If so, let him lay his hand on his heart, and say what thing!

But quitting all that, of which the human soul cannot well speak in terms of civility, let us observe now that Education is not only an eternal duty, but has at length become even a temporary and ephemeral one, which the necessities of the hour will oblige us to look after. These Twenty-four million labouring men, if their affairs remain unregulated, chaotic, will burn ricks and mills; reduce us, themselves and the world into ashes and ruin. Simply their affairs cannot remain unregulated, chaotic; but must be regulated, brought into some kind of order. What intellect were able to regulate them? The intellect of a Bacon, the energy of a Luther, if left to their own strength, might pause in dismay before such a task; a Bacon and Luther added together, to be perpetual prime minister over us, could not do it. No one great and greatest intellect can do it. What can? Only Twenty-four million ordinary intellects, once awakened into action; these, well presided over, may. Intellect, insight, is the discernment of order in disorder; it is the discovery of the will of Nature, of God's will; the beginning of the capability to walk according to that.[54]

Even before there was any sign of improvement in the lot of the working people — on the contrary, when things went worst — men of Christian conscience were struck by the educational and

[54] *Critical and Miscellaneous Essays*, IV, pp. 193–194. The actual sum was not £30,000, but £20,000, granted by the government in 1833.

spiritual plight of the poor. As early as the second half of the eighteenth century the Sunday school movement took shape under the leadership of Baptists and Methodists.[55] Secular Sunday schools also gave help to those strong enough in body to learn on the only free day of recreation.

In 1808 the work of the Quaker Robert Lancaster led to the foundation of the British and Foreign School Society. It was so successful that the Anglican Church began to feel its social obligation. It supported its minister Andrew Bell, who had founded an orphanage at the Indian city of Madras, and felt that the missionary care given to the young Indians might be extended to the poor Christians at home. Thus, in 1811, there came into existence the National Society for Promoting the Education of the Poor in the Principles of the Established Church throughout England and Wales. Even the titles of the two societies reveal the difference in spirit. The first title is general; the second, dogmatic and condescending.

In order to master the ever-increasing influx of children into schools with a minimum of cost and a minimal number of teachers, those in charge divided the throng, generally assembled in one big hall, into smaller groups and appointed older pupils to teach the younger ones the just-acquired rudiments of knowledge. The system of pupil monitors has often been praised as an advance in education. Indeed, it may have been some kind of answer to the problem of keeping children under control while teaching them the foundations of learning. What this system really amounted to is described by two of the best historians of the English people.[56]

Even education, in which the "shopocracy" at least professed an interest, was but little improved. The percentage of illiterates was 41.6 in 1839 (men 33.7 and women 49.5) and it remained virtually unchanged until 1846 and probably later. Indeed, there is reason to argue that the educational position of the working class was actually worsened, by a foolish "discovery" which was widely adopted at this period. The old dame and parish schools had frequently been bad, but they were also sometimes good, though always unpretentious. But the systems of Bell and Lancaster, which their

[55] G. M. Trevelyan, *British History in the Nineteenth Century, 1782–1919.* (London: Longmans, Green, 1922), p. 160.
[56] G. D. H. Cole and Raymond Postgate, *The Common People, 1746–1946,* 4th ed. (London: Methuen, 1949), p. 308f.

propounders said were "with great propriety" called "the STEAM EN-GINE OF THE MORAL WORLD," annihilated any possibility of education. The device merely consisted of teaching blocks of information, generally in the form of answers to a series of questions, to a group of "monitors," who then taught them to another group of children, and so forth. So knowledge was "multiplied;" if an ill-disposed examiner asked the questions in the wrong order, the sham was disastrously exposed. Fortunately this rarely happened.

It is a notable example of the gullibility of the historian that this probably retrograde step is still frequently referred to as an advance. Mr. and Mrs. Hammond have disinterred specimens of the catechisms inflicted upon the children. One must suffice:

> Monitor: You read in the lesson "The enamel is disposed in crescent-shaped ridges." What is the enamel?
> Boy: The hard shining part of the tooth.
> Monitor: What part of our tooth is it?
> Boy: The covering of that part that is out of the jawbone.
> Monitor: What do you mean by disposed?
> Boy: Placed.
> Monitor: The root?
> Boy: "Pono," I place.
> Monitor: What is crescent-shaped?
> Boy: Shaped like the moon before it is a half-moon.
> Monitor: Draw a crescent. *Boy draws it on the blackboard.*
> Monitor. What is the root of the word?
> Boy: "Cresco," I grow.

But, whatever the faults of the new educational experiment may have been, at least it caused wider and wider circles to ponder over the problem of the education of the poor. Many of the working parents, both being employed in factories, were unable to take care of their infants. Thus there arose, on nondenominational religious grounds, the infant-school movement. Robert Owen (1771–1858), director of a large cotton mill at New Lanark, founded The New Institution, which provided free education for the workers' children of from five to ten years. Soon one of his teachers, J. Buchanan, built a similar establishment at Westminster, which in turn motivated Samuel Wilderspin to devote his energy to an infant school at Spitalfields, London, and to the foundation of the Infant School Society.

Wilderspin, in whose thought on educational methods one can already distinguish the influence of Pestalozzi, applied very adroitly two persuasive arguments: first, prevent the growth of juvenile criminality by "bending the twig while it is young"; second, educate the lonely and oppressed by means of love rather than fear.[57] Actually, the slogan, "Open a school and close a jail," has accompanied the public elementary school up to the beginning of the twentieth century, giving it the flavor of a socially somewhat inferior enterprise.

However, despite the persuasiveness of Mr. Wilderspin and his friends — and in 1825 there already existed fifty-five infant schools [58] — many objections were still being raised. Infant schools might take "the work out of the parents' hands . . . lull them into a false security . . . encourage the poor to marry, without considering whether they possessed the means of supporting their offspring." [59]

The whole problem of the schooling of the impecunious was discussed in a fashion not unsimilar to that of the liberation of the slaves in the United States. While one group cited the Bible in favor of new schools, the other appealed to it by warning that schools might lead the humble "into the excitement of emulation." Also, the question was raised whether a child might "gain too much experimental knowledge in the first eight or ten years of its life to render it unfit for a Christian servitude" and make it inclined to "break down the various orders of society." [60] And there appeared continually the question whether a nondenominational education might alienate the young from the faith of their parents. Wilderspin answers:

No; the children are too young to become imbued with any peculiar religious sentiment, and it has therefore been considered advisable for none to be refused admittance because their parents may belong to some particular sect.[61]

Nevertheless, religious jealousies were the main obstacle to the creation of a general system of public education. At the time when

[57] S. Wilderspin, *Infant Education; or Remarks on the Importance of Educating the Infant Poor, from the Age of Eighteen Months to Seven Years*, 3rd ed. (London, 1825); see also Francis A. Young, *The Life and Work of Samuel Wilderspin; A Study in the History of Popular Education* (Thesis, Harvard University Graduate School of Education, 1949).

[58] S. Wilderspin, *Infant Education*, p. 284.   [60] *Ibid.*, p. 281.
[59] *Ibid.*, pp. 11, 18, and especially p. 273f.   [61] *Ibid.*, p. 279.

many of the nonconformists demanded nondenominational public schools, for all children, and when some already advocated secular education, the Established Church claimed that education belonged to its province, as has the Catholic Church from its origin up to our time. Though around 1830 the monopolistic power of the Established Church on public positions and other privileges was broken because the new capitalistic middle class belonged largely to the dissenters, it insisted until 1871 on religious tests for masters in the two old Universities of Oxford and Cambridge. And it would probably have remained still longer in the trenches had not the University of London, founded in 1828 on a nondenominational basis, built up a formidable competition against the old institutions. Even today the Church wields a power over educational legislation that is way out of proportion to the number of churchgoers; this power is due largely to the fact that, in matters spiritual, there is no effective organization to take its place. In a storm even an old roof is better than none.

The movement for better schools was aided by the fact that the first decades of the nineteenth century brought England more and more out of its isolationist attitude, which had been increased by the country's growing aversion to the cruelties and failures of the French Revolution. Men of social and cosmopolitan interest, among whom Lord Brougham deserves particular mention, brought to their country the news of the educational experiments of Pestalozzi and von Fellenberg in Switzerland, of the school reforms in Holland, and of the educational progress in Prussia and other states of Germany.[62]

Furthermore, some of the most famous headmasters of the older public schools made a strong impression on the country by initiating reform. Thomas Arnold (1824–1842), of Rugby, Edward Thring (1853–1887), of Uppingham, and others observed with a mixture of admiration and anxiety the development of secondary education in Germany and decided to change their schools from fashionable boarding places to institutions with truly scholarly as well as moral aims. Their example influenced similar schools all

---

[62] A valuable description of this whole development, together with an excellent bibliography, can be found in Hugh M. Pollard, *Pioneers of Popular Education, 1760–1850* (London: John Murray, 1956).

over the country and paved the way for further important investigations.[63] In the middle of the nineteenth century public anger at the complacent exclusiveness of the two old Universities of Oxford and Cambridge had risen to such an intensity that, despite all their insistence on the right of self-determination, parliamentary commissions were appointed. This led in the 1850's to a reform of instruction, an increase in chairs, and the admission of dissenters to the B.A. degree. (The M.A. degree became accessible after 1871.) From this time on, though not without some pushing by various commissions, Oxford and Cambridge gained the international prestige they had had in earlier centuries.

With the leading independent institutions entering into a spirit of reform, the government itself could not forever remain aloof. In 1833 under the first reformed Parliament, the principle of governmental noninterference in educational matters was broken, at least in part. The two main educational agencies, Dr. Bell's National Society under the Established Church and the nondenominational British and Foreign School Society representing the dissenters, received a state grant-in-aid of £20,000. In 1839 a special central body in the form of a committee of the Privy Council was set up under the directorship of James Kay, later Sir James Kay Shuttleworth (1804–1877). His committee had to consider "all matters affecting the education of the people," to distribute government grants, and to arrange for inspection of the schools by "Her Majesty's Inspectors." We have here the seeds of the later Ministry of Education. As a welfare officer in the industrial city of Manchester, himself a trained physician, James Kay could speak from firsthand knowledge about the life of industrial youth. Under his guidance the educational division of the Privy Council gained more and more recognition, and the state grant-in-aid, which increased up to £663,000 in 1858, became used not only for school buildings, but also for the training of teachers and school inspectors.

In 1858 a royal commission under the Duke of Newcastle,

[63] See Edward C. Mack, *Public Schools and British Opinion*, Vol. I, 1780–1860; Vol. II, since 1860. (New York: Columbia University Press, 1939 and 1941).

Public Schools Commission, 1861–1864, concerning the administration of nine great Public Schools; Schools Inquiry Commission, 1864–1867, concerning the other Secondary Schools; the Bryce Commission, 1894–1895, which improved the admission requirements to the universities and thus also the standards of the secondary schools.

though unable to persuade the religious denominations to create a national school system, could persuade Parliament to empower "County Boards" to levy an educational tax to be distributed among the rival voluntary societies. The Forster Elementary Education Act (1870), disavowing any intention to interfere with the voluntary character of education, nevertheless set up publicly elected "School Boards" side by side with the voluntary agencies in order to fill the obvious gaps. It was the main task of the school boards to see to it that there were a sufficient number of school places for all children to attend school between the ages of five and twelve. Finally, under Disraeli, the "Act to make further provision for Elementary Education" (August 1876) made education compulsory, though not tuition-free, up to the age of twelve.[64] It also allowed loopholes for children after the age of ten, in certain cases even for children "above the age of eight years," to accept employment either for the year or for certain months. However, with the Act of 1876 the state became the guardian of the education of English youth. As has already been indicated, the two educational laws of 1870 and 1876 almost coincide with the legislation that recognized the trade unions as legal corporations.

As in other countries at the end of the century, dissatisfaction with the monopoly of the classical languages in secondary education increased, for with it went the one-sided interpretation of liberal education against which John Locke had protested at the end of the seventeenth century. In addition, the professional world had changed. It was no longer dominated by clergymen, lawyers, and the headmasters of the old public schools, who only grudgingly allowed for a sprinkling of utilitarian subjects in the training of their pupils. There appeared on the educational scene all kinds of upstarts who owned big factories, negotiated international loans, controlled shipping companies and railroads, appointed chemists and engineers, and thought that the practical should come first, and the ornamental later. The utilitarian trend was supported by the new humanitarianism in education. Would it not produce a happier youth and a better type of men — this was now the discussion

---

[64] "An Act to make further provision for Elementary Education (15 August 1876)," in *The Public General Statutes Passed . . . 1876 . . .* (London, 1876), pp. 472–492. Fees were not abolished until after 1891.

— if youth were treated with kindness instead of with the rod and if their individual talents were cultivated rather than neglected?

Herbert Spencer's widely read essays on *Education* asked the question: "What knowledge is most worth?" Boldly he compared the teaching of classical languages with a sort of social tattooing and wondered whether the hardship the boys of the English aristocracy underwent "at Eton, Winchester, Harrow, etc." by accustoming them "to a despotic form of government and intercourse regulated by brute force, tends to fit them for a lower state of society than that which exists. And chiefly recruited as our legislature is from among those who are brought up at such schools, this barbarizing influence becomes a hindrance to national progress." [65]

The rebels against the traditional conceptions of the education of the privileged were supported by scientists, before whose eyes there opened a vastly widened universe with untold chances for intellectual curiosity, disciplined research, and practical application. Darwin's *Origin of the Species* (1859) and *Descent of Man* (1871) were not merely scientific events. Though the evolutionary principle had been anticipated by great mystics and philosophers of the past, in its naturalist nakedness it evoked a spiritual crisis similar to the one caused by Copernicus three hundred years before. Once more — so the theologians feared — man was removed from nearness to God into an obscure corner of a causally determined, material cosmos. The divine nature of the spirit seemed to be lost.

Neither Darwin, however, nor one of the other great English scientists of the time, Thomas H. Huxley, believed that the mysteries of life were solved with the progress of science. Huxley even reversed his opinion about the descendance of man, in spite of his famous Oxford duel with Bishop Wilberforce at the meeting of the British Association (1860). About Huxley, Herbert Spencer writes in his essays on *Education* [66] that he finished a course of lectures with the following remark:

True science and true religion are twin-sisters, and the separation of either from the other is sure to prove the death of both. Science prospers

[65] Herbert Spencer, *Education: Intellectual, Moral, and Physical* (London, 1861), pp. 1–3; fn., p. 111.
[66] *Ibid.*, pp. 50, 51.

exactly in proportion as it is religious; and religion flourishes in exact proportion to the scientific depth and firmness of its basis. The great deeds
of philosophers have been less the fruit of their intellect than of the direction
of that intellect by an eminently religious tone of mind. Truth has yielded
herself rather to their patience, their love, their single-heartedness, and their
self-denial, than to their logical acumen.

Huxley, just as Herbert Spencer, was a thorough advocate of
educational reform, to such a degree that from 1870 to 1872 he
served as a member of the newly established London School Board
and spoke during the latter part of his life before many societies
on the problems of education. Health was for him the basic requisite of personal culture; a sense for the practical as well as for
the aesthetic values of life was of the same importance as literary
knowledge; and intellectual discipline could be gained by the teaching of science as well as, or better than, by the teaching of any
other subject matter. But he avoided the orthodoxy that in modern
times seems to have spread from dogmatic theological over into the
scientific camps. He wanted the Bible to be read, not only because
of its literary value, but also because he wondered "by what practical measures the religious feeling, which is the essential basis of
conduct, was to be kept up, in the present utterly chaotic state of
opinion in these matters, without the use of the Bible." [67]

Finally, the Bryce Commission of 1895 emphasized the advisability of uniting "intellectual training and personal discipline" with
"special regard to the profession or trade to be followed." Such a
combination would "make a person of more value to society and
the state." [68] In calling for a balanced curriculum that would include literary, scientific, and technical subjects, the Bryce Commission marked the beginning of the transition from the classical
to a profession-oriented program of secondary education.

This ideal, as we have seen, was not new. Among the other
advocates, the poet Matthew Arnold, son of the famous Dr. Arnold
of Rugby and himself an inspector of schools, had written in 1865:

It is a vital and formative knowledge to know the most powerful mani-

[67] Thomas H. Huxley, *Science and Education*, in Vol. III of *Collected Essays*
(New York and London: Appleton, 1914), p. 397.
[68] *Report of the Commissioners (James Bryce and Others) on Secondary Education*, I, 136, in *Reports from Commissioners, Inspectors and Others*, Vol. 30
(London, 1895).

festations of the human spirit's activity, for the knowledge of them greatly feeds and quickens our own activity; and they are very imperfectly known without knowing ancient Greece and Rome. But it is also vital and formative knowledge to know the world, the laws which govern nature, and man as part of nature. This the realists have perceived, and the truth of this perfection, too, is inexpugnable.[69]

With the prestige of the Bryce Commission behind it, the trend toward the widening of education expressed itself not only in terms of the program of studies, but also in terms of structure. In 1899 a national Board of Education was created which combined various departments concerned with the physical and intellectual welfare of youth. In 1900 local school boards were allowed to pass by-laws to extend the period of school attendance to the age of fourteen. Finally, through the Education Act of 1902,[70] which became the cornerstone of the educational system of England and Wales, "Local Education Authorities" were established which, working under governmental auspices, took over the responsibilities exercised so far by the local school boards. The local bodies were also authorized to provide "education other than elementary after consulting with the Board of Education." Thus, the guardianship of the state, initiated by the law of 1876, became a function firmly built into the administrative branch of English government. While still allowing, in contrast to highly centralized state systems, a large degree of freedom on the part of communities and teachers, it guaranteed the gradual abolition of abuses to children in early employment, as they still existed up to World War I.

This war forced the English nation into a measure it had so far proudly avoided, namely, compulsory military service. As a compensation for accepting the duty to fight and die on the battlefields of France, the masses now demanded a further advance in public education. They insisted on the change from a class-structured school system, with more than 95 per cent of the population confined to merely elementary training, over to a national school system, which would bring the more advanced forms of education,

[69] Matthew Arnold, *Report on the System of Education for the Middle and Upper Classes in France, Italy, Germany, and Switzerland*, in *School Inquiry Commission*, Vol. VI (London, 1868), p. 593.

[70] "Bill to Make Further Provisions with Respect to Education in England and Wales, 1902" (Great Britain: *Bills Public*, No. 280, Vol. I, Sess. 16, London, 1902).

except the universities, into the reach of the able youth of the people.

The result was the so-called Fisher Act (1918),[71] which had in view "the establishment of a national system of public education available for all persons capable of profiting thereby." Provisions were going to be made "in order to secure that children and young persons shall not be debarred from receiving the benefits of any form of education by which they are capable of profiting through inability to pay fees." A youth who did not go into secondary education had to attend a continuation school after graduation from the elementary school at the age of fourteen. The Prevention of Cruelty to Children Act of 1904 was amended to the effect that children under twelve not be used for singing and performing or be otherwise employed. With small restrictions, fees for elementary schools were abolished.

However, the Fisher Act also retained the old concept of the secondary school as "liberal" in contrast to vocational or, by indirection, "illiberal" studies. This distinction had first been expressed, contrary to the recommendations of the Bryce Commission, in the Board's Regulations for Secondary Schools, of 1905–1906. According to these regulations a "Secondary School" (in England, in contrast to the United States usage, also called "Grammar School") was defined as a "Day or Boarding School offering to each of its scholars, up to and beyond the age of sixteen, a general education, physical, mental and moral" and aiming at the development "of the whole of the faculties" of the pupil, rather than confining this development "to a particular channel" or "fitting a boy or girl to enter business in a subordinate capacity." [72] Thus even after World War I only a small proportion of pupils, around 1920 about 10 per cent, transferred from the upper grades of the elementary into the secondary schools. They had to pass competitive examinations; if successful they received "free places." Only 1 per

[71] "An Act to make further provision with respect to Education in England and Wales . . . 8th August 1918," in *The Public General Acts Passed in the 8th and 9th Years of the Reign of H. M. King George V*; . . . (London: H. M. Stationery Office, 1919), Chap. 39, pp. 124–156.

[72] (Great Britain) Board of Education, *Regulations for Secondary Schools from 1st August 1905 to 31st July 1906* (London, H. M. Stationery Office, 1905), pp. i and vii.

cent or less of these former elementary-school pupils entered the university.

However, the tidal wave of democracy and with it the restructuring of the schools for the adolescents continued to grow. Two reports, the so-called Hadow Report of 1926 entitled *The Education of the Adolescent* [73] and the so-called Spens Report of 1938 [74] showed for the first time in the history of English public education due regard for the physical, psychological, and intellectual qualities of the adolescent, enlarged the scope of education from a primarily intellectual toward a more comprehensive understanding of the learning process, and tried, through a reform of curriculums and organization, to diminish the gap between the education of the élite and the education of the masses.[75] The primary and the nursery-school levels were also re-examined.[76]

Whereas around 1900 the German Herbart had influenced English educational theory, there now emerges "progressive education" under the influence of experimental psychology and the pragmatism of the American John Dewey. Partly as a result of the "admirable statement" of Professor John Dewey "regarding the misleading antithesis between culture and utility" and partly as a result of other independent observations the old idea of the separation between practicality and liberal education is relinquished. "We accept fully the position that school studies should fit boys and girls for the practical affairs of life, and that if they do not do so they must be badly planned or badly conducted." Yet, the conservative element in the English character provides the balance. Despite "the authority of Dewey" and the "seductive" doctrines of "problem method" and "project method," the modern "activity program" must not destroy the value that lies in the consistent pursuit of individual subjects. For the traditional school subjects

[73] (Great Britain) Board of Education, *Report of the Consultative Committee on the Education of the Adolescent* (London, H. M. Stationery Office, 1926).

[74] (Great Britain) Board of Education, *Report of the Consultative Committee on Secondary Education . . .* (London, H. M. Stationery Office, 1939).

[75] See, especially, R. H. Tawney, *Some Thoughts on the Economics of Public Education* (London: Oxford University Press, 1938) and, by the same author, *Secondary Education for All; A Policy for Labour* (London: The Labour Party, 1922).

[76] *Reports of the Consultative Committee of the Board of Education on the Primary School* (1931) and *Infant and Nursery Schools* (1933).

are not just inventions of narrow-minded educators. We "stand" — so the authors say — "for traditions of practical, aesthetic and intellectual activity, each having its own distinctive individuality; and we hold that the profit a pupil derives from them does not come from casual or episodical contacts, but by his being, so to speak, put to school to them, and so getting to make their outstanding characters part of the equipment and habit of his mind." This "training" carries with it "a special kind of ethical permeation" and "may be quite properly described also as 'mental discipline.' For it involves the submission of the pupil to the influences of the great tradition; it is his endeavour to learn to do fine things in the fine way." [77] How much could American school men have learned from this wise judgment!

Both the Hadow and the Spens Reports, especially the latter, are excellent examples of educational thought and statesmanship. They contain historical and theoretical excursus, superior to similar official utterances in other countries. Unfortunately, the practical effect of both reports was limited. The Spens Committee regretted that Hadow's recommendations had largely remained on paper, and Spens's advice, though welcome as a sign of further progress toward a modern school system, remained theoretical. For it came out a year before the greatest test the English nation had to undergo in its long history, the Second World War. This test and the shock that went with it were not only of political and military significance; they were also of a profound social and educational nature.

In one of his books — all of which are most important for the understanding of modern England — H. C. Dent says:

Little as there has been of structural change in the educational set-up during the war (though there has been more than most people realize) the educational order of 1939 has passed beyond recall. It died on September 1 of that year, the day on which evacuation began. It can never be reborn; there has already been too much of change.

A few paragraphs later Dent continues:

Education is the basic activity of society. It conditions, and is conditioned by, all the other activities — political, economic, industrial, social, religious, personal . . . The development of a society cannot be but fundamentally affected — for good or for ill — by the education its members

[77] Spens Report, p. 159f.

receive; on the other hand, the nature, and consequently the value, of that education is determined — at least in a democratic society — by the state of society and by the attitude which society as a whole takes toward the whole problem of education.[78]

Now, in war and evacuation, the English discovered that, in spite of all the educational reforms and in spite of the political unity achieved during the past century, they still had lived as a deeply split nation, with the feeling of communal responsibility stopping before the tenement houses of the poor. But, when the overcrowded city districts suddenly sent their population over the whole of England, men realized that the greater number of even the poorest of the evacuated "were as clean, decent, well-behaved, and well-mannered as were the members of the families which received them." [79] They also discovered that in certain districts the Education Act of 1936, according to which every child had to remain in school until the age of fifteen unless he could obtain a certificate sanctioning his entry into "beneficial employment," had never become reality. And there appeared, to the horror and shame of the respectable families in small urban and rural districts, children and mothers to whom even the rudiments of physical culture were unknown. Dent gives extracts from reports written by receiving communities which reflect the living conditions in certain congested industrial areas and which, he says, could be paralleled by hundreds of others from the most varied sources.

Except for a small number the children were filthy, and in this district we have never seen so many verminous children, lacking any knowledge of clean and hygienic habits . . . Bed-wetting was very general among the children . . . They all used bad language, had no idea of telling the truth, and were quite undisciplined . . . Their clothing was in a deplorable condition, some of the children being literally sewn into their ragged little garments. The majority were opposed to all the generally accepted rules of decent living, and some returned home as soon as a hot bath was suggested. [According to a careful report] . . . the evidence suggests that those with unsanitary habits due to lack of training represented from 5 to 10 per cent . . . As many as 50 per cent may have been verminous.[80]

[78] Harold C. Dent, *Education in Transition . . . 1939–1943* (London: Kegan Paul, Trench, Trubner, 1944), pp. viii, ix f. Other books by H. C. Dent: *A New Order in English Education* (London: University of London Press, 1942); *Change in English Education* (London: University of London Press, 1952).

[79] Harold C. Dent, *Education in Transition*, p. 11.

[80] *Ibid.*, p. 8f.

The people were forced to acknowledge that there was not only an enemy at the door of the nation but peril from within, and the results of this twofold experience were not only heroism on the battlefields and in the raided cities, but also a revolutionary burst of social conscience — the inner renewal of a nation.

In 1942 the country of Adam Smith and Jeremy Bentham surprised the world by the already-mentioned Report on Social Insurance and Allied Services, presented by Sir William Beveridge. The so-called Beveridge Plan was a scheme of social insurance against interruption and destruction of earning power and special expenditure arising at birth, marriage, or death, built on six fundamental principles: flat rate of subsistence benefit, flat rate of contribution, unification of administrative responsibility, adequacy of benefit, comprehensiveness in regard to persons covered and to their needs, and classification in view of the different ways of life in different sections of the community.

Just as revolutionary as the Beveridge Plan in regard to social welfare was the Education Act of 1944 [81] in regard to the schools. Administratively it is a product of great political wisdom. It acknowledges the importance and power of the religious tradition but also pays attention to the secular elements in the nation's culture.[82] It strengthens the national system of education by creating, instead of the older Board of Education, a national Ministry of Education, to be the central coordinating and planning authority, with exception of the universities. At the same time it preserves, and to a degree even strengthens, the old English principle of decentralization, in that the relation of the central authority to local authorities is based on consultation and cooperation provided by inspectors of education who act as liaison officers.

The second, and probably most remarkable, achievement of the Education Act of 1944 is the simplification of the structure of the national school system. Instead of the bewildering complexity that so far had characterized English education in consequence of

[81] *Britain 1950-1951. A Reference Handbook* (Central Office of Information, London) pp. 230-240. Harold C. Dent, *The Education Act, 1944* . . . (London: University of London Press, 1944): "A Bill to Reform the Law Relating to Education in England and Wales. Presented by Mr. Butler," Bill No. 18 in Great Britain (Parliamentary Papers) *Bills Public*, Vol. I, 1943-1944.

[82] Deming N. Hoyt, *Church-State Relations and Education in England since 1900* (Thesis, Harvard University Graduate School of Education, 1953).

its growth from private and religious initiative, the school system is now divided into stages of "Primary Education," for pupils under twelve, "Secondary Education" for pupils over twelve up to graduation, and "Further Education." This constitutes the declaration of the willingness of the English people to break down the old class division of secondary schools for the privileged, on the one hand, and elementary and vocational schools for the masses, on the other hand.[83] All postprimary schools (beginning around the age of eleven) are now called "Secondary Schools" (a name so far reserved only for the grammar schools with the ultimate purpose of preparing pupils for the university). The new secondary schools are divided into "Modern Schools" (eleven to sixteen years) for those who intend to enter a practical vocation immediately, "Grammar Schools" (eleven to eighteen years) for the academically interested students, and "Technical Schools" (eleven to sixteen years for the technically gifted).[84]

[83] To what degree the English schools were, and to a large degree still are, class-determined appears from the statistics contained in an article, "Independent Schools and the Liberal Professions," by N. A. Hans (*The Yearbook of Education, 1950*, London, 1950, pp. 219–238). According to Hans, who bases his findings on *Authors' Who's Who, 1948*, 51.1 per cent of the clergy and 62.9 per cent of the politicians came from the nine "Great Schools" (Eton, Harrow, Winchester, etc.) and the fifty-one other "Public Schools" represented at the Headmasters' Conference; 32.8 per cent of the clergy and 16.1 per cent of the politicians came from "other" English schools, some of them patterned on the old Public Schools. Oxford and Cambridge provided 68.7 per cent of the clergy and 68.6 per cent of politicians, whereas the University of London and the provincial universities procured only 24.9 per cent of the clergy and 11.8 per cent of the politicians.

The main conclusions which Professor Hans draws from his various statistics are that about 66 per cent of the leading members of all the liberal professions, discussed in his article (clerical, academic, legal, medical, technical, literary, and political) are alumni of sixty Public Schools represented at the Headmasters' Conference; that about 62 per cent of them were educated at Oxford and Cambridge; that this percentage has remained stationary since the eighteenth century; and that the Public School-Oxford-Cambridge group are socially different from those educated at "other schools" and provincial universities.

For the leading role of the Public Schools and the old universities and their alumni, Professor Hans offers a mixture of the following reasons: heredity, better training, and social privilege. One should add to these the conservatism that all societies, and the English in particular, reveal with respect to changes in their educational systems.

[84] For a brief introduction into the Education Acts of 1944 and 1946, see J. C. Hogg, *ABC Guide to the Education Acts 1944 and 1946*, 3rd ed. (London: Philip and Tacey, 1946); see also W. P. Alexander, *Education in England. The National System and How It Works* (New York: St. Martin's Press, 1954), and H. C. Dent, *Growth in English Education, 1946–1952* (London: Routledge and Kegan Paul, 1954).

"Further Education," with a cover age from sixteen to eighteen years, was planned for people who after graduation from a modern or technical school wished to round out their vocational and general preparation. The authors of the act thought especially of "County Colleges" for young people up to the age of eighteen, no longer in school full time. Actually Part II, clause 39, of the Education Act declared it the duty of every local education authority to secure the provision of adequate facilities for (a) "part time education colleges for young persons who are not in full time attendance at any school or other educational institution," (b) "full time and part time education in technical, commercial, and art subjects for persons over compulsory school age," and (c) "leisure time occupation, in such organized cultural training and recreative activities as are suited to their requirements, for any persons over compulsory school age able and willing to profit by the facilities provided for that purpose."

For any type of primary and secondary school maintained by local education authorities tuition fees were to be abolished; in addition, the schools were to be connected with all agencies responsible for the nation's physical health.

To a degree, all this means a leveling of the school structure, and the more conservative English newspapers were full of warnings against the dangers inherent in this process. Was the new Ministry of Education perhaps on the way to pulling down the higher rather than to raising the lower levels of talent? Would a minimum of administrative control together with a maximum of qualitative encouragement provide sufficient guarantees for feeding the universities with a well-prepared youth? The answer is complex. The degree of success will depend not on the Ministry alone, nor even on the local education authorities, but on the attitude of the teachers and their immediate superiors. If the grammar schools resist the lure of large numbers and refuse to lower their standards in order to satisfy the desire of poor students for social prestige, then they can be the guardians of fair and just selection needed so much in our democracies. And, if the modern and technical schools will recruit first-class teachers capable of stimulating the practical mind with the desire for cultural advancement, then the nation will look with the same respect at the schools that have supplanted the old elementary training as at the more theoretical institutions. The English will then have achieved in the field of education what they have achieved in their political life, namely, a combination of quality and equality. But if, as in the United States, the English schools that should prepare students for higher studies become overwhelmed by large numbers, they will not only defeat their own purpose, but also press down the level of the other schools, for the latter will lose their challenge from above. Furthermore, they will help to create the so-called "academic proletariat" that has been the danger of many nations in the recent decades of democratization.

And — in order to go the full circle of mutual influences — just as the quality of the grammar schools will depend on the high demands of the admission authorities in the universities, so also the quality of the modern and technical schools, that is, the older elementary and vocational institutions, will depend on the achievements of further or adult education. For an ambitious youth will not be afraid to attend the "minor" types of schools and enter more quickly into a money-earning occupation if he knows that there are later chances for advancement in learning and earning.

The future will show whether the English schools and their people are up to the task of educational statesmanship that waits for them. There is much interest and often excellent public discussion; [85] the training and the work of teachers receive thorough attention; and there is an experimental spirit. Against strong original opposition, the English have even begun to build "omnibus" secondary schools (at least for girls) that bring together under one roof pupils of eleven or over with most diverse interests, from typical academic pursuits to dressmaking and catering. But the budgetary difficulties encountered by every nation after a long war, and apparently also public indifference, have severely curtailed the initial plans for further education. The few county colleges, founded after 1945, may no longer exist when this book is published. And, as already indicated, on the work of these colleges, inspired partly by the Scandinavian folk high schools, depends

---

[85] One of the main sources for the student of English education is the *London Times Educational Supplement.*

to a large extent the success of the education of the working population.[86]

Recently, doubts have been expressed whether the modern schools, because they assemble students of too many interests and differences in talent, will be able to develop a clear and organic curriculum.[87] And there are other signs of disillusion, as they always occur after years of enthusiastic reform. Thus we find in the English *Year Book of Education 1952* the following paragraph:

It seems as if everything that is tried tends to achieve not only what is aimed at, but also and simultaneously the precise opposite. One recommends fundamental education for the masses in order that they may be enfranchised and rise to greater heights. But literacy also makes them more vulnerable to irrational propaganda and to the lure of the ignoble. One proposes more technical education in order better to equip populations to use the resources available. But stress on technical education helps to produce technicians with little understanding of the complexity of human problems which their own activity creates. One proposes to do away with selective secondary education, in order to draw leadership from socially underprivileged groups, in order to enrich the common life by drawing upon larger reservoirs of ability. But thereby one impoverishes the educational offering, lessens the quality of the schooling available to the children of poor parents who need it most. And so on — it seems as if measures of educational reform are of necessity polar in their nature.[88]

But this pessimism does not seem to prevail. The most recent White Paper on *Secondary Education for All*[89] records with satisfaction the following facts. Since 1944 "children have been staying on at school longer"; the number of full-time students in technical colleges has risen from 47,000 to 76,000, and the number of university students "is now double the pre-war figure" (c. 95,000); the school population has increased "well over a quarter"; the number of "trained and recruited teachers . . . has risen by 85,000 since the war to a total of 260,000"; and the school buildings have been improved. Yet, despite all public interest, classes are

[86] Daniel W. Marshall, *England's Plans for County Colleges* . . . (Thesis, Harvard University Graduate School of Education, 1952).

[87] See M. L. Jacks, *The Education of Good Men* (London: Victor Gollanz, 1955).

[88] From *The Year Book of Education, 1952* (London: Evans, 1952), Sec. I, Chap. I, "The Reform of Education." See conclusion, pp. 26–27.

[89] *Secondary Education for All. A New Drive* (London: H. M. Stationery Office, 1958).

still too large, and there is not sufficient opportunity for the fostering of individual talent and for grouping children according to
their particular capacities. As a consequence of this emphasis on
individual accomplishment, the Ministry of Education is critical of
comprehensive or similar schools (as they have been recommended
by the Labour Party), especially if the organization of such schools
"brings to an end an existing grammar school, which may well have
a long and distinguished history." The two opposing errors must be
avoided, namely, "that each school must do everything, and that
each type of school must have a fixed and self-contained territory
into which no other must enter." Nevertheless, the comprehensive
school of the American type, including junior and senior high
school, seems to gain interest and support, even from the Conservative Macmillan government. In January 1958, there were forty-
nine officially recognized comprehensive schools, and the number
has steadily increased.[90] Most recently (December 1959), the Central Advisory Council for Education, headed by Sir Geoffrey
Crowther, has demanded the raising of the age for compulsory
education from fifteen to sixteen years.

However great the influence of the modern school reforms may
be, they alone will not model the future of the English. As should
have become evident from these pages, more than others the English have regulated their lives, not by theory, but by custom and
practical wisdom, and thus they have been able to weather social
transitions without too severe crises. Many of the institutions they
had in distinction from other nations, such as primogeniture, were
more or less good luck. And it was definitely against the intentions
of the older ecclesiastical forces that no church monopoly could
establish itself. Nevertheless, it was due to social morality, prudence, and open-mindedness that the monarch raised men and
women to peerage from most different origins and occupations,
that members of privileged families and of the intelligentsia could
join the workers' movement without being ostracized by their
peers, that the Fabian Society (Bernard Shaw, Sidney and Beatrice

[90] *Learning to Live. A Policy of Education from Nursery School to University.*
(London: Labour Party, 1958), Appendix II and p. 28. See also in this connection
the informative article by Edmund King, "Comprehensive Schools in England:
Their Context," *Comparative Education Review*, October 1959.

Webb, Sidney Olivier, Graham Wallas) [91] could become a clearing-house between conservatives, liberals, and socialists, that the House of Lords was turned from an instrument of aristocratic power into a council of older and experienced statesmen, and that there is much more freedom of the individual parliamentarian to deviate from party decisions than in other countries and therefore less danger of politics becoming an impersonal machine.

Certainly, modern English education, as well as other recent social measures, represents democracy built into an essentially conservative society. At the end of World War II, the superficial observer expected the old Public Schools to disappear. With the coming school reform there would be no need of them. In addition, who would have the money? Actually, the applications to these schools have constantly increased. Like the old universities, they hold up a tradition that, though not always glorious, has nevertheless provided a standard of disciplined learning and deportment. The old families who considered those schools their social property, but now cannot compete with more efficient newcomers, resent the invasion of new elements. Yet, the system of selection, coupled with extended scholarships, should take care that only the best of the new will climb to the top. And if they finally enter Oxford and Cambridge — still the dream of the ambitious despite the excellent scholarly quality of the newer universities — they will not only be trained academically, but also inhale the atmosphere of the old gentlemen's colleges.[92]

Probably the large majority of the people, even the less privileged, would not like it otherwise. And social prejudices will still go on — where would they not? Like gossip, snobbery is a trend thoroughly woven into human nature. Everybody is against it, as he is against sin. But, like sin, we would miss it, if it did not exist.

There is a revealing paragraph in Rose Macaulay's novel *The Towers of Trebizond.*[93] When the Russian secret police interrogate an adventurous lady, Aunt Dot, about the schools for the

---

[91] See Ernst Stabler, *London Education 1890–1910, with Special Reference to the Work of Sidney and Beatrice Webb* (Thesis, Harvard University Graduate School of Education, 1951).

[92] See G. Z. F. Bereday, *The Role of Wealth and Education in English Class Structure* (Harvard, 1953).

[93] New York: Farrar, Strauss and Cudahy (1956), p. 254.

English workers, knowing about them mainly from Dickens' *Nicholas Nickleby*, one of the Russian standard books on the subject, she replies:

> Ancient history . . . You might as well read *Oliver Twist* for information about modern Public Assistance, or *Newgate Visited* for prison life. There are no schools like that today. The children of the workers go first to primary schools, then either to modern or grammar schools. Modern schools seem to have a bad name for some reason, and grammar schools a good one. They are both attended by children of the workers. The *bourgeoisie* usually send their children to other schools, paid for by themselves.
>
> "Capitalist schools," said the interrogators, and Aunt Dot admitted that this was so.

Nevertheless, the modern schools have become great experimental centers, and the grammar schools are now attended by sons of workers.

Our modern world needs a nation that from its own history, with all its bloodshed and defeats, but also with all its victories and acts of prudence, has learned the art of self-correction under high standards. Unless this earth goes through cataclysms that throw all mankind back into barbarism, the nations of the world have much reason to study English history and education and to learn from it.

VI

France

Whereas England is the classic country of decentralization, France is the classic country of centralization. To England fell early the unexpected yet eventually benevolent lot of being conquered by a foreign prince, who by his and his followers' superior culture established a monarchy strong enough to allow a high degree of decentralization without the continual threat of feudal revolts. France did not enjoy this good fortune. The domain of the House of Capet, which, with its residence at Paris, in 987 succeeded the direct line of Charlemagne, was originally restricted to the Île de France and the Orléanais, a region smaller than the territories of the great vassals of Normandy, Brittany, Burgundy, Aquitaine, Flanders, and Champagne. Only by playing these powerful rivals against each other could the monarchy, which had become hereditary in the eleventh century, gradually reduce the might of the "big barons." The skillful politics of the rightly admired St. Louis IX (1226–1270) gave the country a period of relative rest, but only ten years after his death new internal wars broke out; England claimed Normandy, and from 1339 to 1453 the Hundred Years' War between the English and French dynasties destroyed large parts of the country.

Not before the second half of the fifteenth century did a Machiavellian monarch, Louis XI (1461–1483), succeed in subjecting the big vassals. Even in the seventeenth century the genius of a Richelieu was required to keep the power of the nobles in check. Nevertheless, Louis XI laid the foundation for the absolute monarchy or unlimited royal government of which France henceforth became the great example. Where regional independence had been a continual threat to unity, only radical control with the concomitant destruction of local self-administration could provide security. This, at least, was the opinion of the professional jurists whom the monarchy took into its service and who used their knowledge of Roman law to strengthen royal power by arbitrary confiscations and radical centralization of authority. Though a precarious solution, for it deprived the provinces of political initiative and self-administrative experience and made an octopus out of Paris, it was probably the only device that could have worked in the France of the late Middle Ages. Perhaps even Louis XI would not have succeeded, had not in earlier centuries the crusades and other campaigns diminished the strength of the nobility.

During the sixteenth and seventeenth centuries absolutism became fully riveted into the life of the nation, with Louis XIV, *le roi soleil*, as its highest historical apotheosis. There is no proof for his famous statement: "L'état c'est moi." Nevertheless, it expresses the truth. It added to the glory of the crown that with the life of its bearer there coincided the lives of France's greatest dramatists, Molière, Racine, and Corneille, of the famous Catholic apologist and orator Bossuet, and of some of the great masters of the plastic arts. Paris and Versailles became the centers of culture, the high spots of every *grand tour*, the envy of every European dynast. The diplomats from Madrid to St. Petersburg spoke French, and everyone in the whole of Europe who was interested in some display of culture, from the little schoolmaster to the lace-knitting and harp-strumming daughter of a nobleman or bourgeois, laid value on stammering at least a few French words.

Yet, even as the edifice of French absolutism reached its greatest height, dry rot was already eating into its timber. We are reminded of Lord Acton's famous words that while power corrupts, absolute power corrupts absolutely. Politically and socially, the regime of Louis XIV was, in spite of initial success and glory, of doubtful value for the people. As always under imperialistically minded governments, the frontiers of the realm had to be "secured" against "foreign aggression," though at the time of Louis XIV no country intended aggression against France. This securing rounded out French territory; it brought, in full peace, a precious loot from unprotected German fields, namely, Strasbourg with the Alsace. This new possession had then to be further secured by the devastation of the Palatinate. The result was a growing hatred between Germany and France, with the innocent inhabitants of the borderlands pushed around between two rival powers even up to our own day.

When Louis XIV died in 1715, his glorious victories had exhausted the country. The treasury was empty. The aristocracy had been degraded to a mere royal entourage to which even marital honor counted little when interfered with by the grace of the monarch. "To share with Jupiter is no dishonour" (*Un partage avec Jupiter n'a rien de tout qui déshonore*).[1] The once proud and independent nobleman sought distinction by being close to the King and enjoyed bucolic plays in the gardens of Versailles, while squeezing the last farthing out of the impoverished peasant, from whom he became increasingly alienated. Conformist piety seemed compatible with utter license, even to the higher clergy. The precarious religious freedom of the Protestants, secured under Henry IV by the Edict of Nantes, was abolished. Those who did not convert were subjected to physical torture and the enforced conversion of their children, or they had to leave the country, thus depriving it of the potential contributions of one of the finest parts of the population. The Catholic Church allowed the monarch to establish himself as the supreme arbiter in matters religious and, more violently than it would have done itself, to suppress such signs of inner rejuvenation as the theology of Bishop Jansen and the school of Port-Royal. The once great theological faculty of Paris tried to abolish the last vestiges of intellectual freedom. Whereas the masters and students of the thirteenth century dared be rebels, the theologians under Louis XIV and his successor declared in two decisions of 1683 and 1717 that the king received his power exclusively from God and could, therefore, not be excommunicated.[2]

[1] André Maurois, *A History of France*, trans. Henry L. Biusse (London: Jonathan Cape, 1949), p. 216.

[2] Stephen d'Irsay, *Histoire des Universités Francaises et Étrangères* (Paris: Auguste Picard, 1933–1935), II, 55.

As in all communities where the symbols of faith and leadership degenerate, the people became cynical. Authority always kills itself first before it is killed by others. Neither the bourgeois of Paris who paid the taxes, without political representation, nor even the courtier could fail to see the flagrant contrast in a monarch who claimed to be the apostle of God and lived against his Commandments in every respect. And the people prayed: "Our Father who art in Versailles. Thy name is no longer hallowed. Thy kingdom is diminished. Thy will is no longer done on earth or on the waves. Give us our bread, which is lacking to us." [3]

Because of the total neglect of the political education of the people, French absolutism prepared not only for the Revolution of 1789, but also for the Revolution's final failure. Under the guise of democracy, the Revolution rapidly succeeded the old absolutism; it even surpassed it by exposing the helpless country to the murderous tyranny of the party leaders of Paris.

There is something paradoxical in this Revolution, explicable only by the fact that its leaders reached toward a rationally perfect society, while practically and emotionally they were in the state of adolescence. They were intoxicated rather than ripened by great ideas they had learned from books and orations. They did not know how to handle the dynamite of mass feelings and political ambitions. They were fortunate that belligerent interference from other countries gave them a chance to direct these sentiments into the enthusiasm of patriotic glory. Several revolutions have been led to victory this way.

In the times before the absolutism of Louis XIV democratic ideas had not been totally foreign to the French. *Le droit de la nature* had been referred to in the Middle Ages. At the end of the fifteenth century (1484) Philip Pot, Lord of La Roche in Burgundy, had already, though without success, asked for popular suffrage and the constitutional rights of the people. A hundred years later, the great jurist Jean Bodin had spoken of the separation of state and church. The Protestant Huguenots, whose ranks had been decimated by the Massacre of St. Bartholomew's Day (1572), read the *Vindiciae contra Tyrannos*. But in the eighteenth century

[3] Maurois, *A History of France*, p. 224.

the liberal Frenchman had to look abroad, to the England of Locke and the Geneva of Rousseau. And, as with all borrowed ideas, there was no sound transfer of theory into practice. In 1789 the citizens of Paris could listen to magnificent oratory; the revolutionaries and, for a while, even the reactionaries rode on waves of romantic love for every brother on earth; a Declaration of the Rights of Man and of the Citizen was issued; the golden flag of principles flew over every assembly and decision. There was a greatness that mankind will never forget, but there was not the mature wisdom that the English had developed in the course of their political growth. If Louis XIV had not revoked the Edict of Nantes — in other words, if there had been pluralistic sectarianism as existed across the channel — the French people might have found a compromise between centralizing Catholic monarchism and bureaucracy on the one hand and liberal democracy on the other. But, when the Revolution came, it was too late.

Since the decapitation of Louis XVI in 1793, France has gone through thirteen major changes in its political system, not to speak of the rapid succession of cabinets during each era. The inner division that the absolutism of the sixteenth and seventeenth centuries tried to avoid by the extirpation of the Protestants has since the days of Voltaire been replaced by the conflict between secularism and Catholicism, about which I will speak later.[4] Looking at all these internal contrasts and conflicts, one of the foremost modern French writers, Paul Valéry, introduces his essay "Images de la France"[5] with the idea, that there is no nation "more open, nor probably more mysterious than the French" and that it is extremely difficult to describe it in a simple manner. "One can characterize it by any collection of contradictory attributes."

Everything in Valéry's essay is correct, except the idea that only the French nation is a collection of contradictions. We will soon see that the German philosopher Friedrich Nietzsche said the same about his own country.

[4] See below, pp. 154f.
[5] *Regards sur le Monde Actuel* (Paris: Stock, 1931), p. 105. English trans. Francis Searle, *Reflections on the World Today* (London: Thames and Hudson, 1951), pp. 86, 87.

But what, then, gives the observer of the French people and the student of its literature the impression of a nation of the highest cultural self-manifestation, in spite of all discord?

This element of unity is created by the consciousness of a national glory supposedly unsurpassed by any other nation in the world, the claim to guardianship of the universal values of the human race, and the conviction of a cultural mission that appears to be all the greater, the more the dreams of France as a world power disappear. Whether one listens to a group abhorring all that has to do with Protestantism, the Enlightenment, and the Revolution such as the Action Française, led by Charles Maurras, or to a Catholic romantic such as Chateaubriand, or to a writer who deplores the suppression of the Protestants such as André Maurois, or to an admirer of the Cartesian and rationalist tradition such as Buisson or Bouglé, or to a philosopher such as Bergson, or to a socialist who turns Catholic such as Péguy, or a convinced democrat such as Jean Delvolvé — for each one France is endowed with a creative genius above that of any other nation; it is — as far as is humanly possible — the realization of all that is supremely humane in humanity. It is more or less by inadvertence that the Lord has also allowed other nations to make some contribution to civilization. Even such a sharp critic of the defects in French culture and a sincere admirer of Asiatic religions as Jacques Marquette describes Paris as "la capitale morale du monde civilisé." [6]

The Sense of Nationality

A profound sense of nationality developed early in France because it had to defend its frontiers against foreign invaders and its inner unity against powerful vassals. And one of its monarchs, St. Louis IX, became the shining symbol of Christian chivalry to the whole Western world.

The magic of Ste. Chapelle of Paris built for Louis IX in order to enshrine the Crown of Thorns flows not only from the ideality

[6] Jacques Marquette, *Une France Nouvelle pour le Monde Nouveau* (New York: Maison Francaise, 1944), p. 207.

of its Gothic structure and the profoundness of its stained windows. Like Mont St. Michel, it is the image of a period in which, as rarely in history, some chosen men were able to express to the degree of perfection the aesthetic and spiritual longing of their period. But, whereas we leave Ste. Chapelle with a feeling of total harmony, even if our opinions about holy relics may be different from those of the crusaders, the dark dungeons built into the rocks of St. Michel remind us of the strange combination of devotion, superstition, and cruelty so characteristic of medieval men, and perhaps of humanity as a whole. We are reminded of the same cruel contradiction by the other great figure who for the French unites saintliness and patriotism, Jeanne d'Arc. The divine inspiration of a peasant's daughter of Orléans turns the victories of the English on French soil into defeat and restores the faltering prestige of the crown. But the thanks of Church and monarchy are a witch trial and burning at the stake.

In comparison with the transcendental halo that surrounds Louis IX and Jeanne d'Arc, the more recent symbols of French nationalism are of secular character, some of them of ambiguous value even for the most ardent patriot. However, one cannot deny some greatness to Louis XIV, the Revolution of 1789, and Napoleon.

The Roman Heritage

The French sense of nationality has been enhanced by their belief in their Roman heritage. They feel that they are the heirs of Rome. The Greeks and Italians may deserve this title from the physical, but the French deserve it from the cultural, point of view. When in a trial (1404) the great chancellor John Gerson defended the rights of the University of Paris, he traced its origin back to Greece and Rome, from which Charlemagne had transplanted it "with great effort to the city of Paris in France." Even Egypt, Adam, and Abraham are drawn into the ancestral lineage.[7] The partnership of Charlemagne, as successor to the Roman emperors, with the University of Paris has also been asserted by the famous humanist Bulaeus[8] and other historians.

[7] Joannes Gerson, "Querela nomine universitatis ad Senatum parisiensem . . . Anno 1404," in *Opera Omnia* (Antwerp, 1706) IV, 573.
[8] César Égasse Boulay, *Historia Universitatis Parisiensis* (Paris, 1666–1675), I, 91.

The deep sense of guardianship of the ancient heritage appears especially in times of disaster. Thus Henry Massis, one of the defenders of Maurras against the accusation of collaboration with the Germans, reports of Marshal Pétain, the tragical figurehead of the Vichy government:

Marshal Pétain told us: It is the spiritual forces that guide the world . . . The new regime [that of Pétain] will preserve the Greek and Latin heritage of France and its radiating power in the world . . . France occupies so great a place in the civilization of the Occident that the latter cannot subsist without her.[9]

The supposed affinity between the ancient culture and that of France often serves as the explanation for the Frenchman's appreciation of clarity and felicity of expression. A number of sayings and pedagogical exhortations repeat the notion that nothing can be true that is not clear, nothing can be clear that is not also aesthetically pleasant. Only recently have French writers admitted that there can be beauty in the twilight of groping and truth in the admission that one has not yet achieved the final formulation. Of Léon Daudet, Henry Massis says that he possessed "le sens synthétique." Though there was in him the "thirst for the infinite" (which led him to German thought), nevertheless the precise, the concrete, and the real attracted him with invincible power.[10]

This tendency toward the classical, identified with the rational and with *bon sens*, distinguishes, according to general French opinion, the thought of France from that of other nations. Cartesianism is believed to be typically French because of its emphasis on method (an emphasis, however, that Descartes shares with every great philosopher of the seventeenth century). In contrast, Rousseau is suspect to the Latin type, not only because he is a Swiss and a Protestant, but also because he is the symbol of a romanticism that prefers the vagueness of great allusions to disciplined expression. Of course, Pascal may be right in saying that the reasoning of the heart may be truer and more comprehensive than the reasoning of the intellect, but he said it clearly and beautifully; in addition, he was a mathematician, whereas Rousseau was a kind of intellectual

[9] Henry Massis, *Maurras et Notre Temps* (Paris-Genève: La Palatine, 1951'), II, 153.
[10] *Ibid.*, II, 39.

knight-errant. In modern times Henri Bergson's emphasis on the value of intuition, as well as the German-influenced existentialism of Gabriel Marcel on the Catholic side and of Paul Sartre on the secular, deviates from the classical line. Naturally, for the conservative French this is but another sign of degeneration.

Even in a field where rationality is considered merely the handmaid, sometimes even the enemy, of imagination, namely, in art, order and discipline are a supreme measure of quality. Those of the poets and novelists whom the nation esteems as its classics reveal within the easy flow of rhythm a sense of trained choice and severe order. Writers of other countries have also aimed at such perfection, but it would not be the proper criterion for a Shakespeare or the young Goethe. And there is in no other country an institution like the Académie Française as the central authority in matters of literary standard.

Undoubtedly the most influential of the French aestheticians is Nicolas Boileau-Despréaux (1636–1711), the protégé of Louis XIV, friend of Molière and Racine, and author of *L'Art Poétique* (1674) and other aesthetic writings. Inspired by Aristotle and Horace, he analyzes the various types of poetic composition from the lyric to the epic and tragical forms. He may also exhibit Platonic and Stoic influences, for there exists in Boileau's mind a divinely pre-established harmony between nature, *bon sens* or reason, the good and the true. Even the human heart has to adjust its beating pulse to the lawful rhythm of the universe.

"In trying to attract, avoid offense to reason" (*Plaît par la raison seule, et jamais ne la choque*).[11] Even dramatic passion must express itself according to rules. "No beauty outside truth; the true alone is graceful" (*Rien n'est beau que le vrai: le vraie seul est aimable*).

> The false is always flat, annoying, full of boredom;
> But nature has the truth; your instinct tells you so:
> And she alone deserves man's love and admiration.
> (*Le faux est toujours fade, ennuyeux, languissant;*
> *Mais la nature est vraie, et d'abord on la sent:*
> *C'est elle seule en tout qu'on admire et qu'on aime*).[12]

[11] Despréaux Nicolas Boileau, "L'Art poétique," in *Oeuvres* (Paris: Firmin-Didot, 1878), Chant III, pp. 211–213.
[12] *Oeuvres*, "Epitre IX," pp. 165–167.

The poet who follows this advice will achieve the highest qualities of art, namely, rational clarity, simplicity, self-identity, unity, and perfection.[13]

In a more philosophic way, the Abbé de Condillac (1715–1780), influenced by Locke, reiterates in all his works his belief in the unity of all mental processes. Thus the perfection of the French language, so he says in his *Art of Writing*, is due to the clarity and precision it has acquired through the development of philosophical thought since the Renaissance and Pascal.[14] And at another place he says:

I have already shown that the art of writing rests on the principle of the closest connection of ideas because in effect the art of thinking has itself no other foundation. To the degree to which we are able to follow that liaison, to the same degree our mind develops further; it conceives everything at its place; it embraces a multitude of objects at the same time; and in perceiving them neatly it can also explain them with precision . . .

The advance of mind is the same everywhere; only the objects change, and whoever understands one thing and, in addition, knows how he has understood it is also capable of understanding many others.[15]

In the last analysis, all these ideas can be traced back to the overwhelming impression of Descartes's *méthode* on the seventeenth and eighteenth centuries, and they have remained in the advanced forms of French education up to the present.

Just as Descartes' influence was great in philosophy, so also was Boileau's in the field of poetry — though, fortunately, it was not so enduring. Especially in Germany, the power of a Lessing, of the "Storm and Stress" rebellion against artificiality, and of the young Goethe and Schiller was required to overcome the stifling effect of his authority. And the whole international revolt of the period of romanticism against the arrogance of rationalism must be understood in the light of this development. But, though even in France there will be today only a few who admire Boileau's didactical verses as works of art, no doubt, behind the scene he has been alive for a long time.

[13] See "L'Art poetique," in *Oeuvres*, Chants I, III, IV.
[14] "L'Art d'Écrire," in *Oeuvres* (Paris: Ch. Houel, 1798), VII, 409.
[15] Condillac, "Histoire Moderne," in *Oeuvres*, VI, 474.

FRANCE

Catholicism

The history of France is to a large part the history of Catholicism. In France was spilled the blood of the early martyrs, Irenée, St. Blandine, and St. Denis. No one can read without profound sympathy the account that Ernest Renan gives of the persecutions of the Christians at Lyon at the time of Marcus Aurelius.[16]

In France were born the two great ecclesiastical organizations that regenerated a sunken Church and papacy, the Orders of the Cluniac Benedictines (founded 910) and of the Cistercians (founded 1098). These orders spread their influence over almost all Europe, and St. Bernard, the Cistercian Abbot of Clairvaux (1090–1153), became for Western Christianity the symbol of holiness and religious fervor. To France belonged the man against whom St. Bernard directed his polemical zeal and moral ire, Abelard (1079–1142). A mythical figure in European poetry for his tragical love for Héloïse, he represents one of the first personalities in the Middle Ages with a distinctive flavor of modernity. Not without some inner reason, though incorrectly, he has been called the founder of the greatest university that the medieval world possessed, the University of Paris. For the historian of thought he is the author of *Sic et Non* (Yea and Nay), the book that, though primitive in its method of showing contrasting opinions in the theological tradition, was nevertheless the first sign of the revival of dialectical thinking. Both St. Bernard and Abelard were contemporaries of the crusaders.

Yet, in spite of being "the beloved daughter of the Church," France, as we already saw in the discussion of the Middle Ages, never subordinated its national interests to papal claims. When in the fourteenth century the popes became irritating to the French kings, they were kept under strong control at Avignon. The French clergy played the leading role in the reform movement of the fourteenth and fifteenth centuries which, if victorious, would have changed the history of Western Christianity, for it would have placed the popes under the superiority of a European congress of

[16] Ernest Renan, *Marc-Aurèle et La Fin du Monde Antique* (Paris: Calman-Levy, 1891), Chap. XIX; English trans. with Introduction by William G. Hutchinson, *Marcus Aurelius* (London: Walter Scott, 1903), Chap. XIX.

bishops; it would have meant ecclesiastical decentralization instead of centralization; and it probably would have prevented the development of a Luther or Calvin.

In the later centuries, then, the relation of the monarchy to the Church is much less, if at all, one of religion than one of a security pact between two powers, each of which needs the other for its existence. In 1516 Francis I and the Pope concluded a concordat that determined ecclesiastical policy up to the Revolution, for it deprived the Church of France of its financial independence. The income from its rich resources went henceforth into the treasuries of pope and king, who allotted to the clergy the budget needed for the support of its members, its services in schools, and its edifices. The mutual dependence thus established between the courts of Rome and Paris explains why, on the one hand, the monarchy had to suppress ruthlessly the Protestant Reformation and any other sign of antipapism, and why, on the other hand, the popes had to suffer the sometimes humiliating treatment on the part of the French monarchs, especially of Louis XIV. It also explains why from the sixteenth to the eighteenth century the religious vitality that characterized the France of the Middle Ages gave way to an era of conformity, of a conventional religious art and oratory, of Machiavellian cardinal-diplomats as the highest functionaries of the king, and of a cringing university that drove all new ideas outside its walls.

The Enlightenment

As we find in French schools and culture the influence of Catholicism, so we also discover the effects of the Enlightenment. Its general characteristics have already been explained in an earlier chapter. Here one can deal only with those events that have changed the ecclesiastical-monarchical edifice of older France into a divided structure, with a Catholic style on the one side and a secular style on the other.

This can be done more or less in catchwords. France participated in the Renaissance. Great skeptics such as Montaigne and satirists such as Rabelais designed new ways for the interpretation of the human situation: wise resignation rather than dogma and prejudice, laughter and grotesque rather than the pathos of preaching. Against official ecclesiastical politics, the Renaissance of France embraced the teaching of Erasmus of Rotterdam. There came the Protestant crisis with its criticism of established beliefs and institutions, and during the seventeenth century the philosophy of Descartes was accepted even in ecclesiastical circles. At the end of the seventeenth century England's philosophical and scientific empiricism began to exert its influence, and during the following decades, rather than reading poetry, devotional literature, and adventure stories, the French read Voltaire's *Candide*, with its cynical denial of divine Providence, and his *Lettres Anglaises*. These, like the later work by Montesquieu on the *Esprit des Lois*, described England as the country of progress and civil liberty. Speaking of Descartes, Voltaire said: "He left France because he searched for truth, which there was persecuted by the miserable official philosophy" (*philosophie de l'école*). When speaking of Newton, Voltaire said:

It was his great fortune not only to be born in a free country, but at a time when the impertinence of the scholastics was banned and reason was cultivated, and when the world was eager to be his disciple rather than his enemy.[17]

Later the educated French eagerly read Rousseau's heretical *Confessions of a Savoyard Priest* and his *Social Contract*. They bought Diderot's *Encyclopédie*, which had almost all the great liberals of France as collaborators. What united the writers of the twenty-seven volumes, which despite all attempts at confiscation could soon be found in the libraries of enlightened people, was the great faith of the eighteenth century's rationalists: man's thought and life are not dependent on supernatural authority; God, or wherever the creative power may be found, has given him the gifts of reason and observation to discover the laws of nature; true morality and the chance for social progress lie in living according to these laws; and whatever a person may think about the ultimate mysteries of the universe, it cannot be explained by supernatural speculations, but only by men of science. For what has been the effect of religious dogmatism? Superstition, persecution, and religious wars.

[17] Voltaire, *Lettres Philosophiques*, Édition Critique . . . par Gustave Lanson (Paris: Societé Nouvelle . . . , 1909) II, p. 3f, "Sur Descartes et Newton."

One cannot say that *les philosophes*, as they were called by their contemporaries, always followed their own principle. They were inclined to see malice when there was only error, and stupidity when there was only custom; they had no sense for the symbolic; most of them had a one-sided picture of man in that they believed he needed only to be taught the truth in order to live accordingly. Their interpretation of man was, in a way, more superficial than that of traditional Christianity, which, despite all the superstitions that had crept into it in the course of time, understood sin, guilt, and catastrophe as the inevitable accompaniments of human life. Many of the philosophers opposed a stagnant creed either with destructive criticism or unrealistic optimism, or with both in the same breath. They never tried themselves in practical politics and administration. Their concept of nature was in a great stream of thought begun by the Stoic philosophers and was productive of deep insight into the life of man and society. What greater ideal can humanity have than to understand the inner working of the creation of which it is a part, and to live according to this understanding? But there was the danger that nature, and man's nature, might be understood as a materialistic and mechanical enterprise, or as a generalization to be used by everyone according to convenience. And, for all its apparently empirical aspects, it was loaded with emotion. History was conceived by some of the *philosophes* as a mathematical problem with the solution either right or wrong. There was no wisdom of the middle. Thus, when minor men took over, first to destroy the old and then to build a new France, they had the outline for a book, but not for a country with a people in uproar. To be sure, few, if any, of the *philosophes* had really intended a revolution. It came to them as a surprise — a mixture of the rebellion of hungry and exploited masses, of the resentment of a politically powerless middle class, and a protest against tyrannical orthodoxy. And, since supernaturalism had exhausted itself, some kind of materialism became the embodiment of the new.

Yet, despite all the immaturity and clumsiness of the revolutionary leaders, the world owes to the ideas developed by the rationalist thinkers of France, as well as of England and Germany, the gradual emancipation from the torture, from witch trials and from inquisitions. And, however superficially the idea of progress may sometimes have been interpreted, the confidence that man's thinking and initiative may be capable of improving the lot of humanity is one of the great blessings of our era. As all ideals, so also the ideals of liberty, fraternity, and equality have been misused. They have promoted not only mutual respect and democratic living, but also class hatred, dissatisfaction, the cult of mediocrity, and the tendency to pull down everything that is up. But the more we understand these ideas, the more we may see in them the outcome of a long evolution to which many men have contributed in many ways. As a matter of fact, the political revolutionaries were the last; the first were the prophets of the great religions. And this is exactly what the French *philosophes* failed to understand.

EDUCATION

The Church and the Revolution

The forces that molded or split the French mind also molded or split French education. Up to the Revolution little was done for the education of the large masses except where some communities or some priests and Catholic orders took care of those who wanted to learn to read or to write. What is peculiarly French is secondary education. It is a product of the Renaissance, or, more definitely, of philological humanism with its mixture of *pietas* and *eloquentia*. In Strasbourg, then a center of German culture and largely Protestant, the educator Johannes Sturm, or Sturmius (1507–1589), had organized a humanistic school that became the pattern of similar institutions in large parts of Europe and the prototype of the German classical Gymnasium. Though originally Protestant, it was welcomed by the Jesuits as a model to inculcate the minds of the young with the classical and religious training advocated by the Order. The famous Jesuit *Ratio Studiorum* is historically connected with the Latin School of Magister Sturmius at Strasbourg.[18]

Despite centralization in other aspects, the French government was not afraid to leave the education of the privileged youth mainly to the Jesuit Order. Its founder, Ignatius of Loyola, had met with

---

[18] *St. Ignatius and the Ratio Studiorum*, ed. Edward A. Fitzpatrick, trans. A. R. Ball (New York: McGraw-Hill, 1933). On Sturm's relation to the Jesuit schools, see K. A. Schmid, *Geschichte der Erziehung* (Stuttgart, 1884–1902'), III, 37.

his first disciples on the Mont St. Geneviève in Paris; thus it was considered of more or less French origin, though Loyola was not only by birth, but also by mentality, typically Spanish. Furthermore, the Jesuit Order itself was disciplined and centralized and thus able to indoctrinate the youth entrusted to it with the uniform spirit the government wished to create. This spirit and organization had not only helped to suppress Protestantism when (around 1570) about one third of the French population adhered to it; it had also been influential in destroying the tendencies toward independence within the Gallican Church, an accomplishment for which the Jesuits were thoroughly disliked by some of the older religious orders. Finally, Jesuit instruction was not so deficient as later described by its critics. At least up to the beginning of the eighteenth century it served its purpose. The Jesuit *collèges* insisted on the kind of classical scholarship that suited the French sense of Roman heritage; they also took care of good and formal manners; they provided knightly sports and games, and theater, and a highly competitive spirit within unquestioned authority. What more could the absolutist government demand of a school system that cost so little?

The crisis came after the first decades of the eighteenth century. The spirit of the Enlightenment influenced the secular clergy, the officialdom, and even the court. The professors at the University of Paris found unbearable the censorship exercised under Jesuit auspices by the theological faculty. Their once great institution had become ridiculous in the eyes of educated men. Other universities also voiced protest. In his essay, "Les Trois Empereurs en Sorbonne," Condorcet says:

Since the invention of the printing press the theological faculty of Paris has arrogated to itself the right to express, in bad Latin, its judgment about books that it dislikes . . . And in order to multiply the readers and the jeers it has constantly humiliated itself by translating its opinions into French . . .

The faculty was, therefore, obliged to admit that, though the foundation of faith must always remain the same, one may nevertheless enrich it from time to time by new articles with which the circumstances would never have permitted our Lord Jesus Christ and the saint apostles to busy themselves.

This idea about the necessity to adhere to certain dogmas in order to avoid damnation, and the idea that eternal torture will be reserved for the nonbelievers and even the ignorant, is the fundamental cause of fanaticism and intolerance.[19]

Not only the freethinkers, but also the highly religious Pascal and the Jansenists (who represented a kind of Calvinism within the Catholic creed and had for this reason been persecuted) turned against the Order. Public opinion was aroused; men suspected the Jesuits, who served as royal confessors, of secret political influence; they were linked with a financial scandal that caused considerable loss to the upper and middle classes. No doubt, even the Franciscans and Dominicans looked with a measure of satisfaction at the increasing tension. Dogmatically, they had always had different opinions about grace, and, politically, they had looked with envy at the growing power of their Christian brethren.

Thus, in 1762, King Louis XV, though involuntarily, urged the Pope to dissolve the Order. The Roman See, under Pope Clement XIV, yielded.[20] In other Catholic countries also, anticlericalism had grown. In 1759 the Society had been banished from Portugal and Brazil, and in 1767 King Charles III expelled the Jesuits from Spain and its colonies. Paradoxically enough, Frederick II of Prussia, the Protestant agnostic, and Catherine II of Russia, a member of the Orthodox Church, protected them. The Order was restored in 1814, when the wave of rationalism yielded to the romantic movement.

About the time of the banishment of the Jesuits there appeared a large literature demanding general education of the people under the auspices of the national state. The *Essai d'Education Nationale ou Plan d'Etudes pour la Jeunesse* was published in 1762 by Caradeuc de La Chalotais, a member of the parliament of Bretagne. According to a contemporary, it sold twenty thousand copies within a month of publication.[21]

[19] Antoine-Nicolas de Condorcet, *Oeuvres complètes* (Paris, 1804), VI, 347–349.
[20] Brief *Dominus ac Redemptor Noster*, July 21, 1773, in D. Carl Mirbt, *Quellen zur Geschichte des Papsttums und des Römischen Katholizismus*, 3rd ed. (Tübingen: Mohr, 1911), No. 457, p. 312.
[21] English rendering of the essay with the title: *Essay On National Education, or Plan of Studies for the Young*, by Louis Réné de La Chalotais, trans. H. R. Clark, with Historical Introduction (London: Arnold, 1934); see also F. de La Fontainerie, ed., *French Liberalism and Education in the Eighteenth Century. The Writings of LaChalotais, Turgot, Diderot, and Condorcet on National Education* (New York: McGraw-Hill, 1932).

Other works followed, with men of such fame as Turgot, Diderot, Talleyrand, and Condorcet among the writers. The latter's *Rapport et Projet de Décret sur l'Organisation Générale de l'Instruction Publique*, presented in 1792 to the National Legislative Assembly, was adopted as the basis of policy by the revolutionary parliament. In regard to religious education, the opinions of the writers vary, with Diderot and Condorcet hostile to dogmatic religious education within the expected new public-school system, though probably not to religion as such. Condorcet's most famous work, the *Esquisse d'un tableau historique des progrès de l'esprit humain* (Outlines of an Historical View of the Progress of the Human Mind), could be interpreted as the rationalist counterpart to St. Augustine's *City of God*. In the latter work, human history is seen as the way toward salvation through the destruction of the empire of the world and man's surrender to God's final judgment, whereas in the first the way toward salvation leads through man's confidence in his rational powers, which so far have been crippled by a superstitious transcendentalism imposed on humanity by priests and feudal classes.[22]

By which positive means can the new rational and self-confident man achieve progress in conformity with his "natural" destiny? According to the educational writings of the time, the first obligation is a new organization of society. This idea had already inspired Jean Jacques Rousseau's educational novel *Emile* (1762). Despite all his radicalism, imagery, and rhetorical exaggerations, Rousseau's was an extremely sharp mind. Certainly he did not believe in the actual circumstances of his novel — a child to be educated and a tutor alone on an island. He created the island situation in order to indicate symbolically that nothing but a complete rejection of a corrupt society could bring about a new generation and a new future. The more practical educational schemes here under discussion are more optimistic than Rousseau's. Though, in a way, they do believe with him that mysteriously "All things are good as they come out of the hands of their Creator," they do not believe that "everything degenerates in the hands of man."[23] They believe

[22] The most characteristic work of this kind is *Les Ruines* by the atheist, Comte de Volney, published in 1791.
[23] First paragraph of *Emile*.

in man's capacity to create a new state of civilization, which, rather than joining the forces of degeneration and reaction, will join the forces of progress. Not pessimism but progress became the gospel, in France more than in any other country.[24]

Condorcet's *Esquisse* intends to show the successive renaissances of the human race,

the path it has followed, the steps that it has made toward truth and happiness. These observations of what man has been and what he is today will help us to understand the means by which he can ascertain and accelerate the new advances that his nature permits him to hope for in the future.

This is the aim of the work that I have undertaken. Through reason and reference to facts it will prove that nature has set no limit to the gradual perfection of the human faculties; that the perfectibility of man is really indefinite; that the progress of this perfectibility, so far dependent on reactionary forces, knows of no other boundary than the duration of the globe on which nature has thrown us.[25]

There is, in Condorcet's *Report on Public Education*, a passage that reminds us of later anarchism as well as of the Marxian concept of the classless and stateless society.

No doubt, the time will come when scientific societies, instituted by public authority, will be superfluous, and hence dangerous; when even all public instruction will be useless. This will be the time when there will be no reason to be afraid of general error; when the causes of passionate prejudice will have lost their influence; when the light will be spread equally everywhere and in all the classes of society; when the sciences and their application can work without the yoke of superstition and without the poison of false doctrines; when, finally, every person will find within his knowledge and the rectitude of his mind sufficient arms to repulse the ruses of charlatanry. But this time is still far away. Our task, however, is to prepare for and accelerate its coming; and while creating the new institutions [necessary for this purpose] we must incessantly try to hasten the happy moment when they will no longer be necessary.[26]

How can one hope to ever raise the mores of the people unless one provides for its future teachers and leaders an exact and rigorous analysis

[24] See J. B. Bury, *The Idea of Progress: An Inquiry into Its Origin and Growth* (London: Macmillan, 1924), and J. Delvaille, *Essai sur l'Histoire de l'Idee de Progrès jusqu'à la Fin du XVIII° Siècle* (Thesis, Paris, 1910).

[25] *Esquisse d'un tableau historique des progrès de l'esprit humain. Texte revu et presenté par O. H. Prior* (Paris: Boivin, 1933), pp. 2–3.

[26] *Rapport et Projet de Décret sur l'Organisation Générale de l'Instruction Publique. Présenté à l'Assemblée Nationale . . . par M. Condorcet* (April 20–21, 1792), pp. 54–55.

of the moral sentiments and of the ideas and the principles of justice that result from it.[27]

Since there is only one reason, and since the new state of enlightened citizens will accept it as highest authority, the advocates of the new secular society unhesitatingly accept political centralization, unaware of the fact that thereby they invite a new possibility of tyranny. Naïvely they believe that *la souveraineté du peuple*, represented through its parliament, will protect the citizen from being abused. But what is going to happen if the state falls into the hands of evil men? Or what are the leaders going to do if their citizens prefer to remain in the traditional state of stupidity, if they even like superstition, or if certain groups feel that they profit more in calculating by prejudice and ignorance than by intellect? Then the new state has the right to force the recalcitrant individuals into natural happiness or, if they do not wish to be happy according to the prescribed pattern, into prison, just as the old Church felt justified in forcing the heretic back into supernatural salvation or, if he did not wish to be saved, into the flames of the stake.

All the plans for a new education, including the one Talleyrand in 1792 submitted to the National Assembly,[28] reveal a touching confidence that the new education from the elementary school up to the learned institutions will thrive primarily on science. The programs are stuffed with geometry, calculus, physics, and the applied sciences. Languages, especially the ancient languages, recede. Instead, men hope to educate youth toward effective participation in the present society through teaching a secular form of morality, based on man's nature and the understanding of the laws of the universe. Condorcet recommends a subject, new for his time, but increasingly common today in our high schools and universities, *la science sociale.*

Thus in the schools the fundamental verities of social science will precede their application. Neither the French Constitution nor even the Declaration of Human Rights will be presented to any class of citizens like tables that have descended from heaven and must be adored and believed.[29]

[27] *Ibid.,* p. 20.
[28] *Rapport sur l'Instruction Publique, Fait au Nom du Comité de Constitution a l'Assemblée Nationale.* . . . par M. de Talleyrand-Périgord, Ancien Evêque d'Autun (Paris, September 10, 11, and 19, 1791).
[29] Condorcet, *Rapport et Projet de Décret,* p. 7.

All the reports are convinced that the schools of the old regime were wretched, and there is no doubt that the dissatisfaction was rather general. They recommend a division of the school system into elementary, secondary, and higher education in the form of scientific associations and research institutes. For men had apparently given up all hope that the old universities and colleges could serve the new regime.

Through a series of decrees these old institutions were gradually strangled to death. As a matter of fact, the expulsion of the Jesuit Order in 1773 had severely impaired all the advanced schools. They now lost their independent income through the abolition of the tithe and the suppression of religious congregations (1790). The *Constitution Civile du Clergé* changed the status of the priests from servants of the Church to servants of the state, which had little sympathy for them. In 1792 all secular corporations were forbidden. Finally a committee of the Convention asked that the universities, which in reality had already ceased to exist, be officially suppressed.[30] Only the famous Collège de France escaped, as it also remained free from the grip of Napoleon. Apparently, its pure and disinterested scholarship placed it outside the fears of men who could think only in political categories.

Against strong ecclesiastical resistance the laws of 1794 (under Robespierre) provided secular elementary and secondary education for the whole people. But they remained on paper. Instead the Revolution founded in some departments so-called "Ecoles Centrales," which were a mixture of secondary and higher education, and established "Ecoles Spéciales" in place of the old universities, to serve especially the medical and technical professions. It is difficult to say how much was really done for the education of the people, in the name of which all the destruction had been performed. Certainly, it was not much.

In the *Moniteur* of September 27, 1791, Talleyrand wrote that throughout France the universities had suspended their operations

---

[30] For literature, see L. Liard, *L'enseignement supérieur en France, 1789–1803* (Paris: A. Colin, 1884–1902); C. Hippeau, *L'Instruction en France pendant la Révolution. . .*, 2 vols. (Paris: Didier, 1881–1883); Stephen d'Irsay, *Histoire des Universités Francaises et Etrangères*. 2 vols. (Paris: A. Picard, 1933–1935); L. Bernhard, *Akademische Selbstverwaltung in Frankreich und Deutschland, ein Beitrag zur Universitätsreform* (Berlin: J. Springer, 1930).

and that the colleges were "without subordination, without professors, and without students." And in 1796 (year IV of the Revolution) Pierre Daunou sent to the National Convention a report that even for its time is unique in its mixture of honesty, revolutionary phrases, hypocrisy, and distortion of facts.[31]

In 1789, so he says, education was "vicious, but, no doubt, it was organized." For centuries the universities, the scientific societies, the *lycées*, and the theaters had been the pride of the nation, "vast depots of scholarship and glory." But the ignominious old regime poisoned the very sources of education, kept the people in ignorance, degraded the enlightened men of the nation, and brought corruption everywhere. The Revolution soon changed the lower schools into institutions for "the progress of public enlightenment," while the intermediate institutions gradually disappeared, together with the corporations by which they had been financed. Finally, the higher institutions were "engulfed in their own corruption and in the aristocratic immorality with the sinister germs of which they had been infested." Consequently, they did not wish to work with the new regime that refused to acknowledge their old privileges; anarchy in education was the result.

But, so Daunou continues, there were other reasons for the decay of educational institutions. "In these years of peril and war, the French had no time to study any other art but that of victory on the battlefield, and one must agree that in this area they made rapid and vast progress." However, one must also admit that "the frenzies of public mentality, the divagations of opinion, the quarrels of parties, the wars of factions, the continual distractions of thought, even the intentions to ameliorate public instruction" helped to create the deplorable state of things.

Many of the causes to which Daunou refers are true, but, being one of the radical rationalists himself, he could not see the deeper layer of error, namely, the complete lack of insight into the organic continuity of civilization, which cannot suddenly be destroyed like a machine and then replaced by a more modern one. He could not see that the dogmatism that considered any independent corporation dangerous because it did not fit into the new design of a uniformly engineered society was bound to produce a

[31] C. Hippeau, *L'Instruction en France*, I, 470f.

cruelly totalitarian, rather than a democratic, system of government. Finally, a mind such as Daunou's was unaware of the fact that a policy of education based exclusively on the ideas of patriotism and utility was bound to destroy the very premise of a liberal civilization, namely, freedom to think without concern for immediate practical results.

Napoleon

After the revolutionaries had wrecked the whole national household, the strong man had to come to restore some order. Often he comes from outside, not yet engulfed in the quarrels of the old parties, combining distance with the recklessness and military power that permit him to get rid of party politicians. All these requisites were fulfilled by Napoleon Bonaparte. He came from Corsica, had spent most of his life in the army he had led to victory, possessed the mixture of rationality and bombast his French contemporaries liked, and even understood how to dress up his incipient dictatorship with the garlands of the glorious Revolution. Indeed, from the point of view of the expelled Bourbons and the other European monarchs, he was the revolutionary par excellence, and his disrespect for dynastic traditions and for thrones, except his own, proved them right.

As a political architect and legislator, Napoleon found himself in the situation of a city planner in a destroyed city; the old houses were rubble. Thus he could reorganize the administrative map of France. He attracted the best minds of the country to build up a highly trained officialdom; he gave the nation a legal code (*Code Napoléon*) which became the exemplar of modern Continental jurisprudence; and he built public education firmly into the framework of the new regime. For, as for Plato and Aristotle, it was for him but another part of statecraft.

Of all political questions, this one [on the importance of the teaching profession] deserves perhaps the most attention. There will be no political stability as long as there is no teaching body based on stable principles. So long as children are not taught whether they must be republicans or monarchists, Catholics or freethinkers, etc., the State will not constitute a nation but rest on vague and shifting foundations, ever exposed to disorder and change.[32]

The Université Impériale, established in 1806 [33] (now Université de France), is the strongest symbol of France's tendency toward centralization. Its name indicates not a single university but the totality of all publicly supported and controlled schools in the country. In the times of Napoleon, only the higher and secondary schools were included; today the elementary schools also belong to it. In no way was Napoleon troubled about the concept of academic freedom. This idea (*liberté de l'enseignement*), the first notion of which we find in Spinoza's *Tractatus Theologico-Politicus*,[34] had been discussed during the Revolution, but in reality it existed for him as little as it existed or had ever existed in other countries, including the United States.[35] Only in Germany was it slowly emerging. For the French Emperor the new educational system was a national institution, designed to support and preserve the new monarchy. The *écoles spéciales*, founded by the Revolution, were maintained for the time being because lawyers, physicians, and engineers were needed. Everything else that reflected the ideology of Condorcet had to disappear, though Napoleon's educational scheme in many respects resembled that of the enlightened philosopher. Louis Fontanes, who after the fall of Robespierre had been made professor of literature at the Ecole Centrale des Quatre-Nations, became Napoleon's adviser in matters of education and Grand Master of the University of Paris. He tried to sweeten the bitter role of servitude imposed on the professors by the following words:

His Majesty wishes a body the teaching of which should be sheltered from the little fevers of political opinion; which always marches ahead

[32] *The Mind of Napoleon. A Selection from His Written and Spoken Words*, ed. and trans. J. Christopher Herold (New York: Columbia University Press, 1955), p. 117.
[33] "Loi relative à la formation d'une Université Impériale. . . . du 10 Mai 1806," *Bulletin des Lois* (Paris: Imprimerie Impériale, IV, No. 91, p. 527).
[34] "A Theological-Political Treatise," in *The Chief Works*, Vol. I. Translated from the Latin, with an Introduction by R. H. M. Elwes (London: G. Bell, 1883).
[35] See Richard Hofstadter and Walter P. Metzger, *The Development of Academic Freedom in the United States* (New York: Columbia University Press, 1955); see also Robert M. MacIver, *Academic Freedom in Our Time* (New York: Columbia University Press, 1955).

even if the government fails to watch; and the administration and statutes of which are so incorporated in the life of the nation that no one should easily lay his hands on it. — If these hopes are realized, His Majesty will find in this body a guarantee against theories that are dangerous and subversive in regard to the social order, in one sense or another.[36]

In establishing a national institution in the most centralized sense, buttressed by a whole scaffolding of controls ending in the Ministry, Napoleon created also a rigid system for the selection of candidates to teaching positions in the universities and the higher classes of the *lycées*, the so-called *agrégation*. The diploma of *agrégé* is acquired after the candidate's successful passing of *concours*, a highly competitive national examination, given once a year in Paris by special committees appointed and supervised by the Ministry. A visitor of that Ministry will see the walls of the entrance hall and the staircases plastered with announcements concerning these examinations, which not only make the successful applicant eligible for the most coveted positions in the public service, but give him (besides the expectation of marrying into one of the preferred families) the *right* to be appointed. If there is no immediate opening available, the salary is paid nevertheless. The number of those finally admitted to the élite of the *agrégés* in the different professions is, roughly speaking, only about 30 per cent of the candidates. Of course, one has to keep in mind that the *agrégation* is not a typical examination, but, as the term indicates, a concourse where the number of vacancies in the respective professional sector determines the number of successes. (Similar forms of selection, unknown to the American, exist also in other countries, for example, Italy and the U.S.S.R.)

Though an administrative genius such as Napoleon can put his permanent stamp on the external structure of education, no mere decree can change its inner spirit, for the latter depends on the total culture of a country. Even administratively the Emperor succeeded only because he led education into the path the nation had already chosen for a long time, namely, of concentration of its affairs in the bureaucracy of Paris. Yet, there were still professors who minded the control and remained untouched by Fontanes' rhetoric.

[36] Stephen d'Irsay, *Histoire des Universités Francaises et Etrangères*, II, 172.

Ecclesiasticism and Secularism

The split Napoleon could heal least of all was that between church and state, or between ecclesiasticism and secularism. The concordat with the Holy See, which he concluded in 1801 as regent of the consulate, and the re-establishment of the Catholic Church in 1802 disappointed the revolutionaries, who still liked to consider him one of their own. Moreover, it did not satisfy the clergy, which always looked with suspicion at his educational policy. Since then with every change in government, from republicanism to monarchy and from monarchy back to republicanism, the nation has been exposed to the struggle of opposite spiritual forces. Much more than the diatribes flung from one hostile political camp to another, the life and writing of the Abbé de Lamennais (1782–1854) reveal the tragedy of the situation. A devout Catholic, convinced of the eternal mission of his Church as the judge over the powerful and the source of consolation for the poor (of whom there were many after the wars of Napoleon, the reactionary regime of the Bourbons, and the dawn of industrialism), he was nevertheless convinced that only complete liberty in matters of conscience, teaching, and association could secure a wholesome development for his country and the whole world. In order to secure these "trois grandes et imperieuses nécessités de l'époque" [37] the Church, he thought, had to disentangle itself from the unholy alliance with the state which had caused not only the downfall of the old regime, but also endless war, incredible misery, and distortion of the gospel. He was working for a Christian liberalism.

On July 18, 1830, a few days before the outbreak of the July Revolution that ended the Bourbon regime, Lamennais wrote in a letter to the Count de Senfft:

A large part of the clergy and almost the whole episcopate looks on but does not see, hears but does not listen, for it is caught in its old and stupid prejudices. In tying as inseparable the cause of religion to the cause of power which oppresses it, it prepares with all its forces a general apostasy. Nothing else, then, can the Church expect but violent persecution if the irritated liberals triumph, and chains as shameful as heavy if the opposite party carries the day. Indeed, profound and noble politics! [38]

[37] Félicité de Lamennais, L'Avenir, October 17, 1830.
[38] Quoted from Abbé Charles Boutard, Lamennais, sa Vie et ses Doctrines (Paris: Perrir, 1913), II, 109.

Much better a poor clergy esteemed by the people than a rich one supported by the government of the state.

Lamennais' journal *L'Avenir*, after only thirteen months of publication, was condemned and discontinued on orders from Rome. He answered the act of suppression with his *Paroles d'un Croyant* (Words of a Believer), in which in apocalyptic words of beauty and power he described the horrors through which mankind would have to go unless "the living power of liberty" merged with the spirit of Christ, which is love, justice, and charity.

In the encyclical *Singulari Nos* of 1834 Pope Gregory XVI condemned the *Paroles d'un Croyant*.[39] Thus was frustrated a great man's endeavor to end the schism between liberty and religious authority which had haunted Europe since the days of the Renaissance, and even earlier.

In a much more detached attitude, yet essentially with the same inner passion, another great Frenchman looked at the conflict between Catholicism and modernity. Ernest Renan (1823–1892), who was first educated for the priesthood, decided under the influence of German philosophy and critical historicism to become an independent scholar. He no longer could harmonize his expert knowledge of the biblical languages with the traditional teaching of the Church. His *Life of Christ*, picturing the founder of the Christian religion as a natural man in a natural setting, aroused a storm of hostility that, as always in such cases, only increased its influence. Though he had to suffer for his courage until his monumental works on the apostles, on Judaism, Islam, and Christianity made him one of France's most respected savants, he acknowledged the merits of his early religious and theological education. "Fundamentally," he said, "I feel that my life has always been governed by a faith that I no longer have."[40] He hoped for a church both purified and open-minded.

Jesus founded the eternal religion of humanity, the religion of the spirit,

[39] Concerning Lammenais' fight for a religiously based liberalism, see Frederick Eugene Ellis, *The Attitude of the Roman Catholic Church towards the Problems of Democratic Freedom and American Public Education.* . . . (Doctoral thesis, Harvard University Graduate School of Education, 1948).

Les Paroles d'un Croyant, first published in 1834, went through at least nine editions during the same year.

[40] "Souvenirs d'Enfance et de Jeunesse," in *Oeuvres Complètes*, ed. Henriette Psichari (Paris: Calman-Levy, 1948), II, 730.

freed from all priesthood, all cult, all ceremony, accessible to all casts, in one word, absolute. "Woman, believe me, the hour cometh, when ye shall neither in this mountain, nor yet at Jerusalem, worship the Father." [41]

In Renan's opinion, Christianity was going through a stage of sterility. "Our time is so little religious that it has not even produced a real heresy." The Church in its actual existence reminded him still too much of that "frightful adventure of the Middle Ages, that interruption of a thousand years of human civilization" which had been caused less "by the barbarians than by triumph of dogmatism over the masses." [42] Thus he had little understanding for the religious passion of a Lamennais, who in his opinion lacked both rationality and historical knowledge. He also disliked Lamennais' contempt of Protestantism and the Germanic peoples. If Lamennais had acquainted himself "with the old barbaric laws collected in the *Corpus Juris Germaniae Antiqui*," he would have seen that these peoples "far from being bound to destroy" have contributed more than others "to establish liberty, the right of the individual against the state, and the political institutions of which the modern nations are justly proud." [43] Also, despite his deep religious faith, Renan, in contrast to Lamennais, did not believe the Catholic Church of his time to be capable of reconciling itself with the spirit of intellectual and political fredom. "Liberal clericalism" was for him an inner contradiction.[44] The two men, Lamennais and Renan, were of opposite character. The first, like Luther, whom he condemned, was a radical to the degree of fanaticism when he had discovered his mission; Renan, like Erasmus of Rotterdam, combined consistency of purpose with balance, historical perspective, and a sense of humor. In a fine article on the origin of the French language he says:

I believe there is much truth in the word of an eminent linguist of our time that the three causes of foolishness to be found even with otherwise most sensible people are etymology, love, and theology.[45]

[41] "Les Peuples Semitiques," in *Oeuvres Complètes*, II, 330. The biblical reference is to John 4: 21.

[42] "Souvenirs d'Enfance et de Jeunesse," p. 719.

[43] "M. de Lamennais," in *Oeuvres Complètes*, II, 141.

[44] See "Du Libéralisme Clérical," "L'Avenir Religieux des Sociétés Modernes," and other essays, all of great importance for the historian of French and European culture and of French and German education during the nineteenth century.

[45] "Les Origines de la Langue Francaise," in *Oeuvres Complètes*, II, 461.

FRANCE

I have selected Lamennais and Renan as perhaps the two finest symbols of the conflict of the minds in postrevolutionary France. But for illustration I might just as well have chosen the great French novelists from George Sand to Anatole France, whose work reaches over into our century and up to such contemporary writers as Georges Bernanos.

In the merely political realm, however, the relation of the government of France to its Church acquired an increasingly clear contour. The Revolution of 1830, which abolished the clerical-reactionary regime of the Bourbons, and the ensuing more liberal and bourgeois July monarchy (1830–1848) realized that the excitement of the unruly masses had to be directed into more positive channels. The Protestant historian and statesman Francois Guizot was named Minister of Public Instruction, and the Guizot Law of 1833 compelled every community to maintain an elementary school. With this creation of a universal and public educational system the issue of religious freedom in education became by necessity more urgent. The later Third Republic, after the first years of inner threats and insecurity, directed its policy consistently toward the separation of church and state. The school laws of Jules Ferry, voted between 1882 and 1886, introduced compulsory and free elementary education without religious instruction; religious orders were forbidden to cooperate in the state school system.[46] The most important step took place in 1905 when under the growing influence of the Socialist Party the separation of state and church was perfected. Public funds, since then, cannot be used for salaries of clergy; religious organizations are not permitted to meddle in the public schools; and religious orders must have the authorization of the state.

But, like Napoleon's, so also the administrative measure of the Third Republic did not solve the problem of religion in education, were it only for the simple reason that it is, in fact, insoluble. The Catholic Church, to which the large majority of the French people nominally belong — only about one million are Protestant — considers education as an integral whole to be permeated in all

[46] Henry Wallon, "Philosophie de l'Enseignement en France," in Marvin Farber (ed.), *L'Activité Philosophique Contemporaine en France et aux États-Unis.* (Paris: Presses Universitaires de France, 1950), II, p. 351f.

its parts by Catholic faith and spirit.[47] Consequently, only under special circumstances, which may apply to regions where its followers form a small minority, will the Catholic Church tolerate a secular system as a training ground for its youth. Many Frenchmen, of course — like many Italians — are everything else but pious believers. Nevertheless, they respect the tradition. They want to have a religious marriage; they want their children to be baptized; and there is no other spiritual organization of comparable public influence. Only a few break the ties openly. Thus, as with the Anglicans in England, the Catholic Church in France has a negotiating power far beyond its actual authority over the souls of men.

On the other hand, the government is by constitution bound to be secular, and on this point the majority of the political parties, especially those on the left, insist. Nor have the adherents of the *mouvement laïque*, or the secularists, or, if we want to say so, the heirs of the Enlightenment and the Revolution, been thoughtless about the spiritual education of youth. Their concern is with moral values. Some of the finest French minds, philosophers, sociologists, and psychologists, such as Emile Durkheim, have struggled with the question of how to enhance and teach morality without recourse to supernatural revelation. The conflict seems to rage more in the minds of writers, clergymen, and educators than in the minds of the people at large; yet it has divided the country. Otherwise Ferdinand Buisson, educator, and chairman of the Commission for the Separation of Church and State, famous for his *Dictionnaire de Pédagogie*, and, like the moralists of the eighteenth century, an enthusiastic believer in the omnipotence of education, could not have said in his *La Foi Laïque* (Secular Faith) of 1913:

It is not true that there are two Frances, or two peoples within one. It is not true that the nation, our mother, has engendered two irreconcilable races. The school will carry the light. Under its rays the phantom will disappear and we will discover that in France there are only Frenchmen, who today are all equal, and who tomorrow, whatever happens, will all be brothers.[48]

[47] See *The Great Encyclical Letters of Pope Leo XIII* (New York: Benziger, 1903).
[48] *La Foi laïque, Extraits de Discours et d'Ecrits (1878–1911)* 2nd ed. Preface by Raymond Poincaré (Paris: Hackette, 1913), p. 49.

FRANCE

The Political Conflicts of the Twentieth Century

Unfortunately, Buisson was too optimistic about the uniting force of the school, as he was also too hopeful about the influence of the League of Nations he helped to found. The struggle between parties, sections, and nations has continued. Most of the elementary-school teachers, who rightly were dissatisfied with their salaries, the school buildings, and the food and health of their children, belonged before the Second World War to the syndicalist movement, which was close to communism. They supported the many strikes that shook French economy; they demanded socialist action. The bourgeois, bitter because of the loss of monetary stability, became increasingly conservative; instead of defending democracy, he only looked at the two extremes of communism and rising totalitarianism. In a mixture of hatred and envy he observed Mussolini's Italy and Hitler's Germany where, at least, there was order and no strikes.

The number of books sold by Charles Maurras and other members of the Action Française was amazing. They glorified a period of French history that existed only in their dreams: a prerevolutionary, anti-Protestant, and antirationalist France that "after Rome, but more than Rome, united order and instinct, art and nature, thought and life." [49] This France of the sixteenth to the seventeenth century represented a national spirit "so complete, so brilliant, and so perfectly humane that it has become the legitimate heir of the Greek and Roman world." [50] One only wonders why in such a perfect world the poor peasants could believe that they were really hungry, the middle class protest against the tax exemptions of nobility and clergy, and men with a sense of justice fight judicial murder. Like Chateaubriand, the author of *Le Génie du Christianisme, ou Beautés de la Religion Chrétienne* (1802), Maurras admired the old Church without any admixture of historical and philosophical criticism; yet, he accused Chateaubriand of being a "hideous Protestant clothed in the purple of Rome," probably because Chateaubriand's legitimist monarchism had not prevented

[49] "Auguste Comte," in *Romantisme et Révolution* . . . (Paris: Nouvelle Librarie Nationale, 1922), p. 127.
[50] *Mes Idées Politiques* (Paris: Arthème Fagard, 1937), pp. 82–83.

him from criticizing monarchy when it was wrong.[51] Of course, a type such as Maurras condemned the Jew as "un agent révolutionnaire"; everything that had to do with social progress, such as democracy and the rights of man, labor legislation, the public education, were signs of humanitarian decay.

It would not be worth while to mention a morbid movement like the Action Française in a book on the education of nations if it had not had two disastrous results, namely, the creation of an asocial snobbishness among French students and an inner demoralization that went far beyond its immediate political influence. One of the most acute observers of modern France, the Swiss Herbert Luethy, has rightly remarked that the mixture of elegant style, obscurantism, and hatred which spread from the mental milieu of the Action Française had the effect that

a whole French social *élite* put on their uniforms as officers at the outbreak of the second world war fully believing that their country was ruled by a dishonourable pack of thieves, swindlers, and traitors, and that it was rotten to the core; and the collapse came to them like a judgment of God, which they had expected, and for which they had almost hoped.[52]

This demoralization of a country under the pretense, sometimes even with the serious intention, of improving it seems to be an international calamity. In Germany slander, coming from conservative and capitalist groups, opened the way for Hitler. And, reading certain American attacks against their public schools, one sometimes wonders how far criticism can go before it changes from a legitimate form of judging the nation's institutions to a process of undermining and bewildering the people.

During the Second World War, Maurras collaborated with the Vichy regime of Marshal Pétain who in 1941 published a pamphlet on national education.[53] This pamphlet is much more cautious than Mr. Maurras's pronunciamentos; it avoids the religious issue, but it exhales the spirit of patriarchalism and of protest against modern liberalism, democracy, and industrialism so characteristic of the

[51] *Romantisme et Révolution*, p. 246f, 275.
[52] *France against Herself* . . . Translated from the German by Eric Mosbacher (New York: Frederick A. Praeger, 1955), p. 36.
[53] Le Maréchal Pétain, *L'Education Nationale*, with an Introduction on "L'esprit d'une education nouvelle" by M. Albert Rivaud. Comité France-Amerique (Éditions Fernand Sorlot, 1941).

writers of the Action. Pétain himself had since 1934 criticized the public secondary school system and expressed his sympathy with the Catholic groups. The pamphlet sets up straw men and indulges in generalities that are either full of ambiguities or, so far as they are right, contain nothing new.

There was at the base of our educational system a profound illusion, namely, the belief that it sufficed to instruct the intellect in order to form the hearts and strengthen the character . . . School discipline must support the discipline of the family; in this way alone can men and nations grow strong.

Yet, French educational literature — as every good educational philosophy and practice — had always emphasized this point.

Another grave error in our public instruction was that it was a school of individualism . . . that it considered the individual the only authentic and, in a sense, absolute reality . . .

But the French elementary teachers stood for socialism, not for individualism, and if there was anything to complain of about the secondary schools and perhaps the whole school system it was their conformity.

We will devote ourselves to the destruction of the prestige of a merely literary pseudoculture, which only breeds laziness and uselessness . . . [Instead of our elementary schools] a much larger role will be given to manual work the educative value of which is too often underestimated.

This is exactly the point emphasized by the more progressive French educators. However, if manual work is used as a weapon against literacy, it promotes cultural regression. The consequence of the intended reform, so says Pétain, will be that

the best elements of each social class will no longer be falsely pushed, uprooted, and oriented toward that which has been called "le nomadisme administratif" . . . Each profession and trade will have its élite, and we will encourage with all our power the formation of such élites on the local and regional level . . . [This will produce] an arrest, if not a regression, of excessive industrialization . . . Thus we will, on the one hand, try to restore the tradition of artisanship in which for many centuries France has been triumphant; on the other hand, we will try to reroot as much as possible the Frenchman in the soil of France.

There is certainly need of replacing the false élite of social climbers by an élite of men who excel in their work, of whatever kind it may be. But the defeat of France was largely due to its retarded industrial development; even today foreign economic observers criticize French methods of production.

Administrative decrees never speak for themselves alone. They will often express ideas worth considering, but their true value depends on whence they come, who is going to execute them, and whether they reveal or conceal their real goal. The political philosophy of Pétain expressed the idea of return to a guild society, which, in consequence of a growing aversion against mechanical parliamentarianism, appeared also in Germany, Austria, and Italy. A "clerico-monarchical clique," to use an expression of Albert Guérard, had existed in the higher echelons of the army and bureaucracy during the whole of the nineteenth and twentieth centuries. Though not directly responsible for the condemnation of Captain Dreyfus in 1895,[54] at least it looked at the injustice with indifference, or even with pleasure. This clique was in essence opposed to the ideas of the Revolution, and, if history had allowed it to decide, it would not have objected to the restoration of a Catholic monarchy. Even Vichy's plea for decentralization cannot be taken seriously, for what else can a government advocate which is in disfavor in its own country?

Marshal Pétain, the profoundly tragical hero of Verdun, who had no need of personal ambitions but sacrificed himself for his country, was condemned by his nation. It needed him as a scapegoat. But the strife of parties continued. While Pétain and his friends at Vichy tried to lead France back to a patriarchical society, a group of Frenchmen, under the leadership of René Capitant, Commissioner for National Education in the free areas, and the famous physicist Paul Langevin, assembled in Algiers in order to draw up a plan for a radical reform of the French educational system.[55]

[54] See Albert Guérard, *The France of Tomorrow* (Cambridge: Harvard University Press, 1942) and Nicholas Halasz, *Captain Dreyfus: The Story of a Mass Hysteria* (New York: Simon and Schuster, 1955).

[55] Final publication: *La Reforme de l'Enseignement. Projet soumis à M. le Ministre de l'Education nationale par la Commission interministerielle d'étude.* Brochure éditée par le Ministere de l'Education nationale (Paris, July 1947).

The results of the Commission pour la Reformé de l'Enseignement were pub-

About the practical proposals of this plan I will have to speak later on. In this context it is of interest that it bore without any doubt the mark not only of a strictly secular, but also of a highly collectivist, conception of popular education. Paul Langevin, who died shortly after the liberation (1946), was a communist. The project aroused the highest enthusiasm from the radical left and, needless to say, vehement opposition from the conservative and Catholic sides. But it also led the liberals into the battlefield. However great the differences, they joined the rightists because the Langevin plan was, also from their point of view, a blow against the best of the French tradition. Jean Rolin, a *lycée* professor, whose work on *Les Libertés Universitaires* [56] had been rewarded with a prize of the Académie Française, wrote a small, outspoken book in which he assembled all the arguments against materialist Marxism a humanist Frenchman could devise. The Langevin project, he said, means totalitarianism, class struggle, and materialism. It deprives the school system (*l'université*) of its soul and fosters "spiritual sterilization." For it eliminates the influence of the family, drives the humanities out of the program, and bows before mechanical industrialization. Finally, it is utopian because financially impossible; it is nothing but another "opium for the people." [57]

In the meantime the Catholic-conservative camp had become increasingly active and vociferous, this to such a degree that it endangered the continuation of the secularization laws of 1882 and 1905. During and after the last war the Catholic Church offered its houses to children who, in consequence of the destruction, would have been without schools. The regular and secular clergy helped wherever possible in the protection and education of the young. Since the German occupation was more hesitant to intervene in the affairs of the Church than in those of the political authorities, there was more shelter from pressure and violence under the crucifix than under the national flag. Also, as often in times of distress, religious feelings heightened. Furthermore, since

---

lished in a special number of the *Bulletin Officiel du Ministère de l'Education Nationale* (Paris, November 16, 1944).

[56] Paris: Édition de la Nouvele France, 1947.

[57] *Le Marxisme à l'École. Considérations sur le Projet Langevin et la Réforme de l'Enseignement* (Paris: Édition Spes, 1949).

the public secondary schools insisted on severe entrance examinations, considerations of career and prestige may have caused many a parent to send children of limited talent to private schools of religious or secular character with easier entrance requirements or more individual instruction. On the other hand, the government itself had to acknowledge that in some of these private schools, confessional or secular, educational experiments were carried through that contributed to the understanding of the child and his learning.

Since the public treasury has so far been unable to provide a sufficient building program, the ecclesiastical authorities have demanded support. There are a total of almost six million pupils on the elementary level, of whom, according to governmental sources, 17 per cent are enrolled in private (which means mainly Catholic) schools; on the secondary level 42 per cent attend such institutions. In addition to the large number of students, these establishments are mostly of residential character so that the burden of increased living costs also fell upon their budgets.

Thus, in his ministerial declaration as Premier-designate in August 1951, René Pleven was forced to face the issue of how to preserve the constitutional principle of the separation of state and church and at the same time to give support to the secondary schools, in which almost one half of the pupils were educated and which the government itself would have been unable to replace should the parents have wished it so. Certainly, on the basis of their own troublesome experiences, many statesmen of Christian countries sympathized with Mr. Pleven when in the heat of the debate he urged "both sides unfailingly to remember how important it is that no imprudence or violence of language run the risk of inflaming passions that might tear France asunder."

The result of the debate was a compromise. The constitutional principle was saved, or at least respected, by the avoidance of direct support to private schools on the part of the state, while the practical necessity of extending help to these in fact absolutely indispensable institutions was honored by the provision of maintenance scholarships. These scholarships (1,000 francs per capita), not to be allotted to the schools as such, were given to all students attending either public or private secondary schools. (Approval of the government bill on the second reading by the National Assembly was by 378 votes against 236, September 21, 1951.)

Through these scholarships parents with lower incomes are presented with the opportunity to send their children to secondary schools of either public or sectarian character. To guarantee equality of standards, scholastic and technical criteria were set up which the private schools have to meet before being permitted to teach "national scholarship students." About the same time a bill was also approved that extended the privilege of state aid to pupils of from six to fourteen years attending private elementary schools. For this purpose a special fund was created, financed by a 0.3 per cent increase in the production tax.[58]

Classicists versus Realists and the Modern School Reforms

The other problem that has excited France since the days of the Revolution almost to the degree of religious fever was, and still is, the conflict between a traditional-classical and a modern-realistic program of studies.

There were about one hundred Church-dominated *collèges* that represented French secondary education in the middle of the eighteenth century. They taught some mathematics and natural science, but the emphasis was on Latin. I have already described the general protest against this kind of education. When, in the first years of his regime, Napoleon began his work of reconstruction, he attempted a compromise by introducing two sections of secondary education, one of the classical type with Latin as the center, the other (which as a military man he preferred) with mathematics and the sciences in the foreground. But, just as the Americans rejected Franklin's modern "English School," and the Germans neglected their "Realschule," so the French stuck to the tradition they first had criticized. Instead of sending their children to the new state-supported institutions, called "Lycées," they sent them to private schools with a primarily humanistic program.

Yet, in France also the role of science in modern society exercised its pressure on the minds of people and on the schools. A long

[58] In December 1959 the government showed its willingness to yield still further and to give the private schools an unspecified amount of money in return for only a nominal state control. This has rekindled the "school war" to a degree that is dangerous even for the system of de Gaulle.

series of changes in curriculums and school structures began which it would be tedious to picture in detail.[59] Under the Bourbon restoration sections for modern languages and science were introduced, and the Second Empire (1852–1870) under Napoleon III, who favored the industrialization of France, divided the program of the *lycée*, after two years of common instruction, into a literary-historical and a mathematical-scientific branch. The reason for this reform, however, was not only pedagogical. The politically reactionary government of the Second Empire was afraid that the study of the humanities made the students inclined to favor liberal and socialist ideas.[60] Léon Bourgeois' reform of 1890 organized an *enseignement moderne* besides the traditional *enseignement classique*, and in 1899 — about the same time as in other European countries — the Minister of Education Georges Leygues definitely broke the monopoly of classical instruction by acknowledging modern subjects as possible requisites for entrance to the universities. This was the most decisive measure introduced in French advanced education.

About the same time Gustave Lanson wrote an article in the *Revue Internationale de l'Enseignement* (June 15, 1901) with the title "La Reforme de l'Enseignement Secondaire. Les Veritables Humanités Modernes." It is difficult to translate because of the different connotations the terms "scientifique" and "scientific" carry with them. When I render here "scientifique" with "scientific," it must be understood to apply not only to the natural and empirical sciences, but to methodical scholarly pursuits in general. Consequently, the concept of "scholarly," or the German *wissenschaftlich*, should always be kept in mind; otherwise Lanson's article will be misunderstood. In essence, it recommends a spirit of rigorous discipline, whatever study may be pursued. It derogates in no way the humanities but speaks against a merely genteel tradition that puts the decorative, aesthetic, and speculative elements of education above the principle of scholarly research. Lanson wants a fusion, not a division.

[59] A thorough discussion of the subject can be found in Clement Falcucci's *L'Humanisme dans l'Enseignement Secondaire en France au XIXᵉ Siècle* (Toulouse: Edouard Privat, 1939).

[60] See Otto Völcker, *Das Bildungswesen in Frankreich. Geschichte und Gegenwart* (Braunschweig: Georg Westermann, 1927), p. 93.

Is it necessary to prove that first of all we need today men with a scientific spirit? By that ambitious term let us understand minds that have a taste and sense for truth, that in all their actions are carried by a serious desire for clear and exact knowledge, that are conscious of the difficulties and perils hidden in the pursuit and elaboration of truth, and that in defiance of the whole world, including their own inclinations, take all possible precautions against misleading others and themselves. These precautions are that which one calls method. Methodical research for truth, this is the exact phrase for what we mean by the scientific spirit. It should dominate our secondary schools also; all their endeavors should be subordinated to the conviction that their common aim and direction reside in molding minds in such a fashion that during the whole life and in all their interests they follow the idea of systematic pursuit of truth.

The true modern humanities are of scientific nature in the largest sense of the word, which comprehends the historical as well as the exact and natural studies. High culture, namely, that which prepares for life and action — in whatever domain, economic, political, special, and moral — is it perhaps this merely literary culture that develops a certain grace of spirit and trains men to play with ideas? Or is it rather a scientific culture that holds our minds close to the idea of truth and teaches them the ways toward it?

Yet, there has been no end to the controversy. During the years immediately following the First World War, a reaction against the modern trend began. Its most radical expression was the short-lived *reform Bérard* (1923). According to this scheme all students had to take four years of Latin and two years of Greek during the first four years of the six-year *lycée*; the last two years were divided into *option latin-grec*, *option latin*, and *option langues*. Mathematics and the scientific subjects were to be taught besides the humanistic subjects. At some places provision was to be made for two additional years devoted to either a more philosophic or to a more mathematical instruction. Violent objections were immediately raised: the students would be overworked; there was no respect for the practical side of education; furthermore, two years of Greek, a very difficult language, to be taught in the *options latin* and *langues* would be useless. As a matter of fact, the German classical Gymnasium, to which the *reform Bérard* came close, carried the Latin-Greek combination as compulsory up to the last grade.

The *reform* was never put into practice, for after one year the *regime Bérard* was replaced by a more liberal-socialist government.

It is interesting only as the last glimmer of an attempt to force the young French élite into a rigid classical program. Henceforth a more conciliatory policy took hold, mainly under the influence of one of the wisest educational statesmen of the past decades, Anatole de Monzie (1876–1947). Though we need today, de Monzie said, a more realistic as well as a more classical education, there should nevertheless be a spirit of inner harmony in that both ought to be inspired by the ideals of *unité* and *culture générale*. The pupil of the classical brand should not miss the discipline of mathematics and empirical research, and the pupil of the exact sciences should not grow up without the discipline and the refinement of taste that the humanities provide. Thus, he finally acknowledged what A. A. Cournot had already asserted in 1864, namely, that the values of true classical education may change in time and space. But its character and essence will remain the same wherever one succeeds in forming a "system of liberal studies (*un système d'études libérales*) considered to be a necessary requirement for the cultivated mind and a common foundation for the various academic professions." [61] Thus, theoretically at least, the French ideal of education is no longer that of the *honnête homme* of the seventeenth and eighteenth centuries (who had to master his Latin), but an equilibrium between an understanding of the humane tradition and the laws of nature.

But, so the adversaries of reform said, and have always said, it is sheer illusion and self-deception to believe that an ideal such as the French-Latin heritage can remain alive if it loses the contact with its source. Giving up the classical languages of the *lycée* is a betrayal of France's cultural mission. The famous philosopher Henri Bergson saw the influence of ancient studies even in the very practical life of the nation. The "esprit de précision," so he declared, has made France famous not only in the field of letters, but also in the field of industry, especially in the production of luxury articles. Give up Latin in the secondary school, and sooner or later you will lose the fine artisan. [62]

To men of such convictions, and they were numerous in the

[61] *Des Institutions d'Instruction Publique en France* (Paris, 1864), p. 39.

[62] Address to the Académie des Sciences under the title, "Les Études Gréco-Latines," *Revue de Paris* (May 1923), pp. 5–18.

higher echelons of society, the report of the Langevin committee was a sign of barbarism. For it declared that education in the past had been far too theoretical, that it was unadapted to the conditions of modern industrial society and in constant danger of producing unemployable and dissatisfied intellectuals. The goal should be to provide, on a broad basis of general education, more vocational and technical knowledge and to give it the same prestige as the older classical studies, a measure that inevitably would have changed the whole spirit of French education.

There is, of course, also a social factor involved in the difference of opinions about the classical studies. For up to the very present the emphasis on the classics has gone hand in hand with a rigid separation of the secondary schools, destined to lead the élite of the nation to the university, from the schools for the common man. Every change in the school program, from the humanist-historical toward the scientific-technical curriculum, called into the arena the defenders of an aristocratic tradition against the advocates of democracy, the right against the left. The Revolutions of 1830 and 1848, the reign of Napoleon III, the two world wars — all had their repercussions on the educational scene. After 1918 the movement of Les Compagnons was started, mainly by officers whose social consciences had been stirred by sharing the life and suffering in the trenches with their fellow men from farm and factory. It demanded a more unified educational organization, called "École Unique," more or less according to the American pattern or the one recommended by the German "Radical School Reformers" (*Entschiedene Schulreformer*). Influential politicians and even some professors of the Sorbonne supported Les Compagnons. However, after some minor concessions the extraordinary conservatism of the school bureaucracy and the respectable classes spread a veil of indifference over the country. In addition, after the long war, men were tired and wanted peace.

In a way, many proposals of the Langevin committee marked a renewal of the spirit of Les Compagnons as it had emerged during the First World War. But now it was more radical in nature. The intentions of the Langevin group appear most clearly in an essay by Dr. Henry Wallon, who, after the death of the scientist, acted as its acknowledged spokesman. According to Wallon the reform, conceived at the time of the liberation, represented not merely an educational but a definitely political scheme.

> We can prepare for the political revolutions against oppressive capitalism [according to Wallon represented by the United States and its educational philosopher John Dewey] only to the degree to which we can make our children understand the vices of the present regime and the difference between the limited and limiting instruction as it is given now and the possibilities that could be provided by a larger and more vigorous school system.[63]

For that purpose the followers of Langevin recommended an obligatory and tuition-free public school up to the age of eighteen with a basic and common *cycle*, from six to eleven, with a *cycle d'orientation*, from eleven to fifteen, which, besides subjects of common concern, would include optional subjects (physical education, fine arts, science, modern and ancient languages, mathematics, etc.). After the age of fifteen a "division" (*disjonction*) of the thus-far united school would become necessary. Pupils with theoretical talents would enter the section leading to higher studies; those with practical interests, the technical section; and

> those who prefer manual occupations, work in concrete production, and direct contact with material would go into apprenticeship centers (*centres d'apprentissage*).

An enormously generous and elaborate system of stipends and scholarships was to enable the poor scholar to participate in the advanced forms of learning.

The recommended system is not really so different from that of the "capitalist" United States, which, according to the contributors to *La Pensée*, imposed the Marshall Plan on poor France only to destroy its national independence.[64] Yet, as already indicated, behind the similarity is a profound difference of political philosophy. The *liberation* of France, as conceived by Langevin and his friends, was intended to be the beginning of a communist France and Europe, with Soviet Russia as the leading power,

[63] Henry Wallon, "Réforme ou Sabotage de l'Enseignement. Le Projet Brunold," *La Pensée. Revue du Rationisme Modern* (Fondateur, Paul Langevin). *Nouvelle Serie*, No. 48–49 (1953), pp. 8–10.

[64] Henri Claude, "Le Plan Marshall et la France," *La Pensée*, No. 48–49 (1953), pp. 11–12.

whereas behind the American school system there stands a democratic nation.

However, whether Langevin or not, as in other European countries so also in France the fight between those who wish to preserve the traditional rigid division between the schools for the élite and the schools for the masses and those who wish to establish a school system of equal opportunity will gradually lead to compromises on the part of the first. There is no need here to describe the parliamentary debates and governmental reform plans that illustrate this process, especially since the Fifth Republic under de Gaulle has created — so let us hope — the degree of inner stability and administrative efficiency so badly needed for the recovery of France. We read that de Gaulle's Minister of Education, Jean Berthoin, has proposed an educational reform that to a large degree is indebted to the reform plan of René Billères of 1957. It is to be put into practice in 1960. According to this reform compulsory education for children who enter primary school in the fall of 1959 (at the age of six) will be raised from fourteen to sixteen years; the *classes d'orientation*, or guidance classes, originally introduced by the prewar Minister of Education, Jean Zay, but then neglected, will be reintroduced for pupils at the age of ten or eleven in order to help them in the right choice of their career; preuniversity secondary education will be divided into a classical, scientific, and technical course; greater incentives for scientifically talented pupils will be provided; and the whole school structure will be organized to counteract the kind of selection for higher studies that favors one-sidedly children from more privileged families. It will be a part of this "break-through" program to give graduates from secondary, technical, vocational, and scientific schools the same chance of admission to higher studies as the graduates from the old liberal institutions. This equalization of certificates may be rather theoretical because the decisive factor will be whether the students who do not come from the *lycées* and *collèges* will be able to compete with the owners of the old admission card to the university, namely, the *baccalauréat*. But, just as the decision of the English to call all postelementary schools "secondary" certainly does not put the student of a technical or modern school on the same intellectual and social level as a student of Eton or even a grammar school, but is nevertheless a step toward democratization, so also the new French measure will give the nation a higher sense of justice and unity.[65]

At the end of World War II, Jacques Marquette criticized the French school system in bitter terms. This is what he said: France "la mère de la civilisation occidentale," had before the war an elementary school system of extraordinary inferiority which constituted "un scandale permanent." Despite the gratuitous secondary school and all kinds of beautiful theories about the raising of the élite out of the people, three quarters of the population were still excluded from participation in higher cultural values, while at the same time the old folklore had disappeared. Too few schools prepared youth for industry; the *collèges* and *lycées* were much too theoretical and encyclopedic; the cramming for the *concours* exhausted the creative talent of the future professor, and so on.[66]

The aristocrat Marquette, the communist Langevin, and the new member of de Gaulle's cabinet Jean Berthoin agree on many points. Even if one takes into account that especially in eras of disillusion every national school system is decried as more or less responsible for the crisis (at the present America is going through a similar state of things), certainly in France the time has become ripe for a thorough re-examination of the educational issue. For, even if the just-mentioned proposals of the Ministry of Education have some effect, so far not much has been done to improve the elementary grades. On the contrary, more than before World War II, France has shifted the burden of schooling the young to parochial institutions, which, according to Marquette, are apparently not worse than the "inferior" public schools. Certain religious orders are now even allowed to take care of the professional preparation of their teachers.

If all this delaying of decisions has been called lethargy by

[65] For a brief description of modern French secondary education and a discussion of other phases and problems, see *Education in France*, published by the Cultural Services of the French Embassy. See especially No. 4, p. 9; see also the instructive article by Olive Wykes, "The Crisis in French Education," in *Melbourne Studies in Education 1957–1958*, ed. E. L. French (Melbourne University Press, 1958).

[66] *Une France Nouvelle pour le Monde Nouveau* (New York: Editions de la Maison Francaise, 1944), pp. 14, 83, 86, 87.

Frenchmen themselves, it has, at least, deep roots in history. It reflects the fact that France has never overcome the contrast between the times and mentality of Louis XIV, on the one hand, and the French Revolution and our modern period, on the other.

People profess allegiance to the revolutionary ideals of liberty, equality, fraternity, and to the modern notion of democracy; yet, as Marquette remarks, "in spite of its reputation as a democracy France is one of the countries where distinct class stratification is most noticeable." [67] Read almost any one of the famous modern playwrights and novelists, Georges Bernanos, Jean Cocteau, François Mauriac, Marcel Proust, Jean Paul Sartre, not to speak of earlier authors such as Georges Sand and Honoré de Balzac (who assumed the embellishing particle "de" without there being any ground for it in his ancestry). It looks as if the upheaval of 1789 had tried to take away some romantic element without which many Frenchmen (and perhaps many people in all Western nations) do not want to live.[68]

The France that many of its citizens agreed with André François Poncet was in danger of being "stricken from the role of great peoples" [69] has now, in consequence of the revolution in Algeria, a new leader in the person of de Gaulle. He satisfies the romantic urge, appears to be determined to prevent extreme power from gliding into dictatorship, combines vision with realism and patience with energy, and wishes to adapt his, in this respect recalcitrant, people to the necessities of our technological era.

But he will also have to reckon — and will, after some house cleaning, probably even be glad to reckon — with the old bureaucratic and highly trained officialdom that since the times of Napoleon gave the nation a measure of stability despite revolutions, wars, and quarreling parliaments. This officialdom, together with the leading groups in French society, will always favor a school system that sees its noblest purpose in the education of an intellectual élite. In this it will be supported by the highly respected

[67] *Ibid.*, p. 81.
[68] A charming and loving description of French cultural and social life in the capital and the province has been given by Friedrich Sieburg in *Gott in Frankreich?* (Frankfurt-am-Main: Societäts-Verlag, 1929); English trans. Allan Harris, *Who Are These French?* (New York: Macmillan, 1938).
[69] *Le Figaro*, October 17, 1955.

bodies of the universities and the academies, however leftist some of their members may be in other respects. Even the collectivism of the Langevin committee foresaw a rigorous selection for the leaders in science and industry, thus advocating principles we see today realized in the rigid selective system of the Soviet Republics.

It is, of course, difficult to estimate exactly the influence of schools on the spirit of a nation. Certainly, the hierarchical structure of French education, permeated by the postulate of broad understanding of the humane values as expressed in the idea of *culture générale*,[70] has kept the academic man rather distinct from the man without humanistic education. Though in the seventeenth and eighteenth centuries the French concept of the "gentilhomme" and the English concept of the "gentleman" were the same, the second, because of its emphasis on character rather than on schooling, was more capable of democratic transformation than the first. France is in this respect more similar to Germany and other Continental countries than to those of the Anglo-Saxon tradition. And, no doubt, France, like Germany (not to speak of Italy and Spain), has neglected certain educational obligations incumbent on a modern nation.

On the other hand, the hierarchical structure of French education has helped to give a nation so often politically disunited a sense of unity and even uniqueness shared even by social groups that participate little in the labors and blessings of advanced schooling. Hence, its effect is not so "undemocratic" as may appear to the American. France has excelled by its achievements in the realms of art and intellect. Neither France, nor any other country on the European Continent, will regain the political world power it once had. The future of Europe lies in its capacity to combine the wealth of a great cultural tradition with open-mindedness to the realities of the twentieth century. Certain values necessary for this combination do not become immediately obvious to the narrow utilitarian. Yet, they are the ones that make life richer.

[70] See Celestin Bouglé, *The French Conception of "Culture Générale" and Its Influence upon Instruction* (New York: Columbia University Teachers College, 1938).

VII

Germany

THE FORMATION OF A NATION AND WORLD WAR I

IT is difficult to evaluate objectively the cultural achievements of a nation from which not long ago started the revolt against Western civilization connected with the name of Adolf Hitler.

In *Beyond Good and Evil* (*Jenseits von Gut und Böse*), Friedrich Nietzsche says:

> The German soul is exceedingly manifold; it is of diverse origin, more a scramble of pieces than an organic structure: this is due to its history. A German who [with Goethe's Faust] would dare assert: "Two souls, alas, are dwelling in my breast" would badly violate the truth; more correctly, he would lag behind reality by many souls. As a nation of the most prodigious mixture and concoction of races, perhaps even with a predominance of the pre-Arian element, as a "people of the center" in every possible sense of the word, the Germans are more incomprehensible, more comprehensive, more contradictory, more unknown, more incalculable, more surprising, and more frightening than other nations are to themselves. They elude every definition, and for this reason alone they are a cause of despair for the French. It is characteristic of the Germans that they never cease to ask the question: "What is German?" [1]

Though Paul Valery is right in his already-quoted statement about the enigmatic character of the French, Nietzsche has certainly as many reasons for his statement about the Germans.

Concerning the mixture of races — whatever the word "race" may mean when applied to human groups — all modern nations

---

[1] Translated by the author from *Jenseits von Gut und Böse*, sec. 244; Eng. ed., *Beyond Good and Evil*, trans. H. Zimman (New York: Boni and Liveright, 1917).

are composites of various strands. Just as great rivers live not merely on their original springs but mainly on tributaries that join them in their courses, so also the English, the Chinese, the Russians, the French, the Germans represent a confluence of many streams. If Hitler had really tried to purify the German blood from alien influences and not only to eliminate his political opponents and the Jews, he would have been forced to murder the large majority of the German people, including himself, because he came to Germany from a part of Austria in which the mixing of races had gone on for many centuries. In addition, he would have been forced to direct his attack against the artistically and intellectually most productive parts of Germany, the southwest with its large Latin and Alpine elements and the east from Thuringia to Saxony and Silesia with its large Slavic substratum. However, the criteria of horsebreeders do not apply to the human race.

The race myth is, unfortunately, not merely a product of the Germans; in more or less cruel forms it is spread over all the world. The Germans received the myth first from the French Count Gobineau,[2] a highly cultured humanist who was proud of his Norman origin but never thought of racial persecution. Later many Germans read with delight the Teutonic and anti-British literature of Houston Stewart Chamberlain, an uprooted Englishman who had become a Wagnerian devotee and the husband of a daughter of the famous composer. He resided in Germany and before his death thanked destiny for the advent of Hitler. The myth was elaborately organized into the Nazi ideology by Alfred Rosenberg and finally carried to its brutal consequences in the concentration camps of Auschwitz and Buchenwald.

The German people has paid dearly for allowing this poison to creep into its body. There still is a very small, but moribund, minority of old black guards and fanatics. But the new Federal Republic has shown that it will not allow the revival of political insanity whether it comes from the right or from the left. The memory of millions of victims and the enormity of sacrifice all over the world will lose more and more of its terrifying impact on the human mind, for it is the grace of forgetting that has helped men again and again to ascend from the abysses of misery. Never-

[2] *Essai sur l'Inégalité des Races Humaines* (1853–1855).

theless, the reign of Hitler will remain with the German people as
the days of the guillotine will stay with the French — with the
difference, however, that the French Revolution was the perversion
of the great idea of liberty, whereas the Hitlerian ideology was
tyrannical from the very beginning. This is, ultimately, the deepest
lesson of mankind's recent revolutions: that there are dark and
hysterical forces that, unless quenched when there is still time, may
erupt like volcanoes and shed their lava over the remotest stretches
of the human landscape.

In reality, the "prodigious mixture and concoction of races,"
proudly referred to by Nietzsche and hated by Hitler, was the
inevitable result of Germany's situation in the middle of Europe
and, at the same time, the source of its cultural and economic
wealth. The German frontiers have constantly fluctuated. The old
German Empire up to the middle of the twelfth century had its
eastern boundary near the Elbe and Saale Rivers; at the middle of
that century there began the conquest of the Slavic east with such
success that two centuries later German power reached to the
Narva River and Lake Peipus, that is, deeply into the present domain
of Russia. Many of the Polish towns were under German influence,
with German the official language in such cities as Cracow and
Lemberg, now Lwow.[3] Today again it is difficult to say where the
German eastern boundaries will finally be drawn, whether at the
Oder or Weichsel Rivers, or perhaps even near the Elbe. The constant shifting of the western front, especially between Germany
and France, is too well known to be narrated here in detail.

But, wherever at different periods the custom houses and the
frontier guards may have been, they never determined the exchange of cultural goods. Every major European power has added
color to the German mind, even if there was no direct physical
contact. In the south there was Italy, up to the Renaissance the
cultural leader of Europe, and the Latin countries in the west,
especially France, had for some time an overpowering influence on
Germany. The northern seas connected the German realm with
England and the Scandinavian countries, and in the northeast
Poland and Russia opened their enormous plains to German initia-

[3] See Johannes Haller, *Die Epochen der deutschen Geschichte* (Stuttgart and
Berlin: J. G. Cotta, 1943), p. 143.

tive. Through Austria, up to the nineteenth century the most prominent German principality, the country's tentacles touched upon the Balkan countries, most of which were for a long time dominated by Turkey. Twice, the second time most dangerously in 1683, the Sultan's troops stood before the walls of Vienna. No wonder that, since the time when the Renaissance humanist Jakob Wimpheling (1450–1528) wrote the first somewhat comprehensive book about German history, the *Epitome Rerum Germanicarum*, the nation has constantly swerved between the danger of absorption by alien customs and ideas and, as a form of national reaction, chauvinist rejection of anything foreign.

The cultural exposure of Germany to foreign influence was enhanced by the fact that, in contrast to England and France, it did not succeed until 1870 in uniting its big vassals under a dominating government. There was only one faintly patriotic clause inserted in the Treaty of Westphalia (1648) which concluded the disastrous Thirty Years' War and gave the German princes complete sovereignty, namely, that alliances of these princes be not directed against empire or emperor — a ridiculous sham, since for some hundred years, especially during the Thirty Years' War itself, these self-made monarchs had given their support to the highest bidder, irrespective of whether he was a friend or enemy of the country.

Thus up to the beginning of the nineteenth century German ground became the battlefield of foreign powers that fought for superiority over Europe. France especially did everything in its power to preserve and increase German disunity. In view of the history of division and subdivision, foreign invasions and interferences, and of the narrow diplomacy of little territories, often so small that even in an old coach they could be traversed in a day's journey, it is understandable that the one who finally achieved German unity, Otto von Bismarck, was venerated as the nation's savior. Yet he was in no way unopposed; his path was full of stones and thorns.

Liberal opposition against Bismarck lasted up to his dismissal by the young Emperor Wilhelm II in 1890. This opposition was partly that of free traders against a man who advocated tariffs and state monopolies. Liberal protest was directed also against his plan for a universal workman's insurance as an integral part of federal social policy. He nevertheless got a majority for his bill for insurance against injury (1884) and his bills for the institution of sick funds and insurance against old age and disability (1887), social measures that preceded those of other countries by decades.

However, Bismarck's plan to take the wind out of the sails of the Marxist Social Democratic party by this form of state socialism did not bear fruit. This party, then still a member of the Socialist Workers International, had grown constantly in spite of the Anti-Socialist Act, passed under Bismarck's leadership in 1878 by the right-wing liberals and the conservatives. It declared illegal all associations, meetings, and distributions of printed matter directed against the existing form of state and society, placed socialist agitators under severe police supervision and threat of punishment, and empowered the government to proclaim a state of siege in districts menaced by strikes. Yet, when in 1890 the antisocialist law was abolished, the party of the persecuted emerged stronger than before. The only effect had been to alienate the workers from the alliance of state and church as well as from the army, the officers of which had so often commanded their troops against the striking workmen. Thus, national unity and international power became connected with strife and conflict within the new nation.

Moreover, like France, the new German Empire could not avoid the religious issue. Notwithstanding the common aversion against the socialists, the Catholic Church challenged the new regime by demanding the right of interfering in matters of education, civil legislation concerning marriage, and the attempt at restricting the freedom of the clergy. Bismarck counteracted with severe legislative measures; the so-called *Kulturkampf* (battle concerning the cultural rights of state and church) began.[4] It ended practically in 1879, and finally in 1887 with an agreement between the German government and Pope Leo XIII. Though the Catholic Church had to give up some of its demands, here also the chancellor had to acknowledge defeat; as he had alienated the workers from the imperial government, so he had also estranged large parts of the Catholic population.

Though Bismarck may be called the creator, he certainly was

[4] Georg Franz, *Kultur-Kampf* (Munich: D. W. Callwey, 1954).

not the educator, of the German nation; he was too thoroughly steeped in old conservative-agricultural concepts of society to understand the emerging industrial era; he was too convinced of the leadership of an hereditary aristocracy to believe in the self-government of the people; he was too critical of political parties and too disappointed by their initial opposition to his goal of German unification to consider it his task to lead the people toward free and responsible political cooperation. There hardly could be found a more devoted servant to his country and his emperor, a man who believed so honestly that he was on the side of God, but also a man in whom service and faith were so closely allied with cynicism in regard to the means — and the supreme means was power. But we all know how easily in the life of men and nations means turn into ends; he was not alone.

And in this respect he was supported by his people. After hundreds of years of disunity and humiliation the Germans discovered that under the guidance of the *Kanzler von Blut und Eisen* (chancellor of blood and iron) they had become the leaders of the Continent. There began *das Säbelrasseln* (the rattling with the sword). In spite of the opposition of the center and leftist parties, a militaristic nationalism corrupted the nation, even the army itself. Many of the officers of 1870 were men of high culture. Most of their successors of the twentieth century saw no need for that luxury. The chancellors after Bismarck, either encouraged or tolerated by the young Emperor Wilhelm II, arrogantly and stupidly squandered the prestige and confidence the founder of the Reich had tried to establish. Furthermore, the victory of 1871 had brought large sums of money into Germany which encouraged speculation and a rapid, often unsound, expansion of industry. The so-called *Gründerperiode* (period of hazardous enterprise) followed the slow and careful work of earlier men of business.

At the outbreak of World War I the Germans discovered that they had alienated almost the whole world. They stood alone on the side of already-tottering Austria. After a long series of heroic victories they found out that they had not even the great generals they thought they had. Being products of a narrow military education, these men were ignorant about the relationship of war to international politics, economics, and industrial production, and there were no leaders in the civil government to check the power of the men in uniform.

While after 1870 Germany, despite all relapses, became prosperous and a most powerful competitor in the world market, and while its universities became the patterns of scholarly research in every field of existing knowledge, all that which one might properly ascribe to culture in the finest sense of the word declined. Lyric poetry represents the finest barometer of a nation's inner life. But around 1880 most of the popular poetry was artificial in comparison to the strength and depth of the poets of two or three generations before. Only Switzerland, with Gottfried Keller and Konrad Ferdinand Meyer, constituted an exception among the German-speaking nations. A resurgence of original ideas in disciplined poetic form did not occur before the turn of the century.

And, while an appreciative audience listened to classical music performed by great orchestras, the typical home music, represented by the piano-thrumming *höhere Tochter* (daughter of a higher-class family), was just as mawkish as the poetry she read. The wonderful old German folk songs and folk dances were forgotten until the beginning of the twentieth century, when they were revived by the youth movement.

Great minds felt lonely. In the midst of all the so-called progress, Schopenhauer, neglected during his own lifetime (1788–1860), became the favorite philosopher of the sophisticated. Unable to discover any deeper human meaning in all this unleashed energy, they became pessimists.

Jakob Burckhardt (1818–1897), one of the great historians of all times, looked with profound suspicion at all this new busyness with its lack of quality. As a member of the aristocratic democracy of Basel, he was inclined to identify the new trend with rising egalitarian mass democracy, as Europeans of the time believed it to be characteristic of the United States. Since he speaks not only about Germany, but also about the whole Western civilization, a somewhat lengthy quotation may be permitted here. Under the date "March 1873," he says in his admirable *Weltgeschichtliche Betrachtungen*:

The first great phenomenon to follow the war of 1870–1871 was a further extraordinary intensification of money-making, which went far beyond the mere making good of gaps and losses, and was combined with the exploitation and activation of an infinite number of sources of wealth and the inevitable fraudulent schemes connected with them . . .

Art and science have the greatest difficulty in preventing themselves from sinking into a mere branch of urban money-making and from being carried away on the stream of general unrest. The utmost effort and self-denial will be necessary if they are to remain creatively independent in view of the relation in which they stand to the daily press, to cosmopolitan traffic, to world exhibitions . . .

What classes and strata of society will now become the real representatives of culture, will give us our scholars, artists and poets, our creative personalities?

Or is everything to turn into big business, as in America? . . .

One wonders how soon the other countries will follow suit . . .

And finally, the question of the Church. In the whole of Western Europe the philosophy issuing from the French Revolution is in conflict with the Church, particularly the Catholic Church, a conflict ultimately springing from the optimism of the former and the pessimism of the latter.

Of late, that pessimism has been deepened by the Syllabus, the *Concilium* and the doctrine of infallibility, the Church, for obscure reasons, having decided to offer a conscious opposition to modern ideas on a wide front.

The great decision can only come from the mind of men. Will optimism, under the guise of power and money, continue to survive, and how long? Or, as the pessimist philosophy of today might seem to suggest, will there be a general change in thought such as took place in the third and fourth centuries? [5]

In essence, are we not still asking the same questions Jacob Burckhardt discussed with his students at the University of Basel?

Philosophy became sterile. It had exhausted itself with the great system-makers from Kant to Schopenhauer. There were Neo-Kantians, Neo-Hegelians, and similar schools of thought, but their analytical endeavors had no influence on the people. The most widely read philosophical book — if it deserves that name — was the speculative adventure of an outstanding biologist and follower of Darwin, Ernst Haeckel (1834–1919). In 1899 he published his *Weltraetsel* (English translation: *The Riddles of the Universe*, 1900), applying in the most dilettante and primitive fashion evolutionary ideas to the problems of metaphysics and religion. The

[5] Translated and excellently introduced by James Hastings Nichols under the title, *Force and Freedom. Reflections on History* (New York: Pantheon, 1943), p. 297f. See also Jakob Burckhardt, *Briefe zur Erkenntnis seiner geistigen Gestalt*, ed. F. Kaphahn (Leipzig: A. Kröner, 1935).

philosophers protested against it; yet, it became a best seller not only at home, but also in other countries. Its crude materialism appealed to the half-educated, who always characterize themselves by their belief that one can buy an inexpensive key to the world's mysteries. The cheap pamphlets that Hitler read in his youth in Vienna and Munich bore the fatal stamp — natural evolution and nothing but that, survival of the strongest, atheism — though Ernst Haeckel, professor at the University of Jena, would have shuddered at the mere thought of providing scientific material for a Hitler. He wanted to free the world from prejudice, but he helped to create it in another form.

Yet, at the time of Haeckel's greatest influence — the first decade of the twentieth century — there was a renaissance. A new philosophy emerged under the leadership of men such as Wilhelm Dilthey, Max Scheler, and Edmund Husserl. The influence of Henri Bergson made itself felt. The German theater emerged from its traditionalism and became, especially through the early plays of Gerhart Hauptmann and the drama of the Norwegian Henrik Ibsen, the platform where the social problems of the time could be discussed. Poets such as Richard Dehmel, Rainer Maria Rilke, and Stefan George gave German verse a new form, depth, and breadth; the plastic arts became ready for the works of Barlach, Kolbe, and Lehmbruck. Franz Marc, Lovis Corinth, and Ernst Kokoschka created a new style of painting. The Bauhaus movement began. The youth movement, however romantic, wanted a new style of life, free from the sloppy complacency, the Philistine hedonism, and the empty traditionalism they believed to see in their teachers and parents. The drinking habits and the dueling, characteristic of the vacuous mentality of the typical old student corporations, became a matter of distaste for an increasing number of students.

Here is the tragedy. While Germany tried to find its way back to a deeper understanding of life, and while the Western nations increased their fruitful exchange of ideas, frightened and befuddled European diplomacy lost control over the powers of economic greed, imperialist expansion, and nationalist militarism and bungled the European peoples and finally the whole world into a war from which Western civilization has never recovered. As an English statesman phrased it: "The lights went out over Europe." When the battlefields were cleaned up, three great empires that so far had been essential in the balance between Europe and other continents were destroyed: Russia, Austria, and Germany. Russia became communist; Austria, which despite all its defects had provided a measure of stability among the Danube countries, fell into pieces (to be first swallowed up by Hitler, and then by Stalin); and Germany became a republic that did not believe in itself. Italy, in spite of a spurious victory, was near inner collapse and soon submitted to Mussolini's fascist form of totalitarianism. All this happened at a time when, according to the American slogan, the world was to be made "safe for democracy."

THE WEIMAR PERIOD, NATIONAL SOCIALISM, AND THE GERMAN REPUBLIC

The story of the so-called Weimar Republic, like that of the French government after 1789, is a classical example of the predicament of a people that without sufficient political education tries to heal a sudden break in its tradition. France's first democratic venture ended in the dictatorship of Napoleon; that of Germany, in the tyranny of Hitler.

When the shocks, caused by the Emperor's flight to Holland, the defeat, the revolutionary upheavals, and the Treaty of Versailles, had somehow abated, it rapidly became obvious that the German people lacked the instinct for unity and the sense of sacrifice and responsibility necessary to rebuild a shattered commonwealth. After a few seeming concessions to the dangerously excited masses, the conservatives and the powers of industry and capital soon regained their dominating influence. With order restored, they forgot that the Social Democratic trade unions had saved the country from chaos and communism. The decorum of the vanished princely courts and the glories of soldiery still lingered in the minds of the leading families. Instead of searching into the causes of their defeat, they made "the new system" responsible for the fact that the republican army, reduced to one hundred thousand by the victorious nations, no longer provided a reservoir of social prestige and security for their sons. The army itself, staffed with officers of the old regime, soon conquered political influence far beyond its actual size. Skillfully it played on romantic sentiments, the heroic remembrances of battles, and the herd instinct of the widespread veterans' organizations. Despite all protests from the left, it was soon permitted to prepare for the conditions for Hitler's rearmament. The insane legend of the *Dolchstoss* (stab in the back) told the people that the peacemakers in the war parliament, the mutiny of the navy, and the socialist workers were responsible for the defeat. With silence or historical distortions men covered the fact that the revolution came after General Ludendorff, the leader of the army, had asked the enemy for an armistice and fled in disguise to Sweden. A few years later the same man, together with his colleague von Hindenburg, became the symbol of military glory. He offered the Germans his pagan-Teutonistic philosophy, a sort of new Wodan cult of an incredibly low intellectual standard. With Hitler he marched in the batallions of the famous Munich *Bierkeller Putsch* (November 1923), which the army still chose to suppress, though reluctantly. It felt that the time for "liberating" Germany from the democratic regime had not yet come.

The higher officialdom survived unshaken the change from the Wilhelminian era to republicanism, partly because, like the French bureaucratic hierarchy, it was necessary for orderly government, partly because the Weimar Republic respected the statutory rights of the old, even the most reactionary and obstinate, official to the degree of suicide. The moment a sense of safety had entered the ministries, everything possible was done to boycott the bearer of a new idea. The higher courts condoned or punished mildly any crime against the Republic when it came from the right, even when the defendant was an assassin, while it clearly showed no desire for clemency when the offender came from the left. Thus exactly those who should have preserved the sense of justice confused the law-abiding German people. And, whereas the elementary-school teachers stood on the side of the Republic (though many of them, after 1930, were willing to support national socialism), the teachers in the secondary schools believed they owed it to their social prestige and their position as reserve officers to be on the conservative side and to educate the future members of the professions against democracy. As a matter of fact, there were more liberals among them before World War I, especially in southern Germany, than after. Those who frankly professed their liberal or socialist leanings were ostracized by their colleagues. Among the professors in the universities and other higher institutions, the situation was not very different. The press, with few exceptions, was in the hands of antirepublican groups. It served, not as a democratic, but as an antidemocratic educational force.

Taken all together, the more privileged classes committed a stupid crime against the political Constitution, which actually had protected them by securing order in the social crises after the war, a crime that finally turned against them. Politically shortsighted as they were, they did not see that, all in all, they had been extremely well treated in the days of the upheaval of 1918, and that the counterrevolution they worked for would not lead back to the monarchy they hoped for, but to despotism. However, why not a bit of despotism, provided one can profit from it? Thus they supported Hitler, though they were well aware that he and his gang were criminals. From Sophocles' *Antigone* on, one finds the saying in many languages that those whom the gods wish to destroy they first smite with madness.

However, all this could not have happened without the existence of two conditions. First, the parties behind the Republic, doctrinaire and inexperienced as they were, did not understand the meaning of political freedom — freedom not being a platform safe and open for everybody who wishes to undermine it, but a mutual covenant in the interest of the whole nation as a part of humanity. Second, the Social Democrats, who were the only convinced bearers of the democratic idea, had had little chance to train political leaders before World War I. With very few exceptions, all of them had attended only elementary and vocational schools, and their cabinet ministers in the new German states were uncomfortable in the chairs of their conservative predecessors. In dealing with the firmly entrenched higher officialdom, they wavered between arrogance and insecurity. They still were talking about Marxism and the proletarian *Klassenkampf* (class struggle) before their constituencies, while realizing in their offices that with this political philosophy they could not lead a nation which under their own guidance had preferred democracy to the Russian dictatorship of the proletariat.

In contrast to England, there had been no Fabian Society. German labor had been forced to recruit itself almost exclusively from the proletariat; the Emperor's hard words about the "vaterlandslosen Gesellen" (fellows without a fatherland) had been accepted by the respectable citizen. State, church, and society, all three together had missed the chance to incorporate the socialist movement into the country's cultural heritage. The proletariat stood outside, politically as well as religiously; the Weimar Republic proved incapable of reconciling the contrasts.

There was, in addition, a technical factor that hampered the functioning of the political apparatus. In its dogmatic attitude about political justice the new democracy adopted the proportional electoral system with the result that, the major political parties often being equally divided, small and cranky parties could regulate the needle of the balance. Thus the coherent exercise of power by a somewhat steady parliamentary majority was not possible. This was the case especially in the parliaments of the smaller states, which, in consequence of the German past, were closer to the minds of the people than the Reichstag at Berlin.

Yet, it would be wrong to call the Weimar period a period of despair. There were many among German youth [6] and also among older people who had fought the war to defend their fatherland, not out of enthusiasm for imperial Germany and its power complex. They had been in the youth movement, which in its initial state was a romantic attempt at a cultural renaissance. Insofar as they had not been killed in the war, they now — like Fichte after the defeat by Napoleon — tried to develop a new social ethics:[7] religious socialists tried to reconcile socialism and religion; [8] and a slowly developing form of neoconservatism attempted a synthesis between socialism and tradition. Foreign visitors were impressed by the vitality of the cultural discussion and the limitless freedom of

[6] Hanna Hafkesbrink, *Unknown Germany; an Inner Chronicle of the First World War* (New Haven: Yale University Press, 1948).

[7] See Werner Picht, *Jenseits von Pazifismus und Nationalismus* (Munich, D. W. Callwey, 1932); Werner Picht and Eugen Rosenstock, *Im Kampf um die Erwachsenenbildung 1912–1926* (Leipzig: Quelle and Meyer, 1926); Theodor Litt, Das Verhältnis der Generationen ehedem und heute (Wiesbaden: Dieterich, 1947).

[8] Paul Tillich, *The Interpretation of History*, Part 1, trans. N. A. Rasetzki; Parts 2, 3, and 4, trans. Elsa S. Talmey (New York: Scribner's, 1936). J. C. Rossaint, *Neues Deutschland. Bund Christlicher Sozialisten* (Stuttgart: Das Neue Wort, 1947).

criticism and analysis. But, in the absence of a uniting goal, it often turned into mere theoretical excitement and linguistic exercise.

Perhaps the greatest harm was done to democracy by the inability of the republican parties to control the inflation. The legend soon spread that it was a trick of the new government to rob the citizen of his earnings. But even without such rumors it is understandable that a young man who after four or five years of war service worked in an underground mine to earn the money to continue his studies became rebellious against his society when his savings during the work year did not enable him even to buy a postage stamp. In the year before the end of inflation in November 1923 the value of the money had diminished by 1,500,000,000,000 marks. (The exchange rate of a dollar at the height of the inflation was 4,200,000,-000,000.) Everybody was a billionaire, but a billion marks would not buy a loaf of bread.

A few years after the inflation there came the depression and unemployment. Men who after years of work and study had earned a doctorate degree and expected a corresponding social and professional position were fortunate if they could sell socks behind a counter, while young laborers, who thought they could rely on their skill, found themselves idle, without purpose, without pride, living on a dole hardly above starvation level. Much too late the republican parties discovered that under such conditions the people could not identify itself with a new form of government on which there hung the stigma of defeat. Public work projects, large-scale educational measures connected with definite purposes, arousal of the kind of enthusiasm that enables men to make sacrifices under the spell of an idea: all these — as was the case with Russia — would have been necessary to avoid the disaster. The few work camps that finally were founded were like a drop on a hot stove. At many places they served as training grounds for the Brown Shirts of Hitler, whose propaganda had already crept into the yawning psychological vacuum. Hitler took the harvest from the seeds of hatred sown by conservatives and communists alike against the "rotten democracy"; he organized batallions of young people, for whom even marching in a uniform was a relief from boredom; he conjured up the glory of the past and the mirage of a new millennium. Diabolically he appealed to the superior will power of a "new generation" against the "intellectual cowardice," "international pacifism," and "sick effeminacy" of democracy. When profitable, he covered his barbaric paganism with pious phrases, demanding the restoration of Christianity. Despite all warnings from within and without, the churches went a long way with him. He was never excommunicated. His lies were believed, first by a desperate minority, and then by a growing number of bewildered people, not because men examined what he said, but because they wanted something to believe in, even at the cost of reason, perhaps even at the price of life.

There is no need to tell the story further. In January 1933 the Reich President von Hindenburg appointed Hitler to become Chancellor; in March of the same year Hitler won the federal elections with the support of von Hindenburg, who, with his enfeebled mind and under his son's influence, had already become the captive of the National Socialists. Political analysts have discussed the question of the degree to which the German people as a whole stood behind Hitler. The election of 1933 may serve as one indication. The National Socialist Party had 43.9 per cent of the votes. Only with the support of the conservatives could Hitler claim a constitutional majority. The Social Democratic Party had 18.3 per cent. However, after the incendiary burning of the Reichstag building by Hitler's and Goering's henchmen, publicly attributed to the socialists and communists, all electoral propaganda on the part of the left-wing parties had been forbidden. In addition, at least in the rural districts the election results were forged; in many cities terrorist pressure had already begun to work; and many decent people voted for Hitler because they believed that von Hindenburg and conservative power would prevent the Nazis from carrying out their brutal plans. There had never been any real internal terror among the Germans; they had never decapitated a king. The suppression of revolutionaries by the old princes was cruel, but by no means comparable to the civil wars of England, France, and the United States. Imagination was too weak to foresee the future. Even many of those who voted for Hitler were by no means followers of the system as it developed after the seizure of power. The flies had gone into the spiderweb, and, once they were under its terror, they became stupefied and paralyzed. Those who still dared move were the first to be killed. The individual no longer counted. He could not make himself heard, for there was for him no press or radio. Very soon every opponent of the new regime was under observation. He became a danger to his friends; his family was exposed to hunger and ostracism, even to the concentration camp. There was many a brave man who refused to give in, who protected those in danger, who dared speak from the pulpit or the podium. But after a few years they were silenced or driven into small conventicles. Even those churchmen who protested their Christian conviction to the end were unable to change the barbaric laws and war measures of the system. Only if there had been vigorous collective action in the very beginning, supported by forces in other countries, might some change have been effected.

All the more deplorable is the cowardly behavior of the leaders of those institutions that, at least at the beginning of the terror, could have acted as a body. The assembly of the rectors of the universities failed to protest against the dismissal of highly esteemed but politically or racially inopportune colleagues. The officer corps, which had always spoken of *deutsche Soldatenehre* (German soldiers' honor), did not chase the men from the garrison who came on the order of the Nazis to erase the names of Jewish or leftist war heroes from the regiment's monument. The Supreme Court permitted the slaughter of justice and the trampling down of civil rights. High officials preferred the signing of the most vicious documents to decent retirement with the pretext, and often also with the serious conviction, that worse men would come if they did not remain at their place — which was not even incorrect, for some of these officials still could exercise some humane influence.

After the surprising diplomatic successes of Hitler, perhaps also during the first victories in war (though there was on the whole no spontaneous enthusiasm for it), the number of the followers increased. After all, what the republican governments with all their negotiations never would even have dreamed of achieving was granted to Hitler. The most ruthless power, so it seemed to many, was more highly regarded and even respected by foreign nations than decent negotiations. Some years after Hitler's conquest of Germany the whole civilized world seemed to be in a state of coma. And so the terror could spread from Germany over other countries until, after unspeakable sacrifice and destruction all over the world and the systematic extermination of Jews and political opponents within the realm of Hitler's power, the *Führer* had to kill himself in his Berlin bomb cellar.

Hitler's and his conservative friends' reactionary counterrevolution against German democracy and human morality has brought about or at least accelerated the most extensive changes in man's history — the first revolution of global character; the definite end of Europe's supremacy, already initiated by World War I; the rise of two main and ideologically opposed world powers, the United States and Russia; the power of communist doctrine as an international factor of greatest significance; the shaking off of colonialism in Asia, and sooner or later also in Africa; the foundation of a Jewish state; the awakening of Islam; and, in all probability, the emergence of powers of a new form of neutrality, such as India and Yugoslavia, which through skillful coalitions may determine the future of humanity more decisively than their strength of arms indicates.

Of course, Western Europe, especially if one counts the British Isles within its political orbit, has by no means left the stage. In consequence of the development of modern industry, war-torn nations soon recover physically, though still too slowly in view of the needs of the population. Nevertheless, houses are built, the fields soon carry a large harvest, and the traffic system allows for quick distribution.

The decrease of the mortality rate of infants allows the population to fill up quickly the gaps caused by even the most murderous battles. What science and industry cannot replace, however, is the energy and maturing experience of the millions of men who, mostly in the ages between twenty and thirty-five, have been wounded or killed through battle or disease. Ten years after the fighting, they would have entered into the responsible positions in politics, administration, scholarship, and other professions that require a long training. They would have transmitted their own learning to the younger generation; they would have provided a source of sound family life and of mental and emotional energy. The terrible bungling and fatigue Europe displayed between the two world wars were largely due to the absence of more than eleven

million who died of wounds and diseases in the War of 1914–1918. [9]
If one includes indirect losses in the civilian population, the casualties of World War I may amount to more than twenty-five million.
In all likelihood, without this terrible bloodletting the totalitarian menace would not have descended upon mankind. The havoc wrought upon humanity by World War II defies exact statistics.

The decisive question is: will Germany, and the whole of Europe, be given a great new goal to strive for with a chance of success? On the political plane, the goal is a united Europe. And here, as was the case with the German Customs Union that prepared for the unity of Germany before 1870, the material interests of industry may support the moral hopes of man. In the chapter on France the farseeing plans of some of its statesmen were mentioned; they are met by those of influential men on the German side. The design of a common market and similar measures in western Europe is now increasingly helped toward realization by men who around 1930 hoped to profit by the Hitler regime. Is it then too bold to suppose that the west of Europe, and within its orbit Germany, may be ripe for a new political and cultural future?

EDUCATIONAL DEVELOPMENT

Environmental Influences

The division of Germany into many small principalities did not allow for the development of schools and movements that could foster political maturity and independence. In addition, as in other European countries — except England with the institution of primogeniture — the large group of noblemen with its privileges concerning rank and position took away from the middle classes the chance for administrative functions of importance. Yet, the political decentralization permitted, in contrast to France with its all-absorbing capital, the growth of many centers of cultural life. Even in feudal times, with the predominantly agricultural life, the German cities exercised a cultural and even a political influence not known in other nations. In the period of absolutism, following

[9] Samuel Dumas and K. O. Vedel-Petersen, *Losses of Life Caused by War*, ed. Harald Westergaard (Oxford: Clarendon Press, 1923); P. A. Sorokin, *Man and Society in Calamity* (New York: Dutton, 1946); Warren S. Thompson, *Population Problems* (New York: McGraw-Hill, 1953).

the Renaissance and the Reformation, the various princely courts vied with each other for the costly honor of imitating the great courts of the West, especially the court of Louis XIV. Even very small principalities such as Saxe-Weimar or Saxe-Coburg-Gotha were, at one time or another, homes of the arts, not only for decorative purposes, but for the genuine fostering of the humane values. The reign of Charles Augustus of Saxe-Weimar (1775–1828) is still today one of the finest symbols of artistic and intellectual productivity. For to his residence of Weimar, with the University of Jena in the neighborhood, he attracted men such as Goethe, Schiller, and Herder.

The decentralization of culture had its beneficent influence also on cities without princely residences. Places with not more than twenty to thirty thousand inhabitants laid value on financing a permanent theater with actors working on favorable contracts and able to show their talents in a large variety of performances from classical drama to comedy. Especially the universities profited from the noble competition of the various states and cities. There were thirty-four universities and technological institutes in 1937. They differed greatly in size but little in quality. They all produced outstanding scholars. The chair of a philosopher at Heidelberg, or Marburg, of a mathematician or physicist at Goettingen, or of a theologian at Tübingen was just as much, sometimes even more, the goal of scholarly ambition as the chairs at the larger universities of Berlin, Leipzig, and Munich. There was no such thing as "Paris" for a German scholar.

Decentralization and the cultural freedom within the various territories of Germany caused also, at least in part, the remarkable development of German educational theory and of the German school system. As early as the thirteenth century the magistrates of such cities as Zwickau, Leipzig, Worms, Lübeck, Hamburg, and others tried to wrest their schools from the Church, which clung to its old educational monopoly. But only at a few places, such as Cologne, had this lay initiative a lasting effect. The trained personnel still belonged to the clergy, and the citizens were unwilling to burden their budget with attractive salaries. During the fifteenth century schools deteriorated almost everywhere. Only through continual though rarely effective control by the princely governments could a semblance of order be maintained. Learning reflected the general decline of clerical morals and the fact that the older scholasticism was out of gear with the advancing civilization. But this was so in every country except northern Italy, where city universities welcomed the spirit of the Renaissance and a new empiricism.

Humanism, the Reformation, and the Great Educators

The change from sleepiness to new excitement came with two spiritual movements born out of the Renaissance, humanism, and the Reformation. It took some time before the first reached Germany. Aenea Silvio de Piccolomini (1405–1464), the papal legate to Vienna and later Pope Pius II, was one of the early harbingers who brought the spring from Italy to the German people. In his *De Liberorum Educatione* (On the Education of Youth) he recommends a combination of physical and intellectual training; philosophy takes its place beside religious instruction; eloquence, even the systematic training of the voice, grammar in the sense of the art of correct and elegant mastery of Latin, the study of the Greek and Roman historians and poets, not only for their wisdom, but also for their beauty — these are the educational values recommended by the Italian. They were taken up by the German humanists, who around 1500 began to criticize and partly improve education in the secondary schools and the universities. Of course, the northern humanists were less of the worldly Italian "gentleman" type than they were scholars. Erasmus of Rotterdam (1467–1536), the greatest among them, edited the Greek New Testament and the Church Fathers and wrote prolifically on social and educational issues, while Johannes Reuchlin (1455–1522) renewed, not without danger to his person, the knowledge of Hebrew among Christian theologians. But, despite their interests being largely historical, these scholars cherished an image of man closer to the Renaissance than to the medieval ideal. They initiated the slow change from the older world view toward the compromise between religion and secularism that has become the characteristic of Christian humanism. In Germany as everywhere else, however, humanism was still built on a very thin stratum of the population, for only a portion of one per cent enjoyed any advanced education. The whole daily life of man was still breathing in the Christian tradition, and, while other nations could bear a larger dose of doubt, and even of cynicism about the corrupted Church, the Germans apparently needed faith and something to hold onto. They were desperately concerned with their nearness to God, not as interpreted by scholars and priests, but as felt in their hearts and troubled consciences. Impatiently they were waiting for the new prophet with the pure word that could lead deserted humanity back to divine grace.

This man was Martin Luther. Since I am here concerned with the evolution of a nation's culture, his theology proper cannot be dealt with in detail — though the two cannot be separated from each other. Catholics and even Protestants have blamed Luther for willfully disrupting the peace of the Church. Had it been capable of inner rejuvenation, peace could well have been preserved. As it came about, Luther and the other great reformers of his time saved Western Christianity from decay. The Catholic Church itself needed a terrific shock to make order within itself. The sting of Protestantism has constantly stirred its conscience. Finally, the so-called religious wars in which Catholics allied with Protestants in order to fight Catholics, and Protestants with Catholics in order to fight Protestants, would have arisen anyhow as a result of the rivalry between the German princes and the big European dynasties. The whole of Europe, at this time, lived through the transition from obsolete feudalism to the new absolutist order; this was in itself a revolution of no small measure. Without it, the reform would not have been possible.

And, though no one can say whether the Swiss Reformation under Zwingli (1481–1531) and the French under Calvin (1509–1564) would have been the same without Luther, some kind of revolt would certainly have occurred in their countries. Otherwise one could not explain the rapidly spreading influence of these men. A merely imitative movement remains small and dies quickly. Nor could Henry VIII of England have dared the separation from Rome (whatever his personal motives), had he not been able to count on his people's aversion to the papacy. In other words, not one individual alone, or a few rebels, caused the upheaval. It was already there when they appeared.

But every great expression of thought frees latent energies because it lends form to the thus-far unshaped. So also Luther released forces that moved the German people, whom the older Latin nations liked to look down on as half-civilized frontiersmen of a sort, into the center of the spiritual arena. Rightly the papal nuntius Oleander reported to the Papal See that in comparison with the new movement "the rebellion of Henry IV against Gregory VII was lovely like violets and roses." [10]

The stress of inwardness, the central role of personal faith in man's salvation, and the doctrine of Christian freedom by necessity moved the cultural development and education of Protestant Germany into new channels. In his sermons at Wittenberg, Luther declared that every Christian must find his own way of believing just as everyone has to find his own way of dying. This would have meant a kind of spiritual anarchy had there not been the Bible as an authority higher than any church. But the Bible itself is a complicated book, open to many explanations, which is one of the reasons why the Catholic Church withheld it from the layman. And this institution had at its foundation not only the Bible but the councils and the hierarchy as arbiters in matters of faith and, at the same time, Aristotle as the supreme teacher in matters of philosophy. Luther, on the other hand, recommended only Aristotle's works, *On Logic, Rhetoric,* and *Poetics,* and condemned his *On the Soul,* his *Ethics, Physics,* and *Metaphysics.* Rightly, and here in unconscious conformity with the popes at the time of the emergence of systematic and Aristotelian scholasticism, he felt the profound difference between the world view of the pagan and the gospel of Christ.

In this regard my advice would be that Aristotle's *Physics, Metaphysics, On the Soul, Ethics,* which have hitherto been thought his best books, should be altogether discarded, together with all the rest of his books which boast of treating the things of nature, although nothing can be learned from them either of the things of nature or the things of the Spirit . . . I venture to say that any potter has more knowledge of nature than is written in these books. It grieves me to the heart that this damned, conceited rascally heathen has with his false words deluded and made fools of many of the best Christians. God has sent him as a plague upon us for our sins. [11]

---

[10] *Luthers Werke,* ed. Arnold E. Berger (Leipzig and Vienna: Bibliographisches Institut, 1917), I, 143.

[11] "An Open Letter to the Christian Nobility," in *Works* (Philadelphia ed.,

When Oleander wrote his letter to the Pope, trouble had already arisen in the universities; for a while, until Melanchthon preached the return to Aristotle in a new spirit, there was no objective and ordering intellectual system to hold minds together. Strange sects appeared. The Anabaptists arose in Thuringia, Luther's own homeland; they also created chaos in the beautiful city of Münster. In 1524 the peasants of Swabia and Franconia revolted in a wild fury of destruction against the cruel suppression by their nobility. They laid their Christian-political creed down in the Twelve Articles, which in the name of Christ demanded freedom from serfdom and suppression. The peasants asserted that they did not wish the gospel to be considered a cause of rebellion or uproar against rightful authority — which soon it became — but as the word of love and peace. Nevertheless, they demanded that the whole community have the power to elect a pastor, that they be given the right to hunt and fish and to use the woods and the land, that services no longer be heaped up from day to day and daily increased, that the state of villenage be lifted, and that, on the whole, tendencies of the lords to suppress the peasants and to deprive them of their acres, their sources of living, be stopped.[12]

Here lies Luther's tragical dilemma. With his insistence on man's spiritual freedom and the reordering of German society in a Christian spirit he never meant rebellion against established political authority. As stated earlier, he, like the Catholic Church and John Calvin, considered authority God-ordained. In addition, if he had supported the Anabaptists' communist experiments and the Peasants' Revolt, he would have created a disastrous estrangement between the Reformation and the German princes, on whose support it depended. Yet, even under the greatest stress, to what degree can one separate religious from political freedom, and divine from social justice? For not only suppression of faith, but also hunger and serfdom, are an offense against the soul.

Luther's dilemma has remained with German Protestantism up to our time. It preached Christian liberty from the pulpit but became frightened whenever established authority was attacked.

1931), II, 146. See also the extracts from Luther's writings in Robert Ulich, *Three Thousand Years of Educational Wisdom.*

[12] E. Balfort, *The Peasants' War in Germany, 1525–1526* (London: Swan Sonnenschein, 1899).

Thus it lost both liberalism as well as socialism; in the eyes of progressive thinkers and scientists it was an instrument of retardation. The self-liberation of the established Protestant churches from state domination did not begin until after the cataclysms of the two world wars. It is true that the Catholic Church also allied itself in Catholic countries with the conservative forces. Yet, in every crisis it could take recourse to its supernational structure and theory. The supreme head from which the final decisions had to come was not within the state. With the dissolution of papal territorial sovereignty in 1873 by the new United Kingdom of Italy — the greatest blessing ever bestowed on this Church — the Papal See became free from dynastic interests of its own. (The Concordat of 1929 through which Mussolini restored the papal state has merely symbolic value.) Thus the Catholic Church could approach the problems of rising nationalism, class conflicts, and labor struggles with a higher degree of independence than nation-bound Protestantism. For, though Leo XIII's famous encyclical *Rerum Novarum* of 1891, in behalf of Christian relations between industry and labor, would not have been issued without the fear of the Church of losing the workmen to the socialist parties, it nevertheless preceded similar actions by the German Protestant churches. This, of course, does not deny that individual ministers felt the obligation to fight poverty and injustice. But their efforts remained largely as charity.

If thus, in regard to the social problem, Protestantism lost for a long time its original impetus, nevertheless, religiously and intellectually, even politically, it was a dynamic force. Its clergy soon forgot the idea of an *ecclesia semper reformanda* and stiffened into a new hierarchy, but the vital flame of its origin could not be suppressed. In whatever shape and country it remained or became alive, Protestantism helped to make people independent. Commercial and industrial initiative grew first in Protestant areas, and so did democracy — if not within the Lutheran, then within the Zwinglian and Calvinist, orbits. The French liberal encyclopedists, as all French liberals, represented, as it were, an emigrant movement within Catholic territory, whereas in England and the United States, liberalism, though first looked askance at by the established clergy, grew organically within the general intellectual and spiritual climate. The great poetic and philosophical movements of Germany's eighteenth century occurred within the Protestant realm, and the Catholic part followed.

The same has been the case in the wide area of education.[13] First of all, Luther helped to provide one of the basic instruments of national education, a common German literary language. In choosing for the translation of the Bible the Middle High German of the Saxon Chancery, used also as the German diplomatic language by the larger principalities, Luther and his friends established an instrument of mutual literary communication. In addition, through the power of his style and his stress on pure and clear German he established a pattern of inspiration for later literary production, just as the King James Bible did in England.

"It has often happened," he says in his treatise "On Translating," "that for two or three or four weeks we have sought and asked for a single word, and sometimes have not found it even then." [14] There was resistance against Luther's German in Catholic Bavaria and the lower Rhine; also Switzerland with its native Alemanian had difficulty (and, in a way, still has) in adjusting itself to this medium, and the Netherlands developed its own literature. But, when, in the seventeenth and eighteenth centuries, all the great German writers used the language of Luther, Germany had achieved unity, at least in the written word, a fact that, indeed, had no small influence on its emergent political unification. The many dialects have remained, though continually influenced by the literary language; at the same time they are the wells from which the written style receives refreshing waters.

But Luther's educational influence far transcended his linguistic merits. His Protestantism depended not merely on reading, but on the active cooperation of the people. Thus he wrote his various popular explanations of Christian faith and worship, intended to influence the inner life of the family. His two Catechisms of 1529 have become the permanent bases of Lutheran religious instruction. He was one of the founders of the deepest source of German religious inspiration, the Protestant hymn. Finally, in great

---

[13] For English translations, see Frederick Eby, *Early Protestant Educators. The Educational Writings of Martin Luther, John Calvin, and Other Leaders of Protestant Thought* (New York and London: McGraw-Hill, 1931).

[14] "On Translating: An Open Letter. 1530," in *Works*, (Philadelphia ed., 1931), V, 14.

political style, he wrote his two addresses, "To the Christian Nobility of the German Nation," 1520, and "To the Councilmen of All Cities in Germany That They Establish and Maintain Christian Schools," 1524, the latter of which contains Luther's educational manifesto.

Since, so Luther says, parents cannot be trusted to assume educational responsibilities, schools have to be established by the Christian authorities. For the Reformation has sequestrated ecclesiastical property and thus done away with many of the older church-controlled schools so that the youth are in danger of idleness. Moreover, these old schools were ripe for reorganization in any event. With the typical exaggerations of the time and the humanists' vituperative criticism, Luther exclaims: "For it is my earnest intention, prayer and desire, that those ass-stables and devil's schools should either sink into the abyss or be converted into Christian schools." [15]

In these schools classical languages as well as German have to be taught,[16] but no longer with the old grammars of Donatus of the fourth century and Alexander de Villa Dei of the thirteenth, but with modern humanist methods. The larger cities should found libraries, not only for the learned professions, but also for the laymen, because the new Protestant society needs the help of educated adults. However, Luther's main concern was the education of the imperiled youth. Thus he concludes this letter with the words:

> Herewith I commend you all to the grace of God. May He soften and kindle your hearts that they may be deeply concerned for the poor, miserable and neglected youths and with the help of God assist and help them to the end that there may be a blessed Christian government in German lands as to body and soul, with all plenty and abundance, to the praise and glory of God the Father, through Jesus Christ our Saviour, Amen.[17]

Luther's call was not without effect, though reality fell short of his demands. As a report on school visitations in Saxony (*Unterricht der Visitatoren*, 1528) proved, the smaller cities were not yet ready for a thorough reform; the Universities of Erfurt and Leipzig were in a deplorable state, and so were some of the schools for the adolescents.[18]

All these experiences caused the reformer to insist more and

---

[15] "To the Councilmen," in *Works*, IV, 107f. [17] *Ibid.*, pp. 129–130.
[16] *Ibid.*, p. 112. [18] *Ibid.*, pp. 129–130.

more on the right of the civil authorities to enforce obligatory education, at least for the more capable children. Thus there arose, in the year 1530, the classical formulation of the ideas on which henceforth Protestant Germany based its right to intervene in the family life of its citizens.

But I hold that it is the duty of the government to compel its subjects to keep their children in school, especially those [promising] children who were mentioned above. For it is truly its duty to maintain the offices and classes that have been mentioned, so that preachers, jurists, pastors, writers, physicians, schoolmasters, and the like may continue, for we cannot do without them. If it can compel its subjects who are fitted for the work to carry pike and musket, man the walls, and do other kinds of work, when war is necessary; how much more can it and ought it compel its subjects to keep their children in school, because here there is a worse war on, a war with the very devil, who goes about to suck out secretly the strength of cities and princedoms and empty them of able persons, until he has bored out the pith, and left an empty shell of useless folk, with whom he can play and juggle as he will.[19]

Reforms, however, were impeded not only by the laziness of the parents and the thriftiness of the governments and the townspeople, but also by the fact that the teaching profession was held in low esteem. Therefore Luther's admonition:

a diligent and pious schoolteacher, or master, or whoever it is that faithfully trains and teaches boys, can never be sufficiently rewarded, or repaid with any money, as even the heathen Aristotle says. Nevertheless, this work is as shamefully despised among us as though it was nothing at all. I myself if I could leave the preaching office and other things, or had to do so, would not be so glad to have any other work as that of schoolmaster, or teacher of boys, for I know that this is the most useful, the greatest, and the best, next to the work of preaching. Indeed, I scarcely know which of the two is the better.[20]

The Reformation has been criticized for destroying by its religious fervor the just-budding flowers of German humanism, with its great aesthetic, literary, and scholarly possibilities. Before the Reformation, Erasmus of Rotterdam was the most celebrated man in the intellectual world. He was the most literate among the literati, the wittiest among the witty; popes and princes not only

[19] "A Sermon on Keeping Children in School," in *Works*, IV, pp. 177–178.
[20] *Ibid.*, pp. 173–174.

respected, but also feared him. Certainly, in his opinion, the Church was rotten, but the tradition was too great and precious to be broken. He hated the brutal disturbance of a gradual Christian-humanist self-renewal. Wittenberg, the heart of the new movement, was for Erasmus not only geographically but also culturally a place *in termino civilitatis.*[21] Yet, his fame was soon eclipsed by the Saxon monk. And the humanist poets (of whom, by the way, even Erasmus did not think too highly) became somewhat lonely among a people on whom the poetry of the Psalms (published in a special German edition in 1524) made a much deeper impression than Homer and Vergil, and especially their imitations. And why not? Even aesthetically the Psalms are at least on the same level as any great piece of Greek and Roman poetry, and so are some of the Protestant hymns.

But, in spite of its religious emphasis, Protestantism did not cast aside the philological studies. On the contrary, it embedded them into a deeper matrix than can be provided by an exclusively aesthetic and erudite culture, which always is doomed to quick decay and imitative sterility. In his "To the Councilmen of All Cities in Germany" Luther says:

> And let us be sure of this: We shall not long preserve the Gospel without the languages. The languages are the sheaths in which this sword of the Spirit is contained; they are the casket in which we carry this jewel.[22]

Henceforth the German theological faculties, more than those in any other country, have demanded the knowledge of Latin, Greek, and Hebrew from their students. It was the Protestant clergy that insisted on the study of the ancient tongues in the secondary schools, and thus influenced not only the other professions, but also the cultural standards and aspirations of the country as a whole. Without Protestantism the German *humanistische Gymnasium* could not have acquired its monopoly on preparing the candidates for higher studies and preserved this monopoly almost to the end of the nineteenth century. Thus, instead of speaking of the destruction of humanism by the Reformation, one could maintain with greater justification that Protestantism sheltered and

---

[21] Friedrich Paulsen, *Geschichte des Gelehrten Unterrichts*, ed. R. Lehmann (Leipzig: Veit, 1919–1921), I, 187.
[22] "To the Councilmen," p. 114.

helped it toward full maturity. The seed Luther had planted into German soil, namely, searching inwardness together with respect for the ancient heritage, developed later into the last classical period of our Western civilization, or one of the last great searchings of the Western soul into the depths of eternity, the poetry of Schiller and Goethe and the philosophies of Kant, Hegel, Fichte, and Schelling.

Besides philosophy and the literary arts, educational theory and practice also grew mightily within the Protestant climate. Outside of it John Amos Comenius (1592–1670) could not have written his *Great Didactic*, in which with a great sweep of intuition he laid down the systematically arranged rules of teaching. Educational historians stress his "sense realism" because of his emphasis on the psychological or natural conditions of learning, a tendency he found supported in the writings of Francis Bacon. But in looking one-sidedly at his empiricism (still far away from modern scientific method) we must not forget that the wellspring of his educational activity and philosophy is religion of the Pietist Protestant type. He studied at the Protestant Universities of Herborn and Heidelberg. And without Luther's and Calvin's influence his pedagogical and speculative thought would not have reached from central Europe over to Holland, the Scandinavian countries, England, and finally America. Just as Comenius was not of German nationality, neither were the Swiss Rousseau and Pestalozzi; but they were Protestants with the radical sense of inwardness. The educational movement of German "Philanthropism," which turned the interest of the teacher to the individuality of the child, was Protestant. From the Protestant soil of Prussia came also the reorganization of the German school system with the clear division of elementary, secondary, and higher education. And without the eagerness of the German schoolmaster to incorporate into his classroom practices and his own professional education the new theories of the steady evolution of the child's mind and learning, the modern public school would have been incapable of handling pedagogically its ever-growing number of children.

On the shoulders of Pestalozzi, Friedrich W. Froebel (1782–1852) advanced our understanding of the child further. Like his Swiss teacher's, so also his own ideas, while intended for and tested in practice, were nevertheless not products of the scientific laboratory, but were essentially of an intuitional nature. They originated from a Protestant form of idealism as expressed in Schelling's conception of the ultimate identity of mind and matter. In his *The Education of Man* Froebel envisaged education as that specifically human activity by which man participates purposefully in the evolution of the world from lower to higher stages of consciousness. Every step in this divine-natural unfolding is as characteristic of the whole as every other. Thus, childhood and play are not merely preparations for adulthood, to be passed over as quickly as possible, but are significant stages, to be respected and cultivated. Finally Froebel's contemporary Johann Friedrich Herbart (1776–1841) made the step from intuitive to scientific understanding of the process of learning. He was the more pedestrian, systematic, and untiring scholar, but it was his disciples who took the *verba magistri* as a gospel and thus distorted his true intentions. For to Herbart, as to Pestalozzi and Froebel, any education that disconnects itself from a comprehensive philosophical understanding of man and his role in the universe seemed amateurish and by necessity aimless. Metaphysics, logic, psychology, ethics, and education have to form a whole.

We often take for granted what has been achieved by the efforts of these great pioneers of modern education. But, despite all the shortcomings of our modern schools, what parents of today would like to have their children in schools unaffected by the ideas of the eighteenth and nineteenth centuries? Even the most conservative teacher, provided he is a good one, would shudder if he had to work in the typical climate of a pre-Pestalozzian school and see himself always symbolized by the rod as his main means of discipline.[23] It is not the fault of the great pathfinders but the fault of those who ignorantly talk about them, or do not even know their names, that a sentimental concept of childhood has developed in some minds. And one may safely say that the sentimentality increased to the degree that there decreased the religious and idealistic motivation until the individual became an isolated piece of life without cosmic relation.

[23] See G. F. Lamb, *The English at School. An Anthology* (London: Allen and Unwin, 1950).

GERMANY

During the middle and end of the nineteenth century the German schools were considered the patterns for educational reforms in other countries. Among others, Victor Cousin, of France, Matthew Arnold, of England, and Horace Mann, of the United States, traveled to Germany and wrote reports on its educational accomplishments.[24]

The Crises in German Education

Yet, the past decades have shown that despite their great tradition the German schools have failed to bring about the level of national and cultural integration a sympathetic observer might have expected. In trying to explain this fact I deal with a topic that, though here related to Germany, raises profound questions in regard to other countries and, ultimately, to our whole civilization. To what degree do schools determine a nation's future? England, as we saw, had a very bad, or an almost nonexistent, national school system. Yet, it developed into the most mature of the European nations. More specifically, to what degree can schools alter, or be blamed for, politically and culturally undesirable conditions in a given population? To what degree do schools really influence human behavior? Would other nations under identical adversities have behaved similarly to the German, or better or worse, and why? We enter here an area for which nobody has yet discovered a reliable guide. Yet, there can be no cultural policy without at least some tentative considerations.

In his *Seventh Annual Report* [25] to the Massachusetts Board of Education (1844), Horace Mann, after praising the Prussian and, more or less, the whole German school system, gives some answers to a question he supposes largely justified, namely, why despite "such a wide-extended and energetic machinery for public instruction, the Prussians, as a people, do not rise more rapidly in the scale of civilization."

According to Horace Mann, the pupils leave school too early, namely, at fourteen, and there is a dearth of suitable books for the reading of older children or younger men.

[24] Robert Ulich, *A Sequence of Educational Influences* (Cambridge: Harvard University Press, 1935), p. 40.
[25] See *The Common School Journal*, VI (1844), pp. 166–167.

But the most potent reason for Prussian backwardness and incompetency is this — when the children come out from the school, they have little use either for the faculties that have been developed, or for the knowledge that has been acquired. Their resources are not brought into demand; their powers are not roused and strengthened by exercise. Besides, it was not until the beginning of the present century, that the Prussian peasantry were emancipated from a condition of absolute vassalage. Fourthly, as it respects the vices of the Prussians, the same remark applies to them as to those of all the continental nations of Europe; — they are the vices of the sovereign, and of the higher classes of society, copied by the lower without the decorations which gilded them in their upper sphere.

An analysis of these lines reveals the pride of the nineteenth-century American, in whose republic there were no monarchs and no feudal classes, but general mobility and a chance for everybody to strengthen his powers "by exercise." Strangely enough, Mann forgets that in 1844 slavery existed in his own nation, that by far the largest majority of its children did not attend school beyond the age of twelve or fourteen, and that many of his own compatriots were not so sure whether the European Continent was so low "in the scale of civilization" that it could not favorably compare with the United States. Furthermore, in contrast to the socially backward parts of eastern Prussia, with its long-continued serfdom under the old Junker regime — always considered the most retarded part of Germany — there were in the west the Rhineland, Westphalia, and Friesland and in the south Bavaria and Württemberg, with their proud and free farmer population.

Yet, despite all patriotic one-sidedness — probably emphasized in order to make the praise of foreign and the criticism of American education palatable to his citizens — Horace Mann rightly refers to a most important factor in the education of the German as well as of other nations. There was, deep into the nineteenth century, a lack of opportunity for the average citizen to apply his education in public responsibility. Reciprocally, the schools themselves did little, or could do little, to arouse in their pupils the desire to transfer knowledge into political initiative. The necessity of interaction between school and community had been the central theme of one of Pestalozzi's main works, *Lenard and Gertrude*. But the teachers who put this postulate into practice were looked at with suspicion by the government.

For a long time, political reaction was supported by spiritual retardation. The monarchies knew well how to use the Christian gospel for their own purposes, whether interpreted in the Catholic or Protestant fashion. They selected for indoctrination those Christian virtues that taught humility, not only before God, but also before men, and the relativity of earthly values to the transcendental goal of life. It would be wrong, however, to reduce this emphasis to a mere ideological trick on the part of the civil administration and the clergy. It was, so to speak, part of the general climate that up to the nineteenth century dominated in all countries of Europe. Although enjoying the more preferred role in the drama of earthly life, most members of the ruling classes believed seriously in the essential tenets of Christianity, and under the guidance of this faith many men and women who could have chosen a more comfortable path lived a life of severe discipline and sacrifice.

Whereas the elementary schools were decidedly Christian, the higher levels of education, reserved mainly for the privileged and professional classes, were largely based on the humanistic ideal. As we saw, it had, at least in part, been absorbed into Protestant education. Around 1800, humanism received new inspiration through a fresh and vital interpretation of Greek and Roman literature and the great revival of German thought and poetry. Wilhelm von Humboldt, the friend of Goethe, provided the German pattern for the reform of secondary education. By no means intentionally anti-Christian or antireligious, it was nevertheless oriented to an essentially Platonic and aesthetic interpretation of the classical, especially the Greek, spirit. Yet, both the Christian heritage, on which the elementary school was built, and the humanist ideal of higher learning failed to inspire the souls of men toward the end of the nineteenth century, or even earlier.

Germany had no organized *mouvement laïque* as in France, with the aim of separating the churches from the state and school because the independence of the various states in cultural and educational matters prevented the secular elements from concerted action. In addition, the rivalry between the Catholic and Protestant parts of the population kept each in fear that a slackening in the denominational issue might strengthen the other group.

But politics in religion does not make a nation religious. Until

the Center Party organized a large part of the Catholic workers —
though not all by far — into its religiously dominated labor unions,
the constantly increasing industrial proletariat was in danger of
becoming wholly affiliated with the Socialist Party, which, in the
main, had adopted Marx's dialectical explanation of social history
and a sort of materialist monism. Questionnaires given to Berlin
elementary-school graduates around World War I established
clearly that religious instruction, though given for fully eight
years, had not touched their souls. Not even the simplest facts
were remembered. And, while the French labored to build up a
course in secular morality in their nondenominational schools,
nothing of this kind was done in Germany. The Constitution of
the Republic (1919) officially separated the schools from the denominations. However, the pertinent Article 146, a result of much
bargaining between the right and the left, was phrased in such
a way that the individual states and their communities could preserve the old system. Those few schools that left religious instruction to house and church were called "atheist" and shunned by
respectable parents. Here as almost everywhere, men did not hold
to the past because they believed in it, but because they were afraid
of the new.

Just as the religious character of the elementary schools persisted more or less hypocritically, so also the humanism of the advanced schools had become more a convention than a commitment.
The new image of man that Wilhelm von Humboldt had had in his
mind — the gentleman whose well-rounded education and continual development reflected the great spiritual achievements of
humankind — this image had been buried under the weight of imitative linguistic exercises. As so often in schools that thrive one-
sidedly on the past, spirit had faded into grammar, and the schoolmaster had killed the prophet.

Here Nietzsche, himself a professor of classical philosophy, appeared as the most penetrating critic. Though biased as always, he
saw clearly the shallowness of the claim of *formelle Bildung* (formal education) set up by the classicists against the advancing
sciences that were supposed to be without deep humane meaning.
What else, so he asked, can any good education do but form the
mind? If it conveys merely subject matter, it is not education, but

drill. Unfortunately, he continued, that is almost all the classical Gymnasium now provides.[26] "Never in the German Gymnasium have I found even a thread of what one could call truly classical education (*klassische Bildung*)." This is in no way astonishing in view of the fact that the Gymnasium has lost contact with the classical writers of its own nation and, consequently, also the discipline of German style. For only through the understanding, cultivation, and appreciation of one's own language can one perceive the beauty of the older authors. Thus the Gymnasium is neither German nor classical; it is a hybrid. Even the university has lost its cultural meaning, for "Built on the fragile and crumbling foundation of the present conception of the Gymnasium, its own edifice is slanting; it will not hold before the first gust of the whirlwinds. Observe the so-called free student, this herald of academic independence; guess what he really is from his instincts and his desires! What do you think about his true education if you measure it on these three yardsticks: first on his concern for philosophy, then on his appreciation of art, finally on his understanding of Greek and Roman antiquity as the essential and categorical imperative of all culture?"[27]

But what would Nietzsche say about any national school system of today, and about America's in particular? What happens to national and educational institutions that pretend to live on ideals they no longer take seriously? They lose what Nietzsche rightly regards as the essential goals of all education: moral strength and honesty of character.

The crisis that, first seen only by a few, had hovered for decades over Germany and all Europe became violently apparent with the First World War. After the defeat, educational literature, abundant in the German nation for centuries, increased by leaps and bounds. A National Education Conference (*Reichsschulkonferenz*) was held in 1920. Its report is one of the most revealing sources for the educational spirit of the postwar period.[28]

[26] "*Über die Zukunft unserer Bildungs-Anstalten*," in *Werke* (Leipzig, Naumann, 1896), IX, pp. 264, 265. For a historical analysis of the German intellectual development from Goethe and Schiller through the present, see Hans Kohn, *The Mind of Germany; the Education of a Nation* (New York: Scribner's, 1960).
[27] "*Über die Zukunft unserer Bildungs-Anstalten*," pp. 326–327.
[28] *Reichsschulkonferenz 1920, ihre Vorgeschichte und Vorbereitung und ihre Verhandlungen* (Leipzig: Quelle and Meyer, 1921); *Reichsschulkonferenz in*

The Gymnasium, which had already lost its monopoly on university preparation during the 1890's, had to give way more and more to secondary schools representing the mixed type of classical, modern, and scientific studies. As in France, the debates between the traditionalists and the modernists raged through German ministries, teachers' assemblies, journals, and newspapers. Among the moderate progressives the ideas of Pestalozzi were revived, while the more radical *Bund der Entschiedenen Schulreformer* (Association for Resolute School Reformers) tried to find a guiding principle for the new school by connecting its curriculum with the work and spirit of the modern industrial society.[29] Together with John Dewey and his followers, this German group influenced the early Russian experiments and was, in turn, influenced by them. In all German states the attempt was made to create a more flexible program of secondary education, to open it to larger groups of the population, and to link it more closely to the elementary schools. More and more people protested against the situation that 50 per cent of the people, constituting mainly industrial workers, provided only 6 per cent of the university students. For there was no reason to believe that the 94 per cent of students from the upper and middle classes were altogether of superior intellectual quality.[30] This lack of equilibrium, however, was in no way worse than in other European countries. As a matter of fact, in 1930 Germany sent more students from a greater variety of social groups to institutions of higher learning than other European countries. In Germany, out of ten thousand persons twenty attended such institutions; in France, fifteen; in Italy, ten; in England, nine. In addition, Germany at this time suffered from heavy unemployment of the academic classes.[31]

Those in favor of a more unified structure, or an *Einheitsschule* (unified school), tried to learn from the American single-track or single-ladder system. All these attempts at a higher degree of

ihren Ergebnissen (Leipzig: Quelle and Meyer, 1920); *Deutsche Schulreform: Ein Handbuch für die Reichsschulkonferenz* (Leipzig: Quelle and Meyer, 1920).

[29] *Entschiedene Schulreform; Abhandlungen zur Erneuerung der deutschen Erziehung* (Berlin, Nos. 1–51, 1922–1928).

[30] Adolf Löwe, "Das Gegenwärtige Bildungsproblem der Deutschen Universität," in *Die Erziehung*, Jahrgang VII (1931), pp. 1–19.

[31] See Walter M. Kotschnig, *Unemployment among the Learned Professions* (London: Oxford University Press, 1937).

social justice in the schooling of the nation were combated by the conservative elements. In regard to cultural and social matters, the upper classes always received strong support from large groups of the middle strata of the population and from the associations of secondary-school teachers. For these, like all organizations without organic vitality of ideas, specialized on self-defense. They were afraid of losing prestige by being too closely connected with the less well-paid and less esteemed elementary-school teachers. At the same time the representatives of the secondary schools fought the men who, in view of the obsoleteness of the old teachers' seminaries (normal schools), insisted that they graduate from a full-fledged secondary school and attend pedagogical academies or special university departments for their professional training.[32]

All the hopes toward further educational reform were shattered by the victory of Hitlerism. There is no need to describe here in detail the various measures by which that regime tried to use the schools for planting itself in the minds of youth. Indoctrination, in the sense of the systematic transmission of the values held in esteem by the older to the younger generation, is a common and necessary practice. Otherwise cultural continuity would be impossible. Yet, there is a decisive difference between this practice in democracies and totalitarian systems. First, indoctrination that is truly democratic aims at enhancing the dignity and freedom of the individual within a framework of values believed to be conducive of this end. Totalitarian indoctrination, on the other hand, aims at securing the vassalage of man under a tyrannically construed set of regulations. Second, since such regulated beliefs do not grow organically from the people's tradition, they cannot be taught in a natural dialogue between teacher and pupil but have to be imposed upon both, either by promise of enticing reward, or by threat of severe punishment. Under such a system special schools for the youth of the party and for future "leaders" are established which as far as possible keep the pupils away from parents and from discussions of universal interest. Such schools will use at the same time education by fear and menace as well as education by persuasion, methods

[32] For a detailed description of the educational policy of the Weimer Republic, see Robert Ulich, "Germany," in *Educational Yearbook* of the International Institute of Teachers' Colleges (Columbia University, 1936).

we might call reactionary as well as methods we might call progressive; and the arts and impressive pageantry will be mixed with military drill. All that it finally amounts to is "conditioning," not education.

Reorganization

When Germany was defeated, the educational system had to be reorganized from scratch, materially and mentally. Schools were either nonexistent or in complete chaos. Many of the buildings were destroyed; there was no equipment — even pencil and paper were lacking; the children were bewildered and hungry; of the sixteen universities, eight technological schools, and eight scientific higher schools now within the area of the Federal Republic and West Berlin, only six could operate fully right after 1945, fourteen were 50 to 75 per cent demolished, and the rest were totally destroyed. In addition, hundreds of thousands of German families driven out of Poland, Czechoslovakia, and other countries had to be housed in half-destroyed towns and villages. Understandably, though unwisely, the occupying powers first excluded from the schools all teachers who belonged to the National Socialist teachers' organization, irrespective of whether they had joined it voluntarily or under threat of dismissal and persecution. Only after about three years of special trial and proof of political fitness, could a dismissed teacher be re-employed. In the meantime the victorious powers engaged in the so-called "re-education" of the German people; especially the United States sent a considerable number of men and women to the defeated country. Unfortunately, the large majority of them did not understand the enormous complexity of the situation, nor did they speak or read German. Naively, they sought to transfer American institutions right into German, and if possible, European soil. By their blundering they diminished the psychological effect of the generous material help extended by America to German schools and children.[33] If any lesson should have brought home the necessity for careful selection of competent men thoroughly acquainted with the problems of comparative and international education, it was

[33] William Ernest Hocking, *Experiment in Education: What We Can Learn from Teaching Germany* (Chicago: Regnery, 1954), and Erich Weninger, "Die Epoche der Umerziehung, 1945–1949," in *Zeitschrift für Pädagogik*, 1 (Weinheim: Beltz, 1959).

this one. However, not all was in vain. Some lasting friendships were formed, and the American libraries and America Houses built a strong link between the European and the American nations. Even the laughter and irritation about Senator Joseph McCarthy's delegates, who began to search for controversial or communist-infiltrated literature in American institutions, could not spoil the confidence that friendly officials had acquired in the meantime.

The progressive elements among the German teachers, so far as they had survived, hoped that the vacuum created by Hitler's downfall might offer the opportunity for a thorough reform of the German school system. But, though not communists like Langevin, their ideas nevertheless suffered the same defeat as his. When the occupying powers outside the Russian-dominated Eastern Zone — about which I will speak briefly later — recognized the difficulties in establishing a national school system from outside, they left the task to the German groups they trusted and apparently needed most, and these were, as after 1918, the generally conservative. Thus the school system that emerged slowly but steadily out of the ashes was more or less that of the pre-Hitler Weimar period. In almost all states the pupils entering the academic schools are separated after four years of elementary training, at the age of ten, from the about 80 per cent who complete the eight- or nine-year elementary school and then attend either a part-time or full-time vocational school up to the age of eighteen. The secondary schools are divided into (1) the old "Classical Gymnasium," (2) the "Modern Language Gymnasium" (*Realgymnasium*), which retains Latin, but omits Greek and emphasizes instead foreign languages, mathematics, and sciences, (3) the "Mathematics-Natural Science Gymnasium" (*Oberrealschule*), which requires two modern languages and special emphasis on science and mathematics, and (4) various forms of "Build-Up" schools (*Aufbauschulen*). These schools had been established after World War I with the purpose of giving children from towns or villages without an advanced school the opportunity to complete six years of elementary training at home and then to enter a secondary school. Thus the Germans hoped to abolish the injustice of geographical locations that forced parents to pay the generally high price of a private pension for their children to study in the next larger locality. During the past decades, however, there has been a considerable increase in private secondary schools with boarding establishments. These were little known in Germany up to the nineteenth century, with exception of some denominational institutions. But these private schools are also expensive.

The trend away from the old Greek-Latin classical education (with the appreciation of Latin, nevertheless, remaining) shows in the fact that the modern language Gymnasiums exceed the other secondary schools in number; the mathematics-natural science Gymnasiums come next, being two thirds of the first in number. However, the old classical Gymnasium will not be abolished. A goodly number of parents are still convinced that the introduction of the young into the great classical heritage is of irreplaceable value and that much of what the other schools offer can be learned later. They may well remember that the great scholars, whether mathematicians, scientists, or humanists, who in the nineteenth and the beginning of the twentieth centuries made the German universities internationally famous came from the old Gymnasium.

Fortunately, the educational ministries of the German states seem to be aware of the value of a school type that had already developed in the eighteenth century, but was neglected by Wilhelm von Humboldt's reform of secondary education and thenceforth had to struggle for recognition, namely, the *Realschule*. Like the other secondary schools, it branches off from the elementary schools after the first four years, but it leads only to the sixteenth year and prepares its pupils in a well-rounded nonvocational education for the medium-level careers in business, public administration, and technical work. It requires one foreign language, a good mastery of the mother tongue, and a certain proficiency in science and mathematics. Though graduating its students two years earlier than the American high school, its scholastic achievements are certainly on the same level as the college-preparatory divisions of the American institution. This is not said in order to recommend the *Realschule* for imitation in this country with its highly developed industrialization and its consequent lack of opportunities for apprenticeship. But it is said in order to emphasize how much more could be done with American youth if our high schools gave their intellectually equipped students a well-organized and consistent education.

Right from the beginning of German educational reconstruction, the religious issue was as hotly debated as during the Weimar period. The occupying powers ordered that the schools be reopened as interconfessional schools. Whereas the Protestant churches would, on the whole, not have been opposed to continuing this state of things after the establishment of the Federal Republic, the Catholic Church insisted on the division of elementary education according to denominations (Protestant and Catholic). There are certain exceptions, and, fortunately, in contrast to the period up to World War I, the teachers can no longer be compelled (except by indirect pressure) to give religious instruction, nor can unwilling parents be forced to send their children to religious classes. Fortunately, also, the secondary schools have remained nondenominational, as they had been for more than a hundred years; there the concept of liberal education has proved to be stronger than the division of children according to the creed of their parents. As all German public schools, secondary schools also include religious instruction according to confession, but the various classes are given within the same school. Catholic influence has greatly increased with the separation of the largely Protestant East from the Western part of Germany, or the German Federal Republic.

And this now leads to the internationally most dangerous factor in the development of postwar Germany.[34] Almost eighteen million Germans, of whom according to careful estimates not more than 5 per cent would vote for the Communist Party if they were free, live under the Soviet-supported puppet regime of the German Democratic Republic and have to send their children to schools about which, in spite of a democratic façade, they have nothing to say. There is a constant tendency for East Germans to escape to the West. "Between 1949 and 1955 alone, over 1.7 million Germans either emigrated or fled from the so-called DDR (Deutsche Demokratische Republik) to the Federal Republic." Between February 7 and 13 of 1959, a total of 2,375 refugees from the Soviet Zone of

[34] Helmut Arntz, *Facts about Germany* (Munich: Press and Information Office of the Federal German Government, 1957); see also P. S. Bodenman, *Education in the Soviet Zone of Germany*, Bulletin No. 26 (U. S. Department of Health, Education and Welfare, 1959).

occupation asked for asylum in the Federal Republic. The number of university students decreases constantly, and the shortage of physicians has become catastrophic.

Those who defend an equalitarian and collectivist point of view might welcome certain features in the educational structure of the Russian-occupied Zone. Covering, at least on paper, the years from six to sixteen or eighteen, it comprises a "Basic School" (*Grundschule*) with a three-year practical and a four-year academic branch. The latter is subdivided into a so-called "classical," a "modern language," and a "scientific" branch. From the fifth grade upwards, when instruction in special subjects begins, Russian is compulsory; from the ninth grade upwards, a second language is required (English, French, Latin, Polish, Czech); from the tenth grade upwards, Greek is added to Latin in the classical division; and from the eleventh grade, Latin is added in the modern language track. This means that the idea of the old classical Gymnasium, or of a thorough acquaintance with the classical languages, is totally abandoned because it can never be achieved with two years of Greek and two or three years of Latin. Instead, in order to press East Germany into the Russian orbit, the Slavic languages are emphasized. The training of elementary-school teachers, which in the Weimar Republic, except in Bavaria, had been raised to the level of higher education, has been reduced to the level of the old seminary, or normal school. Teachers for the intermediate level (grades five to nine) must attend a two-year pedagogical institute after completing a course at a secondary school, but they can also have been trained at a "workers and farmers academy" or at a night school. The teachers for the upper level (grades nine to twelve) receive their preparation, after secondary school, at a four-year pedagogical academy or a university.

Religious instruction, needless to say, is not given, but the religious bodies are permitted to introduce their children into the religious heritage by instruction outside the school.[35] Private schools, of course, are also forbidden.

[35] A useful, though no longer completely up-to-date, introduction into the school systems of the German Federal Republic and, to a degree, also into that of the Soviet Zone is available in *Education in Germany: An Introduction for Foreigners*, ed. Erich J. Hylla and Friedrich O. Kegel (Frankfurt-am-Main: Hochschule für Internationale Pädagogische Forschung, 1954).

From a theoretical vantage point one could argue that the educational system of East Germany represents an interesting experiment of the *Einheitsschule* (unified school) as recommended in
principle by socialist school reformers, such as Langevin, and as
planned also in Czechoslovakia. If conducted in a really educational
spirit, it could prove, or disprove, the contention that a thoroughly
executed single-track mass education, as exists nowhere else in
complete actuality, vitalizes a people's intellectual energy. We hear
that certain educational conferences in East Germany, visited also
by teachers from other Eastern countries and controlled by Russian educators, were stimulating, especially in regard to teaching
methods. But, as cannot be otherwise expected under totalitarian
control, the schools of the Soviet Zone are, as much as the German
schools under Hitler and perhaps even more, used for the propaga-
tion of the dominant ideology, without the slightest opportunity
for teachers and pupils to work together in the spirit of free discussion. The value of truth is expressly denied as an outmoded bourgeois concept, and the history of Germany, Europe, and the whole
world is completely distorted; for years the children of professional
and otherwise socially preferred families have been prevented from
higher studies and even from the upper grades of secondary schools.
Ostensibly shown loyalty to the Communist Party and to Russia is
one of the main roads to success. And the universities, rather than
opening the possibility of free investigation, are under perhaps even
sharper and more cruel control than the other schools — inevitably
so because the student's inquisitiveness and critical sense are more
difficult to tame or to deflect than is the curiosity of children.
Consequently, persecutions of teachers who wish to save the last
remnants of academic freedom are frequent. Even professors who,
first exiled by Hitler, have voluntarily returned because of Marxist
sympathies are now accused of disseminating counterrevolutionary
opinions among their disciples and are forced to try to flee to the
Federal Republic. Students who in assemblies dare ask inopportune
questions are sent to prison or disappear. Spies are everywhere.
Apparently no stone remains unturned in the effort either to make
the area ready for resigned submission under an alien tyranny, or,
since this never works completely, to create in the center of

Europe an atmosphere of boiling bitterness and revolutionary wrath.[36]

On July 29, 1957, the three major Western powers (Britain, France, and the United States) together with West Germany issued a solemn declaration demanding the reunification of Germany. It began with the following words:

> Twelve years have elapsed since the end of the war in Europe. The hopes of the peoples of the world for the establishment of a basis for a just and lasting peace have nevertheless not been fulfilled. One of the basic reasons for the failure to reach a settlement is the continued division of Germany, which is a grave injustice to the German people and the major source of international tension in Europe.

In the atmosphere of distrust in which nations of today live, many negotiations on the whole broad front of international problems will be necessary before the demands of this declaration will become a reality. In the meantime an unusual combination of discipline, courage, and resistance will be required from the German people. For without these qualities either communism will throw its net wider and wider over Europe, or, as in Hungary, open conflicts will break out. And in the case of Germany it will be almost impossible to isolate them from the rest of the world. The present struggle over West Berlin will be the test of the political wisdom of our modern world.

CONCLUDING REMARKS

Whatever may be the causes of this attitude — climatic, political, educational — the Germans like to work. Without it they become desperate. Hitler throve on unemployment. After the stabilization of the currency in 1948 it was easy for German industry to find orders. Cities were destroyed, property was lost, communication was disrupted, and there was American credit on which to build new plants and buy new machines. Yet, the amazing recovery would be inexplicable without German energy, which, if given the right chances, will be the most potent factor in demo-

[36] The West German Association of German Students (*Verband Deutscher Studentenschaften*) publishes in its *Hochschul-Informationen*, partly in English translation under the title, "University News," the documents and events concerning the universities in the Soviet Zone. They show the unsuccessful attempts of the East German Government to coerce the universities under its control through constantly changing and increasingly unacademic regulations.

cratic self-redirection. From the unskilled worker to the leading engineer, from the students on the elementary level up to the university, there is willingness and effort. In addition, work prevents the older generation from thinking about a horrible past and from becoming cynical. For who, when looking back over the decades since World War I, would not be tempted? Broken lives, broken oaths, misused and misdirected love and faith, and heroism turned into destruction — all this is not easily forgotten.

Here now lies the frightening responsibility of education, not only in Germany, but in all Western countries, for they also, though in different degrees, have felt the impact of eruptive forces on the old order. Yet, more than others with the exception of Russia, Germany saw its whole tradition in extreme jeopardy. The violence of a Hitler would not have succeeded if the social body had still been healthy. And, despite many prayers, many lonely fighters, innumerable silent sacrifices for the sake of truth and decency, and some officers' plots toward the end of the war, national socialism was not destroyed from within; it fell in battle.

Will the old tradition of Christianity, of idealism, humanism, and of selfless devotion now emerge with sufficient new vigor to fill the gap? The physical task of reconstruction, a new prosperity, and work alone do not provide a really humane culture. It needs a deeper foundation. Nor will scientific research and scholarship, in which Germany again begins to excel despite the destruction of so many of its universities,[37] provide alone a sufficient basis for cultural rejuvenation, Metaphysics is required to change physics and inventions into human blessings and theoretical knowledge into moral commitment. The past has shown it.

No one can say whether and whence the new spirit will come. But certain conditions can be stated. No nation can and should live in a continual state of repentance. If that were the case, all nations would have to mourn in sackcloth and ashes. Only hypocrites can demand that from the new generations of a people. Nevertheless, there must be no superficial forgetting, but profound remembering. What happened after 1918 must not happen again, namely, that

[37] A useful survey of current research in Germany is provided by the journal, *Universitas. A German Review of the Arts and Sciences.* Quarterly English Language Edition (Stuttgart: Wissenschaftliche, Verlagsgesellschaft, since 1956). By 1957, 8000 foreigners were studying at German universities.

defeat is whitewashed with all kinds of subterfuges and reservations. And this time it is not only the defeat but all the horrors against the spirit of humanity that have occurred. They must be forgotten in the sense that they do not humiliate the souls of the innocent, but they must be remembered as a lesson to humanity, as a lesson that the unimaginable can come to pass if distorted minds are permitted to pervert the image of man, to soak human reason with the poison of muddled emotions, and to change patriotic sentiment into the fury of hatred.

Furthermore, neither will religious doctrine, as such, make man religious nor humanist instruction per se make him humane. Both can be barriers rather than vehicles to progress if they enclose the person's conscience into a mere crust of words; the bigger the words, the greater the danger. There were so-called good Christians who had read the Bible and gone to church, so-called humanists who had read Plato, Sophocles, Goethe, and Schiller, who nevertheless voted for Hitler. To avoid sterility, traditions must be purified of false ballast: religion must be freed of doctrines that can no longer be honestly believed, and humanism of elements that appear useless to modern man, even if he is not a utilitarian. There is no salvation except in ideas that enter into the formative center of the individual. Museums are good only if they are houses of mental recreation; otherwise they are cemeteries.

In comparison to this deepest problem of German, and all Western, education, changes in the external organization and structure of the school system may be important, but they are not decisive. The final success depends on the spirit that flows from the best of the nation into the institutions of learning and from them ordered and clarified back into the people at large. Several times during the past century the political and spiritual foundations of the German nation have been shaken. But, even despite a Hitler, the inner core seems to have been less affected than it seemed during the tyrannical thirties and forties. As cannot be expected otherwise, strong contrasts reveal themselves.

Unfortunately, some are now inclined to consider national socialism merely an episode, a bad interruption of a once great tradition. This is understandable, but unproductive and superficial, for like a person a nation can little allow lacunae in its history. Others, like so many Frenchmen after the Revolution, indulge in a romantic convert spirit and condemn the rational heritage of the Enlightenment, not realizing that it was not reason, but unreason that brought the Nazis into power. Others, influenced by the "anxiety" concept of German existentialist philosophy, cannot turn their gaze from the tragical depth in human nature. All optimism and belief in the possibility of progress seems to them shallow. They are almost as suspicious of democracy as they are of communism because both, from their point of view, cater to the sentiments of the *Massenmensch* (the mass man). There is probably some truth in every skepticism (though the most easy truth), but it can lead to a comfortable retreat from the urgencies of political life. No nation can thrive on a dichotomy between inwardness and action, for when separated from each other the first becomes cowardly withdrawal, and the second loses the control of conscience.

On the other hand, there now appear an increasing number of books and journals attempting to anchor the German mind in a configuration of values that, without neglecting the good in the heritage of the past, also point at the tasks of the future, reminding the reader that courageous and rational trial is better than constant fear of failure. The monthly *Deutsche Jugend* (German Youth), which in its high quality is certainly not representative of every German young man and woman, nevertheless indicates the emergence of that faithful realism that has always been the surest guarantee of constructive action.[38]

Also, the unrealistic spirit of stability at any price which has settled over German school politics is now being challenged. Together with some modernizations of the curriculum certain structural modifications have been made. In place of the former perpendicular dualistic system (elementary and vocational schools, on the one side, and elementary and secondary schools, on the other), a system of three tiers, or horizontal layers, has been established. One can now distinguish between a primary level, a middle school with beginning differentiation in structure and content, and a higher secondary level with marked differentiation.[39] Some writers point at the reforms of England and at the fact that even in France the plans of Langevin and Billères have, at least in part, been taken up

---

[38] Munich, *Juventa Verlag* (since 1953).

[39] See Franz Hilker, "Die Pädagogische Situation in der Bundesrepublik Deutschland," in *International Review of Education* IV, no. 3 (1958).

by de Gaulle's cabinet. Might it not be imperative that Germany also ask itself whether its present school system, built in principle during the nineteenth century, is still adequate in view of the social changes that have taken place during the past decades?[40]

The result of this restlessness has been a Reform Plan, published in 1959 by a nongovernmental agency, the German Committee on the Reform of Education.[41] The authors are mainly concerned with the restructuring of the, from their point of view, still-antiquated German school system, but they are fully aware that there can be no meaningful debate of this intricate topic without a thorough consideration of the aims and the program of studies to be pursued by the various schools attended by students with different aims, different talents, and different social backgrounds. Rightly the plan points at the following defects:

1. A deplorable lack of articulation and integration of the various school types.
2. The neglect of the elementary school (which in the nineteenth century was the pride of Germany), especially of the upper grades; and the lack of coordination between it and the more advanced schools, on which the pupils, except in a very small number of cities, have still to decide at the premature age of ten (after four years of schooling) in contrast to age eleven or twelve in other countries.
3. The neglect of opportunities for the education of students who aim at a somewhat advanced position in practical life without prior university studies.
4. The inadequacy of the programs of study in the schools preparing for higher education (Gymnasia).

At the present state the Gymnasia are both too difficult and too easy. They are too difficult in that, of the pupils who enter the first grade at the age of ten (c. 20–25 per cent of the school population), only 30 per cent graduate, which is an inadequate number in light of the increased demand for well-trained men in modern pro-

[40] See especially Helmut Becker, *Kulturpolitik und Schule* and *Bildung zwischen Plan und Freiheit*, and other publications in the series *Fragen an die Zeit*, ed. von Theodor Eschenburg (Stuttgart: Deutsche Verlagsanstalt).

[41] *Rahmenplan zur Umgestaltung und Vereinheitlichung des allgemeinbildenden öffentlichen Schulwesens* (Stuttgart: Ernst Klett, 1959). For a longer description of the *Rahmenplan*, see Ursula Kirkpatrick, "The *Rahmenplan* for West German School Reform," *Comparative Education Review*, June 1960.

fessional life. At the same time the increased number of students (around 1900 not more than *c.* 3 per cent of the school population attended) does not allow the Gymnasia to keep the standards of earlier times. Therefore the plan recommends beside the Gymnasia — which, in contrast to the present structure, would begin after six, not four, years of elementary training and would be divided into a seven-year "natural science" and seven-year "modern language" branch — a highly selective and demanding secondary school for especially gifted pupils (*Studienschule*). This school, beginning at the age of ten, would be dedicated to the older European classical tradition, with Latin, Greek, and mathematics emphasized in one branch, and French, instead of Greek, emphasized in another.

The Reform Plan is as comprehensive in scope as a report intended to arouse general interest can be. It is courageous in that it tries to organize the German school system according to the social and intellectual changes that have occurred during the past century. And, in suggesting the *Studienschule*, it respects the classical tradition of European thought, though recognizing that the ancient languages can no longer demand the place they occupied in earlier times. The plan also retains the number of thirteen years as necessary in the preparation for higher studies, whereas most other countries require only twelve years.

In view of the mentality of the old associations of the German secondary-school teachers and the conservative social powers behind them, there can be no doubt as to a thorough resistance especially against two features of the plan: first, the prolonged attendance of the obligatory common school from four to six years, even for young candidates to the Gymnasia, and, consequently, the reduction of the latter from nine to seven years; second, the separation of the *Studienschule* as a higher type of academic institution (nine years, ages ten to nineteen) from the Gymnasia. Men will argue that both measures will lead to a further lowering of the standards of the Gymnasia, and, since they prepare for the university, eventually also of the standards of higher education. But, whatever the outcome, the new German Committee on the Reform of Education has filled the gap caused by the inertia of Germany's academic population in regard to a democratic reorganization of the schools. No one can predict today whither victory will lean, whether to the progressive or the resisting forces. In either case, Germany has now joined the development that the student of comparative education can discern in all progressive nations, namely, the gradual replacement of a school organization based on an older class-dominated society by a structure that tries to combine social justice, differentiation, and selectiveness.

But all endeavors on the higher levels, including the again-flowering adult education, can do little without the cooperation of the teachers. They have to rewrite the history textbooks; this is a work not of mere compilation, but of re-examination and reorientation of the nation's traditional values. Apparently, much has been done in this respect.[42] Yet, still more influential than lessons in history and the social sciences will be the social and political attitude of the German teachers themselves. On them will depend to a large degree whether the old divisions in the German people remain open, or whether that kind of inner unity will be created which alone makes it possible for a nation to contribute its full share to the work of humanity.

Germany's situation "in the center," of which Nietzsche spoke, is not merely a geographical fact. It contains the challenge to use this situation for a meeting of the minds of Europe and the world, in spite of all the differences of political and spiritual systems. The cataclysm that overcame Germany during the period of tyranny and murder may then be turned into one of those lessons through which mankind, while recognizing the abysses into which it may be driven, also discovers its powers of construction and reconstruction. One fact is certain: if the community of Western civilization loses its contact with Germany, whose regions are nearest to and partly within the Russian-dominated realm, the fate of Europe will be sealed.

[42] The following publications are of special note: *Internationales Jahrbuch für Geschichtswissenschaft* (Braunschweig: Albert Limbach, beg. 1951). Publishes important essays on the international problems of history. *Deutschland und Frankreich im Spiegel ihrer Schulbücher*, ed. Internationales Schulbuchinstitut an der Kant-Hochschule Braunschweig (Braunschweig: Albert Limbach, 1954); Ernst Weymar, *Die neuere Geschichte in den Schulbüchern Europäischer Länder* (Braunschweig: Albert Limbach, 1956); *Deutsch-Französische Vereinbarungen über strittige Fragen Europäischer Geschichte.* Neudruck (Braunschweig: Albert Limbach, 1958); Otto Ernst Schüddekopf, *Die Internationale Schulbucharbeit* (Braunschweig: Albert Limbach, 1956); *Deutschland und England 1918–1933.* Empfehlungen zur Behandlung der English-Deutschen Beziehungen in der Zwischenkriegszeit. (Braunschweig: Albert Limbach, 1957).

VIII

The United States of America

T HE United States has often been called the country of immigrants. This explains the fact that there is no sovereign country belonging to Western civilization that, seen from one point of view, has been so dependent on influences from abroad as the United States, but that, seen from another point of view, has produced so indigenous a political and educational system.

To speak of the influences first: Massachusetts or the Bay Colony, the most educationally minded of the early provinces, developed its school system on the Protestant conviction that every Christian should live in an immediate and personal relation with his Lord. Consequently, he should not remain ignorant of God's plan concerning the nature and purpose of man. Rather, he should have access to God's word, contained in the Bible, without a hierarchy of priests standing between him and divine grace. This, of course, as in Protestant Germany, involved the creation of a broad elementary school system, for in order to escape eternal damnation people had to be able to read. The Massachusetts Law of 1647 ordered that every township of fifty or more householders should appoint a person "to teach all such children as shall resort to him to write and read" and that every town of more than one hundred householders should set up a grammar school in order to fit youth for the university.

In addition, just as Calvin in Geneva insisted on a close relationship between church and state, so also colonial Massachusetts developed during the seventeenth century a kind of theocratic system, with the community of the saints or the elect forming at the same time the church and the body politic. This was no democracy in the modern sense of the word, nor did the Puritans differ from any other Christians of the time in their assurance that they alone knew what the Lord had meant with the creation. Yet, through the common deliberation in the town meetings and through the early legislation on a public tax-supported school system, Massachusetts prepared the ground for later democratic developments — just as little intended by the founding fathers as European democratic development by Luther and Calvin.

As a matter of fact, the Virginia Colony, the founders of which had settled at Jamestown in 1607, thirteen years before the Mayflower landed at Plymouth and twenty-three years before the Arabella arrived at Boston, has a much truer claim to being the cornerstone of American liberty than the Puritan settlements. Unlike the North, Virginia granted religious freedom to members of all faiths who would take the oath of allegiance to the British crown (though Sir William Berkeley, Governor after 1642, persecuted the Puritan minority). Virginia had a charter that granted representative government, and except for some few critical years (1611–1616) it had trial by jury. But Virginia was largely Anglican and therefore less interested in the education of the common man than were the Puritans; it soon had a plantation and slave system with wide geographical distances between the inhabitants. The wealthy families preferred small private schools with tuition, or the tutor, according to the advice given by John Locke in his *Thoughts Concerning Education*. Some of them sent their sons to England for a gentleman's education. Only at a few places did parish schools provide a degree of literacy for the poor.

Without much difficulty the more privileged part of the population of early Virginia could have resettled in monarchical England, whereas the Puritans would have been a dangerously alien element. Even for Cromwell, with a nation behind him that felt the first lure of world power, the concept of a commonwealth as developed by his Puritan brethren of New England would have been too stiff, too moralistic, too antiquated.

Yet, in order to survive mentally and physically in the wilderness, the Puritans needed the same sense of being chosen or elect that helped the Jews to survive under the persecution of ancient and modern nations. As a matter of fact, for few Christian sects was the Old Testament with its idea of a covenant between Jehovah and his people so much of a reality as for the New England Calvinists.

There was still another element of cultural strength in the Puritans. Like Milton, they lived not only in and with the Bible, but also in and with the heritage of Greece and Rome. Hence their emphasis not only on a broad elementary school system of Christian character, but also on a classical training for the prospective leaders of their society. Boston Latin School was established in 1635, and Henry Dunster, the first president of Harvard, formulated in 1642 the following entrance requirements.

> When any Schollar is able to understand Tully, or such like classicall Latine Author extempore, and make and speake true Latine in Verse and Prose, *suo ut aiunt Marte*; And decline perfectly the Paradigm's of Nounes and Verbes in the Greek tongue: Let him then and not before be capable of admission into the Colledge.[1]

If, then, religion and the classics were the pillars of education, science was by no means foreign or suspect to the Puritans. Rather than being afraid of its mechanistic implications, they considered its discoveries new revelations of God's grandeur. The fact that at the same time they would have witches was not unique with them. There were many men in the sixteenth and seventeenth centuries, among them the great French political philosopher Bodin, who combined a high degree of rationality with the crudest belief in magic.

We do not know exactly to what degree the rather impressive school laws of early New England (1642, 1647, 1650) really brought all children into schools. To conclude from the number

---

[1] *New England's First Fruits* (London, 1643). Fully reprinted in Samuel Eliot Morison, *The Founding of Harvard College* (Cambridge: Harvard University Press, 1935), pp. 419f and especially p. 433.

of later injunctions, many of the pioneer families believed more in the training of youth through family life and hard work than through schoolmasters. The quality of these decreased, moreover, after 1700, when the Puritan hierarchy had to yield to a more worldly government.

The old Latin grammar school was the pattern for secondary education all over the American colonies. It continued a classical tradition that, as the letters of Jefferson and the Adamses show, still produced in sensitive minds a grand style of writing, thinking, and living. Nevertheless, just as in other countries, it became increasingly pedantic and remote from the interests of the majority of even the more privileged youth. Thus, after 1700, private schools were opened which catered to the interests of trade and commerce by teaching not only the traditional subjects but also navigation, applied mathematics, surveying, and other topics of interest to the emerging class of merchants. And in 1749 Benjamin Franklin wrote his *Proposals Relating to the Education of Youth in Pennsylvania*, in which he recommended two main innovations: one, emphasis on English and modern foreign laguages (French, German, and Spanish); the other, emphasis on mathematics and "natural and mechanic philosophy." Thus, besides a Latin department, his proposed "Academy" was to contain an "English" and a "Mathematical School." The methods of instruction should lead the student to scientific experimentation, observation, and application.

> While they are reading natural history, might not a little *Gardening, Planting, Grafting, Inoculating*, etc. be taught and practised; and now and then excursions made to the neighboring plantations of the best farmers, their methods observed and reasoned upon for the information of youth? The improvement of agriculture being useful to all, and skill in it no disparagement to any.[2]

Though Franklin's idea of a more utilitarian education preceded the spirit of the time because of, to use his own words, mankind's "un-

[2] *Benjamin Franklin: Representative Selections*, ed. F. L. Mott and C. E. Jorgenson (New York: American Book Co., 1936), pp. 205–206. See also *Writings of Benjamin Franklin*, ed. A. H. Smyth (New York: Macmillan, 1905–1907), II, 395; Robert Ulich, *History of Educational Thought* (New York: American Book Co., 1945), pp. 225–241; Ulich, *Three Thousand Years of Educational Wisdom*, pp. 426–462.

accountable Prejudice in favour of ancient Customs and Habitudes,"[3] it nevertheless prophesied a new era. Between 1759, the year when Franklin's Academy opened in Philadelphia, and 1850, academies, all fashioned according to a variety of practical purposes, increased to more than six thousand in number.[4]

Franklin's life and thought themselves are the best source for discovering the new spirit that permeated the colonies during the era of the Enlightenment. Religiously, what a difference from the diaries, sermons, and the pedagogy of the Mathers of the seventeenth century! Throughout the original states during Franklin's life the old religious "establishments" began to be shaken, partly because the population became more and more heterogeneous, partly because widening contacts with different cultures undermined dogmatic assumptions held absolute so far, and partly because the ideas of natural law and freedom of conscience — both so important for the understanding of the American Constitution — required tolerance and respect for the serious opinions of one's fellow man.[5]

In Franklin's and his friends' minds, all influenced by Locke, Hume, and the French *philosophes*, there no longer live the ideas of original sin, of total depravity, of predestination, and of the unquestionable authority of the Scripture, but a courageously illogical mixture between a somewhat mechanical deism and the conviction that the Lord will personally look upon those who first of all try to help themselves. A moral life is more important than theological and metaphysical speculations concerning an ultimate world about which we know little anyhow. But God, or Nature, or "Nature's God," gave us the wonderful gift of reason, of observation and experiment. Yet, there is no arrogant scientism in Franklin's mind. In a letter to Peter Collinson of the year 1747 he writes: "If there is no other Use discover'd of Electricity this however is something considerable, that it may *help to make a vain man* humble."[6] Franklin possesses a wise and earthy humor, but he refrains from the

[3] *Writings*, X, 30.
[4] See J. D. B. De Bow, *Statistical View of the United States . . . Being a Compendium of the Seventh Census* (Washington, D. C.: B. Tucker, 1954).
[5] See R. Freeman Butts, *The American Tradition in Religion and Education* (Boston: Beacon Press, 1950).
[6] *Representative Selections*, p. 194; *Writings*, II, 325.

cynicism of a Voltaire. Rather he is Newtonian in his respectful attitude toward the laws that the divine Creator has planted into the universe, and, to a degree, in the soul of every human being.

There is much difference between Franklin and the other great statesman and educational figure of the Revolutionary period, Thomas Jefferson.[7] The first is the self-made man, looking for the useful and the moral in things and people, an astute and successful businessman, systematic in behavior and in thought (which made him one of the fine scientists of the age), the best exemplar of the new Northern middle class. The other, a landowner without real interest in the rising business class, enchanted by "the precious remains of antiquity" (not only in architecture, but also in thought), by the beauty of men, buildings, sculptures, and gardens, a potential architectural and scientific genius who nevertheless preferred accomplished amateurship to specialization, interested in increasing his plantation, but spending money easily, is the true example of the old aristocrat from the South.

Yet, there is also much similarity in the two. Mysticism, even of the great type, is foreign to them. They hate dogmatism in matters of faith, as they hate tyranny in matters of state. Their religion, though an essential part of their personalities, is unsentimental. Jesus represents one of the revelations of divine wisdom, but they refuse to argue about his being the Son of God. Locke, Hume, and Newton are much nearer to them than Plato; Jefferson writes to Benjamin Rush on April 21, 1803: "I name not Plato, who only used the name of Socrates to cover the whimsies of his own brain."[8] Rousseau had no influence on either of them; he was for them too romantic. Both loved books. Jefferson had a library of six thousand volumes. But for both ideas were only as good as they proved themselves in action. On the other hand, fact and action were only as good as they appeared before the tribunal of reason. Both were willing to sacrifice their personal existences for the freedom of their country, but both were also sufficiently familiar with the human

[7] See Ulich, *History of Educational Thought*, pp. 242–257, and *Three Thousand Years of Educational Wisdom*, pp. 463–479. For a selection of Jefferson's educational writings, see *Thomas Jefferson and Education in a Republic*, ed. Charles F. Arrowood (New York: McGraw-Hill, 1930).

[8] *The Writing of Thomas Jefferson*, Definitive Edition, ed. A. E. Bergh (Washington, D. C.: Thomas Jefferson Memorial Association, 1907), X, 383.

race to know that in the hands of unworthy and uninformed men freedom will soon be lost, turning either into chaos or into tyranny.

Hence, just as we can observe in the newly emerging nations of today, so also in the new United States the minds of the great statesmen turned to education as the best protector of the republic. Washington said in his Farewell Address of 1796:

> Promote then, as an object of primary importance, institutions for the general diffusion of knowledge. — In proportion as the structure of a government gives force to public opinion it is essential that public opinion should be enlightened.[9]

And Jefferson wrote in his beautifully terse prose:

> It is an axiom in my mind that our liberty can never be safe but in the hands of the people themselves, and that, too, of the people with a certain degree of instruction.[10]

Whereas Franklin's interest in education begins before the middle of the eighteenth century, Jefferson's writings on the same great national issue coincide with the fight for, and the initial struggles of, the new republic for its existence.[11] It is characteristic of Jefferson's whole personality that his "Bill for the More General Diffusion of Knowledge" of 1779 builds, on a broad and democratic foundation of elementary schools for all, a selective system of advanced grammar schools and of higher education. The selection becomes more stringent the higher up the publicly supported student (for stipends will be necessary if he comes from poor parents) intends to climb on the educational ladder.

Jefferson's bill was finally passed by the Virginia Assembly in 1796, though in effect defeated through amendments that gave the power into the hands of the individual communities. Like Franklin's "English School," Jefferson's scheme was ahead of its time. It has been called aristocratic in the sense of being against the spirit of democracy. This is correct if democracy is mistaken for equalitarian mediocrity, but many of us will believe with Jefferson

---

[9] *Washington's Farewell Address* . . . ed. Charles R. Gaston (Boston: Ginn & Co., 1906), p. 12.

[10] Letter to Washington, January 4, 1786, in *Writings*, XIX, 24.

[11] "Bill for Establishing Religious Freedom," 1779; "Bill for the More General Diffusion of Knowledge," 1779; "Bill for Establishing a System of Public Education," 1817.

that democracy particularly needs high and rare quality to avoid the cult of the mass man. Rightly he says in a letter to John Adams of October 28, 1813:

For I agree with you that there is a natural aristocracy among men. The grounds for this are virtue and talents . . . The natural aristocracy I consider as the most precious gift of nature, for the instruction, the trusts, and government of society . . . May we not even say that that form of government is the best, which provides the most effectually for a pure selection of these natural aristoi into the offices of government? [12]

Franklin, who died twenty-three years before this letter was written, would have agreed with it. The only difference between him and Jefferson might have been that Jefferson considered classical studies, and among them Latin more than Greek, the cornerstone of Western civilization. "It would be very ill-judged in us," so he said in the *Notes on Virginia*, if we followed the examples of Europe where "the learning of Greek and Latin, I am told, is going into disuse." [13] No diploma, from his point of view, should be given to a graduate of the University of Virginia

who has not passed such an examination in the Latin language as shall have proved him able to read the highest classics in that language with ease, thorough understanding and just quantity; and if he be also as proficient in the Greek, let that too be stated in his diploma. The intention being that the reputation of the University shall not be committed but to those who, to an eminence in some one or more of the sciences taught in it, add a proficiency in these languages which constitute the basis of good education, and are indispensable to fill up the character of a "well-educated man." [14]

But even here Franklin might have agreed with Jefferson, for he protested only against the monopoly claimed by the ancient languages in advanced education, not against the languages as such. And Jefferson himself wrote in a letter to John Brazier of August 24, 1819:

For the merchant I should not say that the languages are a necessary. Ethics, mathematics, geography, political economy, history, seem to constitute the immediate foundations of his calling. The agriculturist needs ethics,

[12] *Writings*, XIII, 396.   [13] *Ibid.*, II, 205.
[14] From the Minutes of the Board of Visitors of the University of Virginia, October 4, 1824, in *Writings*, XIX, 444. See also Jefferson's letter to John Brazier of August 24, 1819, in *Writings*, XV, 207–211.

mathematics, chemistry and natural philosophy. The mechanic the same. To them the languages are but ornament and comfort . . .[15]

And both would have buried their differences under the supreme principle of education stated by Franklin when he said:

With the whole [process of instruction] should be constantly inculcated and cultivated, that *benignity of mind*, which shows itself in *searching* for and *seizing* every opportunity to *serve* and to *oblige*; and it is the foundation of what is called GOOD BREEDING; highly useful to the possessor, and most agreeable to all.[16]

In view of the enormous changes the United States and its schools have undergone during the nineteenth and twentieth centuries, is it still even worth while to recall the memory of a Franklin and Jefferson? The answer is "yes," and for the following reasons.

First, both men are not merely historical figures who have done their work in helping to give the American people its political independence and Constitution and in reminding them of the educational foundation of democracy. Today Franklin is still the symbol by which to illustrate certain features of the American character: it is utilitarian, not in an egotistic sense of the word, but willing to sacrifice personal interest for the usefulness of the whole. There is no country where a rich man would be so criticized for keeping all his earnings for himself as the United States. A great number of universities, schools, museums, hospitals, as well as the whole religious life of the communities, are supported by voluntary gifts. It would be advantageous for international understanding if the many critics of "American materialism" in other countries knew of this situation and imitated it. Franklin is also characteristically American, or, as one could say, the American is also characteristically Franklinian, in his desire for action, for trial and experimentation, and in his belief in the possibility of progress, provided men behave rationally. Many Americans, as perhaps Anglo-Saxons in general, resemble Franklin also in their distrust of absolutes and in their willingness to compromise in matters philosophical. The logic of a good and successful life, individually as well as communally, may not always be the same as the logic of the thinker; yet both may be right. The pragmatic

[15] *Writings*, XV, 211. [16] *Ibid.*, II, 396; *Representative Selections*, p. 206.

humanism of William James and John Dewey has its origin in the thought of such men as Benjamin Franklin.

Difficult though this may be for the Continental European to understand, this pragmatic attitude, with all its shades over into relativism, is by no means unprincipled. It represents a form of faithful idealism. It rests essentially on the eighteenth century's concept of natural law, which, if traced back to its origin, appears to be rooted in both the Greco-Roman and the Christian interpretations of the rights of man. The Declaration of Independence, after referring to the "Laws of Nature and of Nature's God" contains the following sentence:

> We hold these truths to be self-evident, that all men are created equal, that they are endowed by their Creator with certain inalienable Rights, that among these are Life, Liberty, and the Pursuit of Happiness.

It is the peculiar fortune of the American nation, one which penetrates its political consciousness more than any verbal schooling could do, that, though blessed with great leaders in the period of the Revolution, it considers its birth, its Constitution, and its government as the work and expression of the whole people. What a difference from the life of nations whose forms of government carry with them the memory of warring monarchs, of defeat, of the imposition of a ruling caste, or even of conquest by a foreign power!

Besides Franklin and Jefferson, it is Lincoln to whom the American citizen of some intellectual standard feels admiringly related. To the people of Sangamon County Lincoln said:

> Upon the subject of education, I can only say that I view it as the most important subject which we as a people can be engaged in . . . For my part, I desire to see the time when education, and by its means, morality, sobriety, enterprise and industry, shall become much more general than at present, and I should be gratified to have it in my power to contribute something to the advancement of any measure which might have a tendency to accelerate the wider education of our people.[17]

There may be differences of opinion whether George Washington, the great general and statesman, plays as great a role in the hearts

[17] Abraham Lincoln, "Address to the People of Sangamon County, March 9, 1832," *Complete Works*, ed. J. D. Nicolay and John Hay (New York: Francis D. Tandy Co., 1905), V, 7.

of the nation as the men just mentioned, despite his prominent role in the textbooks and the stories for children. Somehow he lacks the popular common sense of Franklin, the intellectual charm of Jefferson, and the mixture of deep humaneness and religious transcendence that radiates from the life and face of Lincoln. Take these three, or, if you want, include Washington, as the fourth, and you have the ideal of the good American, his real and great educators. They have provided the ethical foundation without which America would hardly have been able to maintain its moral and national identity.

Though in the following section I will relate the growth of the American school system to the increase of the population and to the change from an agrarian to an industrial society, it would be wrong to overemphasize these material factors. Unless a nation's vitality is gone, it creates ever-new situations and responds elastically to them. In the middle of the nineteenth century America was no longer the country of the Puritans (which it never had been entirely); nevertheless, the high aspirations remained. Often without the loss of religious zeal, indeed, still Christian in a sense, Americans engaged in all kinds of humanitarian movements, from prison reforms to lyceums, from antislavery societies to back-to-nature appeals. In essence, they tried to find out how much of the promised supernatural millennium could be realized within the realm of nature. From the Constitution to Franklin D. Roosevelt's New Deal, the transcendental and the secular always joined hands in the struggle for man's freedom, however differently understood. Inevitably, the schools and the training of teachers had to be included.

THE SCHOOL SYSTEM IN A GROWING NATION

So much happened in the U.S.A. between the formative years of the republic and the two world wars that it might have been too severe a challenge for the integrating power of any other nation. Whereas in 1790, the year of Benjamin Franklin's death, the population was almost entirely rural, today only about 30 per cent live on the soil. Even they work under mechanized conditions that set them farther off from a Jeffersonian landowner than the latter is from a Roman farmer or a man who today plows his fields in the valleys of the Himalayas. The nation has expanded from the thirteen original states to the fifty states reaching from the Atlantic to the Pacific; it has increased from about four million in 1790 to about one hundred and fifty million in 1950.[18]

After the middle of the nineteenth century waves of population rolled toward the Middle West and the West. In 1840 Chicago had forty-five hundred inhabitants; in 1880 it had half a milion; in 1890, a million. Some cities almost doubled their population every year. The railroad mileage was 23 in 1830, 2,818 in 1840, and 30,626 in 1860. In 1869 one could travel on rails from the East to San Francisco.

This process of opening up a continent was accompanied by a second factor, which probably more than anything else changed the character of the American population and its school system, namely, foreign immigration. Until 1830 immigration did not add significantly to the growth of the population. But in the decade between 1841 and 1850 the total immigration rose to 1,597,604 as compared with 495,736 during the preceding decade, the increase being largely due to the famine in Ireland and the political unrest in Germany.

In 1930 slightly less than one fourth of the entire population was foreign-born or native inhabitants with one or both parents foreign-born. In 1790, the year of the first official census, 90 per cent of the white population was of British (including Scotch and Irish) stock; the Germans were near 6 per cent.[19] The number, however, may not be correct, since many immigrants, especially Germans, had adopted Anglicized names. In 1850 the Irish formed nearly half the foreign-born. In 1900 the northwestern Europeans, with Irish included, represented only 66.4 per cent, and after 1880 Italians, Russians, Poles, Austrians, Bohemians (the latter two mostly of the Slavic part of the population), and Hungarians entered in ever-greater numbers. From 141,132, in 1919, immigration increased to 805,228, in 1921.[20] There was no free land and

[18] Clifford L. and Elizabeth H. Lord, *Historical Atlas of the United States*, rev. ed. (New York: Henry Holt, 1953), pp. 198–199.

[19] U. S. Bureau of the Census. *A Century of Population Growth* (Washington, D. C.: Government Printing Office, 1909), p. 117.

[20] U. S. Immigration and Naturalization Service, *Annual Report*. Table I: "Immigration to the United States, 1820–1948."

no frontier so that many of the poorer immigrants were forced to crowd in the growing slums of the big cities. The ports of arrival were the larger cities, and some kind of living could more easily be secured there. The dispersion of foreigners to other parts of the country, therefore, was a slow process.[21] At the same time employment became increasingly difficult, even for returning veterans. Thus, after some initial legislation Congress passed the Act of 1924, which introduced a highly reduced quota system and which, because based on the population census of 1890, practically excluded all immigration from Asia and Africa.

The increase in population from other than Germanic stock changed the mentality of the nation. The United States of today is pluralistic and even full of contradictions in its spiritual structure. The optimist-rationalist strain of thought that comes from Franklin and Jefferson and, despite his profound transcendentalism, also from Lincoln, still remains. But one may ask whether it is still dominant among the educated.

According to the 1958 Yearbook of American Churches, published by the National Council of Churches, church and synagogue membership had risen to more than 103,250,000 in 1956. It has doubled during the past thirty years and is constantly rising, while the population has risen 40 per cent. At the present, sixty-two out of one hundred Americans of all ages are members of a church or a synagogue. The Protestants in their totality number more than 60,000,000; the Roman Catholics, more than 34,500,000 members.

Parallel with the stronger interest in religious institutions (which does not necessarily indicate a correspondingly genuine interest in religion) there can be found all kinds of mental patterns shading from indifference and agnosticism to the most multifarious modes of superstition. This variety of views exists in all modern countries, but there is probably none with such vital sectarianism as the United States.

Boston, once the citadel of the Puritans, is now, like New York, one of the foremost Catholic world centers. The Protestant churches of the United States taken together still embrace almost two thirds of registered Christians with an ever-fresh sectarianism

---

[21] William S. Rossiter, *Increase of Population in the United States 1910–1920* (Washington: Government Printing Office, 1922, Census Monographs No. 1).

constantly agitating the minds of religious seekers. In 1956, on one of the historical residential streets of Cambridge, a Mormon church was erected, directly across the street from a Quaker meeting house, and not far away from Harvard University, from the various old Protestant churches and theological schools, from a Christian Science church, and from the domicile of the Catholic Father Feeney, who was defrocked because of his dogmatic fanaticism. All over the country one finds Russian and Greek Orthodox churches, and in the city of Washington, D.C., a voice from the minaret of a mosque will admonish the faithful to observe the holy month of Ramadan.

All these changes in industry, population, and religious outlook went on in a country whose path toward prosperity was all but steady. The incorporation of new territory and the conquest of the West were not always accomplished by peaceful and morally dignified means; the Civil War from 1861–1865 was one of the most severe inner crises any modern nation has been able to survive. Perhaps the reconstruction immediately after this war left deeper wounds in the souls of the Southern citizens than the war itself. Finally, the participation in two world wars placed the nation in a position of international responsibility never dreamed of and even undesired in earlier times. Thus waves of liberalism and internationalism changed to waves of political phobia and isolationism, which, though going under the name of democracy, often revealed a frighteningly totalitarian spirit. The panics of 1837, 1873, 1893 and the stock-market crash of 1929, each with years of unemployment in its wake, brought the country close to financial ruin. And, as can hardly be astonishing with a people of such wild and gigantic growth, speculation and corruption undermined the nation's self-confidence and moral quality from time to time.

How did education — this is now the main question — adjust itself to these vicissitudes? During the 1830's it became increasingly clear to the socially minded that the prevailing educational system of elementary schools with incompetent teachers, the Latin schools in the larger cities, and the academies for the mostly nonprofessional middle class were inadequate to cope with the tasks of the growing nation. Americans looked for patterns from abroad and found them, especially in the German elementary, secondary, and higher schools. Many reports were written, and, deploring the state of teachers' education in his county, the Reverend Charles Brooks (1795–1872) began his public lectures on the Prussian system of normal schools in 1835. Two years later, Horace Mann, often called the father of American public education, took office as secretary of the newly established Massachusetts Board of Education. He found the common school system "degenerated in practice from the original theoretical view of the early Pilgrim Fathers" and criticized a generation that through

the opportunities unparalleled in the world's history, which the establishment of the Federal Union had opened to all classes of men to obtain wealth, had lost sight of the idea of having the rich and the poor educated together.[22]

Whatever the influences from other countries — and they increased during the nineteenth century, especially those from Germany in regard to higher education — the idea "of having the rich and the poor educated together" was in that time uniquely American. Despite rising discrepancies between the emerging social classes it was part and parcel of the creed that Franklin and Thomas Jefferson had bequeathed to a new republic, that "liberty can never be safe but in the hands of the people . . . with a certain degree of instruction."

At the end of his Twelfth Annual Report Horace Mann formulated his final credo of public education in its various religious, social, and moral aspects. He writes:

Such, then, in a religious point of view, is the Massachusetts system of Common Schools. Reverently, it recognizes and affirms the sovereign rights of the Creator; sedulously and sacredly it guards the religious rights of the creature; while it seeks to remove all hinderances, and to supply all furtherances to a filial and paternal communion between man and his Maker. In a social and political sense, it is a *Free*-school system. It knows no distinction of rich and poor, of bond and free, or between those who, in the imperfect light of this world, are seeking, through different avenues, to reach the

[22] Massachusetts Board of Education, *Reports 1838–1848.* 3 vols. (Boston, 1839–1849). Contains Reports 1 to 12 by Horace Mann. Robert Ulich, *A Sequence of Educational Influences* (Cambridge: Harvard University Press, 1935). See also *Reports on European Education by John Griscom, Victor Cousin, and Calvin E. Stowe,* ed. Edgar W. Knight (New York: McGraw-Hill, 1930).

gate of heaven. Without money and without price, it throws open its doors, and spreads the table of its bounty, for all the children of the State. Like the sun, it shines, not only upon the good, but upon the evil, that they may become good; and, like the rain, its blessings descend, not only upon the just, but upon the unjust, that their injustice may depart from them and be known no more.[23]

Beautiful and sincere as these words were, they differed shockingly from the real situation. In 1857, the year that the National Teachers Organization was organized in Philadelphia, two thirds of the teachers of Pennsylvania were under twenty-five years of age, two fifths had taught less than three years, two thirds were probably only temporarily appointed. The salaries over the whole country were barely on a living standard.[24]

Yet, the years of "degeneration" as Horace Mann himself had called them, in comparison to the prestige that education had enjoyed during the period of the Pilgrim fathers, were also the years of regeneration. For in the middle of the century state departments of education and normal schools were founded; the teachers became conscious of their profession, began to read journals, and assembled in associations and institutes; textbooks were improved; instead of the old and sometimes incredibly filthy houses new school buildings were erected, and they harbored more and more children, organized in grades, instead of crudely lumped together, as before. Perhaps the deplorable state of schools at the time of Horace Mann had, historically speaking, even its positive side. The people themselves could, and had to, build their schools — from scratch, so to speak. This, together with the ideal of social justice, may have been the reason for the rejection of the European system of separate elementary and secondary schools in favor of a single-ladder, universal, and tax-supported public school in which, ideally at least, every sufficiently talented child has the same chance to climb from one rung to the next.

There was, needless to say, opposition on the part of the well-

[23] Horace Mann, "Twelfth Annual Report of the Secretary of the Board of Education," in *Massachusetts Board of Education, 12th Report* (Boston, 1849), p. 140. See also *The Republic and the School. Horace Mann on the Education of the Free Man*, ed. Lawrence A. Cremin (New York: Columbia University Teachers College, 1957). Contains extracts of Mann's *Twelfth Report*.

[24] Edgar D. Wesley, *NEA: The First Hundred Years* (New York: Harper, 1957).

to-do. Why should they be forced to pay local taxes for schools that the children of the poor could attend without any contribution on the part of their parents? The matter was finally settled (1874) by the Supreme Court of Michigan in the so-called Kalamazoo case, in which the Court granted the community the right to tax itself for the maintenance of its secondary schools.

It was also in the seventies that the National Education Association (founded in 1857 as the National Teachers Association by various state teachers societies for the purpose of effective national representation) began to exercise a growing influence on general educational policy. Out of this endeavor grew in 1880 the National Council of Education. It soon started an era of reports and inquiries that had more influence on American schools, from the elementary to the tertiary level, than similar documents in other countries. Certain reports of England are comparable because of the fact that both countries had to replace the missing central educational hierarchy by self-initiative and self-government. In the United States, however, the cooperative attempt by interested men at improving the schools was by necessity still more important. For, first, America lacked the long and somewhat hierarchical social tradition of England; second, it had no schools that, liked or not, nevertheless set the pattern, like the old public schools in England; and, third, it had to adjust its schools to a people with cultural differences unknown to other countries.[25] The constitution of the Council stated as its objective "to reach and disseminate correct thinking on educational questions." For this purpose, so the statement continues, "it shall be the aim of the Council, in conducting its discussions to define and state with accuracy the different views and theories on the subject under consideration, and secondly to discover and report fairly the grounds and reasons for each theory or view, so far as to show, as completely as possible, the genesis of opinion on the subject."

Of the various reports issuing from the Council's activities three became landmarks in the history of American education, the

---

[25] The following considerations are largely based on the *Proceedings of the National Education Association* and on a report entitled "On the Conflict between the 'Liberal Arts' and the 'School of Education,'" submitted to the American Council of Learned Societies by Howard M. Jones, Francis Keppel, and Robert Ulich. Reprinted in *The ACLS Newsletter*, Vol. V, No. 2 (1954).

Report of the Committee of Ten on Secondary School Studies (1893), the Report of the Committee of Fifteen on the Training of Teachers and on the Correlation of Studies in Elementary Education (1895), and the Report of the Committee on College Entrance Requirements (1899).

I am here especially interested in the Report of the Committee of Ten, which worked under the chairmanship of President Charles William Eliot, of Harvard University. This document represents, so to speak, the end of the four-year high school as an academic and selective institution. Up to 1890 this school, though organically linked to the eight-year elementary school, had nevertheless remained the training ground for the more privileged of the nation who aspired at some sort of professional education. According to the Annual Report of the Federal Security Agency (1952),[26] in 1890, only about 7 per cent of the eligible youth of a total population of sixty-three million were enrolled in secondary schools, that is, in terms of percentage, less than there are now enrolled in the academic secondary institutions of bifurcated European systems. The Report of the Committee of Ten shows that the teachers of the ancient languages, and of the liberal arts in general, still claimed the high school as their old and proper domain. However, they were already on a polite defensive against all kinds of undesirable newcomers such as the natural sciences and the more applied subjects of learning.

Indeed, the great change came soon. After 1890 the high-school population doubled every ten years until the maximum was reached in 1940 with an enrollment of more than seven million. Then, in consequence of the lower birth rate in the economically troubled thirties, the school population declined for some years. Since 1954 the number of pupils again has increased by leaps and bounds. In 1957, eight million were in high schools, and in the early 1960's the number may rise to ten million. No longer 7 per cent as in 1890, but 80 per cent of the eligible boys and girls are now in some form of secondary education, and, though with great differences in various localities, between 50 and 60 per cent of the pupils graduate. Since, together with the growth of the population in an

[26] *Annual Report, 1952* (Washington, D.C.: Office of Education, Federal Security Agency), p. 14.

increasingly technical society, the tendency toward prolonging the years of professional preparation also grows, the colleges will become more and more inundated. Currently, slightly more than 30 per cent of the college age group are in colleges of some kind or in universities (about two and a half million), whereas in England, to use it as an example of other European countries, about 5 per cent of the total age group attend institutions of higher learning. Around 1960 four million students may be in our colleges, and before 1970 there may be six million or more.

No longer is there any semblance of Jefferson's selective scheme, or of anything that Franklin, who by himself learned several languages, would have considered an advanced education. And how can it be otherwise since the measure of intelligence of the high school students ranges from those close to the moron up to the highly talented? In other words, the American secondary school has become a school of and for the people, and attending college will for the American middle class change more and more from a privilege into a requirement or a matter of custom.

The socialization of the high school, or its function of educating the rank and file citizen without much claim to scholarly pursuits, became evident in the Report on the Cardinal Principles of Secondary Education of 1918.[27] It defines the goal of education in the following terms:

The purpose of democracy is so to organize society that each member may develop his personality primarily through activities designed for the well-being of his fellow members and of society as a whole . . .

Consequently, education in a democracy, both within and without the school, should develop in each individual the knowledge, interests, ideals, habits, and powers whereby he will find his place and use that place to shape both himself and society toward ever nobler ends.

The high school is to achieve this noble goal by instilling in pupils (1) health, (2) command of fundamental processes, (3) worthy home membership, (4) vocational training, (5) citizenship, (6) worthy use of leisure, (7) ethical character.

In comparison with the Report of the Committee of Ten, this

[27] *Cardinal Principles of Secondary Education.* Report of the Commission on the Reorganization of Secondary Education (Washington, D. C.: U. S. Bureau of Education, 1918).

means a complete shift in emphasis from the earlier scholarly interest in subjects toward a social interest in producing a normal, physically and morally healthy individual. Values that the older selective high schools could take more or less for granted because they were taken care of by the family are now placed into the foreground. The scholarly purpose has receded before the aim of normalcy and adjustment to life.

This change was supported by both a philosophical and a psychological trend. Philosophically and methodologically during the main part of the nineteenth century, American education took its principles from the Pestalozzian movement, from Froebel, from Hegelianism, as represented by William T. Harris and his friends, with their center in St. Louis, and from Herbartianism, as taught by the brothers Charles and Frank McMurry. Each of these European, especially German, movements of thought received a specific national hue in America. St. Louis Hegelianism took the more optimistic and activist sides from the master's dialectic, and the Herbartians cared more for Herbart's psychology and theory of learning than for his complicated metaphysics. The prevailing tenor was still idealistic, and the specific dignity of man was understood to lie in his capacity to think and act in harmony with the inner laws of a rationally understood universe. The critically minded were already attracted by Herbert Spencer's *First Principles* (1862), *Principles of Sociology* (1877–1896), and *Essays on Education* (1861). [28] In the latter he protested against the uselessness of the typical classical studies and the harsh discipline in the English public schools, thereby giving support to the democratic trends in American education. And, as in every country, so also in the U.S.A. the work of Darwin created both fury and admiration. By jumbling the ideas of these two Englishmen, every group could read out of them whatever justification it needed for its particular propensity: rugged individualism for the entrepreneur, collective action for the socially minded and for labor, the appeal to will for the voluntarist and the idea of immutable law for the determinist, a new gospel for the atheist and the hope of eternal progress for the secularist Christian. [29]

[28] *Education: Intellectual, Moral, Physical* (1861).
[29] See Richard Hofstadter, *Social Darwinism in American Thought* (Boston: Beacon Press, 1955).

After 1900, the pragmatism of William James and especially of John Dewey became the guiding force for the progressive American teacher, though one must be cautious with generalizations. The bulk of professional literature does not always indicate the actual disposition of men's minds. Much more than the theoretician may think, American teachers still cling to the old religious or idealist traditions, and an increasing number of them are Catholic.

However, especially in the field of education, John Dewey became the foremost spokesman of the *Zeitgeist* of the first four decades of the twentieth century. He combined in his thought Hegel's idealist evolutionism and respect for institutions (which he transferred to democracy) with Darwin's theory of natural evolution, with scientific experimentalism, with the pioneer spirit of a society that had shifted from agriculture to industry and labor, and with the missionary zeal of American democratic nationalism. As a philosopher, Dewey was of minor rank if compared with the really great men of thought; as a cultural apostle, he had an immediate influence on his environment that only a few university professors have ever had.

Unfortunately, like all men who think of thinking as a way of action and consequently wish to influence other people, he tolerated too benignly a kind of discipleship that spread his name into groups generally impervious to difficult abstractions, but that at the same time oversimplified his ideas and thus perhaps did them more harm than good in the long run. And, whatever the merits of his philosophy, in his opposition against the old metaphysics he failed to make explicit the metaphysics inherent in his own system of thought and thus allowed the isolation of the surface from the depth of his ideas. Certainly, under the name of progressive education, child-centered schooling, creative teaching and learning, modern and, on the whole, better pedagogical methods were advanced, from which even conservative schools profited more than they like to admit. At the same time such noble and perennial requisites of civilization as duty, authority, devotion to ideals even if connected with sacrifice were dimmed by the vague use of such theories as growth for its own sake, experience, activity, learning by doing, self-development, and democratic living. Whoever carefully reads Dewey's main educational work *Democracy and Educa-*

tion will find that, by centering ideals like discipline and duty around the concept of interest, he does not intend to belittle their importance, but to create a more dynamic conception of human development. However, recommendation of educational subjectivism can easily be read out of his statements, and that was the danger. Hearing the protest against false authoritarian methods, men forgot that there must not only be process and activity, but also an aim; not only interest (which so easily glides over into mere self-interest), but also the willingness to learn and work even under difficulty; not only an understanding for the specific conditions of childhood, but also an understanding for the conditions of the civilization into which the child has to grow; not only freedom from false authority, but also respect for rightful authority.

The other disintegrating influence on a clear conception of what youth can and should learn in school came from the controversy between the traditionalists in education and the findings of modern psychology. Needless to say, the whole issue is closely related to John Dewey's philosophical criticism of conventionalism in education. It is the American version of the struggle between the humanists and the progressives we encountered especially in French and German history. Unfortunately, many conservative advocates of the old liberal arts, especially the teachers of the ancient languages, rather than simply and proudly referring to the inherent values of a great heritage, attempted to bolster up their vanishing prestige and self-confidence by a most doubtful theory of universal transfer. According to this theory, the learning of grammar, particularly of Latin grammar, was supposed to strengthen miraculously all "the muscles of the mind" and to be, therefore, of most general value and utility. Against this essentially materialistic concept of human intelligence, Edward Lee Thorndike, who had begun his experiments in 1901, could assert in his comprehensive work on *Educational Psychology* of 1913–14:

The notions of mental machinery which, being improved for one sort of data, held the improvement equally for all sorts; of magic powers which, being trained by exercise of one sort to high efficiency, held that efficiency whatever they might be exercised upon; and of the mind as a reservoir for potential energy which could be filled by any one activity and drawn on for any other — have now disappeared from expert writings on psychology. A survey of experimental results is now needed perhaps as much to prevent the opposite superstition; for, apparently, some careless thinkers have rushed from the belief in totally general training to the belief that training is totally specialized.[30]

The last sentence in this statement is revealing. Just as Dewey's ideas were often falsely applied by his disciples, so were Thorndike's. There is no evidence that he directed his critical inquiry into the prevailing theories of learning in a spirit hostile to good standards in the liberal arts and related school subjects.

Yet, by some modernists, if we may call them this, experimental psychology was used to disparage any hierarchy of the intellectual disciplines. Unfortunately, this tendency is still with us. It leads to an atomistic education, which, sadly enough, had already been introduced into the American high school by the Report of the Committee of Ten and the Report of the Committee on College Entrance Requirements. For, in order to create some regularity in face of the threatening chaos of high-school subjects, these committees had postulated that a respectable college should admit only those candidates who could show a record of credits for sixteen courses. But, while in the 1890's there was still some reason to assume that sixteen courses would form an organic body of knowledge, after World War I this assumption proved to be illusory. Except for some basic subjects such as American history and English, the sixteen credits now can refer to the most scattered congeries of subjects. It apparently makes no difference to some educators whether the mind of the student has been nourished by material worth learning from a scholarly and humane point of view, or whether it has just been kept busy with something, no matter how trivial.

Thus serious complaints accumulate that the American high schools offer a "grab-bag" education ranging from physics and Latin to basket weaving, mountain climbing and automobile driving, while the colleges turn out a growing proportion of youth who despite sixteen years of exposure to teachers show few signs of academic discipline and learning.

The mechanical reliance on credits, from the high school to the graduate schools of the universities, without due respect for

[30] *The Psychology of Learning* (New York: Columbia University Teachers College, 1913), II, pp. 364-365.

coherence and standard, is the curse of American education. No real reform will be possible unless the program of study is brought into harmony with the development of human intelligence, which requires steadiness, concentration, courage in overcoming difficulties, and a sense of the relation between a single subject and the wider context to which it belongs.

To a degree, since the time when the public high school changed from a selective into a more or less universal national institution, educators have tried to meet the arising difficulties by two measures. First, in order to allow more specialization according to talent, they have divided the high school into a college-preparatory, a commercial, a technical, and, if feasible, in a general division. Secondly, many communities have changed the original structure of eight elementary and four secondary-school years into a six-year elementary, a three-year junior high, and a three-year senior high school program. This structure allows, on the one hand, for greater flexibility in discovering and cultivating the interests of the student and, on the other hand, for his greater concentration on a group of subjects arranged according to his purpose, ability, and interest. As will be shown in one of the next sections, with these measures the American school approaches somehow the more compartmental character of the European system. However, the totally unselective admission to the high school as well as extreme decentralization, which often allows the community to control the school administrator and his teachers without any admixture of scholarly standards, does not permit sufficient insistence on good performance. Hence the waste for many talented students who during the most malleable years between twelve and eighteen could easily have learned one or two foreign languages and more mathematics and science in addition.

Despite sometimes hard, though by necessity rather mechanical, entrance tests, the colleges and universities have been unable to stem the high school's trend away from academic subjects. Hence, in contrast to Europe where the student at a university is given a considerable amount of freedom because one may trust that he has received some intellectual discipline in his preparatory school, the American college and even the university believe they must impose on the young scholar a rigorously regulated schedule, class attendance lists, examinations during and after each course, and all kinds of guidance procedures. There reigns a pedantic and unacademic climate. Would it not be more conducive to a person's development if he were more free when he could profit from his freedom, namely, as a young man, or woman, and more controlled when control might be at the right place, namely, as an adolescent? But these are things about which it is hard to argue with an American. As things stand, the first two of the four years of undergraduate work become increasingly filled with subjects that could well have been mastered in high school. This is especially the case in regard to languages.

No wonder that Americans are now frightened by the unexpected efficiency of Russian schools. The missionary enthusiasm that especially after the two great wars made American educators believe they had the key to democracy in their hands has now given way to a more sober attitude of self-examination.

THE TASKS OF THE FUTURE

No people can rest on the achievements of the past. The United States is now one of the great world powers in an extremely competitive situation, and this position will be lost unless it is based on inner as much as outer wealth.

What the American school now needs is, first, a combination of the principle of equality and of justice to all with the principle of quality. As the American schools operate now, they neglect not only the theoretically gifted but also the practical students. The correction of this defect need not endanger the unity of the American high school; in the future it should still keep together the nation's youth up to the age of eighteen. Unity and diversity do not necessarily contradict; they can even support each other. Separate schools for the young intellectuals and vocational or trade schools for the practical are against the tradition of the country. There should be just as much dignity, humaneness, and satisfaction in helping the practically minded pupil toward his kind of productivity as in helping the theoretically talented toward his form of creativeness. Unless we succeed in this twofold task we will end on a level of verbalization too low for the gifted and too high for the practical.[31]

The second task incumbent on the American school is an organic rather than a mechanical concept and method of organizing both the program of studies and the process of examination and selection. As has already been said, mere credits acquired by the most disparate and incoherent kind of activity do not form a mind, but confuse it.

Third, America needs a combination of the traditional decentralization with concerted national and professional leadership, as it existed to a high degree between 1840 and 1900. Political and administrative centralization in Washington, similar to the kind France has in Paris, is impossible in the United States, and if possible, it would be disastrous. For there exists neither the well-trained officialdom, stemming originally from the old monarchical hierarchy, nor the cultural unity, which, despite all internal differences, still characterizes France, nor the willingness of the people to receive and obey orders from above. But all this is no excuse for managerially minded school administrators or politicians on school boards to exercise their power over better-educated teachers and parents.

Fourth, there must be brought about a closer coordination and cooperation between the colleges and universities, on the one hand, and the secondary schools, on the other. It is paradoxical for a country to have a single-track system and, at the same time, so little mutual attention, interconnection, and sometimes even mutual esteem as exists in the United States between the secondary and tertiary institutions. The result is a situation that sometimes borders on chaos. The state teachers colleges also, which, though belonging to the higher level, now lead an almost isolated existence, must be included in the intellectual blood stream. Otherwise one third of the teaching profession will lead an intellectually isolated existence. Generally, a broader humanistic rather than a primarily technical training of teachers must be aimed at in the various schools of education. But by no means should this lead, as some people advocate, to an absorption of the professional preparation of teachers by other departments, such as psychology, philosophy,

[31] See Robert Ulich, *Crisis and Hope in American Education* (Boston: Beacon Press, 1951).

sociology, and history. Education has become too complicated and demanding a responsibility, both from the scholarly and the national point of view, to be administered in a scattered, left-handed, and consequently more or less amateurish fashion. Certainly, some people are by nature, as it were, good teachers, and others are not. But a born teacher exists as little as a born lawyer or a born physician. In addition, the conditions of modern civilization are such that our schools, whether they like it or not, have to include a number of social obligations that in earlier times were discharged by family, church, and community. They demand much more from the teacher than just the instruction of this or that subject matter, however paramount this purpose is. Therefore, though education in the wide sense of the word is the responsibility of every college or university in its totality, there must be in both central agencies in which the various scholarly and social tasks of the teaching profession receive unity and clear focus. This agency can only be a highly developed department, or school, of education.

There are other aspects worthy of discussion, which, though perhaps external at the first glance, nevertheless determine the spirit of teaching and learning. American youth are one-sidedly educated by women, who form more than 72 per cent of the teaching staff. This is no wonder if one considers that the living conditions in the United States are such that teachers' salaries, though comparing favorably with the profession's income in other countries, are nevertheless too low in purchasing power. If 73 per cent of the male teachers are forced to look for outside occupation to keep their families on a decent standard, other professions will be more attractive. Furthermore, the majority of instructors in secondary schools have a teaching load that exceeds that customary in other countries. There is little, if any, awareness on the part of the American public that a bad scholar cannot be a good teacher, and that the latter needs a private library and time to read in order to escape the ever-threatening danger of routine and incompetence. Finally, the enormous contrasts in the quality of teaching in the various states must be corrected by federal aid without interference in the freedom of the teaching profession. This rich country has, besides school palaces no other nation could afford, still some ten thousand high schools with less than two hundred students. Naturally, they cannot give even the minimum of diversified education that young people of the ages between fourteen and eighteen have the right to expect.

The shock the United States has received from the sudden realization of Russia's advances in the field of education, especially in science, has uncomfortably awakened the nation from its complacency concerning its school situation. Congress has granted considerable sums to be spent in the form of federal aid to schools and universities, and the states will have to match most of the funds; newspapers and journals abound with articles dealing with the best possible training of the considerably more than forty-one million persons enrolled in schools and colleges (an increase of 27 per cent over the past five years); and all the institutions of learning, from the elementary schools to the graduate schools of the universities, are frantically looking for funds in order to attract better teachers. In view of all the one-sided statements issued by an innumerable number of more or less competent individuals and organizations, it was encouraging to read the balanced report of the Educational Policies Commission, prepared under the chairmanship of the President of Indiana University, Herman B. Wells, and published January 3, 1958. Fully recognizing the merits of the American schools, it nevertheless urges a more responsible participation of the American public in the affairs of its schools; a better preparation, higher payment, and increased recognition of the role of the teacher; better counseling; better opportunities for the gifted student; improvement of instruction not merely in mathematics and the sciences, but in all subjects, including languages; better-equipped schools and college buildings; and "a substantial breakthrough in educational finance." Of considerable value also is the Rockefeller Brothers Report on education with the descriptive subtitle: *The Pursuit of Excellence: Education and the Future of America.*[32]

These reports have now been overshadowed by the so-called Conant Report.[33] After examining a number of comprehensive

[32] Report V of Special Studies Project, Rockefeller Brothers Fund, in *America at Mid-Century Series* (New York: Doubleday, 1958).

[33] James B. Conant, *The American High School Today* (New York: McGraw-Hill, 1959).

high schools in eighteen states, Dr. Conant, former president of Harvard University, affirms his belief that the pattern of these schools — critically looked at by the English and other European nations — is capable of satisfactory reform without fundamental changes, under the condition that provision is made for proper size, for a competent staff of teachers and administrators, for a better guidance program, for a better balance between individualized, general, and certain forms of vocational education, for a richer and stiffer curriculum for the gifted, especially in science and languages, and for several other improvements.

Dr. Conant's report is sufficiently empirical, realistic, and at the same time demanding to be a challenge to the school administrators. They should, however, not forget that, according to the author, "the study has made no attempt to answer such questions as 'How satisfactory is the typical American high school?' "

Certainly, even if the author's recommendations in regard to the advanced academic courses were fulfilled, the so-called "college preparatory divisions" in the American comprehensive high schools would still lag behind the standards of those secondary schools in Europe that prepare a young person for higher studies. Dr. Conant remarks:

> In the European pre-university schools an eight- or nine-year rigorous course in languages, mathematics, science, history, and literature prepares the student to pass a state examination for a certificate which admits him to a university. The failures during the long course are many, and a considerable number fall by the wayside, but those who succeed finish with a mastery of two languages, a knowledge of mathematics through calculus and of physics and chemistry at the level of our sophomore college courses.[34]

But Dr. Conant rightly points at the incomparability of the American high school and college with the European preuniversity secondary school and university.

In consequence of their specific purpose, most of the reports written during the past decades give little or no attention to certain questions for which there may be no clear-cut answer, but which, nevertheless, have to be kept alive if education is not to degenerate into routine. What are the basic criteria according to which to

[34] *Ibid.*, p. 2. At certain schools three to four languages are required, but generally with a reduction of science.

judge the education of a nation? As this book has shown, there are many. However, one criterion is paramount, namely, whether a school system creates among its youth a feeling of national belonging within a general climate of universal human values such as decency, respect, and cooperation. Instead of condescendence on one side and servility on the other, does every good citizen feel a sense of equality among the lawful members of the nation? In the light of this criterion one can only agree with Henry Steele Commager, who affirms in his book *Living Ideas in America*:

> No other people ever demanded so much of schools and of education as have the American. None other was ever so well served by its school and its educators.[35]

But one has to go further. America is proud of the mobility of its population and, relatively speaking, of the absence of tight social classes (though there exists, as the vengeful heritage of older times, the problem of segregation). The nation is also proud of its universal school system and of the fact that abundance of living is not merely a privilege of a few. The American industrialist and engineer excel through their technical knowledge. Finally, this country has been given the role of leadership among the non-communist nations.

These are certainly great achievements, but they also involve great obligations. Whither will all this mobility lead? For there is no blessing in mobility, unless it creates deeper forms of happiness than a mutual race and scramble. Does the universality of the school system produce not only more widespread knowledge, but also better taste and more courageous individualism within a framework of worth-while loyalties and a deeper faith in man and the ultimate sources of his existence? Does abundance express itself primarily in the sale of automobiles, or in the greater appreciation of the finer arts of living? Are industrial energy and production merely means for a higher quantity of production, or for a qualitative culture that makes American leadership a matter not only of bigness, but of truly deserved respect among the family of cultured nations? This is a challenge of a magnitude rarely faced by any other nation. The future of humanity will depend on the answer.

[35] New York: Harper, 1951, p. 546. See in this context also G. Z. F. Bereday, *Equality in Education — Its Meaning and Methods* (New York: Harper, 1960).

IX

Russia

SINCE the times of the Greeks and the Romans the part of the globe that, despite the new name of the Union of Soviet Socialist Republics, or Soviet Union, we still like to call Russia has filled the minds of people with a sense of awe and fear. One knew of sunny beauty in the south and icy terror in the north, of steppes and forests and an enormous mountain range, the Ural, east of which there was the unknown; merchants and fur dealers told of rivers that seemingly traversed whole continents, of lakes the size of oceans, of tribes in continual search for food, and of warriors under despotic leaders with courts and retinues of fabulous luxury. The sixteen republics that today form the Soviet Union represent the greatest mixture of ethnic groups in any modern commonwealth. What happens in Russia is not always decided by Russians or by Slavs. Stalin was a Georgian. The Russian Academy of Sciences classifies the population into 169 ethnic groups, divided into ten major divisions. The largest, the Great and White Russians, forms about 56 per cent of the population.

The first event that we might meaningfully connect with the history of Russia as a cultural unit is the conversion of the Russian princes to the Greek Orthodox Church. It occurred shortly before the turn of the first millennium under the leadership of Vladimir the Saint, who came originally from a Norman dynasty that had pushed south to Kiev. Had he chosen Rome instead of Byzantium, the history of the world would have been different. But the Byzantine realm was nearer; it was still an empire; and it had a great and coherent tradition, while Catholic mankind was then a medley of nations, some old and some still emerging, and the Rome of the popes was dependent on a changing constellation of European powers. And it may well be, as Nestor's Chronicle, compiled by clerics in the twelfth century, tells us, that the pomp-loving princes were more attracted to Greek Orthodox than Roman Catholic ritual.[1]

After the fall of the Kiev dynasty in the twelfth century and the devastation of the city by the Mongols in 1239, Russia broke into separate principalities, leaving the country to inner warfare and its frontiers to continual Turkish invasions from the steppe. About the fourteenth century, the tribes north and west of the Dnieper, who had preserved their freedom, brought some order into the chaos. Galicia, Novgorod, and Moscow became new rallying places. Under Ivan III, or Ivan the Great (1462–1505), of the House of Rurik, Moscow became the political center of the country. For from it started the victorious campaign against the supremacy of the Mongols. Moscow became also the spiritual capital, or the "third Rome." For, after the fall of Constantinople (the "second Rome") in 1453, the duke of Moscow was considered the successor of the Byzantine emperors and the representative of the real Christian faith. Church and state now formed that close theocratic unity that was characteristic of Russia up to the Revolution of 1917.

The weight of an historical tradition going back to the times of ancient Byzantium gave, in the eyes of the Russian people, the nation and its monarchy a sacred glory unsurpassed by any other nation. This consciousness of the great tradition lived in the pride of those intellectuals who favored Slavophilism or Panslavism, whether based on political or religious grounds; it was an instrument of appeal used by the government for imperialist expansion and a powerful weapon of defense against aggressors. And, if we may believe a modern analyst of the Russian Revolution such as Nicolai Berdiaev,[2] it lives in the vigor and suffering of the com-

---

[1] See Helen Gay Pratt and Harriet L. Moore, *Russia: A Short History* (New York: John Day, 1947); Leo Wiener, *Anthology of Russian Literature* (New York: Putnam's, 1902–1903), I, 66f.

[2] *The Russian Idea* (New York: Macmillan, 1948), and *The Origin of Russian*

munist Revolution, though this Revolution, according to the same author, is the result of irreligious and secular autonomy taken over from modern Western civilization. Nevertheless, the myth of the past has also served as a link between communism and the Orthodox Church. For, after years of persecution and resistance, the clergy has found it compatible with its spiritual mission to achieve some peace with the regime of Stalin and his successors. In spite of all, it is "Holy Russia."

At the beginning of the reign of Ivan the Terrible (1533–1584), "All Russia" reached from the frontiers of Livonia and Lithuania to the former Greek empire, and the conquest of Siberia began. Ivan called himself Tsar (from the Latin Caesar), and even more cruelly than the absolutist monarchs in other countries he forced the obstinate higher nobility into the service of the monarchy and created a well-trained army. Since then the monarchical idea has never been in serious jeopardy, nor, despite the opposition of the Church, has there stopped the cultural contact with the West to which Ivan had given the initiative. The monarchs who in this respect made the most decisive steps were Peter the Great (1689–1725), in whom the adherents to the old faith saw the expected Antichrist, and Catherine II (1762–1796), who corresponded with Voltaire and his friends and, until the French Revolution changed her mind, aimed at an enlightened absolutism of the kind of Frederick II of Prussia or Maria Theresa of Austria.

It was not only the felt necessity of social reform but also the expansion of the empire toward the West, especially through victorious wars with Sweden in the eighteenth century, that caused Russia to enter more and more into the European arena. Napoleon's remodeling of the European dynasties caused Tsar Alexander I (1801–1825) to intervene against the upstart from Corsica; finally France's defeats during the years 1812–1814, in which Russia played a major role, elevated Alexander to the role of a savior of Europe. Inevitably, the ever-growing international involvement brought about comparisons with the political and cultural life of other countries; Russians traveled to the European

---

Communism (London: Bles, 1948). There should be an English translation of Fedor Stepun, *Der Bolschewismus und die Christliche Existenz* (Munich: Kösel-Verlag, 1959).

capitals; the various military adventures taught the government that an efficient army needed a more efficient industry; it realized the discrepancy between the country's size and resources and its dependency on foreign capital. Russian belles-lettres, under the leadership of Pushkin, the creator of classical Russian literature, Gogol, Turgenev, Chekhov, Dostoevski, and Tolstoy, as well as Russian music, under the leadership of Moussorgsky, Rimsky-Korsakov, Borodin, and Tchaikovsky, made the nation aware of the dismal contrast between its rapid ascent to international fame in the field of the arts, and its backwardness with respect to the social and educational conditions of the large majority of the people. Some of the social reformers, both from the right and from the left, demanded better educational conditions, and Konstantin Ushinsky laid the foundation of Russian elementary education and teachers' training. Several political reforms were brought about, generally against the opposition of the Church. But the continual wavering of the tsars and their governments between slow progress and sudden reaction caused the rise of secret societies, the opposition of the universities, which had developed to great centers of learning, and the growth of an emigrant intelligentsia. These *émigrés*, who had escaped prison at home, became the more dogmatic and intolerant as to what should happen with Russia the more they lost contact with the life of the Russian people. From this group and the underground movement in the country itself the Revolution of 1917 was engineered, made possible by the stubbornness and frivolity of the old aristocracy and the two lost wars of 1904 against Japan, and of 1914, against Germany.

THE COMMUNIST REVOLUTION

Unless communist China sets a new record, the Bolshevik Revolution and the ensuing communist regime has brought about the most radical transformation of a people known in the records of history. It was planned according to the doctrine of Marx and Engels, which resulted from the observation of early industrial capitalism in England and could never have grown out of the predominantly agrarian society of Russia. But Lenin and his Bolshevist friends relied on the social and mental conditions of an industrial proletariat within a nation 80 per cent of whose population was comprised of backward and mostly illiterate peasants, and they accomplished exactly the contrary of what the tillers of the soil had expected. For excepting the interval of the NEP (New Economic Policy, 1921–1927), which allowed a measure of free trade in order to save the country from complete famine, the Leninist Revolution deprived the small farmer of the fields he had taken away from the big landowners at the beginning of the upheaval and pressed him into collectives (though today he is permitted to cultivate as much personally owned land as he can take care of with his family). It forced many of the communist workers into four years of civil war against troops that, at least in the beginning, were better equipped and staffed than the army of the Revolution. Those in the factories had to work ten hours a day and more on a minimum of food. Even the First Five Year Plan (1927–1932), which brought about almost a doubling of the production of coal, oil, and iron, could be carried through only under enormous sacrifices on the part of the workers, while the reluctant farmers saw their harvests taken away by the government. After the initial victory of the Revolution, the "Red Terror" against all anticommunists ceased somewhat, but after Lenin's death in 1924 the struggle between Trotsky and Stalin began. The constantly expanding purges and spying methods the latter inaugurated in 1934 put a large part of the population into a state of insecurity and lawlessness for which we now have authentic testimony in Khrushchev's revealing address of February 24–25, 1956. This address answered the question that had tortured the whole world during the nineteen thirties: Why did the old Bolsheviks confess to crimes that in all likelihood they had not committed?

> Only in one way — because of the application of physical methods of pressuring him, tortures, bringing him to a state of unconsciousness, deprivation of his judgment, taking away of his human dignity. In this manner were "confessions" acquired.[3]

Mr. Khrushchev's speech was prompted politically by internal unrest — the people wanted to eat and live better, not only to pro-

[3] *The Crimes of the Stalin Era.* Special Report to the Twentieth Congress of the Communist Party of the Soviet Union by Nikita S. Khrushchev, First Secretary, Communist Party of the Soviet Union. Annotated by Boris I. Nicolaevsky (New York: *The New Leader,* 1956), especially p. 34.

duce guns — and by international strategy, for definite gains were to be expected from presenting to the astonished world a picture of cooperating decency in comparison to Stalinist brutality. It was also perhaps the outcry of terrorized souls against a past in which they were involved as frightened accomplices. But, whatever the causes, the address proved that under certain conditions the spirit of Ivan the Terrible could again rise in human history, just as the event of Hitler suddenly reminded the Germans of the almost-forgotten horrors of the Thirty Years' War.

There are in Russia, as in every other great nation, literary masterpieces that in a short time tell us more about complex situations than detailed scholarly analyses. The Russian novel, from Pushkin to Gorki, gives us an inexhaustible revelation of the education and mentality of the Russian people under the tsars: the frightening contrasts between the nobility and the serfs, the capitalists and the workers, the internationally educated élite, which was at home in several countries and languages, and the ignorant peasant who hibernated during the winter on his stove and had never seen a book. Marx's phrase "the idiocy of village life" comes into one's mind. Yet at the same time one remembers the depth of religion, the rhythm of songs and dances, and the beauty of colors applied in the weaving of these poor peasants. There are contrasts even in one and the same soul — superstition and profound insight, cruelty and universal sympathy, sexuality and asceticism, love and hatred, and hatred even in love — reflecting in its own extremes the extremes to be found in the human race as a whole.

Even before the Revolution of 1917 many observers liked to speculate on what would happen if the spark of self-awakening were to be thrown into this sleeping mass of potential talent. As early as in 1835 Alexis de Tocqueville, in his famous book *La Démocratie en Amérique*, stated that besides the United States Russia would become one of the world's great powers. "Their starting points are different, and their courses are not the same; yet each of them seems marked out by the will of Heaven to sway the destiny of half the globe." [4] As a matter of fact, since the middle of the nineteenth century feudalism had given way to some re-

[4] *Democracy in America*, trans. Henry Reeve, ed. Henry Steele Commager (New York: Oxford University Press, 1947), p. 286f.

forms; in 1861 the serfs were liberated, at least legally, and some years later the first beginnings of the representation of the people in councils were made. Even in 1899 Lenin admitted that Russia had changed.[5] Yet, it still was tsarist Russia, trying to build every concession to the demands of the people's representatives into an essentially absolutist political framework.[6] This is the reason why the communists opposed even those prerevolutionary governmental measures that were aimed at bettering the education and welfare of the toilers. Not evolution, but revolution from the bottom to the top of society, was the aim.

The roots of this Revolution are many and often contradictory. One can recognize the influence of Stirner's radical individualism, of Bakunin's atheist anarchism, of Nechaiev's utter antimoralism, of Trachev's fascist voluntarism; in short, almost all that during the nineteenth century frightened the adherents of law and order was taken up by Russian revolutionaries, who had their domiciles from Siberia to Switzerland, Germany, and France. But all these vague, sometimes totally unrealistic, doctrines were, at least theoretically, pushed aside by scientific Marxism, as expounded by Lenin.

What is this scientific Marxism or dialectical materialism of the Leninist version? It cannot be the purpose of the following explanation to elaborate on the question whether Lenin interpreted Marx correctly. As many of the latter's disciples and adversaries, the Russian revolutionaries assumed against evidence that Marx was a materialist in the strictly ontological and epistemological sense. Of course, in "turning Hegel's idealism upside down" Marx stated that ideas as we find them in the cultural activities and aspirations of man are not the primary movers of social history. Instead, so he said, these moving forces have to be sought for in man's economic interests. He thus opposed the idealist and religious tradition of the West and relegated the products of mind or spirit to the "superstructure," rather than considering them the foundation of the historical evolution. Yet, he did not pass any judgment on the ultimate nature of mind and spirit themselves, which, as cannot be de-

[5] Maurice J. Shore, *Soviet Education. Its Psychology and Philosophy* (New York: Philosophical Library, 1947), fn. 280.

[6] For the various aspects of the liberation of the peasants and the contrast of their life to that of the privileged, some of whom already had a bad conscience, see Leo Tolstoi's novel, *Anna Karenina*, and the many works of Maxim Gorki.

nied, are indeed involved in economic interests, for there can be no "interest" without some mental activity. The few remarks in Marx's writings that we have on this subject [7] are too brief to allow any ultimate metaphysical assumptions. After all, Marx wrote on political economy, not on metaphysics.

But whatever answer Marx would give — he would probably declare himself an agnostic and therefore give no answer — the lack of clarity in respect to the interrelation between spirit and matter has had the most serious political consequences. For it led the organized socialist movements of the European Continent, which saw in Marx their theoretical leader, toward an antireligious monist materialism of a rather crude type. Certainly, many of the so-called Marxist workers were pious Christians, but even they, from Madrid to Moscow, were mostly against the established churches, seeing that these churches constantly allowed spiritual and religious values to be used for the defense of the ruthless forms of early capitalism, militarism, and colonialism.

In his theoretical writings Lenin made some concessions as to the contributions of capitalist "bourgeois culture" to the intellectual and material welfare of the masses. Yet, on the whole, he took over the negativist criticism of Marx and Engels, which had a high degree of justification in the middle of the nineteenth century. For, as the chapter on England showed, early Manchester capitalism was indeed an inhuman form of production. What Lenin, as a radical revolutionary, refused to see were the possibilities of peaceful evolution. As a matter of fact, the combination of an elastic capitalism, workers' self-help through labor organizations, and the growing humanitarian conscience has proved itself so capable of democratic development that, at least in the advanced countries, the basic demands of a civilized life for all classes of society are being increasingly fulfilled. But Lenin had in view the retarded social conditions of tsarist Russia and the cruel treatment of the workers in the abortive Revolution of 1905. For, after the country's defeat

---

[7] Karl Marx, *Capital: A Critique of Political Economy*, trans. from the 4th German edition by Eden and Cedar Paul (New York: International Publishers, 1929); Karl Marx, "Misère de la Philosophie," in *Kritische Gesamtausgabe* (Berlin, 1932) VI, 117–228. English translation, *The Poverty of Philosophy*, with an introduction by Frederick Engels (New York: International Publishers, 1936). See also Karl Korsch, *Karl Marx* (London: Chapman & Hall, 1938).

by Japan in 1904, thousands of workingmen, led by the priest Gapon, marched to the tune of religious hymns and with icons in their hands to the emperor's palace to put their grievances to "their father Tsar." They left the palace with about a thousand of them killed by firing troops, the Tsar himself being absent. As always in human affairs, one nail drives another. Socialist revisionism, which under Bernstein in Germany and Jaurès in France tried to reconcile Marxist doctrinairism with developing social and industrial conditions, was rejected by Lenin. In full measure he adopted the thesis that the exploitation of the workers by the owners of capital could be ended only by revolutionary explosion. It would be followed by the proletarian dictatorship as the bridge toward the classless society that would make unnecessary the state, so far the instrument of the leading classes for the preservation of their privileges. The end would be a secular millennium of international peace. This hope was based on Lenin's belief that, after the terrors of World War I, the capitalist system was on the verge of collapse and that, once the revolution had broken out at one place, the workers all over the world, especially in Germany, Austria, and France, would hoist the red flag over their government buildings.

Lenin also adopted the Marxian idea that public education, as any other state-supported institution in a class-dominated society, had been given to the workmen only to make them more useful for production, more pliant, and also more ignorant about their own power. As long as the proletariat was not sure of its own victory — which at the same time would be the victory of man over the struggles of classes, for the working class would absorb all others — in other words, as long as there was an historical necessity for proletarian dictatorship, the new policy of education would have to follow the essentially undesirable pattern of early societies of using the schools for political purposes.

EDUCATION AFTER 1917

It is, especially for the period after World War II, extremely difficult, if not impossible, to give an accurate picture of the development and quality of Soviet education. One has always to keep in mind that the U.S.S.R. comprises territories of most different material, ethnic, and cultural traditions. Even the most rigid centralization could not enforce conformity of standards. Moreover official documents cannot always be trusted. The picture becomes especially blurred if, as is now the fashion, Russian education is compared with American education, for the latter also, though mostly for different reasons, is highly diverse.[8]

Immediately after the Revolution of 1917 had achieved a minimum of stability, education was organized to secure communism against the old feudal and bourgeois society that still threatened the new republic and to promote communist world conquest. The Platonic-Aristotelian principle that education is a part of statecraft, which in a deep sense is true and has been followed by every strong government whether secular or ecclesiastical, was now applied with the extreme rigor characteristic of modern totalitarian governments. Indeed, the growth of Soviet power would be unthinkable without Soviet education.

[8] Descriptions of the Soviet school system and related cultural activities can be found in *Education in the U.S.S.R.* (Washington, D. C.: Office of Education, 1957); Nicholas DeWitt, *Soviet Professional Manpower. Its Education, Training, and Supply* (Washington, D. C.: National Science Foundation, 1955); Alexander G. Korol, *Soviet Education for Science and Technology* (New York, John Wiley, 1957). For a valuable criticism of Korol's book, see Ivan D. London, "Evaluation of Some Current Literature about Soviet Education," in *School and Society*, November 8, 1958. See also *Report on Higher Education in the Soviet Union* (University of Pittsburgh Press, 1958); Clyde Kluckhohn, Alexander Inkeles, and Raymond A. Bauer, *How the Soviet System Works* (Cambridge: Harvard University Press, 1957); George S. Counts, *The Challenge of Soviet Education* (New York: McGraw-Hill, 1957). During recent years the language difficulty has been reduced by a number of translations from Russian sources. See especially *Soviet Education*, which is the translation of the Russian pedagogical journal, *Sovetskaya Pedagogika* (New York: International Arts and Sciences Press, since 1958); *Current Digest of the Soviet Press*, U.S.S.R.; *Soviet Survey; Russian Review; American Slavic and East European Review*. See also *Teaching in the Social Sciences and the Humanities in the U.S.S.R.* (Studies in Comparative Education, Office of Education, Division of International Education, U. S. Department of Health, Education and Welfare, 1959); *Soviet Commitment to Education. Report of the First Cultural Mission to the U.S.S.R.* (Washington, D. C.: U. S. Office of Education, 1959); *Bibliography of Published Materials on Russian and Soviet Education: A Research and Reference Tool* (U. S. Office of Education, 1960); G. Z. F. Bereday, W. W. Brickman, and G. H. Read, *The Changing Soviet School* (Boston: Houghton Mifflin, 1960); *The Politics of Soviet Education*, ed. G. Z. F. Bereday and Jaan Pennar (New York: Frederick A. Praeger, 1960); Vyacheslav Yelyutin, Minister of Higher Education of the U.S.S.R., *Higher Education in the U.S.S.R.*, Soviet Booklet No. 1 (London: Soviet Booklets, 1959, and New York: International Arts and Sciences Press, 1960); Nicholas DeWitt, *Education and Professional Employment in the U.S.S.R.* (Washington, D. C.: National Science Foundation, publication expected in 1960). A chapter of this book, entitled "Polytechnical Education and the Soviet School Reform," appears in *Harvard Educational Review*, Summer 1960.

We have, besides Lenin's own words concerning the conversion of the school from a weapon of the class domination of the bourgeoisie into a weapon for the dictatorship of the proletariat, one especially clear expression of communist school policy; it comes from Lunacharsky, one of the early revolutionaries and first Soviet Commissar of Education. Says Lunacharsky in his book on the general situation of national education in the Federal Soviet Republic:

> We know all too well that the American-European school is the school of the bourgeois class. It influences the children's consciousness to such a degree that most of them become incapable of any critical judgment on the injustice of the social order for the service of which they are prepared by their teachers. We too must create a class school, the school of the proletarian class. But, from our point of view, the proletarian class consciousness has at the same time the power to lead mankind toward freedom and happiness. As long as the state exists, the school must be a class school; however, the proletarian class consciousness is identical with the universal interests of mankind. In this way a quality emerges from quantity: it demands that we construct a new way toward productivity; it compels us to build the foundation of a school such as never existed before.[9]

How, so one may now ask, was this foundation built? First, Bolshevism carried through a demand raised by socialism and organized labor since their origin in the middle of the nineteenth century, namely, a universal elementary school system. The fight against the illiteracy of almost 80 per cent of the workers and peasants was one of the first points of the Soviet cultural program. Considering the destructions wrought by World War I, the Revolution and the Civil War, the poverty of the people, the enormous distances, and the lack of teachers, transportation, and facilities, we cannot be astonished that before World War II the task was not yet completed. But today Russia, except in remote districts, is on the same level as the most advanced of the Western countries.

Furthermore, there was the danger that amidst all the hardship

[9] See *Führer durch die Arbeitsschule in Sowjet Russland*, ed. Deutsche Gesellschaft zum Studium Osteuropas (Berlin: Osteurop Verlag, 1927). A similar statement is also to be found in Albert P. Pinkevich, *The New Education in the Soviet Republic*, trans. N. Perlmutter, ed. G. S. Counts (New York: John Day, 1929).

For a list of numerous writings on education by Lenin, see Maurice J. Shore, *Soviet Education, Its Psychology and Philosophy* (New York: Philosophical Library, 1947), pp. 321–339; see also, George S. Counts, *The Challenge of Soviet Education* (New York: McGraw-Hill, 1957), pp. 47, 63f.

of the revolutionary years youth and adults might relapse into the old habits of passivity, of listening to the voices of the past, of doubt in the new ideals. Hence, an additional thread was woven into the network, namely, adult education and the organization of leisure time for the purpose of communist indoctrination. Unceasingly the party used pictures, wall newspapers, itinerating orators, public offices, in short, every available space and place to keep alive the attention of the people. Clubs were founded in industrial as well as rural districts, not only for discussions and reading, but also for teaching the elements of hygiene and child care. For under the tsarist regime Russia had had one of the highest death rates among infants. Compulsory youth organizations, one of the characteristic features of all totalitarian systems, comprised in 1941 about twelve million children of the ages between nine and fourteen [10] under the name of Young Pioneers, while those between fourteen and twenty-six were assembled under the name of Young Communists. The whole Russian society abounds with associations that guarantee strict party supervision over every citizen, young and old. Needless to say, schools for party leaders are indispensable in a totalitarian state.

Inevitably, during this enormous transformation from a largely illiterate toward a literate nation the school structure and its subdivisions underwent such a variety of changes that it is impossible to delineate them accurately according to years and regions. But the following picture may indicate the general trend.

As could be expected in a revolutionary and totalitarian system, as early as 1918 all educational institutions were put under government control. Inevitably, private schools were abolished. Except the institutions on the tertiary level and the lowest schools, educating children from age five or six to nine, all schools were organized under the name of "The Unified Labor School." The lower section comprised four years for children from nine/ten to twelve/thirteen; the middle section, three years for the youth of thirteen/fourteen to fifteen/sixteen; and the higher section, two years for the pupils from sixteen/seventeen to seventeen/eighteen years of age. By far the majority of the children dropped out after the middle division,

---

[10] B. P. Jessipon and N. K. Gonscharow, *Pädagogik. . .* , ed. Deutschen Pädagogischen Zentralinstitut (Berlin, Volk und Wissen, 1953), p. 355.

at fifteen to sixteen. A highly selected number of students were admitted to a three-year university course, intended almost exclusively for the training of scientists.

In contrast to the old existing Russian system of bifurcation between the elementary and vocational schools on the one hand and the elementary, academic secondary, and tertiary schools on the other, the whole structure was built on the idea of establishing a single-ladder system, similar to that in the United States. The new school, integrating general and vocational training, was to represent the unity and equality of the Russian people under the rulership of the workers. It would allow every deserving youth to enter the higher echelons of professional life. For a thorough proletarian shake-up of Russian society, sons of the formerly privileged and professional classes were excluded from the higher grades of schooling.

According to the decree of 1923 a new structure was to be introduced with a first elementary section of four years (eight–twelve) and a second section, subdivided into three years (thirteen–fifteen) and two years (fifteen–seventeen). For the second section competitive selection and tuition fees according to the parents' financial and social positions were introduced.

But more than in any other country it would be wrong to believe that degrees and statutes represented reality.[11] There existed, at least up to 1927–1928 three different school types, in addition to schools for young workers, rural youth, and adults. They were: (1) at the base of the total structure, a four-year elementary school (108,800 schools with about 8,400,000 pupils); (2) a seven-year general school (6,600 schools with about 2,100,000 pupils); and (3) a secondary school (1,800 schools with about 900,000 pupils). In addition then to the secondary school there were the advanced institutions. The whole structure showed a strong vocational trend.

At the end of the twenties the government, which despite civil war and famine had established itself with a degree of certainty, realized increasingly its inefficiency in competition with foreign

[11] See Sergius Hessen's article on the Russian school system in *Handbuch der Pädagogik*, ed. Herman Nohl and Ludwig Pallat (Langensalza: Julius Beltz, 1928), IV, 504–508; *The National Economy of the U.S.S.R.: A Statistical Compilation* (Moscow: State Statistical Publishing House, 1956), p. 228.

countries. The League of Nations was going to break down; aggressive tendencies among the nations of Western Europe became apparent; it was dangerous for the Soviet Republic to have its plants run by engineers imported from Germany and the United States and to have the enormous agricultural and mineral resources of the wide territory insufficiently exploited. Hence, in 1929, the First Five Year Plan was established with the goal of higher industrial output, and with it a third educational phase was introduced, intended to bring education into line with the general trend toward higher achievement.

The fourth phase of Russian education (1932–1937) and the Second Five Year Plan (1933–1937) also coincided, at least roughly. The same was the case with the fifth educational phase and the Third Five Year Plan (1938–1942), which was aimed at building up industrial and military weapons against threatening aggression from Hitler's armies. Both educational phases showed the tendency toward more severe selection and classification in elementary, secondary, and higher education, with the purpose of producing better scholarly results on the higher levels, especially in the fields of technology and science. Finally during the war and the following years Russian education was completely remodeled, with a seven-year school for all and a ten-year school for the more advanced children becoming the central educational institutions.

Each of these phases in Russian education is marked by definite changes in spirit, method, and content. The first phase (1918–1923), and to a diminishing degree also the second (1923–1927/28), may be called enthusiastic or utopian. George S. Counts, in his book *The Challenge of Soviet Education*, uses the terms "experimental" and "romantic." Marx had thought of a society in which everyone had to contribute some hours of industrial work for his livelihood. In addition, he was impressed by the ideas of Robert Owen and by the reports of English factory inspectors, according to which children who worked in plants learned through a combination of labor and schooling as much as and even more than they did in regular day schools. Thus he developed his principle of "polytechnic education," in the hope that the school of the future would offer "an education which, in the case of every child over a certain age, will combine productive labor with instruction and physical culture, not only as a means for increasing social production, but as the only ways of producing fully developed social beings." [12]

This Marxian idea of using labor as the center of the educational process of the young was taken over by the German Radical School Reformers who demanded productive labor schools, but the Russian revolutionary educators including Lenin's wife Krupskaya in contrast to the German progressives, had a real chance to carry the idea into practice. In addition, the Russian leaders, expecting the world revolution and the victory of the Communist International in the near future, were anxious to integrate with their manual-labor principle every method that seemed to be progressive, pragmatic, activist, and based on team work or on the combination of physical and mental development. Thus, besides the German progressives and the leader of the German reform of vocational schools, Georg Kerschensteiner, John Dewey with his emphasis on the interrelation of school and community and on learning by doing, Mr. Collings with his project system, and Miss Parkhurst with her Dalton Plan were considered to offer adoptable schemes for world-saving communist education.

Indeed, one device was carried through in Russia with a measure of success possible only in a proletarian culture, namely, the planting of the school right into the factory. Travelers who in the twenties visited these labor schools were impressed with the spirit of cooperation prevailing there.

On the whole, however, the new enthusiasm soon proved to be headed toward failure. Let us assume that the ideals of new education which since World War I have excited progressive European and American teachers are really productive; if properly understood they are also expensive. For they require much equipment and small classes, consequently a high percentage of teachers who, in addition, must be unusually well trained; they require also time for experimenting and testing and a majority of students whose minds have already been nourished in a favorable home environment. But Russia, despite all its potential riches of material and of talent, was a poor country, defeated in a long war and torn by civil hatred and bloodshed. A considerable part of the intelligentsia had been killed or had left the country; the children of those remain-

[12] Shore, *Soviet Education*, p. 52; Karl Marx, *Capital*, p. 521.

ing, as bourgeois, were not admitted to the higher grades. The available teachers, if trained at all, had been educated and had taught in old-fashioned and authoritarian institutions. Furthermore, there was little time to lose in this period of crisis; and 90 per cent of the children in certain rural districts came from illiterate homes.

Most of all, the methods of education recommended initially by the Russian revolutionaries were developed in liberal-democratic environments. Even there these methods were criticized as unrealistic, if not anarchical. How could they be adapted to a country that had rapidly passed from an absolutist theocracy into civil wars, anarchy, and then dictatorial totalitarianism? Thus one after the other of the great dreams of an educational revolution within a political revolution had to be abandoned.

V. N. Shul'gin,[13] Director of the Marx-Engels Institute of Pedagogy and one of the radicals who considered formal schools as provisional institutions that would wither away together with the withering away of the state under the new proletarian culture, lost more and more in influence. In 1931 his Institute was dissolved. "Pedagogy," or the science of education, became carefully distinguished from the sentimentalities and the romanticism of "pedology." [14] In 1937 even the cherished Marxian principle of polytechnic education was abandoned.

Nevertheless, the first utopian years were not totally wasted, for during this time there was awakened that interest in education that, despite certain relapses, characterizes the population of Soviet Russia. And where has there been a scheme capable of capturing a dormant nation which has not a utopian quality?

Educational realism asserted itself in the regulations of 1927, in contrast with those of 1923. The weight of solid knowledge, especially in mathematics and the sciences, became increasingly acknowledged. On the whole, with each five-year plan a more realistic attitude took place, until in 1943 even coeducation was abolished in order to give the young men a truly manly and the young women a truly womanly education. As before the Revolution, uniforms are now worn by students; and discipline is the new principle. Coeducation, however, has been re-established.

Since it had quickly become apparent, as also in other revolu-

---

[13] Shore, *Soviet Education*, p. 155.   [14] *Ibid.*, p. 176.

tions, that competition, selection, and rewards provide generally more efficient incentives for learning than nice feelings of comradeship, in 1932 academic degrees, entrance and graduation examinations were reintroduced. With almost every new step rules and regulations concerning admissions, marks, and examinations were issued and enforced.

Still in 1948 the official newspaper *Pravda* found it necessary to complain about the population's lack of interest in the new schools. Between one third and one half of all children did not go beyond the fourth grade; in some remote areas they escaped school completely. Truancy was frequent, and developing agriculture and industry took youth away even before they had completed their compulsory four years, then at the ages from seven to eleven. Naturally, at the end of the intermediate grade, covering three years, only a few remained to attend the upper secondary school, leading up to the tenth grade, or the age seventeen/eighteen. Only 700,000 students attended higher institutions, which is about one third of 1 per cent of the total population (*c.* 200,000,000 in 1956). One may also doubt whether all of these 800 higher institutions were really of academic nature. At least a part of them were correspondence schools.[15]

However, this was only three years after a devastating war, in face of a terrible shortage of housing, and it was still better than under tsarist Russia. What more can be expected? The main fact is that during the following years the situation improved constantly. In 1952, in connection with the new Five Year Plan of 1950, the Nineteenth Party Congress declared it the goal of the Soviet Republic to have, by 1960, a universal and obligatory ten-year education, divided into a four-year elementary and a six-year secondary school. (The latter would roughly correspond to our junior and senior high schools.) In 1955, 880,000 graduated from the ten-year school; in 1956 the number of the graduating class had risen to 1,300,000, and more than 5,000,000 attended the grades eight to ten. Running parallel to the upper three years of the general high school with a unified curriculum (Russian language and literature, a foreign language, history, mathematics, and a considerable portion

[15] UNESCO. *World Survey of Education. Handbook of Educational Organization and Statistics* (Paris: UNESCO, 1955), pp. 629–648.

of science), there existed a technical division; and besides the general school special schools of technological character, so-called *Tekhnika*, were established, covering grades one to ten, or ages seven to seventeen. These schools were rightly supposed to be of great value providing liaison officers between the scientifically trained engineer and the practical workers in the plant. At least five such technical assistants are needed for every academically trained engineer.[16] Students of special promise could pass from the *tekhnikum* to the university.

Just as the secondary and technical school systems have received the most encouraging support by the Soviet authorities, so also did the institutions of higher learning. They are highly articulated according to modern professional needs. The University of Moscow, the symbol of communist cultural as well as architectural progress, already had in 1955 about 23,000 students with about 3,000 graduating each year and 10 per cent passing over to graduate work with highly individualistic instruction. The U.S.S.R. has now about 800 institutions of higher learning with 2,000,000 students, in contrast to 1,858 comparable institutions with more than 2,500,000 students in the United States. There are now more than eight times as many universities and other institutions of higher learning as before 1917 (within boundaries prior to September 17, 1939).[17] About three quarters of all students are on state scholarships. "The amount of the monthly stipend is such that the stipend for one to three months covers tuition fees. The amount of the tuition fees equals about a month's average salary of Soviet workers and employees. Thus, the tuition fees in themselves are not very high." [18]

Admission to, and graduation from, universities depend on competitive examinations. Each student, whatever his specialty, must continue to learn a foreign language; apparently much emphasis is laid on the linguistic and anthropological training of emissaries to foreign countries, probably all graduates from schools for specialists. The Russian student attends many more courses than

[16] Korol, *Soviet Education for Science and Technology*, pp. 9, 113–114, *passim*.
[17] *National Economy of the U.S.S.R.* . . . Issued by the Central Statistical Administration Council of Ministers (Moscow: State Statistical Publishing House, 1956), p. 233.
[18] DeWitt, *Soviet Professional Manpower*, p. 143.

the American. Like the *agrégés* in France, who, of course, represent only a very small group, the many thousands of Soviet university graduates are immediately placed in assigned positions that they are bound to accept — the theory being that the privilege of a scholarship involves a corresponding duty to the commonwealth.

According to recent sources [19] there were in 1957–1958 more than 200,000 general schools of all types in the U.S.S.R., with a total enrollment of more than 30,000,000 students, whereas in 1914 not even 10,000,000 pupils were registered in elementary and secondary schools. Technical and other specialized secondary schools, including correspondence schools, enrolled 2,000,000, as did higher institutions, also including correspondence courses. More than 3,500,000 persons studied part time at the secondary and tertiary level and at general schools for young workers and farmers. In 1957 approximately 1,500,000 pupils finished secondary schools, and about 332,000 finished labor-reserve schools.

Because of cultural, environmental, and structural differences it is impossible to make clear comparisons with the American situation. It is especially important to keep in mind the fact that the subject matter of the unique American institution, the college, would in Russia belong partly to secondary and partly to higher education.

About the spirit that some years ago pervaded Russian education we have a first-hand testimony from the Deputy Minister of Education of the Russian Soviet Federated Socialist Republic, who visited the United States in March and April 1956.[20] The early progressive experiments in Russian education were considered a failure; "not one teacher in Russia" would want to continue such experiments. Instead Russia had returned to the traditionalist and authoritarian way.

In order to secure unity and discipline, the trend toward centralization had continued, if not increased. Textbooks had to be approved by central committees of the various republics of the U.S.S.R., which worked closely together with the Academy of Pedagogical Sciences. The policy of the Academy, like that of every

---

[19] See, among others, *Report on Soviet Commitment to Education* and Khrushchev's "Memorandum on School Reorganization," to be discussed later.

[20] See also DeWitt, *Soviet Professional Manpower.*

other agency, had to be approved by the Central Committee of the Party. According to the emphasis on industrialization, extreme value was laid on vocational and technical training; consequently mathematics and the sciences were the most important subjects even in high school.[21] The pupil-teacher ratio had been reduced. While the schools of rich America still average twenty-seven and more students per teacher, the Russian teacher faced only seventeen. The teachers insisted on rigid examinations after the first four years of schooling.

Indeed, these examinations were very severe. A set of Soviet Test Queries[22] in mathematics, physics, and chemistry shows that the Soviet graduates from a secondary school, after only ten years of schooling, compare very favorably with the best of the American high-school graduates. Only a few of the latter could compete with the intellectual élite of young Russia. This is due not only to discipline, but also the fact that Russian children get more hours of instruction in ten years than American children in twelve. The achievements are challenging not only to America, but to any other country.

However, it would be interesting to have accurate answers to two questions. First, how many schools with such standards really do exist in a country so vast and with such a diversity of cultures? Second, how many of the Russian pupils enter the last three years of the ten-year school? So far as we know only one half; of these only one third graduate. And this is inevitable, for it is contradictory to our experimental knowledge about ordinary human intelligence that the mathematical and linguistic levels postulated by the official Russian examinations for the upper grades of secondary school could be achieved by all children. Unless the general intelligence of the Russian people is superior to that of other nations, not more than one half of its youth could be expected to pass. However, our American educators have perhaps failed to test one factor, namely, how much a child can learn when he is put under hard and consistent discipline and pressure.

[21] Korol, *Soviet Education.*
[22] On examinations in Russian schools, see DeWitt, *Soviet Professional Manpower*, Korol, *Soviet Education*, and "Final Examinations in the Russian Ten-Year School," in *Information on Education around the World* (Washington, D. C.: U. S. Office of Education, October 1958).

Nevertheless, the Russian physicians complained that the great work load was detrimental to the health of youth. According to the Soviet Survey of February 1957,[23] a group of leading physicians in May 1956 appealed to the public in a letter dealing with the "unbelievable over-burdening" of school children. At the ages from eleven to thirteen they had to work eight to ten hours a day; at the ages from fourteen to seventeen they had to spend ten to twelve hours for school and homework, so that no time was left for sport, sleep, and legitimate leisure. Apparently, the open letter had — at least in some states — the effect of reducing the number of year-end examinations. They are now to be given only after the seventh and tenth grades and have been simplified as to content and procedure. Also, the Academy of Pedagogical Sciences was advised to "define and clarify" the essentials of the secondary-school program and to "reduce the number of syllabuses and textbooks." [24] In a recent important address on the topic of "Strengthening the Ties of the Schools with Life" Khrushchev himself warned against overburdening school children to the detriment of their health.[25]

Nevertheless, the fact is that, except in remote districts, the Russian schools have not only achieved under the most arduous circumstances an almost complete universal training with an almost complete abolition of illiteracy. They have at the same time, at least in a considerable number of schools, raised their standards to such a degree that, in terms of mere efficiency, they are now on the same level as the most advanced nations of the world. In recent times Soviet educators have also emphasized the moral responsibilities of their schools. The Rules for Children of 1943 stress devotion to the Soviet motherland, diligence, obedience, orderliness, cleanliness, good posture and proper language, and the obligation of the pupil "to prize the honor of his school and his class as his

[23] *Soviet Survey: An Analysis of Cultural Trends in the U.S.S.R.* Published by the Congress for Cultural Freedom, London, which has published a number of important reports on Soviet developments.

[24] Jack Raymond in the *New York Times*, special dispatch from Moscow, June 15, 1956.

[25] "On Strengthening the Ties of the Schools with Life and on Further Developing the System of Public Education in the Country," *Pravda*, September 21, 1958. Khrushchev's address, or "Memorandum on School Reorganization," appeared in translation in *The Current Digest of the Soviet Press*, October 29, 1958. It has been reprinted as Appendix A. in James Bryant Conant's *The Child, the Parent, and the State* (Cambridge: Harvard University Press, 1959).

very own." [26] Russian statesmen also speak of the "idealistic" qualities of Russian culture.

But probably much of what has been said here about the intellectual phase of Russian education already belongs to the past. There are many signs that the communist educators and their leaders have no intention of resting on their laurels. On the contrary, they doubt whether they have really earned them and wonder whether they have made mistakes. For about three years the Soviet schools have undergone a reorganization equal to the other great events in the reform of Russian schools. This reorganization found its first official sanction in the already mentioned address by Khrushchev of 1958 and is generally connected with the movement of "polytechnical education." The new plan still aims at adding an eighth year to the present universal seven-year public school. It would be divided into a four-year primary base and a kind of junior high school of three years, to be followed by a senior high school, also of three years. By far the large majority of children would leave after the junior high school stage that in the course of time may even be extended from three to four years.

In addition, the single-track structure of Russian education will give way to a highly diversified multiple-track system in order to make the greatest possible use of the various talents of the children and to allow for local differences in industrial and agrarian districts. To the already existing special schools for children in music, art, and choreography, schools for adolescents highly gifted in the sciences will be added. Together with a fundamental training in science and literature, communist ethics, health, and good "aesthetic tastes," the seven- or eight-year compulsory school will provide a basic training in the crafts, beginning with simple manual arts during the primary stage and specializing increasingly in the upper grades. But the three-year senior high school, designed to complete the preprofessional training for the gifted youth, will also in no way neglect the polytechnical training. The goal of preprofessional education can also be reached through evening and correspondence courses, for in this way the maximum interaction of theoretical schooling and practical work in factories or in the fields could be accomplished. Khrushchev's plan must be interpreted as an

[26] See Counts, *The Challenge of Soviet Education*, pp. 74-75.

attempt to achieve a balance between the high degree of intellectual-ization, aimed at during the past two decades, and the earlier labor-centered concept of communist education. Ideologically, Soviet educators are attempting to connect the recent reform to Marx's idea of polytechnical schooling, though Marx wanted exactly the contrary, not vocationalism in the form of an early industrial specialization, but a full and rounded out education to fit men for the new classless society. What, we may ask, are the reasons for the new trend?

At several places Khrushchev states categorically that "serious dissatisfaction with the present [1958] state of affairs in the secondary and the higher schools" has arisen from the realization of the fact that "our secondary and higher schools . . . are detached from life . . . our general schools suffer from the fact that we have adopted many aspects of the prerevolutionary gymnasiums, the purpose of which was to give their students enough abstract knowledge to receive a diploma . . . In trying to pull all our young people, millions of boys and girls, through the ten-year secondary school," we must realize that "naturally not all of them can be absorbed by the higher educational institutions and specialized secondary schools." Their health may suffer from cramming, and, when leaving school, too many of them "reluctantly go to work at factories, plants, and collective and state farms, and some of them even consider this to be below their dignity. This haughty and contemptuous attitude toward physical work is also to be found in families."

Consequently, for the future "all students without exception should be drawn into socially useful work at enterprises, collective farms, etc., after completing the seventh or eighth grades" and "the entire system of our secondary and higher education should be so organized as to assure good training of cadres-engineers, technicians, farm specialists, doctors and teachers and factory and agricultural workers — of all the cadres that our state needs."

Khrushchev's suggestions have been transformed into law by the Supreme Soviet of the U.S.S.R.[27] This law also distinguishes between the seven- or eight-year basic school and "a complete

[27] See extract in *The Current Digest of the Soviet Press*, March 4, 1959, and Conant, *The Child, the Parent, and the State*, Appendix B.

secondary education for young people, beginning at the age of 15–16," to be divided into "(a) schools for working and rural youth — evening (shift) general-education secondary schools . . . (b) general-education labor polytechnical secondary schools providing production training . . . (c) technical and other specialized secondary schools." Furthermore, the network of "boarding schools," a relatively new school type, should be expanded and be "organized along the lines of the eight-year school or general-education labor polytechnical secondary school providing production training." The law provides that these measures be carried through within "three to five years, beginning with the 1959–1960 school year." It prescribes reforms for higher education also.

This is, indeed, a kind of counterrevolution within a revolutionary era. It is not anti-intellectual because throughout it insists on the training of a primarily scientific élite, but it attacks, if one might say so, a misplaced educational intellectualism that attempts to drive all the nation's children through a ten-year and academically oriented single-track school system. It represents, without doubt, a political reaction against the apparently observed danger of the emergence of a class system built on educational differences, with a privileged intellectual élite on the top and the mass of the toilers at the bottom. Eventually, so Khrushchev seems to fear, it would change the communist society of comrades into the bourgeois society characteristic of other European countries. The other reason for the reform is the enormous need for manpower caused by the endeavor of the U.S.S.R. to become the leading industrial world power.

It remains to be seen to what extent the Soviet powers will be able to steer the ship of the nation through the Scylla of a specialized school system with the inevitably ensuing differentiation of classes (which even the reform cannot avoid completely) and the Charybdis of equalitarianism with the hardly avoidable danger of inefficiency. Certainly, the new polytechnical education must be interpreted not only as an educational, but also as a political measure of highest significance.

Apparently, Khrushchev and his advisers have no illusions about the difficulties to be encountered by a school system that tries to bind into one three seemingly opposite tendencies: theory and devotion to practical work, general and special training, unity and diversity. There will be many errors and disappointments, but there will be daring and vitality.

With the competitive situation as it unfortunately exists in our troubled world, no educational system has aroused so much attention as that of Soviet Russia, especially in the United States. Our educators and politicians begin to realize that it is not enough to glory in terms such as "democracy" and "the free world," but rather it is essential to use the freedom for high accomplishment. After all, what our educators now suddenly discover in relation to Russia, namely, that youth could learn more than they often learn here, they could have observed for many decades in the secondary schools of Europe. And the whole free world should have learned by now that totalitarian systems, however harsh on the human soul, can nevertheless be frightfully effective in the technical sense of the word. Within a few years Hitler could create an army that fought the world for four years. Science lends itself to teamwork. As a consequence of its superpersonal objectivity it allows for the subordination of the individual to a prescribed goal, and it can thrive under rigid systems of government better than free speculation, poetic imagination, and artistic creation.

The very absence of regard for human freedom, characteristic of totalitarian countries, allows also for a rapid and well-planned allocation of manpower. In many instances, not the individual determines his occupation, but the policy-making authorities. And, where whole populations can be, and have been, shifted from one land to the other, troops of workmen and their engineers ("cadres") can also be moved rapidly from one to the next industrial center. A totalitarian country is like a big army on the alert. Perhaps, sooner or later even science may suffer, for its basic progress also depends on the creativeness of minds. But the laboratory of the physicist and the quiet study of the mathematician may become the only refuge for the productive urge in Russian man; and for the very reason that science is politically, socially, and morally neutral, its results can be used equally for good and evil purposes. Even the early Bolshevists recognized this. They tried to win outstanding scientists from the tsarist era over into their own camp, or, at least, they left them relatively unmolested. This is the reason why the American Report to the President, October 1957, made by the National Science Foundation, could make the following statement:

It would appear that the United States has a formidable competitor in the Soviet Union which, although starting from a relatively low research-and-development level, is progressing at a remarkably rapid rate. In addition to stressing technological aspects of its economy, the Soviet Union seems to be able to draw heavily on an educational and intellectual structure, developed long before the coming of the present political regime, closely resembling European structures with a strong emphasis on basic research. There is also evidence of able, high ranking administrative leadership toward increasing the stature of the country in science and technology.

EVALUATION

With all the changes just-described, has there been any stability within the Russian educational system? Of course, there has. The way has been from romantic and revolutionary inexperience to the realism of efficiency. Lenin, who had carefully observed the history of political institutions, was convinced that a new government's adaptability to changing situations would lead to disaster if it were not combined with insistence on coherent principles and beliefs. His dialectical materialism, more than any other theory, permits rapid changes within the sameness of final purpose.

First, there has remained within Russian education the materialistic and collectivistic concept of man. Though not denying the person's right of progress and happiness, it nevertheless considers him a part of the social organism. If he offends his society as defined and represented by the government in power, he is no longer a comrade, but an outlaw.

Second, the pupil, whether in elementary schools or in adult courses, is trained to be the fighter, the pioneer, or the warrior of the republic. As in the early years of the Revolution, Lenin, Krupskaya, and Lunacharsky, so also in 1948 the Great Encyclopedia defined the mission of the schools in definitely political terms:

To develop in children's minds the Communist morality, ideology and Soviet patriotism; to inspire unshakable love toward the Soviet fatherland, the Communist Party and its leaders; to propagate Bolshevik vigilance; to put an emphasis on atheist and internationalist education; to strengthen Bolshevik willpower and character, as well as courage, capacity for resisting adversity and conquering obstacles; to develop self-discipline; and to encourage physical and esthetic culture.[28]

In order to hold the uniqueness of the Russian educational system before the eyes of the students, the schools of all the other countries have to be pictured in derogatory terms, and, as often is the case, those that have contributed most are the most preferred targets. John Dewey and his followers have often been described by Russian educators as patriotic chauvinists in the service of American capitalist bourgeois imperialism, ready to support any crime against the intelligence and moral conscience of mankind, and for this purpose devoted to training youth away from social reality into a state of complete submission to their class-directed authorities. One sees how differently an educational theory and system can be interpreted when observed from the other side of the fence!

But propaganda not only goes on in schools. It is, so to speak, the heart of communist policy since the time when Lenin in his early articles of 1901 and 1902 [29] stated that theory, propaganda, agitation, and organization should be the instruments of the still extremely small but constantly growing Communist Party. And at the Eighteenth Party Congress in 1939 Stalin declared, "If our Party propaganda for some reason goes lame . . . then our entire State and Party work must inevitably languish." [30] The Agitation and Propaganda Department of the Communist Party ("Agitprop"), which directs all the various activities of indoctrination and persuasion, is one of the largest agencies of the country. According to Frank Bowen Evans the Communist Party and the Soviet government employed, in 1953, 375,000 propagandists full time and 2,100,000 part time.[31] To be sure, the liberalizing movements of other countries never influenced Russia, except through a very small intellectual élite; the country as a whole went from tsarist theocracy almost straight to communist idolatry, as we could see it in the adoration of Joseph Stalin. It will always remain one of the trage-

[28] Quoted from William Benton, "The Voice of the Kremlin. Some First-Hand Observations on Red Propaganda Techniques within the U.S.S.R. and Satellites," in *Britannica, Book of the Year. Feature Articles* (Chicago: Encyclopedia Britannica, 1956).
[29] "Where to Begin" and "What Is to Be Done," (*Iskra*, No. 4, 1901).
[30] Taken from report of William Benton in "The Voice of the Kremlin. . ."
[31] Frank Bowen Evans, ed., *Worldwide Communist Propaganda Activities* (New York: Macmillan, 1955).

dies of our time that not only Russia, but also other parts of the world, especially of Asia, may, in their understandable attempt at rapid social improvement and political independence, turn from old feudalism and colonialism right to communism, from one state of bondage to another. In contrast to complicated liberal democracy, the communist ideology has a deceptive simplicity and promises quick results; and its leaders have taken over from the West industrialization, socialism, and public education, all movements that render it attractive to thus-far neglected peoples.

Despite its rapidly growing population, Russia, in contrast to so many other countries, does not seem to suffer from a lack of teachers. They enjoy high social prestige and a relatively good income. And, having never heard of anything else, they may well believe it the "secret" of the Communist Party that it inculcates its youth "with high ideals, teaches them nobility, modesty, and unselfish love of their country." They may also believe that their country's virtues shine in glorious contrast to the capitalist countries where a "man's imagination can only soar toward banks and check books," and where a considerable number of youth are drug addicts, murderers, rapists, burglars, and extortionists.[32] In recent times Khruschev even used the term "spiritual values," in regard to Russian education, a phrase that would have been impossible under Stalin.

Third, though in the course of the past years more administrative power has been given to the individual republics than before, there has remained the tendency toward federal centralization. Here Russia is not unique. It clearly repeats the Napoleonic scheme of securing — or undoing — the results of a revolutionary period by means of subjecting every phase of schooling to central control. That which is unique is the intensity of the procedure.

Fourth, the concept of labor still exists as the centralizing proletarian principle of education. The hope is to connect the schools as intimately as possible with industry and agriculture. Communist activity and technical efficiency are the supreme goals of education, though men now realize that there can be no technical efficiency on higher levels of production without a thorough theoretical

[32] Quoted from *Soviet Education*, Eng. trans. of U.S.S.R. monthly journal, *Sovetskaya Pedagogika*, Vol. I, No. 2 (December 1958), p. 13.

groundwork. We have no means of judging to what degree this technicalization of education will be detrimental to creativeness in fundamental thinking. Certainly, in regard to industrial productivity Russia has surprised even the keenest observer by its postwar achievements. At the present rates of growth, the Soviet Union will forge ahead of Western Europe's economic output within the next two decades and will shift the balance of power in the world.

History tells us that a nation can succeed materially and industrially and at the same time lose its soul. The technical progress of modern Russia is not paralleled by a similar progress in the arts and the humanities. But here, again, the situation is too complex to allow quick generalizations. However, the fate of Pasternak tells us that just as the teachers, so also the writers have, first of all, to obey.

Fifth, opinions conflict as to the degree to which the pressure teaching of official materialism has succeeded in eradicating the religious interest of the people. Together with the teaching of science, materialist atheism has certainly had a deep effect on the younger generation. On the other hand, despite all the dangers involved in the new compromises with the communist regime — the priests, for example, are well paid — the Orthodox Church may have profited spiritually from the years of suffering and from the loss of the corrupting alliance with tsarism. At least, it is no longer a convention, and this very fact may in the course of time increase its influence. Who knows how many pray at home who do not want to be seen at church?

Though it sounds paradoxical, a good deal of transcendent longing — which seems to be the eternal companion of man — lives even in present communism, used, abused, but in any case reckoned with by its leaders. For they have created a sacred dogma (dialectical materialism) and a myth with a holy shrine (Lenin's tomb); they have tried to replace the old adoration of saints with a personality worship of such an intensity that it turned into an ideological and political danger (the pictures of Stalin); and they have instituted processions, rituals, and theaters for arousing the people's enthusiams in the new cult. All this, together with the claim of scientific objectivity, has given the Marxist-Leninist doctrine a powerful inspirational dynamic. And, if the communist leaders no longer believe in the original gospel, they are not different from the many Christian monarchs of older times who also defended a faith they no longer had, knowing that their political system needed a doctrinal tradition. Communism becomes especially powerful if, as can easily be done in the oppressed nations of Asia and Africa, it allies itself with the modern pseudoreligion of nationalism. The ideal of economic happiness within a classless society of international scope is then married to the idea of political self-determination and liberation from colonialism, even where colonialism already belongs to the past.

Communism — so said one of the delegates of the 54th Annual Silver Bay Conference on the Christian World Mission, July 1956 — is functioning as a powerful and increasing religion. "Communism has more missionaries in Southeast Asia than Protestantism has in the entire world. The Communists spend more on literature in India than our State Department spends on its entire Southeast Asia operation. In one six-month period, 10,000 Chinese high school students left their homes in Malay for Red China . . ." In the meantime, as we know, many thousands of Chinese students leave for Moscow. In other words, the chain closes.

But it is exactly in this situation that education may play an historical role. As was also the case with earlier movements such as the Reformation and the French Revolution, the Soviets believe that progress in schooling will inevitably confirm and spread their message. But the more people learn, the more they will distinguish, compare, ask critical questions, and reject answers they cannot believe. Thus they may discover the inner contradictions that lie in the Russian as in every dogmatic Marxism.

In a treatise that has been called the modern communist catechism, Stalin asserts:

Further, if the world is in a state of constant movement and development, if the dying away of the old and the upgrowth of the new is a law of development, then it is clear that there can be no 'immutable' social systems, no 'eternal principles' of private property and exploitation, no 'eternal ideas' of the subjugation of the peasant to the landlord, of the worker to the capitalist . . . Hence the transition from capitalism to socialism and the liberation of the working class from the yoke of capitalism cannot be effected by slow changes, by reforms but only by qualitative change of the capitalist system, by revolution.[33]

But, if there are only laws of development and of evolution, and if every efficient Marxist must be a revolutionary and not a reformist, why must the order created by Lenin necessarily be stationary and unchangeable? The doctrine that the state would wither away under the new society has already become a pious fraud. If anything, the state has become even more powerful.

In addition, the communist order is no longer socialist, in some respects less so than the modern democracies that allow trade unions and labor parties to participate in the political and economic affairs of the country. Nor is the communist state the all-embracing *pater familias*; it is in the hands of a hierarchically organized party that consists of only 3½ per cent of the population and is continuously exposed to fights among the highest ranks. Why should they necessarily represent eternity in contrast to any other system of government? May they not also be replaced by the inevitable "laws of evolution"? And — unless there is an international conflict of great magnitude or a violent civil war in Russia — it may not even be too bold to guess where this evolution may go. The Soviet worker enjoys increasingly the results of the industrial production. Much though his government may decry the bourgeois, the farmers — who now can read — already complain about the dreariness of the new realistic novel. With rising standards of living the communist laborer himself will become a little bourgeois, just as the worker of the Western countries. Contacts with these countries will increase in the course of time; and the Russian proletariat will use the vocabulary of Lenin with no greater desire to engage in revolutionary adventures than a French liberal who sings the "Marseillaise," or a Daughter of the American Revolution who lays a wreath on the tomb of Washington.

But these are questions that only the future can answer. So far the various political and educational changes in the Soviet Republic have only strengthened the power of communism, and they have not modified the philosophical foundation of Russian education, namely, a materialist dialectic integrated with a desire for national and scientific expansion.

[33] Iosef Stalin, *Dialectical and Historical Materialism* (New York: International Publishers, 1940), pp. 13, 14.

X

The "New" and "Old" Nations and the Persistent Problems of Education

THIS chapter consisted originally of an analysis of the main social and educational events of a number of African and Asiatic countries which after World War II have either emerged as independent nations or undergone decisive transformations: especially China, Egypt, India, Indonesia, Israel, and Japan. Each of them represents particular problems of a political, social, and cultural nature, and, all together, they have created an international situation, unforeseen by statesmen and educators a generation ago. However, in order to avoid the danger of superficiality, this original scheme would have required a second volume, and, more important, would have produced repetitions of relatively similar themes. And, whenever this is the case, one may risk the danger of generalization, rather than tax the patience of the reader.[1]

In addition, by any standard of completeness it would be necessary to include in the picture the new nations of black Africa. Some, like Ghana under the leadership of Nkrumah, or Guinea under Touré, have received independence very recently.

---

[1] A recent publication that deals with problems similar to those discussed in this chapter is that by W. E. Ward, *Educating Young Nations* (London: Allen and Unwin, 1959; published in U.S.A. by Essential Books, Fair Lawn, New Jersey).

Others, in consequence of the retreat of England and France before aggressive African nationalism, will become autonomous, or at least semiautonomous, during 1960 and the following year. Nigeria and a number of territories in French Equatorial Africa and French West Africa fall into this latter group. The political, and consequently the educational, events that will occur in these territories, including even those parts of the world known to a few colonial officers, explorers, and elephant hunters, will throw into the shade even the most surprising historical metamorphoses. People who so far have passively accepted the fate of slavery or semislavery will proudly go to the polls to vote for their candidates, of whom more and more may eventually appear in the French parliament. Tribes, arbitrarily cut into parts by rivaling colonial powers, will try to regain their ethnic unity. Women, so far treated like beasts of burden, will assume their role in society and study in universities at home and abroad. Linguistic groups, some even without an alphabet, will suddenly clamor for literacy. Populations to which even the wheel was a novelty will skip the era of railways and jump into the age of airplanes and of unsettling industrial production. Men will discover that they can participate constructively instead of being ordered. All demand their own government. And all have on their lips the politically vague, but intensely felt, cry for freedom and equality. It may elevate them to cultural heights they have not even dreamt of, but it may also cause them to mistake for the real leader the demagogue who is the worst enemy of African unity.

But, whatever the continent and the nation, its future will largely depend on the quality and the extent of public education. The analysis of the main educational factors, as they have emerged within the new countries, reveals, despite all environmental differences, a number of persistent trends and issues that, once clarified, appear to be of general educational, sociological, and philosophical significance. And, however surprising it may be at the first glance, there is really nothing fundamentally novel in the new nations' developments. For these developments reflect reactions that may appear in every person who is overwhelmed by new constellations of experience. Or, one may understand the events in the new nations more easily by imagining that the political and cultural evolution of the modern Western countries, instead of lasting from the Middle Ages and the Renaissance up to the present, had been compressed into the lifetime of two generations.

Here, I am convinced, emerges another reason for a relatively brief treatment of the new and an extensive treatment of the older Western nations. Even at the risk of appearing arrogant, one must state that it is the education of the West that now spreads over the world, and this to such a degree that it leads to a dangerous self-alienation of the peoples it affects. It is therefore mandatory that our students of comparative education acquaint themselves first with the educational systems of their own civilization; only then can they develop a discriminating judgment of the specific cultural and educational conditions in other countries. It is an old experience that no one can be truly world-minded who is not really at home in his own environment, especially since this sense of belonging creates at the same time that capacity for honest self-criticism we all so urgently need when we direct our attention to the life of foreign peoples.

NATIONALISM VERSUS HUMANITY

The first characteristic of all the new countries, especially when they have emerged from colonial dependence, is a heightened and often-frightening sense of nationalism, which in its passionate radicalism often goes far beyond the emotional limits of sound patriotism. But the same exaggerated feeling penetrated the Western nations when they fought against foreign conquerors, or smarted from the wounds of humiliated pride, or, after many inner struggles, finally achieved unity. One could easily assemble illustrations of it in all these countries, from Russia to Spain and even to America. To what degree the nationalism of the new nations is connected with imperialism, that is, the desire to subject weaker nations, depends on the particular situation.

On the other hand, Sukarno, President of Indonesia, probably spoke honestly when in his address of May 17, 1956, before the United States Congress he denied that the nationalism of liberated countries was identical with the conquerors' complex into which it had often degenerated in the West. Rather it should be viewed as the mainspring of the efforts toward self-respect after centuries of colonial submission. "Understand that, and you have the key to much of postwar history. Fail to understand it, and no amount of thinking, no torrent of words, and no Niagara of dollars will produce anything but bitterness and disillusionment."

Jawaharlal Nehru of India could have spoken the same words. The fact that both Sukarno and Nehru look with envy at certain possessions of European nations which ethnically and geographically belong to their own territory, does not contradict their interpretation of the new nationalism.

On the other hand, especially when, as in the case of China, the new nationalism is connected with the missionary zeal of a new ideology in an overflowing population, it can become dangerously imperialistic. The cruel conquest of Tibet and the clashes on the Indian border offer frightening prospects. But Spain was imperialistic at the time of Cortez; England, at the time of Milton; France, at the time of the Revolution; Germany, under the Emperor and Hitler; and Russia, under the tsars and the communists. It is impossible to disentangle the network of aspirations and ambitions which led these older nations into foreign territories. Some of these impulses issued from religious zeal, the desire to convert the heathens; some from an attempt to open new markets; some resulted from the conviction in having the right political gospel; some, from mere lust for power; and all of them, from some kind of master complex. And, as it happened in the old, so it may also happen in the new nations. It appeared rapidly in Japan before its defeat in World War II.

The nationalism of the new nations is extremely sensitive, just as are individuals in a neurotic situation. Reasons for suspicion certainly exist, but suspiciousness can distort the picture of reality. These countries willingly accept from the more wealthy peoples money, help, and other benefits, but they dislike being the objects of charity, of imperialistic motives, or of political propaganda. Now we all know that the finer grace in help can be turned into bitterness if the giver does not know how to give graciously. Clumsiness on the part of officials of the richer nations has offended many potential friends. There is something precious in personal as well as in international situations, perhaps best expressed in the word "tact." Some people have it, some people can learn it, and some people apparently will never know what it is. On the other hand, it is ridiculous to think that, in our modern situation of international competition, any government can ask its citizens to pay higher taxes and see the money go abroad merely out of a selfless delight of spending. Those who give ask for cooperation; those who do not wish to cooperate should not accept.

The dangers of exaggerated nationalism need not be elaborated. Briefly speaking, they reside in the fact that at a time of untold possibilities of mutual acquaintance and collaboration there may also develop untold possibilities of mutual separation, alienation, and final destruction. Failure to understand the conditions of international cooperation and education is the reason why earlier attempts at bridging the gaps between peoples were not encouraging.

When the shock of World War II revitalized the fading consciousness that there was need of something more than politics to create an international society, there was founded in connection with the United Nations the United Nations Educational, Scientific, and Cultural Organization, generally called UNESCO. Words full of idealism were spoken, and a beautiful Preamble to the Constitution of UNESCO was written beginning with the statement: "Since wars begin in the minds of men, it is in the minds of men that the defences of peace must be constructed." This statement is undoubtedly true, but it is the kind of truth that often leads to false generalizations. For it is not only in the minds of men that wars originate, but also in their hearts and their stomachs, and it is not only ignorance that has created suspicion and distrust — as a further sentence of the Preamble says — but also knowledge. And this knowledge, or falsehood, was spread even in schools. After all, the European nations have known each other rather well for centuries.

As always in cases of flamboyant enthusiasm, there quickly came the disillusionment.[2] The budget, granted to UNESCO by reluctant parliaments, is now about twelve million dollars, a ridiculous sum if compared with the money that even poor nations spend

[2] *Reflections on Our Age. Lectures Delivered at the Opening Session of UNESCO at the Sorbonne University, Paris.* Introduction by David Hardman; Foreword by Stephen Spender (New York: Columbia University Press, 1949). This collection of twenty-three essays reveals the absence of a clear aim in the initial stages of UNESCO.

for other purposes. And the sum would not even amount to that if the United States did not pay one third or more of the total budget. Other difficulties soon confronted UNESCO, especially the jealousy among nations and the suspicion of religious groups in regard to the necessarily nonsectarian spirit of the new organization. However, after the first crises, which would have arisen also with a larger budget, UNESCO has found one important function in training teachers of various parts of the world in "fundamental education." This means in the teaching of literacy in connection with the promotion of health, sanitation, and agriculture. Furthermore, UNESCO distributes information about the educational systems and activities of various countries, promotes the exchange of ideas in the field of education and scholarship, and supports national and international conferences related to mutual understanding. UNESCO serves now also as a laboratory for teaching in neglected areas of the world, an activity the difficulties of which were originally gravely underestimated. If the nations of the world, once freed from the threat of international war, could devote more attention to cultural cooperation, they would find in UNESCO a most valuable instrument. To the student of comparative education and international relations the new organization has already proved to be a much greater help than its predecessors at the time of the League of Nations.[3] It strives toward a future when all the nations of the world will share in the universal legacy of mankind, understanding at the same time that it is not in the plainness of conformity but in the wealth of variety that the creative ground of life reveals itself to the human mind.

THE STATE VERSUS THE INDIVIDUAL

Intimately connected with the problem of modern nationalism is the problem of the relation between the state and the individual. The rise of the sovereign state has been accompanied by the rise of the nationalist sentiment, and in their tendency toward unity and conformity they both represent the more collective element in history as against the solitary and individualist tendencies of the developed human person. The state, represented by its government

[3] See also the bibliography on history textbooks, Chapter VII *supra*.

and the groups that have the greatest influence on it, centralizes, whereas the individual decentralizes. Therefore the relation between the government and the person is to a large degree the same as the relation between centralization and decentralization.

Today, every new nation tries to compete with the West, partly for reasons of power and pride, partly for reasons of physical health, wealth, and material production, partly out of admiration for, or envy of, the cultural and scientific accomplishments of the older countries. But it is doubtful whether one of the West's particular achievements, namely, respect for the freedom of the individual, is included in the emulation. Unfortunately, the Western countries themselves have become increasingly collectivist and conformist, thus betraying and failing to reveal to others one of the best elements in their tradition. Unfortunately, also, the drive toward living up to the West is more virile and dynamic in the political and intellectual leaders within and around the government than in the people at large. It is difficult to mobilize the masses; they want to stay where they are, sometimes even in their misery.

In addition, vested interests fight the new; every revolution is apt to create its counterrevolution. Therefore the government must have power — power to whip up the lethargic, power to carry through the five-year plans for the building of roads, dams, and factories, and power to crush the opposition. The absolutist monarchs who changed the feudal system of vassals big and small used the same power, according to their ways and times. Even where for one reason or another the government wanted schools, they had often to be imposed on the citizens, and fines had to be meted out to the recalcitrant. Jefferson's plans for the reform of education in Virginia were defeated by decentralization.

Hence, most of the new countries incline toward centralization. The French pattern of control of education impressed the Japanese, when after their humiliations by the Americans and British in the 1850's they began to reform their old empire. Indonesia, with its thirty-five million scattered over thousands of miles in thousands of islands, Egypt, still suffering from the most appalling contrasts of wealth and culture, and the recently created African states have to centralize not only politically and economically, but also educationally. Actually, the postwar Japanese education has suffered more than it has profited from the decentralizing measures imposed on it by the American occupation authorities. For they had not enough imagination to foresee that not only the liberal, but also the communist, elements among the teachers might profit from the loosening of control. Even Israel, with its immigrants coming partly from the capitals of Europe and partly from the deserts of Yemen, cannot leave its school system to the hazards of group decisions. And India, where according to the Constitution the responsibility for the public school system rests with the ministries of education of the various states, has nevertheless established an Advisory Board under a central Ministry of Education and thus succeeded in bringing about a certain uniformity. Furthermore, not only in India with its four hundred million inhabitants scattered in seven hundred and fifty thousand villages and speaking more than two hundred vernaculars, but also in other new nations, some agency has to take care of communication, and who else can it be but a central government?

On the whole, in connection with nationalism, centralization — when not excessive — has achieved some of its purposes, even when it showed little respect for individual interests, sometimes perhaps for this very reason. It has stimulated national pride and self-respect and imposed a measure of responsibility on the local communities. In combination with other factors it has improved the status of women by giving them education and political rights and by employing them beside men in public work projects. It has decreased illiteracy much more quickly than would have been the case under different conditions, and governments have also begun to learn that literacy pursued in isolation is no panacea. Unless the learning of letters coincides with the building up of an environment that allows a person to continue his reading for his and other people's benefit, the lessons are, as we know from several millions of people in our own country, nothing but a quickly forgotten exercise.

Finally, only a high degree of centralization has made possible the financing and technical assistance for grand-scale planning in industry and agriculture, and only such planning has enabled some new countries to feed their population and to compete on the world market. Also here the new countries imitate developments they have observed in the older countries, where, in spite of the accumulation and greater elasticity of private capital, it is impossible to carry through such essential activities as atomic research, agricultural production, and international trade without enormous governmental subsidies and controls. The same is the case with education. Even where traditionally it was decentralized, and to a degree still is, as in England and the United States, the universities could not do their work without government money.

But a terrible polarity works in all centralization. It can turn from a means of progress to an all-devouring force. It can even be both at the same time. When Mao Tse-Tung, then President of Communist China, gave his famous "let the flowers bloom" speech, he probably expressed in a flash of generosity the serious desire to avoid the tyranny over the souls of men characteristic of communism. But, when the students and other people applied his declaration of intellectual liberty in their own thinking and speaking, he had to clamp down on them, and on the better part of himself. For, once centralization has passed the small boundary line from helpful assistance and control to tyranny, the tyranny exerts itself even over the tyrant. Education then can no longer be what it should, namely, the helping of a person toward the realization of the best and most humane qualities he finds in himself; it becomes a process of streamlining and of conditioning.

And this peril lurks in every country. Schools have never been free from the danger of producing subservient conformists instead of free citizens. Some kind of indoctrination goes on in every nation, for what healthy society would not wish the values it cherishes to be transmitted to the younger generation? But the difference is not only in degree; it is also in spirit. A good commonwealth wishes to strengthen itself by strengthening the individual in his moral and intellectual wholeness; an evil one wants to use the individual for any purpose it considers conducive to its power. One can phrase the problem also in terms of the relation between efficiency and worth. We all want to have efficient schools in order to produce efficient citizens. But the question is whether this efficiency is merely for carrying out the orders of the government, or for leading a humanely enriching and worthwhile life. And, ultimately, all goes back to the concept man has of man. Is he considered an end in himself, related to transcendent laws we may call divine, or is he merely an instrument to be used by those who happen to have the power? In the continual awareness of this difference and the defense of the rights of man against the usurpations of the state lies the supreme obligation of education, and this continual vigilance is necessary even in democracies.

In connection with the spread of totalitarian dictatorships a question of gigantic consequence emerges on the horizon. Can old cultures be changed into new and lasting ones by order from above, provided, of course, that those on the top have absolute power? Is it, then, false that, as I said in regard to the French Revolution, history finally revenges itself on those who too arrogantly interfere with its inner development? Can one change a nation's character by physically eradicating all opposition groups and ideas? Can one, with the help of radio and loudspeakers, blare forth a constantly repeated set of propaganda phrases? Can one extinguish all desire for a private life by gathering men and women into communes and clothing them with the same uniform? This is now the case in China, which apparently surpasses even Russia in the art of conditioning and social engineering. Were Hitler and his henchmen with their gospel of streamlining defeated perhaps only because they went to war? Certainly their ideas triumph now in other parts of the world and under different banners.

However great our aversion to modern collectivist practices, we cannot, at the present, give a definite answer. Perhaps, when people have lived under collectivist customs, and, in addition, feel that the new policy — which we would call enslavement — is for them a step forward toward national pride, better living, and better schooling, the circumstances may, at least for a while, converge toward the intended result. After crucial elimination of all conflicting forces, the subjects of the collectivist state may form a unity like the parts of a machine, and the machine may work.

But the time must come when the external goal is somehow achieved. Then people may tire of being commanded and may develop an insatiable thirst for being individuals, permitted to enrich their souls through contact with other ideas and free to live with humanity rather than merely with the crowd. Then the present collectivist revolution, extending itself from eastern Europe to large parts of Asia, would be followed by a counterrevolution. It might not be less cruel than the present because the pent-up streams of individuality would rush like wild waters over the broken dams of dictatorial collectivism, until a new order might be achieved. Unless mankind destroys itself in atomic wars, these will be the great problems of the future.

THE ROLE OF RELIGION

It is inevitable that with the rise of nationalism and state control there emerges the question as to the role religion and the churches will play. In this respect several of the new countries, following the doctrines of Marx, identify religion with the old forces of reaction, and in some instances they are not even incorrect. For not infrequently, as we saw, did the clergy enter into the most dubious alliances with suppressive governments and exploiting classes, protect superstitions, and preach obedience when it should have proclaimed liberation. Nor has it hesitated to force the schools and teachers into its service, even when their intellectual and social consciences rebelled. No wonder that the emerging resistance identified the eternal essence of religion with the human — all too human — ecclesiastical institutions, and that the vanguard of the revolt consisted of intellectuals in search of new forms of creativity.

Also here, the countries now in the state of transition offer no new spectacle to the historian. Even governments that claimed to be Christian ran into conflict with vested church interests when they reorganized the political structure: England under Henry VIII, Italy under Victor Emmanuel, Germany under Bismarck. And few countries, if any, are even now free from tensions between their secular institutions, including the public school systems, and the claims of ecclesiastical bodies. Necessarily, the issue becomes much more fundamental and impetuous when the political strife goes hand in hand with a clash of *Weltanschauungen*. Such was the case in France during the Revolution of 1789, and is today the case in all countries allied to Soviet Russia and its ideology. But, whereas it seems that in Russia some kind of balance, though an uneasy one, has been found between the all-powerful state and the submissive Church, in the so-called satellite countries, where communism is alien and the government consists of traitors, all means are still being used to bolster up the weak political foundation by pressure on families and schools. Special devices, such as youth festivals with forced attendance and oaths of loyalty, are invented to discover the nonconformists and punish them by exclusion from higher studies, the professions, and public employment (This, unfortunately, is not new; remember the Corporation Act and the Act of Uniformity in the England of Charles II).

Only in the Islamic countries does religious peace appear to prevail. For, after severe conflicts in Turkey under Mustafa Kemal Pasha, the religion of Mohammed supports the national movements. Yet many members of the intellectual groups from Egypt to Pakistan believe that Islam is responsible for customs and superstitions that have held the people in a state of backwardness and bondage, especially its women. It is unlikely that many of them will retain purdah while others attend modern universities and are seen unveiled at diplomatic receptions. This breakdown of old taboos, more than any political or academic discussion about the rights of women, will change the mentality of the countries involved.

In India, the conflict between the new and the old goes on in the minds of men but has caused relatively little violence. Though the division of the subcontinent into India and Pakistan with all the ensuing cruelties and dislocations was intensified by religious conflicts, the character of Brahmanism and its descendants is essentially nonbelligerent and nonmissionary. In contrast, China betrays the old and venerable Confucian and Buddhist traditions to a degree few persons familiar with the country's heritage would have expected.

One may deplore that in all these conflicts educators, including those in the universities, have shown little independence. There are several reasons for this. The churches possess an organization of their own, with goals and loyalties pointing beyond the state and other earthly powers — though all too often the principles are broken down or ended in compromises. But the institutions of education have been unable to develop an autonomous structure deriving its strength from the recognition of a universal value. The value as such exists; for what can be a more impelling ideal of action than to transmit the best of the human intellectual and moral heritage to the younger generation and thus help them to live a life of truth and responsibility? But too many conflicting interests have always distorted the purity of the purpose: the national and practical claims of the state and the community; the jealousy of the churches, which in earlier times were the spiritual guardians of the schools; the fact that historical truth is not static, but open to different interpretations, which is the reason why there is no symbol for it equal to the perennial symbols of the great religions. Parents desire to have their children formed in their own image and complain when they come home with new ideas. Furthermore, teachers are appointees of the state, or of the community, or of private agencies. Often they are badly paid, especially in elementary schools; in the United States, they are all too easily hired and fired by school boards with political rather than educational interests. On the other hand, their social status — somewhat in between the higher professions and the ordinary wage earner — has hindered them from effective unionization, from resisting undue pressure through collective action. Only in the German and French Revolutions of 1830 and 1848 were teachers a political force of importance. Thus in most cases where they either should have resisted the governments or churches that violated the freedom of human development, or should have supported that defended a just cause, they were merely passively involved, and were always the sufferers. Generally, only heroic, mostly unprotected individuals dared to assert the dignity of teaching and learning.

Whether the new countries will learn from the experiences of the old remains to be seen. But all the changes, even those that seem to us rather external, are symbolic of one fundamental phenomenon, and that is the gradual displacement of divine, transcendental, or supernatural authority unquestionably accepted, by man-made explanations of the role and destiny of humanity. Even where the great religions will be not only tolerated, but actively supported, where the public schools give religious instruction and the statesmen lay value on being seen in churches, man will think about himself and the universe differently from his pious ancestors. This change, going on unconsciously in many minds, will create many moods and interpretations. Partly, it will be caught by the religious systems and establishments themselves through the expansion of their sphere of tolerance to new ideas and ways of life;

partly it will be a religious or a naturalist form of humanism, partly it will be a dialectical or primitively monist materialism. And it will to a large degree depend on education whether the road will go, as some pessimists predict, from religion to humanism, from humanism to materialism and finally to technological barbarism, or whether a new type of man will emerge able to use the wisdom of the past and the knowledge of the present for a future of humanely constructive freedom.

TRADITION VERSUS REFORM

It seems that the new nationalism could be so powerful only because it had to fill a gaping void that came from the sudden disruption of old customs and traditions and thus created the danger and fear of uprootedness. Some of the best expositions of the problematic situation in which the new nations find themselves are the addresses of Nehru, this highly cultured man who more than others articulates, as it were, the self-consciousness of the great Asiatic cultures. In an article contributed to the *New York Times Magazine* (March 1, 1956), he speaks with remarkable frankness of the many contradictory influences that have created what he calls India's "split personality." He first describes his country's "composite culture" (but which culture is not composite?) and the two opposing tendencies in its mentality, "synthesis and absorption" on the one hand and "static separateness" on the other. India, according to him, wavers between the Eastern gospel of detachment and the Western gospel of activism. In this respect, he remarks, the intellectuals have been of no help because they themselves suffer from "a crisis of the spirit, not knowing where to go between the attractions of their own great past, western ideas, and Marxism." In addition, so Nehru confesses, India has not overcome the caste system.

In some way, every new nation is in the grip of similar dilemmas. Myths, magical beliefs, and superstitions still retard the intellectual, physical, and economic progress desired by the leaders; many people who with more reason and energy could live a better life pine under poverty and filth; more rationality, combined with industrial production, could alleviate their suffering. But, though it may be difficult for some Western men to understand, there may be profound comfort in myth. Myth is not only poetry, faith, and depth; it also helps man to bear the burden of life. Take away the mystery without giving a higher alternative, and you create misery even under greater material comfort. Indeed, it should not even be so difficult for us to project ourselves into the mental contrasts of an Asiatic or African peasant or intellectual. In some form or another we still have them in every country. Although we had more time, we still have not yet found the reconciling principle between our religious past and modern secularism. The school systems of almost all Western countries suffer from this unresolved conflict. We still live amidst tensions between myth and science, transcendentalist heteronomy and humanist autonomy, asceticism and worldliness, and, to use Nehru's term, synthesis and separateness. We have no caste system, but we have the separation between different social classes and different ethnic groups. This in some respects may be more cruel than the older caste system, which protected its members from the loneliness characteristic of our enlightened civilization. Many of us have ancestors who during the era of industrialization were driven from their farms into the slums of the big cities, where they had a little more money but no nature, no real neighbor, and no family life. And we have the results of dislocation with us, physically as well as mentally. Otherwise we would not need so many psychiatrists, hear so constantly about modern man's "anxiety," and suffer so much from juvenile delinquency. Truly, even the poor in the United States are, on the whole, materially better off than the Arabian fellahin, though they also may be hungry and sick. But this is not the only standard. Suicide is rare, and partly even unknown, in Asia and Africa. As a matter of fact, even in the Western countries it is more common among the well-to-do than the indigent, the literate than the illiterate, the religiously and environmentally protected than the unprotected.

All these problems, together with enforced expropriations of private property by the new governments and with changes from individual farming into communes (China and East Germany) and from craftsmanship into factory work, have now encroached upon millions of people who for many centuries had lived in a firm tradition of faith, worship, art, and production. Every university instructor knows of the "split personalities" Nehru describes, whether they come from afar or from our own civilization with its pluralistic and contradictory influences.

Thousands of books have been written about the predicaments of modern man, and it would be arrogant to recommend easy solutions. The art of turning revolutionary into evolutionary forces, or potentially disruptive into productive tensions, has been developed in the sphere of the mind just as incompletely as in the sphere of politics. In addition to patience and endurance, this art requires the kind of individual and collective wisdom which understands how to observe and obey the laws that work in man as well as in nature.

The historian Toynbee is right in saying that "the reception of a foreign culture is a painful as well as a hazardous undertaking," [4] but he is wrong when in the same paragraph he says that the reception is always connected with "instinctive repugnance" and "a self-defeating attitude of opposition and hostility." There is instinctive repugnance, but there is also instinctive avidity, the urge to imitate, and the desire "to live up to the Joneses." Let us hope that in the course of time some balance, or some real "acculturation," may emerge. With amazing rapidity the new nations have learned science and technology that it took the West about five centuries to develop. Because of the greater perspective they may be even more able than we to distinguish the true and dynamic that is in Western religion, humanism, and secularism from the obsolete and superficial. If that should be the case then the West may go into the school of the East; in matters of the spirit it has already done so for the past two centuries when Chinese and Indian thought became known to European culture. Christianity itself, let us remember, is not of Occidental but of Oriental origin.

On the whole, let us not be too pessimistic about man's capacity to weather situations of crisis. Crises, after all, are the inevitable accompaniment of virile civilizations. Especially in relation to the distinction between religion and transcendentalism, on the one hand, and so-called secularism and worldliness, on the other hand, many modern writers, especially in the religious camp, indulge in pessi-

[4] Arnold J. Toynbee, *The World and the West* (New York: Oxford University Press, 1953), p. 80.

mism as a kind of perverted mental satisfaction. Or they fall prey to the semantic fallacies that hide in the usual contradistinction between the "religious" and the "naturalist." Profoundly religious aspirations may work in many modes of life, generally called secular or faithless, especially in modern science, whereas crude materialism, theatrical showmanship, and expectations of reward and security — all traits for which the terms "secular" and "naturalist" are much too good — lurk behind many shining religious façades.

It is time that we rid ourselves of time-honored categories that distort reality, obscure more than they clarify, and divide more than they unite. Words and concepts are the most wonderful gift given to man, but they can also be his curse.

XI

Concluding Remarks

PEOPLE have always argued whether the study of history merely satisfies some men's appetite for information and vicarious participation in the great events of humanity, or whether it could have some practical use and serve — to quote the Greek historian Thucydides — "as a key to the future." Certainly, men like to have both the charming as well as the practical aspects of history, and the recent growth of the comparative method in so many of its fields is, at least in part, due to this desire. By combining the vertical with the horizontal approach one hopes to gain an increased insight into the relationships that govern the life of men and societies.

When we combine the historical and the comparative points of view in relation to education, we find first confirmed the rather obvious and often-mentioned fact that the schools and their programs are constantly changing because they are affected by the changes occurring in their political and cultural environment. However, this statement needs qualification. For there exists a relatively high degree of educational stability in cultures and epochs where the end and meaning of human existence are interpreted according to religious, and therefore supposedly eternal, standards and where, comprehendingly, a caste of priests or sages — mostly in alliance with an hereditary aristocracy — determines the structure and context of learning. This, as we saw, was the case in the Middle Ages. It was the case also in old India, China, and the countries under the spiritual guidance of Islam. This situation of stability changes with the growth of secularism and its political concomitant, the national state. Whereas it was possible to describe European education as a whole up to the Renaissance without too much violence to territorial differences, after that period one can no longer picture it as a unified entity. The differences become too great. States and statesmen know of the transitory character and competition of political systems; consequently they wish theirs to be secured as quickly and firmly as possible, and one of the means to this end is the school. In addition, the secular mind is more open to new situations and new knowledge because it is less detached from the affairs of the world than is the religious mind. Thus it wants the schools to catch as much as possible of the conquests of the intellect.

There is a further factor that accounts for the sudden spread of interest in comparative education, namely, competition. Especially since the rise of Soviet Russia as a nation committed not only to a conquering ideology, but also to the training of an élite through education, many governments, so far indifferent to the educational policy of other countries, realize that not only diplomats, generals, and men of business, but also schoolmasters and professors may be important for survival. (France and England understood this years ago after the German victories from 1864 to 1871.) Unfortunately, this growing awareness has, though in different degrees, led men to regard the schools not only as places of intellectual and moral training, but also as political agencies. Even in the United States certain patriots would like to direct a whole battery of oaths against our students, refusing to see that thus they imitate the strategy of totalitarian nations against the democratic liberty of thought. Apparently, one can destroy what one intends to protect. How to serve one's state loyally, and at the same time preserve one's freedom and intellectual dignity, is one of the crucial questions that confronts all institutions of learning.

In spite of the exposure to the vicissitudes of the day, there is still a higher degree of historical continuity in the area of education than in many other fields. Even totalitarian countries that apparently have broken with the past discover, after a while, that not only political indoctrination, but also substantial learning based on a long intellectual tradition, will decide the nation's future. China, profiting from Russia's experiences, has recognized this fact from the very beginning. And, more and more, even dictatorial governments will discover that it is not only bodies and brains over which they have to rule, but beings who want to live as human beings. The Russian farmers declared that they are tired of political and realistic novels; they want to have literature that satisfies their emotions.

But, however constant certain elements in the perennial enterprise of learning, and, however permanent and strong the demands of human nature against the encroachments of modern politics, the fact remains that increasingly in modern times education has been torn out of its safe moorings in the grounds of civilization. It has become a part of grand-scale planning and statesmanship on which the future of civilization will depend just as much as on other and generally more clamorous institutions and activities. And within this broader context it is especially the study of comparative education in combination with its historical aspects from which we can hope to receive increasing insight into the cultural policy of other nations, together with reliable criteria for the evaluation of our own plans of action.

For the United States such insight into the nature of planning [1] is not only a domestic but an international responsibility. The way in which it is discharged will decisively affect our relation to other peoples and thus our own prestige and prosperity. It is pathetic that it was reported as a unique event that one of our ambassadors to a South American nation invited students to his home for a friendly exchange of opinions on controversial matters. Every diplomat should do this kind of thing, for unless he is informed about the education of the men, women, and youth he meets, he cannot understand the people about which he has to report.

For about fifty years, thousands of students from Asia and Africa have studied in our universities, not only to participate in the advance of scholarship, but also to organize their schools according to patterns they consider superior to their own. In addition, we have sent thousands of educational emissaries into other nations, many of whom were shockingly ignorant about the conditions of their work.[2] They have done more harm than good not only

[1] See in this connection the works of Karl Mannheim, especially *Freedom, Power, and Democratic Planning* (New York: Oxford University Press, 1950).
[2] See William Ernest Hocking, *Experiment in Education* (Chicago: Regnery, 1954).

to foreign countries, but also to their own nation, which they were supposed to represent.

One cannot simply transfer the structure and program of schools from one people to another according to preconceived opinions gained from the standards and experiences at home. For only in a remote way can the means and goals of education be derived from an abstract concept of man; they must harmonize with the lives and ideas of men in particular circumstances. The planners and organizers of school systems, whether they work at home or as consultants to foreign governments, will have to take into account the religious beliefs, customs, and traditions of a specific people. And, however much they may be convinced of the existence of overarching and transcultural values in the life of humanity, they will have to gear the programs of teaching to the work of the men and women in their communities, as well as to their individual talents. Just as they will have to create respect for intellectual achievement, so they will have to increase the respectability, now generally low, of practical work through good vocational schools — "good" referring here to the capacity to combine vocational training with the understanding of human values and interests. Many more people than we think in our world of words grasp theoretical problems better through manipulation than through mental exercises isolated from concrete applications.

We rightly consider it the duty of a civilized nation to provide schools for every youth to the extent to which he is capable of profiting from them, irrespective of birth and race. Yet, even in the most advanced countries we are still far from the goal. Moreover, the attempt to intellectualize the whole world is against the natural limits of the average person's intelligence. It can only lead to general mediocrity by pulling the theoretically gifted down and by pushing the primarily practical type above his understanding.

The old countries were wrong in restricting the possibilities of leadership to the socially privileged classes, thereby excluding large groups with potential talent, and they were also wrong in setting up an inflexible school structure that separated the overwhelming majority of pupils in elementary and vocational schools sharply from the very small group of university candidates. But they were right in insisting on the training of an élite. Least of all can a modern democracy live without it. With modifications required by the change of time, Jefferson's plan to recruit an aristocracy of talent out of a broad social foundation is still the only one that will work, because it is just, realistic, and appreciative of excellence. In their own way, the Russians follow it. But in their understandable desire for better leadership several younger nations have built their educational system upside down, that is, they have created too many higher institutions rather than elementary and practical schools. Striking examples are the Philippines at the time when its school organization began under the tutelage of the United States, to a degree India under English influence, and Ethiopia and other African countries to-day. Such conditions inevitably produce the alienation of an intellectual group from the totality of the population (lawyers instead of leaders) and finally an intellectual proletariat, uprooted, unemployed, and consequently dissatisfied and revolutionary. During the depression the unemployed university graduates of Europe formed the vanguard of the most unproductive revolutions. These men were highly educated professionals in a society that was not fitted for them because it could give them no adequate and satisfying work, and for which they were not fitted because specialization and false pride had made them inflexible. In our modern industrial societies overproduction is the danger to man, not underproduction as in earlier ages. Prosperity may change to depression, and it is sounder and easier to raise intelligent though mainly practically trained men to the challenging work arising in years of higher demand, than to keep overspecialized intellectuals or semi-intellectuals quiet and satisfied in years of want.

The life of the next generation will be influenced by the enormous increase of population. If it continues at the rate of the past decades, it may grow from 2,500,000,000 in 1950 to 6,250,000,-000 in the year 2000. Scientists debate whether these masses will find sufficient food; they fear that the genetic constitution of man will suffer from mushrooming caused to a large degree by parents of low responsibility; and there is the question whether these millions of youth can be properly educated and employed. In India, all attempts at better schooling and employment may be defeated by the waves of human masses. The problem of birth control rises demandingly.

To a degree, more people create more work. But, with the development of technological research and automation, invention and creation will be done by a few, while the occupations of others, provided they can be employed at all, will become more and more mechanical, or at least shortened. Can adult education and "education for leisure time" solve the problem? Or will it not be wiser to avoid the ever-growing danger of enforced passivity by an education that, without degenerating into mere manual drill, makes possible self-help in times of stress, teaches people to repair their houses and even to build simple ones, to make their own furniture and to support their household by growing some vegetables. If this seems to be useless and unfeasible in industrially overdeveloped areas, it is, as Gandhi emphasized, certainly advisable in other parts of the world. Even at places and with people where it may seem to be useless, it may be most helpful. Many a man with high intellectual and political responsibilities receives his recreation from some practical hobby. Pestalozzi is still right when he demands the education of the head, the heart, and the hand, and with intelligent youth the last element in the triad of education will not take away undue time and strength from the first two. On the contrary, some practically constructive activity will support the general learning. In the long run one cannot build a culture on overburdened and nervous scientists, on the one hand, and television audiences, on the other hand.

Whatever the situation, education is not for itself, but it is for human happiness, though not understood in an hedonistic sense. It should provide the conditions under which the human goal of inner wealth, personal dignity, and social productivity can be organically connected with an individual's talent, status, and occupation. And what is true of a person is true also of a nation. Organic education, if one may use this term, helps to make a good and happy nation as it helps to make brave men, whereas inorganic education, however great the achievement in isolated knowledges and skills, will end in misery and disappointment. Immense is the responsibility of those entrusted with the direction of the moral and intellectual future of the coming generations.

XII

New Developments

In recent years no revolutionary changes have occurred in the field of education. Rather, the nations portrayed in this book have strengthened, debated, or refuted educational trends that were already germinating at mid-century.

ENGLAND

IN England today Aunt Dot (the symbolic figure mentioned on pages 127 and 128) would still have to give a somewhat evasive answer to the Russian's question about equality in English education. The Public School boys from Eton, Harrow, Winchester, and similar schools still occupy most of the significant positions in government and other important areas of public life. The Establishment is still strong and ardently defended by the conservatives, who advocate the separation of the university-oriented grammar school from the less demanding types of schools and who are therefore up in arms against the further expansion of the comprehensive high school. They are, however, retreating before the will of the nation to modernize its schools according to democratic principles. In 1964 the government announced that all secondary schools would be reorganized on a comprehensive basis. New comprehensive high schools, somewhat similar to the American model, will thus incorporate more and more students after the age of eleven. This means that the grammar school, which now makes provision for approximately 20 per cent of the nation's high school age children, will be under the same administration as the modern school, attended by about 70 per cent, and the technical school, which serves about 10 per cent.

The discussion of a new unilateral system versus the older separatist system also excites the minds of other European nations and, to a degree, the United States with its old and indigenous tradition of the single-ladder school system; it seems appropriate, therefore, to reiterate briefly the arguments in this debate. In spite of national differences in terminology and structure, comparisons can easily be drawn.

In England, the advocates of the comprehensive high school point to the clearly existent social injustice in the schooling of the nation's youth and to the fact that many equally gifted (or perhaps even more gifted) children from less privileged families, if educated in better schools, could serve the nation just as well as those from the higher ranks of society. They complain that the teachers of the modern schools are inferior in comparison to those of the grammar schools. Only the comprehensive high school, they argue, can provide for the off-spring of the masses a culturally and materially more satisfying life. Furthermore, they do not recommend the same education for all children, but a flexible, varied, and multi-streamed school instead, within which each child can be guided according to his abilities. Finally, they state that failures in a few instances say nothing against the value of the majority of the comprehensive schools. After all, if the system works in the United States and, mutatis mutandis, in Soviet Russia, why should it not work in England?

Naturally, the Labour Party stands behind the comprehensive school. It is being blamed for laxity by the impatient, however, not without some innuendo about the Public-School past of various prominent labor leaders. On the whole the English populace, relatively satisfied with new social developments and perhaps apathetic toward larger cultural issues, leaves the school debate mainly to the representatives of the more ambitious middle classes who hate the present discrimination against their children on the basis of caste and money. Ever since the American and French Revolutions these groups have been the protagonists of productive reforms.

On the other side, the conservatives (supported, like the progressives, by specific organizations and lobbies) emphatically assert that the comprehensive school fosters the modern mass culture which increasingly endangers the precious values of individuality. They point out the danger of leveling down the intellectual standards, the inevitably impersonal atmosphere in schools which have as many as two thousand pupils (in the United States the number goes up to seven thousand), the waste of time for superior students, and the usefulness of selective schools as a preparation for higher studies. Drawing on history, they praise the high quality of leadership which the independent schools have provided for the English nation and the advanatges of an elite in any social system, and they warn of the danger inherent in changes of old cultural patterns — not to speak of the growing expenses against an already heavily burdened budget.[1]

The decision concerning change from the differentiated school system to the comprehensive pattern rests with the individual local education authorities. Whether the pendulum swings toward one side or the other will depend on the social and political composition of those groups.

Certainly in England, as elsewhere, the older image of the educated man who is supposed to have been nourished by the great authors of antiquity will give way to the concept of a person capable of coping with his personal and professional tasks within a modern technological society, replete with moral and social conflicts. "Along with scholastic reform this entails the purposeful transformation of many cultural influences and social institutions that do not always at first sight seem to have anything to do with Education." [2]

If there is any need for demonstrating the present transformation in our cultural patterns, the fact that Cambridge, following Oxford, has given up the last vestige of Latin requirements will

---

[1] A provocative discussion of the problem can be found in the July 7 and the July 14, 1966, issues of the English Radio and Broadcasting Journal, *The Listener*. Those interested in the sociology of knowledge will certainly not fail to notice that not only in England but in all Western countries the representatives of the traditional humanities, or of the old "liberal arts," are suspicious of school reforms, whereas the representatives of the new social sciences favor them. Each side, of course, claims to argue on strictly objective grounds.

[2] Edmund J. King, *World Perspectives in Education* (London: Methuen, 1962), p. 113.

serve as an illustration. Simultaneously, despite religious instruction in school (insisted upon by the ecclesiastical Establishment), the influence of Christianity on the minds of the young will continue to recede, though probably not to the point of a loss of interest in religion as such. The roads of the past have come to an end. Modern man's thinking about himself and the universe has changed; but an acceptance of crude forms of "materialism" or "naturalism" has not necessarily been involved. These dogmatisms are as absent today as is religious dogmatism.

However, the generation or regeneration of culture depends on the flow of many sources; the school is but one of them.

FRANCE

Whether or not we consider one-man rule in a modern society desirable, such a rule certainly reveals to us the inabilities of the citizens of that society to arrive at important decisions by means of democratic procedures. Nevertheless, there can be no doubt that "le général" has put an end to the protracted deliberations about reforms that characterized the educational policy of France from the time of World War I and, to a degree, ever since the French Revolution of 1789.

The reform programs of 1959 with Jean Berthoin and of 1964 with Christian Fouchet as Ministers of Education have given to the French people a school system that coordinates the elementary school (age six to eleven/twelve) with various forms of post-primary or terminal education for those who do not desire, or would not profit from, a prolonged education. Provided the reform is effective, these schools, from 1967 on, should retain their pupils up to the age of sixteen and give them, in addition to a basic general education, a similarly basic introduction into the various practical activities of the nation — agriculture and the industrial crafts, for example.

The more ambitious youth will go through a two-year *cycle d'observation* (age eleven to thirteen) and then have a choice between, on the one hand, a three-year course of somewhat advanced general and vocational character (*l'enseignement terminal*), or, on the other, a tripartite *lycée* (classical, modern, technical) with a bewildering variety of curricular subdivisions (age thirteen to eighteen). At the end of such a four- or five-year course (*l'enseignement général long*) the intelligent and persevering student is rewarded with the *baccalauréat*, which only 15 per cent of the appropriate age group receives. The less theoretically minded but practically gifted children may, after the *cycle d'observation*, enter a *collège d'enseignement technique* and after that a higher technical school which is not on the university level.

There also exists, after the *cycle d'observation*, a short general education (*l'enseignement général court*) from which a promising student may be transferred into a *lycée*. But this is an exception. Most graduates enter somewhat advanced activities in agriculture, handicraft, commerce, or industry. Or a student may enter a training school for elementary school teachers (*école normale*): in France, as in England, the "schoolteacher" is prepared on a pre-university level. The adult who wants to go on learning finds, as in most modern countries, many opportunities in the increasingly developed institutions for adult education.

A French youth is confronted with an educational structure of an elaborateness unequaled in any other nation. But once he has made up his mind about his course of instruction he will be guided by teachers who, even though not always stimulating, are nevertheless competent in their subject matter.

On the whole, the educational work of de Gaulle is more a stabilization and redirection of previously existing trends than a creative reform. The policies adopted have been conservative and in some respects even arresting, though partly based on the programs of Langevin and Billères. (See page 171, above.)

When reading M.-A. Bloch's *La Pédagogie des Classes Nouvelles*, published in 1953,[3] one has the feeling that after the liberation French pedagogy underwent a resurgence similar to that which occurred after 1918. The difference between the earlier and this later resurgence is that the ideas and plans which were then even more radical (as exemplified by the demand for an *école unique*) have now been carefully balanced against the traditional concepts of French education. That which Mr. Bloch and his friends ask

[3] Paris: Presses Universitaires de France, 1953. In the series *Nouvelle Encyclopédie Pédagogique*.

for is a combination of French individualism with a new educational socialism. "It is necessary that we pass from a deadening encyclopedism that threatens to become inhuman to a truly human culture (culture humaine) which is at the same time individualistic and social." [4]

At the same time, the advocates of the *classes nouvelles* are demanding careful psychological guidance for the pupil in order to help him discover his individual talent. Furthermore, they are asking for stronger efforts toward freedom, motivation and activization of learning, and a more thorough understanding of the influence of environment on a pupil. They want a closer coordination of the various disciplines of learning and eventually a whole "transformation of the milieu of the school."

Apparently these ideas have influenced the authors of a momentous reference work of 1,176 pages,[5] parts of which were certainly written before the Gaullist educational reform of 1959. The *Encyclopédie*, which expresses both a historical and contemporary point of view, provides a comprehensive description of the various functions and responsibilities of the school in a modern nation. The pervading tenor of the book is well expressed in the concluding chapters that deal with *L'Education et le Monde de Demain* and relate the schools, in a manner so far unknown in France, to the whole social development of the nation. With remarkable sincerity the authors admit that their country, as a result of the growth of the birthrate and of political and economic changes, finds itself suddenly compelled to take quick action. This, "*après une longue inactivité*," has taken the nation by surprise [6] and will require strenuous efforts.

It is necessary, the authors of the concluding chapters assert, to rear a new generation of men and women who are not merely recipients of tradition, but who are also capable of coping with a changing world. The makers of social and educational policy must come to understand that the gravest obstacle to progress is the combination of poverty and unproductive working methods. In-

[4] *Ibid.*, p. 12.
[5] *Encyclopédie Pratique de l'Éducation en France, publiée sous les Patronage et avec le Concours de L'Institut Pédagogique National* (Paris: Ministère de L'Éducation Nationale, 1960).
[6] *Ibid.*, pp. 1160ff.

stead of being afraid of the increasing involvement of the masses in the cultural process, they will have to find ways of integrating even children of low-standard families into the productive work of the nation. What a change from Henri Bergson's insistence on Latin as the indispensable requisite of the French *esprit de précision!* (See page 168, above.)

The modernists are not unmindful of the dangers inherent in sudden changes in the social setting. They are afraid of the moral consequences of a one-sided scientific and technological orientation for modern youth. The more modern science progresses the more, they assert, we become aware of our ignorance of the deep secrets in man and nature; consequently, the more we must insist on instruction in the humanities.

The question we must now ask is to what degree the spirit of the advocates of the *classes nouvelles* and the authors of the *Encyclopédie Pratique* is alive in the schools of the Fifth Republic.

American writers have often wondered at the seeming contradiction between the centralized administration of the French and their veneration of rank and authority on the one hand, and their individualistic spirit on the other. Indeed, it seems as if the monarchical absolutism of earlier centuries has remained in French culture just like the cathedrals which still stand in the centers of the French cities — the one difference being that the cathedrals are becoming emptier and emptier (except for the tourists), whereas the offices of the government grow more and more crowded. De Gaulle is the most striking symbol of the French desire for authority (which, as with the Germans, is the counterweight to an excessive self-centeredness). Nevertheless, he is not and has never desired to be a dictator. He has, certainly, silenced voices of discontent on several occasions in a somewhat dictatorial manner, especially in the army, but he has never abolished the right of political opposition.

Communism, to which some of the most prominent French writers adhere, is a great force in France — greater than its actual parliamentary representation indicates. The elections of March, 1967, proved that since the party's low of 1959, caused by its unpopular subservience to Moscow, it has been rebuilt. Its membership has increased from three hundred thousand to almost half a million, with half of the members under forty years of age and apparently above the average Frenchman with regard to both earnings and education. France has, traditionally, ten times as many communist voters as party members.

Many parents gave their votes to the "Left" (which includes the large social-democratic party) because they were dissatisfied with neglect of the schools by the Gaullist government. Thus, the criticism which the radical Marxist Georges Corgniot levels against the French schools certainly represents more than the voice of an isolated radical. No doubt the French can read the same violent objections to their school system in their press as Americans can when they peruse their own radical Negro press.

Corgniot describes the school policy of the fifth Republic in the following manner: [7]

> One rightly discovers there the plain aspect of reaction: obscurantism and the favors extended to the Roman Church; the denial of indispensable credits for public education, authoritarianism, militarism, etc. But one should not conclude that this is merely a form of mediaevalism. On the contrary, it is a well deliberated form of modern politics, constructed to serve the monopoly of the capital.
>
> On the one hand, the development (of modern industry) requires more engineers and superior technicians, on the whole more scientists, but one needs engineers and scientists who are docile and malleable, as much as possible stripped of general culture, similarly foreign to a rational understanding of the world as to a truly democratic mentality. We have seen that "le gaullisme," following its inherent logic, intends to diminish the role of a liberal culture (culture générale) in the lycées. It wants to have mathematicians, but they should be without culture and without the temptation to think. . .
>
> The inequality in education reflects and solidifies our social inequality. The more the broad social classes endanger the hierarchy of the capitalist order, the more it will erect inaccessible tiers in the edifice of learning.

Of course, this criticism of the French schools is written from the point of view of a man who fundamentally denies the value of modern capitalist democracy. Although on this point the contributors to the above-mentioned *Encyclopédie Pratique* would object, the more liberal among them would agree with him in other ways; for Mr. Corgniot offers abundant proof that despite

[7] *Láicité et Réforme Démocratique de L'Enseignement* (Paris: Editions Sociales, 1963), pp. 184ff.

the official separation of state and church in France (see page 157, above) the Catholic Church still exercises the same considerable overt and covert influence on the education of the country as the various denominations do in other countries. The Church, he says, insists on state support of Catholic schools, but it denies to the working class and its communist party the right to establish their own state-supported private schools.[8] Without the slightest proof the Church has consistently asserted that there is an indissoluble connection between morality and the Christian faith,[9] with the effect that it has taken the French people a long time to believe "that an atheist can be an honest man." But "everybody knows that in the *Résistance* the largest number of the heroes of national independence, who were men of character and self-negation, were furnished by the class that according to the Church is the most heathen, namely, the working class. 'Only the working class,' said Francois Mauriac, 'has in its totality been faithful to dishonored France.' "[10]

It would take too much space to describe further the content of Mr. Corgniot's book. It is highly opinionated, but for anyone interested in modern state-church relations it contains an unusual number of interesting references that apply not only to France but also to other nations, especially Italy and the United States. It is sufficient to say that Mr. Corgniot finds in the French schools "une atmosphere morale deprimante."[11] This is natural considering his point of view, though one may doubt whether he would find the schools of Mr. Ulbricht's communist East Germany more congenial to his spirit.

Nevertheless, a perusal of Mr. Corgniot's book might cause even the convinced democrat to reflect on the impact of an authoritarian government upon the structure and mentality of the schools. It is difficult to deny that the stability which de Gaulle has given the French school is at the same time the stabilization of an excessively cumbersome and complicated structure of learning. Instead of facilitating it may be choking the pupil's freedom of choice. And in spite of the admonitions on the part of the Ministry

[8] *Ibid.*, p. 64.
[9] *Ibid.*, p. 73.
[10] *Ibid.*, p. 73.
[11] *Ibid.*, p. 137.

of Education that the teacher should develop more originality and initiative in handling his subject matter, the rigorous (and centrally controlled) examination system stifles his inventiveness. Many creative Frenchmen still feel that the high intellectual achievements of French schools are bought at the price of genuine joy of teaching and learning.

But whether with or without cheerfulness — the conservatives would say — we want our schools to serve first of all as institutions to convey knowledge and intellectual discipline. Real genius is not so easily killed. Our schools cannot have done so badly: they have helped us to stay together through cruel wars, and through ninety-nine governments during forty years of the Third Republic (1870–1940) and twenty-five governments during the fourteen years of the Fourth Republic, in the perilous years of 1944 to 1958. They have certainly contributed their share to the present vigor and prosperity of the nation, though we must admit that more educational opportunties should be provided for the working population. But let us not lightly experiment with our schools, for they train our youth in the art of toughness, patience, and reasoning and may save us from rebellion when the time comes to get over the bridge from the regime of de Gaulle to a new and uncertain road of republican life.

There is more to it than mere political, or social, or national interest. There is a profound moral feeling. Says one of the greatest teachers of France, Alain (whose real name is Emile August Chartier [1868–1951]) in a sentence the beauty and preciseness of which is difficult to render into another language:

> Je ne promettrai donc pas le plaisir, mais je donnerai comme fin la difficulté vaincue; tel est l'appât qui convient à l'homme; c'est par là seulement qu'il arrivera à penser au lieu de goûter.

> [As my aim, I will not promise pleasure, but the human triumph over difficulty. This is the lure which it behooves man to follow. Only thus will he become a thinker instead of a dabbler.] [12]

GERMANY

It is understandable that after the collapse of 1945 Germany concentrated on the reconstruction of its destroyed cities and their industries. Surprised by the economic miracle after years of despair

[12] Alain, *Propos sur L'Education* (Paris: Presses Universitaires de France, 1963).

and hunger, it forgot that the revival would have been impossible without the knowledge, energy, and experience of well-trained men who had survived Hitler and the war and who knew how to use the few existing resources and the aid from the Marshall Plan to the advantage of the country. Germany thrived, then, on intellectual capital which was left over from the past and which would have to be replenished by a younger generation educated in schools adapted to a new world of international exchange and competition. This would require the broadening of a school system, especially at the secondary and tertiary levels, that in the past had achieved relatively high scholastic standards, but had made it almost impossible for at least 80 per cent of the people (especially members of the rural and working population) to benefit from the more advanced levels of learning.[13]

Suddenly it dawned, almost two decades after the war, first to a very few educators and then also to men in business and administration, that the nation was threatened by educational disaster — a *Bildungskatastrophe* — unless drastic measures were taken. As a result, a number of newspaper articles and brochures appeared in 1964 and 1965 which pointed out, among other disturbing facts, that in those years only 10 per cent of the elementary school graduates completed the ninth year, and that in 1963 not many more than 7 per cent of all secondary school age youth had graduated from secondary schools as compared with about double that figure in Belgium, Finland, France, Norway, and Sweden.[14] There was danger that the gap between Germany and other countries would constantly widen. In 1970, Yugoslavia and France would have trebled and Italy and the Netherlands doubled their high school populations. If the situation of 1963 prevailed, in 1970 all graduates from higher institutions would have to enter the teaching profession if the need for teachers were to be met.[15]

Actually, these comparative predictions are doubtful. In view

[13] Two carefully documented articles on German education appeared almost at the same time: Charles H. Whiting, "Crisis in Higher German Education," *The Educational Forum* (January 1967), and John H. van de Graaf, "West Germany's Abitur Quota and School Reform," *Comparative Education Review* (February 1967).

[14] See Saul B. Robinson, "The Newly Founded Institute for Educational Research," *Comparative Education* (November 1965), pp. 31ff.

[15] See especially George Picht, *Die Deutsche Bildungskatastrophe* (Freiburg: Walter-Verlag, 1964).

of the structural and qualitative differences of national school systems and the interlocking of elementary, secondary, and tertiary forms of education it will always be difficult to provide reliable data. Nevertheless, even if a considerable margin of error is granted, the symptoms described by the critics do indicate a severe malady in German education and a severe threat to its future.

One of the first steps toward recovery has been the foundation of the Institute for Educational Research (*Institut für Bildungsforschung*) in Berlin, with Professor Hellmut Becker as initiator and director. (In several books Professor Becker had, prior to this, pointed out the close interconnection between education and the political and economic development of a country.) Furthermore, the neglected *Deutsche Institut für Internationale Pädagogische Forschung* at Frankfurt has received new support. And finally, the heretofore slumbering governments of the German *Länder* (states) and their ministries of education, as well as a number of intermediate organizations, have begun to act. Thus the dour predictions of the years 1964 and 1965 may not materialize at the end of this decade.

What were the causes of the school crisis in a country that had been respected for almost two hundred years as the model of education from the primary school upward to the university?

The main cause has already been noted: two wars, with the resulting depletion of the youngest and most vigorous parts of the population. To this must be added the culture shock of the Hitler period that changed "Das Land der Dichter und Denker" into "Das Land der Richter und Henker" (roughly translated: the land of poets and thinkers into the land of henchmen and executioners).

It is painful for a conscientious person emotionally attached to the country of his ancestors and their cultural achievements to teach recent German history to questioning adolescents who want answers about the motives and causes behind organized mass murder. When we and the teachers of other countries — especially those with long histories of colonialism and slavery — reach down deeply inside ourselves for the answers to such questions, we should be embarrassed, and we should not allow ourselves to glide smoothly over the dark spots in the stories of our own nations or of humanity as a whole. A slave market in New Orleans, though an event of the past, is also a testimony of what so-called respectable people can do or tolerate. The collective German crime record, however, is the youngest and in its concentration on a brief span of time the most atrocious of all.

An adolescent will also ask how insane fanatics, a small group in comparison to the total population, could subject a supposedly civilized nation to that most shameful form of tyranny which was at least partially welcomed by the German nation. The fact also remains that the liberation of the Germans from their self-imposed bondage had to be achieved through the intervention of enemy nations. The famous and much advertised officers' plot of July 20, 1944, would certainly not have occurred if the army had been victorious and enabled Hitler to extend his tyranny over all Europe. Thousands of young socialists and some religiously in-spired men and women had already died martyrs' deaths before them. Thus, many Germans have lost faith in human culture; others find a spurious kind of comfort and pride in economic efficiency and prosperity.

The teaching profession of Germany today is no longer as socially prestigious as in earlier times. Even at the famous old Gymnasia the teacher is not the scholar who was once given time for private studies and writing; instead, he is forced to teach over-crowded classes for twenty-five hours a week.

Furthermore, social and political arguments prevent a thorough reform of the antiquated German school system. Notwithstanding all social upheavals, except in a few progressive cities, the con-servative forces of Germany are still strong enough to resist major changes. (Ironically, their antidemocratic attitude was reinforced by clumsy and inexperienced American "re-educators" who, im-mediately following the war, tried to impose their concepts of "progressive" education on the bewildered Germans. And the exhibits in bookstores of the American army of occupation were hardly appropriate for convincing Germans of the superiority of American education.)

The German school structure is not as complicated as the French, though its problems resemble the French ones in several respects. But in contrast to other countries, including France, a child in almost any German state who wishes to enter a more advanced school must leave the common elementary track after four years [16] — at an age when he is too young to make valid decisions about his talent and fitness as a pupil in an advanced school. Furthermore, with few exceptions the various forms of the Gymnasium (classical, modern, and scientific) still extend over a period of nine years — in other words, up to the age of nineteen plus.[17] The number of dropouts in the Gymnasia is still staggering, though it has decreased during the past years. In 1962, of the pupils in the third years of the Gymnasium only 41.8 or 6.8 per cent of the total population was graduated. Since then the number has risen to nearly 50 per cent.

Of the graduates of the nine-year Gymnasium almost all enter the universities. But there again the number of failures is considerable, so that at present Germany is providing no more than approximately 5 per cent of its young men and women with an academic training somewhat adequate for meeting the demands of modern professional life. According to the aforementioned article by Charles Whiting, only ten out of every hundred thousand citizens of the Federal Republic possess a science degree, in contrast to forty-six of every hundred thousand in the United States and sixty-seven in the Soviet Union. To be sure, all these statistics are necessarily dubious: there are great differences, for example, between science degrees granted in Sweden, France, the United States, and the U.S.S.R. Moreover, graduates from difficult schools that grant no degrees may be better educated than degree-holders from easier schools. Are all of the more than two thousand institutions of the United States, of which most grant degrees, really institutions of higher education? In this particular respect the German picture may not be as dismal as it appears statistically; in Germany only universities or similar institutions grant degrees. Nevertheless, the academic road is for-

[16] More detailed statistics and certain variations from the rule can be found in the article by John H. van Graaf, entitled "West Germany's Abitur Quota and School Reform," *Comparative Education Review* (February 1967), pp. 75ff.

[17] As indicated above, on page 214, there exists in Germany the so-called "*Realschule*," an intermediate branch between the elementary school and the academic school. It can be compared with the French *l'enseignement général court*, as it prepares its graduates (age sixteen/seventeen) for the middle ranks of society. Most modern countries have a similar school type.

bidding to children of the working population or of parents with uncertain wages, even though some *Länder* (Hesse, for example) have abolished tuition in high schools.

Adding to the difficulty is the fact that in Germany, as in other European countries, the idea of social mobility has not been adopted as readily as in the United States. A person who enjoys some security in his work and income is more content with his social status than the typical American. One may sometimes ask oneself who is the happier.[18]

Unfortunately — also in Germany — interest in political and social prestige interferes with rational educational policy. The organization of the so-called *"Höhere Lehrer"* (the teachers at a Gymnasium or a comparable school) jealously defend their traditionally superior position above the elementary school teachers, who are generally trained in special pedagogical academies outside the universities. This jealousy is understandable to a degree in that everybody expects some reward for prolonged efforts. Nevertheless, the fact remains that with few exceptions the German *Studienrat* (or *Höhere Lehrer*), though well prepared in terms of subject matter, is miserably prepared for his task as instructor, whereas the teacher in the elementary schools knows something about teaching methods. However, the struggle between the two groups contributes to the separation of the more advanced schools from the schools of the people. The prestige complex is even more evident in the universities, because of the antiquated control of the *professor ordinarius* and *Institutsdirektor* over the younger members of the academic body.

All public polls indicate that the university professor still towers at the apex of the professional hierachy. However, the painful shortage of competent young scholars and the gradual rejuvenation of the academic body will enforce a more cooperative system. Furthermore, the five universities now in the planning and construction process will have to be more experimentally and democratically minded than the old ones if they are to attract young teachers of high quality. They will also make room for the many students who, so far, have been forced to work in over-

[18] See Suzanne Grimm, *Die Bildungsabstinenz der Arbeiter* (München: J. A. Barth, 1966).

crowded laboratories with obsolete instruments. On the other hand, particularly after the destruction of the last war, these new universities will have great difficulty in building up adequate research libraries.

No doubt, the regime of Chancellor Adenauer, though extremely successful in many other respects, had little regard for the free pursuits of the intellect. Many good Catholics confess frankly that their Church has been a retarding element in the cultural life of the new Republic. Some bishops seem to live in a medieval mental world; miles behind some of their German colleagues who are the leaders in the ecumenical movement, they still promote the old confessionalism that has been the plague of the German schools for centuries.

One of the greatest hindrances to a concerted direction of German schooling is the lack of a federal ministry of education. (Denominational narrowness is also largely responsible.) There is no central agency to guide the educational policy of the various Länder. As a matter of fact, the Ministry of Education in such a traditionally decentralized country as England, and the Federal Office of Education in Washington, have recently influenced the schools of their nations more effectively than any comparable agency in Bonn — if there is one. Nothing has come from Germany comparable to the English *Robbins Report on Higher Education of 1963.*

During the past decade, however, the conferences of the ministers of education of the various states and the newly established *Bildungsrat* have brought about some unification of the various school systems. Parents can now move more freely from one region to another without too much fear that their children may lose a whole year of life because of unsurmountable differences in the structure and curricula of the schools. Industry, suddenly realizing that it may have to import not only workers but also scientists and engineers from other countries, is also beginning to take a stronger interest in the education of German youth.

Germany can only regain its former role in the cultural life of Europe and maintain its economic prosperity if the culturally and politically responsible groups acquire a deeper comprehension of their educational responsibilities. A school system which a century ago could somehow excuse its overselective and exclusive character on the grounds of its high scholastic achievements is no longer adequate in the second half of the twentieth century.

As many student demonstrations and innumerable articles in the student press prove, German youth has for years and in the strongest terms complained about the obsolete school structure, the physical (and mental) conditions in the classrooms, the shortage of competent teachers, and the inaccessibility of the overworked university professors. This is a youth deeply concerned with Germany's past and future; anxious to learn; and eager to come into contact with other nations.

The authorities finally seem to be yielding before overwhelming pressure; but German officialdom, though reliable, is slow and encumbered by red tape. The political horizon of the older and traditionally conservative generation of officials, moreover, is deploringly limited.

The old and rather inane slogan that children should be worthy of their parents is heard often. With regard to Germany, one is inclined to reverse the sentence.

THE UNITED STATES OF AMERICA

If one wished to make a somewhat accurate generalization about recent developments in the school systems of the United States, it could be derived from the country's desire to create more order in its educational structure. That desire was already evident in the various reports mentioned earlier in this book (pages 252 ff.). Dr. Conant, in the meantime, has added to his report of 1958 (*The American High School Today*) a vivid description of the differences between the schooling of the underprivileged children in the crowded quarters of our big cities and that of the children of the well-to-do in the fashionable suburbs.[19]

In February, 1967, a sequel to the 1958 report appeared, entitled *The Comprehensive High School: A Second Report to Interested Citizens*.[20] In it Dr. Conant states that only 10 per cent of the recently investigated two thousand high schools of average

[19] *Slums and Suburbs* (New York: McGraw Hill, 1961).
[20] New York: McGraw Hill, 1967.

size and environment measure up to the demands raised in the earlier report. These demands, if compared with the intellectual achievements required by high schools in other countries, are rather moderate (see page 253, above). Nevertheless, most observers would agree that the teaching of mathematics is improving, and so, to an even higher degree, is the teaching of science. If a reliable comparative survey could be made, the United States would probably excel in the teaching of social sciences, despite all the debates and uncertainties about the critical introduction of the young into our complicated society.

On the other hand, the teaching of the humanities, except the English language and American history, is badly neglected. In certain schools of the state of California the teaching of Spanish is a fake, the vocabulary not extending far beyond words like "Los Angeles" and "San Francisco." On the whole, the linguistic illiteracy of the average American, and even of university students, makes it difficult for him to project himself into the culture of a foreign country.

In his various reports Dr. Conant purposely abstains from philosophical statements about the aims and values of education. "Over the years," he says in his Inglis Lecture *The Revolutionary Transformation of the American High School*, "I have wrestled with definitions and struggled with chains of logical reasoning; I have been guilty of my share of educational banalities. As a consequence, I must confess to an increasing distrust of the deductive method of thinking about questions confronting teachers." [21]

By placing "definitions," "chains of logical reasoning," and "deductive method" in the same category, this sentence becomes somewhat confusing because these are logically distinct notions. Furthermore, though to a different degree, they are inevitably involved in the making of educational policy, even in scientific research. All educational policy contains certain deductive and intuitive elements; and without some definition of aims, even those beyond the immediate purpose, the parts may lose direction and coherence.

Dr. Conant's statement, no doubt, expresses the aversion of

[21] Cambridge, Mass.: Harvard University Press, 1959, p. 1.

a famous scientist for abstract and nonempirical forms of thinking. This aversion is obvious in all his reports and partly explains their success. But it has harmed the validity of his report, *The Education of the American Teacher*,[22] because the report deals with a field in which fact-finding and conclusions drawn from "evidence" (however that term is construed) can and often do lead to one-sided recommendations.

To be sure, the report has merits: it rightly recommends improvements in the preparation and certification of teachers and in the relation of the teaching profession to universities, state boards, and other administrative agencies. But it has been disappointing and even frustrating to many leaders in the field who have hitherto sincerely welcomed Dr. Conant's criticism in an admirable spirit of self-examination (which might serve as an example for other scholarly departments).[23] They are rightly afraid that the pragmatism which pervades all of Dr. Conant's writings has led him to venture into an atomistic program of action. Such a program would remove the broad philosophical and cultural elements now included in the preparation of teachers and reduce their profession to a mere craft which, after some liberal education and some training in the methods and psychology of teaching, could be learned simply through an apprenticeship — this at a time when other nations are striving for a deeper understanding of the responsibility of the teacher in modern societies that are currently in profound moral and intellectual crisis.

The planned National Assessment Project to be conducted under the direction of Ralph Tyler (Director of the Center for Advanced Study in the Behavioral Sciences, in Palo Alto, California) should be as important for the unification of American education as the Conant reports. There is some fear that this project may be the forerunner of a centralized examination and control system in disguise, different in name and organization but nevertheless similar to that of France, and that it may force the process of education into narrow grooves, crippling the freedom and initiative of the teacher. As it is presently planned, there is

[22] New York: McGraw Hill, 1963.
[23] See especially *Phi Delta Kappan* (June 1964), "Conant's Impact on Teacher Education," and the excellent article by Harry S. Broudy, "Conant on the Education of Teachers," *The Educational Forum* (January 1964), pp. 199ff.

no reason for such fear: the goals will be set, not by a central government agency, but "by a variety of committees representing both educational and lay groups. It will evaluate neither individual pupils nor school systems, but rather will develop some types of national norms against which communities can judge themselves. One can quarrel both with the project's insistence upon having a broad consensus on goals and with its conservatism, but one can only applaud its attempt to inquire into what and how we are doing in our schools. The extent of the attacks against it is a measure of its necessity." [24]

The United States, like the U.S.S.R., has an advantage in its unified educational structure leading from the elementary school to the high school and the universities. Hence it is spared some of the frustrating struggle of the older nations for a socially just and democratic school system. But this democratic quality turns out to be a myth if high schools have no more in common than the name, as is the case if we compare the schools of the state of New York with those of Mississippi, or even if we compare the schools of various districts of the city of New York with each other.

This is the main reason for the strengthening of the Federal Office of Education under Presidents Kennedy and Johnson. For the first time in history the Office has become a policy-making institution that can allot immensely increased sums of federal money to school systems, provided minimum standards are met and local authorities commit themselves to support the Civil Rights Program of Presidents Kennedy and Johnson.[25] Support of the Office will perhaps vary in degree under different presidents and congressional majorities. Nevertheless, its influence will continue and will have a lasting impact not only on education proper, but on the whole culture of the nation.

If sheer numbers mean anything, in 1966 Congress passed the International Education Act and extended the Elementary and Secondary Education Act. The Eighty-eighth and Eighty-

[24] Quoted from the Dean's Report 1965 to 1966, Graduate School of Education, Harvard University.

[25] See the book by the former Federal Commissioner of Education, Francis Keppel, *The Necessary Revolution in American Education* (New York: Harper and Row, 1966).

ninth Congresses enacted more than thirty educational statutes. When President Kennedy took office, federal funds for education amounted to three billion dollars a year; now they are ten billion. From 1961 to 1966 the budget of the Office of Education was multiplied eleven times.[26]

Of course, the contributions of money and legislation, important as they are, may be wasted unless they receive the moral support of the people; and this moral support will depend in turn on the nation's willingness to grant the full rights of citizenship and education to its almost twenty million Negroes. Certainly the recent study by James S. Coleman entitled *Equality of Educational Opportunity* (commissioned by the United States Congress through the Office of Education, and dealing with the effects of racially segregated schooling on American children) will be just the beginning of further studies and demands. The heavily documented study, *Racial Isolation in the Public Schools*, commissioned by President Johnson in 1965 and released by the U.S. Commissioner on Civil Rights in February 1967 shows that, unfortunately, almost nine out of ten Negro children still attend racially imbalanced schools. The study also proves that this imbalance is worst at the elementary level (where it is also most harmful), that it hurts white as well as colored children, and that it can be corrected only by desegregation in housing.

This would not be the first time in human history that prejudices — and not only prejudices, but also very real difficulties in the adjustment of groups of different backgrounds — have prevented men from seeing clearly what they are doing to future generations. But America is not a country to despair: if things are bad at one point they are better at another. Almost every day the newspapers report on some phase of education. More than in other countries, it has become a national concern; and now the great industrial companies, as well as the government, are becoming more and more involved in education. These companies are interested in the financial aspects of an enterprise which, if one includes the factor of manpower, amounts to an expenditure of about fifty billion dollars each year.

[26] See Samuel Halperin, "Significant Events of 1966" and "Education Legislation in the 90th Congress," *Phi Delta Kappan* (February, 1967).

Thus, a gigantic educational industry is in the making — the great publishing houses and communication centers, technological firms, electronic companies, and investment agencies. Some of these entrepreneurs are interested not in quick profit, but in a new and perhaps satisfying cultural venture. Nothing gives a more informative picture of the new educational developments in brief than the issue of the *Saturday Review* containing the report and analysis presented annually by the Committee for Economic Development, "Changing Directions in American Education." [27] This report predicts that after a decade even the most advanced school system of today will be antiquated. The school of the future will contain centralized tape libraries; closed-circuit television systems; electronic teaching machines, which promise to be particularly useful in language instruction; programmed learning systems for detailed, repetitive instruction; scanning devices in each classroom, linked to the library records office in order to free teachers from many routine functions; computer centers for grading, cataloguing, and retrieving information; and a flexible open-circuit television network for current events.

To some of us such a school may look like an enormous factory populated with children. Indeed, the danger is great that with the attack currently being made on educational problems by so many industries, the school itself may become a technological institution — the school commissioner like a general of a technical corps in a modern army, and the principal a kind of top engineer. The final effect of all these projected plans will depend on the answer to the same basic question upon which the future of our whole civilization depends. Will machines become the masters of man or man the master of the machines? Will they free him or will they enslave him? With regard to the past century the answer of the historian will be ambiguous: they have done both.

In such an enterprise as education and our schools, which involves the happiness and free personal development of our children, let us hope that the spirit of man will be stronger than the demon of mechanization.

[27] *Saturday Review* (January 14, 1967).

NEW DEVELOPMENTS

In the previous chapter on Russia we mentioned certain characteristics of Soviet education, among them: the materialistic and collectivistic interpretation of man; the conception of education as a means for training communist fighters; the trend toward federal centralization under control of the party; the emphasis on labor as the proletarian principle of education; and, finally, the hostility against religion.

On the whole these trends have persisted during the past decade. This decade has also confirmed the ability of the Russian government to adhere to the basic principles of Marxist-Leninism even when compelled to modify certain details of policy. This ability has been demonstrated again in the handling of educational maneuvers made by Nikita Khrushchev.

Khrushchev, afraid of the emergence of a new intellectual class that might become detached from the life of the people, re-emphasized the revolutionary idea of "labor," or "polytechnic," training that had been abandoned after earlier enthusiasm about the future of a completely novel "proletarian culture" had waned. (See pages 277ff., above.) As long as Khrushchev was in power, the leading pedagogues dutifully reiterated his idea of labor education. They also tried to revive the paling memory of their greatest revolutionary educator, A. S. Makarenko (1888–1939), who had declared that the school must be "the collective" — indeed "must be the only collective which unifies all the processes of upbringing." [28]

"All-round education" became the slogan. F. F. Korolev, Director of Research at the Institute of the Theory and History of Pedagogy, even compared the new aim of education with the Greek ideal of the harmonious man, the *aner kalos kai agathos*, but with one difference: for the Greeks this ideal had been the privilege of the ruling class; now it was to be deeply embedded in

---

[28] See Helen B. Redl, *Soviet Educators on Soviet Education* (New York: The Free Press of Glencoe, 1964), p. 149. On Makarenko see also Frederic Lilge, *Anton Semyonovitch Makarenko* (Berkeley: University of California Press, 1958), and James Bowen, *Soviet Education, Anton Makarenko and the Years of Experiment* (Madison: University of Wisconsin Press, 1962).

the life of the common man. On its realization (or so Mr. Korolev thought) depended the emergence of a true communist society.[29]

No doubt, one of the reasons for the excitement among educators was the sense of relief that followed the death of Stalin in 1953. Under his regime no one would even have thought of writing an article with the title "Let There Be More Enthusiasts!" as A. D. Aleksandrov did in 1962. And, we read in an important communication of the *Sovetskaia Pedagogica*, "The Plan and Research Problems of the Academy of Pedagogical Sciences of the RSFSR for 1962," the following sentence: "All of us well know that the cult of Stalin's personality had a deadening effect on the development of public education and of pedagogical science. As a consequence of the personality cult our Soviet labor school was gradually transformed into an improved type of the pre-revolutionary gymnasium." [30]

On Khrushchev's initiative the ten-year common school was changed into an eleven-year school, mainly to make room for the new curriculum in which one-third of school time in grades nine, ten, and eleven was spent in the theory and practice of labor-polytechnic-production training. For admission to the universities, two years of practical work after high school were required; the higher education curriculum was lengthened; and correspondence and evening courses were established for the training of specialists.

At the same time school "internats," or boarding schools, were founded and integrated as much as possible with the collectives in industry and agriculture. On January 11, 1964, the *Uchitelskaya Gazeta* could even report on the first factory run exclusively by school children making dolls and clothing.[31] Indeed, the Five Year Program anticipated that the internats, promoted so intensely by Khrushchev as communist model schools, would by 1965 have as many as two and a half million students.[32]

[29] *Soviet Education*. I.A.S.P. Translations from the Original Soviet Sources (New York: International Arts and Sciences Press, January 1962).

[30] The article of Aleksandrov is to be found in *Soviet Education* (April 1962), and the quote from *Sovetskaia Pedagogica* in *Soviet Education* (June 1962). RSFSR is the abbreviation of "Russian Socialist Federated Soviet Republic," which constitutes the federation of the western — that is, the leading — states of Soviet Russia.

[31] Jaan Pennar, "Five Years after Khrushchev's School Reform," *Comparative Education Review* (June 1964), p. 74.

[32] Helen Redl, *Soviet Educators*, pp. 196ff.

But once again it turned out that they were chasing after an ideal. Few teachers had received sufficient training for the new polytechnic education, and in many instances it became, as all bad vocational education does, more of a tinkering with tools than real work. Adequate textbooks were unavailable; rivalries developed between schools and factories. Serious efforts to combine practical and theoretical education resulted in the overworking of pupils. After graduation, many young people did not know how to apply their skills. Furthermore, a shortage of well-trained candidates for the academic professions threatened. In 1962 there were five hundred thousand dropouts in Soviet schools, of which 50 per cent were in rural areas; and repeaters in all grade levels in the RSFSR amounted to one million two hundred thousand.[33]

Thus, after the enforced retirement of the seventy-year-old Khrushchev in October 1964, the party reverted to the educational realism of the 1950's. The number of school years was reduced to ten: in other words, to the same length as before 1958; polytechnical training was sharply reduced, though not completely eliminated; and the admission requirements to the universities were changed. Only a very few of the school internats exist now.

However, this retreat from Khrushchev's more adventurous plans in favor of a policy which the now retired statesman would suspect as a sign of "bourgeois leanings" should not tempt us to presume a general relaxation of the educational temper of the Soviets. On the contrary, when reading the journals and reports on teacher conferences, one gets the impression that a great deal of intense activity, self-examination, and directiveness is going on in Russia today. In fact, if national and ideological differences are taken into consideration, one could draw up the same agenda and list of research topics for a teacher's symposium in the United States or in the U.S.S.R. For instance, the same concern exists with the apparently considerable number of failures and dropouts, with the systematic improvement of the methods of instruction and the preparation of teachers, with the discovery of the pupil's cognitive capacity and interests at different age levels, with the

---

[33] See the excellent analysis by M. Rosen, "Changing Guideposts in Soviet Education," in *New Directions in the Soviet Economy*, Part III, "The Human Resources" (Studies prepared for the Subcommittee on Foreign Economic Policy of the Joint Economic Committee [Washington: U.S. Government Printing Office, 1966]). See also Jaan Pennar, "Khrushchev's School Reform," p. 75.

advisability of using such technical means of instruction as radio, television, and film strips, and finally with the perpetual topic of the moral conduct of the younger generation.

In an article entitled "The Spiritual Needs of Students in the Upper Grades," Iu. V. Sharov declares that a high level of "spiritual needs," like the need for the beautiful and for social activity, is not only "the most important characterological feature of a comprehensively developed and well balanced personality, but is also the most important condition for its formation . . . The problem of developing moral needs," he continues, "is extremely complicated." [34] All over the world, teachers would agree with him; but in regard to Soviet Russia a deeper problem emerges, ably discussed by Allen Kassof in his book *The Soviet Youth Program: Regimentation and Rebellion.*[35]

To what degree can an educational system with its schools and various youth organizations tightly controlled by the omnipotent party of the total state (in other words, administered by functionaries dependent upon orders from above) help create moral strength in the Western sense of the term? There is no reason to believe that Soviet youngsters behave better or worse than those of other nations. However, many Russian educators today seem to miss the true revolutionary devotion of the creative period, not realizing that the system they defend is in itself problematic from an ethical point of view. Morality is not identical with outward behavior or obedience to rules the intrinsic value of which one does not dare examine because one is not allowed to. But since the Renaissance and Reformation (neither of which ever wandered from the West to the Russian East!) we have known that every society which forbids a person to insist on being himself, or on being "free" in the sense of acting according to best of his conscience, deprives itself of genuine ethical substance.

Whenever these human privileges are offended by overcontrol, the costs are high. They create that climate of lethargy and boredom which always emerges when a human being knows that whatever he does is not his own doing. But another symbol of

[34] *Soviet Education.* I.A.S.P. Translations from Original Soviet Sources (December 1956).

[35] Cambridge, Massachusetts: Harvard University Press, 1965.

existential misery may also emerge: namely, a pathological desire for extravagance, showmanship, and that hectic display of originality which buries the creative depth of a person more than it unfolds it. Boredom and violence are not far removed from each other.

The observations of Allen Kassof agree with the impressions of many travelers. The *stilyagi*, often compared with our beatniks, appear in growing numbers on the streets of the cities. People are concerned with the "nihilistic tendencies" of the younger generation. Thus, if we consider the problems of education in our seemingly opposed democratic and communist cultures, the differences seem to diminish. Everywhere a part of youth, often not the worst, has difficulty in finding its place in our rapidly advancing but at the same time spiritually floundering technological environment.

On the other hand, there are encouraging signs that we do not resemble each other merely because of mutual concerns, but also because of more positive developments. For example, Russia now allows some private industries to build plants on its side of the curtain. Scholars, writers, and students are openly exchanging ideas, and the Communist Party permits, though reluctantly, exhibits of abstract art. (So there is at least one point on which it agrees with the Western bourgeois.) In terms of politics proper, Russia today is no longer the Bolshevist nation of Lenin and Trotsky, the terrorized nation of Stalin, or even the nation of Nikita Khrushchev, who after many years of isolation dared cross the Russian boundaries. All official propaganda and indoctrination to the contrary, there is a great deal of evidence that Russians are beginning to think differently about Americans and Americans about Russians.

Even the school systems of the two countries are acquiring some similar features. The Russians are now beginning to appreciate the advantages of a general and the Americans the advantages of some vocational education. Both systems aim at a unified but in itself differentiated course of learning, and in this respect they resemble each other more than they resemble the school structures of the countries of the European continent, which still carry the burden of an old social structure.

Of course, deeply rooted ideological differences often lurk

behind structural resemblances, and they certainly do so in the case of communist Russia and democratic America. Nevertheless, equal organizational patterns always indicate at least a degree of likeness. Both countries believe in the advantages of a unified school system that allows every young citizen, according to his talent, to enjoy the blessings of a rationally oriented education.

To be sure, without their size and their resources neither Russia nor the United States could be where it is today. But South America, China, and India are also spread over enormous territories. To a large degree, it is universal education which distinguishes advanced from retarded countries, as many of the "underdeveloped" countries are discovering.

The world certainly hopes that the power and intelligence of the Soviet states and America will be used not only for technological competition, but also for giving mankind that degree of security which it needs for making this planet a place where hunger and fear are increasingly superseded by health and mutual confidence.

THE TRENDS OF THE FUTURE

The question to be considered now is whether those developments in school systems which have just been discussed will allow us to make certain predictions about the future of modern education. I think they will; but we may well disagree about the desirability of the trends we are able to foresee.

1. Education and the State

More and more often, the opinion of Plato and Aristotle that education is a part of statecraft is confirmed. As has been discussed in earlier sections of this book, whenever a government has tried to mould the people under its rule into a loyal and self-conscious nation the importance of indoctrination of its youth has again been demonstrated. Whether the government has been monarchical or republican, conservative or revolutionary, whether it has left the direction of youth to a cooperating church, or whether the secularization of culture has forced it to place matters educational under its own auspices has made no difference. In each case, the goal has been the same: the making of good patriots and loyal citizens.

Nevertheless, there has remained, except under dictatorial regimes, some educational independence for individual regions and communities; and outstanding teachers have been able to place the stamp of their personalities on the schools they have founded. Today, the chances for such variety are waning. Very few centers of learning can operate without some state aid and, therefore, without some central control. What are the causes of this development?

First, the demands for justice and equality in education, and for the freedom of youth from the handicap of poverty, can be effected only with the support of an institution like the state which comprises the totality, and not merely the mutually jealous parts, of the people. All over the world, the separation of state and society — assumed by Adam Smith and the old liberals to be the rule — is making way for the state enjoined to create and uphold a welfare society (which is supposed to socialize without necessarily creating a socialist or communist politico-economic system). To a degree the state is partial, like any other human institution. Fluctuations of educational policy clearly demonstrate that it reflects the opinions of a majority, which might often be intransigent in regard to minority opinions having equal or perhaps greater value.

A paradox thus appears. On the one hand, the state widens the chances for the development of hitherto neglected talent; on the other hand, it is the great leveler. It levels up; but it also levels down, and even where a minority rules — as in modern dictatorships with their heroes and hero-worship — the minority, no less than the majority in a democracy, attempts to reduce social and educational differences in the life of the nation as a whole. In contrast to democracies, sometimes considered averse to the "outstanding" and the aristocratic, every dictatorship is essentially plebeian whether it comes from above or from below. Its constant fear of youth with independent minds explains why the dictator usually initiates his reign with a hasty attempt to conquer the schools.

As indicated earlier, however, our modern democracies must

guard against the degeneration of their ethos of equity into the monotony of egalitarianism which, along with old class prejudices, is perhaps the reason for the opposition of certain parts of the English population to the government-sponsored comprehensive high schools, and for the tenacity with which the nations of the European continent reject the unlateral school structure of the American pattern. Such egalitarianism may also be part of the reason why, in the United States even more than in other countries, private schools appeal to an increasing number of parents even though their children's attendance often requires considerable financial sacrifice. The case for private schools cannot be proved or disproved in regard to scholastic achievements; in fact, the achievements of the larger public schools may even be better as a whole — often they are in individual cases. Nor are larger schools necessarily detrimental to individual development: small establishments can be confining. Nevertheless, in spite of all that can be said in favor of the public school, many of us feel an instinctive repugnance for educational mass production.

Doubtless, the trend toward state control and collectivization of education is supported by the fact that our modern nationwide forms of schooling (which sometimes extend beyond the political boundaries of a single nation into the arena of international cooperation or competition) need planning and financing on such an enormous scale that only a centralized government can afford the undertaking.

Just as in industry the old individualistic entrepreneur must make room for the "manager" of a big company (who, however willed and skilled, can still be hired and fired), so the well-paid but uniformly trained and uniformly thinking school superintendent appears now in our larger school systems. He is not asked to be a teacher, scholar, and thinker, and he may be even less educated than many of the classroom teachers under his supervision; but, like the business executive, he is supposed to have administrative talent. This managerial trend is not confined to the public schools: the modern American college president is no longer expected to be a scholar, either.

To speak of the financial side alone, English universities were virtually self-supporting until World War I, as were some of the richly endowed higher institutions in other countries. Today, it is a fair guess that 70 per cent of expenditures for scientific research in England and the United States comes from the government; and most countries subsidize their universities completely.

Recently, industry has become the provider of education along with government, especially for the universities, because it needs well-trained scientists who understand how to build computers, nuclear plants, automatic machines, and missiles. However, the alliance between industry and the state may be as little a contributive to the development of independent minds as the earlier alliance between the state and the clergy.

The menace which we have already pointed out in Chapter X of this book — namely, the kinship between state power, collectivism, and nationalism — may imperil, even in democracies, the precarious quality of freedom. To what degree, then, are modern nations educating their youth for a personally and socially courageous and creative life which insists on the right of dissension?

Certainly, all nations need loyal citizens. But the citizens who help their nation to thrive are the citizens prepared to distinguish between those aims and ends of action which do and those which do not deserve their loyalty, regardless of whether or not these ends are being promoted by the state. Only if we have a sufficient number of such citizens do we have reason for welcoming rather than fearing the power of the state. The state is not a thing in and for itself; rather, it is what we make of it. It has been said with some justification that a nation has the government it deserves; citizens educated for conformity, therefore, will have a collectivist society.

There are only two chances for escape from this vicious circle. One is the possibility that the memory of those values which remind man that he is not only a citizen of his country but also a citizen of a spiritual universe beyond all national boundaries may not entirely disappear. This spiritual universe, by no means identical with churches and established religions, may even be strongest when it appears outside our conventional establishments. The second is connected to the first, but in a more concrete and practical way. It is the hope that our political conscience will increasingly widen beyond family, community, and nation to incorporate mankind as a whole into its orbit of thought and action.[36]

2. The Prolongation of Education

The second trend evident in modern education, and just as replete with great possibilities and disturbing problems as the trend toward collectivism, is the prolongation of school age. As a matter of fact, the two are interrelated.

Longer school attendance is generally welcomed as a sign of an advanced civilization, and rightly so. But let us not indulge in the belief that it always results from the initiative of the people. In fact, European governments recently encountered almost the same apathy, if not opposition, toward the introduction of the ninth and tenth years of elementary education as the governments of a hundred years ago encountered when trying to convince the masses of the advantages of the sixth or eighth year.

The real force behind recent prolongation of school age is the necessity to adjust our institutions of learning to the social and vocational changes of the present. We have lost the apprentice-ship system and many other opportunities for early and useful occupation, for which our schools must now provide a substitute. Furthermore, our modern civilization is so complex that even its fundamentals cannot be understood without a rather extended form of training.

We flatter ourselves by thinking that the average man of today is much better educated than his ancestors. In terms of mere knowledge, he is, But it is doubtful whether the schooling he receives contributes to the harmonious development of his personality. One frightening fact alone should cause us to think: during the past decade juvenile delinquency has doubled in several Western countries, and it is rising in Japan and Korea and apparently in every industrializing nation. Sitting on school benches is no substitute for the farm, the workshop, and the sailing vessel of earlier times; there is no adventure in our schools.

Hence, the modern educator has the responsibility not merely

[36] See *Education and the Idea of Mankind*, edited by Robert Ulich under the auspices of the Council on the Study of Mankind (New York: Harcourt, Brace and World, 1964).

to provide *more* schooling, but the *right* schooling — an education that does not simply *inform*, but *forms* a young person — or his school may turn into a parking place. The transformation of the school of today from a center of instruction into a "school for life" (to use the phrase of the founder of the Danish folk schools, Bishop Grundtvig) would require a fundamental reorganization of our whole modern school system. In view of what man needs in order to mature and to order his often restless energies into an organic whole, all our high and higher schools are antiquated; and this will be increasingly true the more we cling to the mythical identification of verbal with real learning.

Relying somewhat on test results from various countries, we may assume that about 20 per cent of the human race are so constructed that intellectual pursuits reach into the living and creative center of their personalities. Those people represent the truly theoretical type. But by far the large majority of men and women learn best when their learning is incorporated into some practical work which for them has a definite meaning in terms of what they are, what they would like to be, what they want to do, and what they are able to do. This requires — preferably within the pattern of a comprehensive high school — an elastic combination of theoretical education with vocational and practical challenges and actual responsibilities, be they in workshop, garden, or field, in working with animals, or in working with human beings in a community.[37]

We arrange and classify all our pupils on the basis of a primarily intellectual scale, placing the "brainy" child at the top. Indeed, in an intellectual culture like ours he belongs there, and we should do for him whatever is possible. But we should not let the others gradually glide down to the bottom of the scale without realizing that most of them also have an inherent chance for a kind of excellence which, if appealed to, would change the constant threat of frustration they feel into constructive action. The millions to be spent for teaching machines and other electronic devices may be all to the good; but unless we replace those lost

[37] I have drawn up a plan for a school that would do justice to the various kinds of human talent in my *Crisis and Hope in American Education* (Boston: The Beacon Press, 1951. New edition, New York: Atherton Press, 1966.)

chances for personal initiative and trial and error with new chances for initiative and commitment in the schools of the future, we will have more and more juvenile delinquency and student riots. Schools are necessary for civilization, but they may also hollow it out from underneath. The great Swiss, Pestalozzi, predicted the inner decline of civilization when he spoke of the curse of a culture that teaches words and phrases without teaching the meaning they expressed when they were created — or, as he called it, their "truth."

Let us therefore find out in the future how much reality and how much myth inhere in our educational doctrines and practices; how much knowledge we impart that generates new knowledge, and how much of it is inert; how often we prepare a young person for life, or how often we postpone his entrance into a rewarding occupation that would give him a sense of self-respect and a place in the social order. If we ask these questions we will find, when we contemplate the nature of man and the tasks which mankind has before itself, that much taxpayers' money now spent on education is sheer waste.

3. Education and Science

So much has been written about "science and the modern world," or about the "two cultures," that an extended debate on this topic would only be a repetition of arguments which have become commonplace.

Nevertheless, we should examine the question of whether our schools, which up to some decades ago were primarily history-oriented, are now becoming oriented toward nature and matter to such a degree that they fail to provide a sound balance between man the empiricist and engineer on the one hand, and man as that strange creature who cannot forget that he has a soul, whatever that may be, on the other hand. Actually, the problem reaches beyond the already antiquated controversy between science and the humanities and into the problems of determining to what extent our schools will rear a generation of men and women and fathers and mothers who are capable of educating their children, and to what extent our universities and schools of education will produce a generation of teachers who are inspired by a sense of cultural mission and who refuse to repeat unthinkingly the slogans of a metaphysically hollowed-out culture.

In view of this situation it is disappointing to notice the difference between past reports on educational policy and those of the present. In spite of pious assertions about humanistic subjects, the emphasis today is one-sidedly on the improvement of science and not on the improvement of man in his totality. One can even notice a nationalistic flavor in such reports which is intensified by our newspaper coverage of educational issues: interest in the promotion of knowledge as a human value seems to inspire contemporary journalists much less than the question of competition with other nations, especially with Soviet Russia. Some of these writers also convey the impression that the nation with the highest number of high school graduates versed in the art of calculus is the most educated nation. In the spring of 1967 the prestige of Japan was unexpectedly heightened by the news that the *International Study of Achievements in Mathematics* had placed it at the top of the list of twelve nations participating in the inquiry, with the United States ranking among the bottom six nations.[38] But the public reads very little, if anything, about the fact that the teachers of Japan are profoundly troubled by the rapid transformation of their society. They are also anxiously debating the effects of the separation of public education and religion, which was imposed upon them by American occupational forces in 1945, as well as the growing indifference of the younger generation to the nation's spiritual and moral heritage. No one knows how to replace the rapidly vanishing old values with new ones that are equally inspiring.

This problem troubles all modern and modernizing nations. We have no universal image of man toward which to order our various educational activities. The hope that science will provide it has vanished: itself science is in a state of profound philosophical uncertainty.

Nevertheless, we may foresee the beginning of a new convergence of ideas, or of a new *Weltanschauung* (if we will ever have one), in the growing conviction among educated men that the universe is one and cannot be divided into a sphere of causality

[38] New York: John Wiley and Sons, 1967.

and a sphere of miracles. Any philosophical system or religion which offends this conscience will be relegated to the realms of superstition and sentimentality — which, we have learned and are constantly learning, may for a while (even for a long while) be more powerful than rationality; but in the course of time the latter will defeat the former.

The disintegration of old traditions that are often indissolubly amalgamated with the whole history of a people makes us wonder whether we can still speak of an "education of a nation" in the customary sense of the term: as the provision of a stable system of values, often metaphysically sanctioned, which have helped a people to retain their identity in times of external trouble and inner bewilderment. The present predicament has been brought about largely by the corrosive doubts created by scientific research which have been actively dissolving cosmologies and myths since the eighteenth century.

But it is still within our power to determine whether we want these doubts to remain primarily negative. The very conviction that the universe is whole and undivided should tell us that mankind, with all its errors and conflicts, is also essentially *one* because it is a part of the whole of nature. Even if we can no longer accept as literal guidelines for the future the myths and national traditions of previous generations, man has nevertheless expressed through them a common thirst for meaning. And even if we recognize that this thirst has embodied itself in forms of thought taken from prescientific and, geographically, extremely limited stages of world history, we must nevertheless not forget that in many ways there is more wisdom hidden in these earlier stages of imagination than in many of the rationalist platitudes of today. Hopefully, the scientist will eventually come to accept the fact that all profound wisdom is and must remain somehow ambiguous; otherwise it becomes commonplace and as such either tautological or trite.

There lives in man an inner substance — call it, if you like, an instinct for moral and physical survival — deeper than all the religions and philosophical speculations based upon it. Amid dangers beyond his wildest imagination man has not only survived, but he has been strengthened in his quest for a better life.

NEW DEVELOPMENTS

It is science in the broadest sense of the term — not separated from, but interacting with, the humanities — that should teach us from which inner resources of mind and nature these forces come and how they can be developed through the right kind of education. Then we may see, in the midst of the confusion within which we live, not only a reason for anxiety, like that which every soldier feels before battle, but also a justification for taking fresh courage. After thousands of millennia of slow development, constantly interrupted by war and mutual suspicion, we may yet learn how to use the gift of human understanding for the ultimate creation of a truly human society in which the nations of the world will no longer fight, but will help each other instead in order to achieve new levels of moral and intellectual growth.

References to relevant books are contained in the footnotes. For the study of comparative education the following suggestions may be useful.

1. Erich Hylla and W. L. Wrinkle, *Die Schulen in Westeuropa* (Bad Nauheim: Christian Verlag, 1953).

Kandel, Isaac L., *Comparative Education* (Boston: Houghton Mifflin, 1933).

Kandel, Isaac L., *The New Era in Education. A Comparative Study* (Boston: Houghton Mifflin, 1955).

King, Edmund James, *Other Schools and Ours* (New York: Rinehart, 1958).

Schneider, Friedrich, *Triebkräfte der Pädagogik der Völker. Eine Einführung in die Vergleichende Erziehungswissenschaft* (Salzburg: Otto Müller Verlag, 1947).

2. *Educational Yearbook of the International Institute of Teachers' College*, ed. I. L. Kandel (New York: Columbia University, 1924–1944).

The Yearbook of Education (London: Evans Brothers, 1934–1940 and 1948–1952; New York: World Book Co., 1953–).

3. *International Review of Education.* 1931–1934, Editor: Friedrich Schneider. Since 1955, Editors Karl W. Bigelow, Roger Gal, M. J. Langeveld, Walter Merck, Friedrich Schneider (The Hague: Martinus Nijhoff).

Comparative Education Review. The Official Organ of the Comparative Education Society. Editor: George Z. F. Bereday, Teachers College, Columbia University, New York.

4. *The New York Times Index. The Master Key to the News.* Issued continuously since January 1913 (New York: The New York Times Co.).

Index to the Times (London: The Times Publishing Co., Ltd.).

5. For the present, consult the various publications of UNESCO and of the United States Department of Health, Education and Welfare, Office of Education, Division of International Education. The publications of these two agencies are especially important for those who want to follow the events in new and emerging nations.

Very helpful are the various publications of the U.S. Office of Education under the title *Education Around the World* and *Information on Education Around the World*. These publications contain extensive bibliographical references to books and articles, especially: *Bibliography. 1958 Publications in Comparative and International Education.* (Studies in Comparative Education. July 1, 1959) and *Selected Bibliography of Recent Materials Related to International Education*, 1960.

Of great value are also the *Studies in Comparative Education*, edited by the U.S. Office of Education. Especially the issue: *Teaching in the Social*

Sciences and the Humanities in the U.S.S.R., with an article by Frederic Lilge on "The Study of Literature in the Soviet School."

See also the various *Proceedings of the Annual Conferences on Comparative Education*, edited by W. W. Brickman (New York: School of Education, New York University). Among them, especially, *The Teaching of Comparative Education*, 1955, with an article by George F. Kneller on "Recent Research in Comparative Education."

See also, *Comparative Education and Foreign Educational Service*, 1957, and *Research in Comparative Education*, 1959.

The student of comparative education should also read the various publications of the United Nations Economic and Social Council, especially the *Report of the Secretary-General of the United Nations and the Director-General of UNESCO* on "Teaching of the Purposes and Principles, the Structure and Activities of the United Nations and the Specialized Agencies in Schools and Other Educational Institutions of Member States." February 1960.

6. There are innumerable modern books that deal with the living conditions and cultural patterns of foreign populations. Many of them can be of great value for the study of comparative education. A masterpiece may be mentioned here: Laurence Wylie, *Village in the Vaucluse* (Cambridge: Harvard University Press, 1958).

Many countries provide various kinds of information and official documents on education, e.g., *The British Information Service*, an agency of the British Government; *Education in France*, New York French Cultural Services. Various publications have been issued by the Press and Information Office of the Federal German Government and by the Japanese Embassy to the U.S.A. See also bibliographical notes in chapter on Russia. Embassies or Legations and Consulates will always be helpful. Some of these publications are written for propaganda purposes and should be accepted with a degree of caution. George F. Kneller, *e.g.*, quotes in his aforementioned article the following statement from *Fifteen Years of Spanish Culture*, 1938–1952, published by the Madrid Diplomatic Information Office: "Spain is the country where the most intense intellectual life exists at the present day. It is, in fact, a great laboratory of progress, civilization, and culture." (p. 217)

7. For background reading, consult the standard histories dealing with the political and cultural development of the various countries.

Also:

1. Brameld, Thedore, *Cultural Foundations of Education. An Interdisciplinary Exploration* (New York: Harper & Brothers, 1957).

2. Brinton, Clarence Crane, *The Shaping of the Modern Mind*. The concluding half of *Ideas and Men* (New York: The New American Library of World Literature, 1959).

BIBLIOGRAPHICAL NOTES

3. Brubacher, John, *A History of the Problems of Education* (New York, McGraw-Hill, 1947).

4. Butts, R. Freeman and Cremin, Lawrence A., *A History of Education in American Culture* (New York: Henry Holt, 1953).

5. Emerson, Rupert, *From Empire to Nation; The Rise of Self-Assertion of Asian and African Peoples* (Cambridge: Harvard University Press, 1960).

6. Kallen, Horace Meyer, *Utopians at Bay* [on Israel] (New York: Theodor Herzl Foundation, 1958).

7. Randall, John Herman, *The Making of the Modern Mind. A Survey of the Intellectual Background of the Present Age* (Boston: Houghton Mifflin, 1940).

8. Reischauer, Edwin Oldfather, *Japan, Past and Present*, second edition, rev. and enl. (New York: Alfred A. Knopf, Inc., 1956).

9. Ulich, Robert, *History of Educational Thought* (New York: American Book Company, second edition 1950) and *Three Thousand Years of Educational Wisdom* (Cambridge: Harvard University Press, sixth printing, 1959).

Several of these books contain extended bibliographies.

Recent Publications

With the addition of Chapter XII, it becomes possible to add this listing of recent and pertinent books. Most of them have extensive bibliographies, should the reader wish to explore further in any one field.

General

Adams, Donald K. *Introduction to Education: A Comparative Analysis.* Belmont, Cal.: Wadsworth Publishing Company, 1966.

Bereday, George Z. F. *Comparative Method in Education.* New York: Holt, Rinehart and Winston, 1964.

Bereday, George Z. F., and Joseph A. Lauwerys. *The Education Explosion.* The World Yearbook of Education 1965. London: Evans Brothers, 1965.

Bowles, Frank. *Access to Higher Education*, vol. I. New York: Columbia University Press, 1963.

Cerych, Ladislav. *Problems of Aid to Education in Developing Countries.* New York: Frederick A. Praeger, 1965.

Comparative Education. Published three times a year since October 1964 (London: Pergamon Press).

Coombs, Philip H. *The Fourth Dimension of Foreign Policy: Educational and Cultural Affairs.* New York: Council on Foreign Relations and Harper & Row, 1964.

Cramer, John Francis, and George Stephenson Brown. *A Contemporary*

Study of National Systems, and ed. New York: Harcourt, Brace & World, 1965.

Curle, Adam. *Educational Strategy for Developing Societies*. London: Tavistock Publications, 1963.

Fraser, Stewart, ed. *Governmental Policy and International Education*. New York: John Wiley, 1965.

Hilker, Franz. *Vergleichende Pädagogik: Eine Einführung in ihre Geschichte, Theorie and Praxis*. München: M. Heuber, 1962.

Holmes, Brian. *Problems in Education: A Comparative Approach*. New York: Humanities Press, 1965.

International Conference on Public Education, XXVIII Session, 1965. Geneva and Paris: International Bureau of Education and UNESCO, 1965.

International Yearbook of Education, vol. 26, 1964. Geneva and Paris: International Bureau of Education and UNESCO, 1965.

Kazamias, Andreas M., and Byron G. Massialas. *Tradition and Change in Education: A Comparative Study*. New York: Prentice-Hall, 1965.

King, Edmund J. *World Perspectives in Education*. London: Methuen, 1962.

Lewis, L. J., and A. J. Loveridge. *The Management of Education: A Guide for Teachers in New and Developing Systems*. New York: Frederick A. Praeger, 1965.

Paedagogica Europaea 1965: The European Yearbook of Educational Research. Amsterdam and Brussels: Agon Elserier, 1965.

Parsons, Talcott, Edward Shils, Kaspar D. Naegele, and Jesse R. Pitts, eds. *Theories of Society*. New York and London: Free Press and Collier-Macmillan, 1965.

Piper, Don C., and Taylor Cole, eds. *Post-Primary Education and Political and Economic Development*. Durham: Duke University Press, 1964.

Röhrs, Hermann. *Die Reform—Pädagogik des Auslands*. Düsseldorf: Küpper, 1965.

Röhrs, Hermann. *Schule und Bildung im Internationalen Gespräch*. Stuttgart: Akademische Verlagsgesellschaft, 1966. Special Issue on Student Politics, *Comparative Education Review*, vol. 10, no. 2 (June 1966).

England

Alexander, Sir William. *Education in England. The National System—How It Works*, and ed. London: Newnes Educational Publishing Co., 1964.

Armytage, Walter H. G. *Four Hundred Years of English Education*. Cambridge: Cambridge University Press, 1964.

Baron, George. *Society, Schools and Progress in England*. Oxford: Pergamon Press, 1965.

Blyth, William A. L. *English Primary Education: A Sociological Description*. London: Routledge and Kegan Paul, 1965.

BIBLIOGRAPHICAL NOTES

The Bow Group. *Strategy for Schools.* London: The Conservative Political Centre, 1964.

Dancy, John C. *The Public Schools and the Future.* London: Faber & Faber, 1963.

Gross, Richard E., ed. *British Secondary Education. Overview and Appraisal.* London: Oxford University Press, 1965.

Jarman, Thomas L. *Landmarks in the History of Education: English Education as a Part of the European Tradition,* 2nd ed. London: John Murray, 1963.

MacLure, John Stuart, comp. *Educational Documents: England and Wales, 1816–1963.* London: Chapman & Hall, 1965.

Ogilvie, Robert Maxwell. *Latin and Greek: A History of the Influence of the Classics on English Life from 1600 to 1918.* London: Routledge and Kegan Paul, 1964.

Ottaway, Andrew K. C. *Education and Society: An Introduction to the Sociology of Education,* 2nd ed. London: Routledge and Kegan Paul, 1962.

Pedley, Robin. *The Comprehensive School.* Baltimore: Penguin Books, 1963.

Taylor, William. *The Secondary Modern School.* London: Faber & Faber, 1963.

Wilkinson, Rupert. *The Prefects: British Leadership and the Public School Tradition.* A Comparative Study in the Making of Rulers. London: Oxford University Press, 1964.

France

Alain. *Propos sur L'Education.* Paris: Presses Universitaires de France, 1963.

Bloch, M.-A. *La Pédagogie des Classes Nouvelles.* Paris: Presses Universitaires de France, 1953.

Cacérès, Benigno. *Histoire de l'Éducation Populaire.* Paris: Editions du Seuil, 1964.

Chateau, Jean. *École et Éducation,* 2nd ed. Paris: Librairie Philosophique J. Vrin, 1964.

Corgniot, Georges. *Laïcité et Réforme Démocratique de l'Enseignement.* Paris: Éditions Sociales, 1963.

Cros, Louis. *The "Explosion" in the Schools.* Paris: Sevpen, 1963.

Fraser, W. R. *Education and Society in Modern France.* London: Routledge and Kegan Paul, 1963.

Halls, W. D. *Society, Schools and Progress in France.* Oxford: Pergamon Press, 1965.

Natanson, Jacques, and Antoine Prost. *La Révolution Scolaire.* Paris: Les Editions Ouvrières, 1963.

EDUCATION OF NATIONS

Schneider, Christian W. *Neue Erziehung und Schulwesen in Frankreich.* Heidelberg: Quelle und Meyer, 1963.

Germany

Edding, Friedrich. *Bildung und Politik.* Pfullingen: Neske, 1965.

Edding, Friedrich. *Oekonomie des Bildungswesens: Lernen und Lehren als Haushalt und als Investition.* Freiburg: Rombach, 1963.

Grimm, Suzanne. *Die Bildungsabstinenz der Arbeiter.* München: J. A. Barth, 1966.

Picht, Georg. *Die Deutsche Bildungskatastrophe.* Freiburg: Walter-Verlag, 1964.

The United States

American Education. Published in Washington, D.C., by the U.S. Department of Health, Education and Welfare. Vol. I., no 1 (January 1965 and later numbers).

Brickman, William W. *Educational Systems in the United States.* New York: Center for Applied Research in Education, 1964.

Butts, R. Freeman. *American Education in International Development.* New York: Harper & Row, 1963.

Cremin, Lawrence A. *The Genius of American Education.* Pittsburgh: University of Pittsburgh Press, 1965.

Frankel, Charles. *The Neglected Aspect of Foreign Affairs: American Educational and Cultural Policy Abroad.* Washington, D.C.: The Brookings Institution, 1966.

French, William Marshall. *America's Educational Tradition: An Interpretive History.* Boston: D. C. Heath, 1964.

Hartford, Ellis Ford. *Education in These United States.* New York: Macmillan, 1964.

Keppel, Francis. *The Necessary Revolution in American Education.* New York: Harper & Row, 1966.

King, Edmund J. *Another Society: Schools and Progress in the U.S.A.* Oxford: Pergamon Press, 1965.

Norton, John Kelley. *Critical Issues in American Public Education.* Pittsburgh: University of Pittsburgh Press, 1965.

Rudy, Solomon Willis. *Schools in an Age of Mass Culture.* Englewood Cliffs, N.J.: Prentice-Hall, 1965.

Thayer, Vivian Trow. *Formative Ideas in American Education: From the Colonial Period to the Present.* New York: Dodd, Mead, 1965.

Welter, Rush. *Popular Education and Democratic Thought in America.* New York: Columbia University Press, 1962.

Wingo, Glenn Max. *The Philosophy of American Education.* Boston: D. C. Heath, 1965.

BIBLIOGRAPHICAL NOTES

Russia

Anweiler, Oskar. *Geschichte der Schule und Pädagogik in Russland vom Ende des Zarenreiches bis zum Reginn der Stalin-Aera.* Heidelberg: Quelle und Meyer, 1964.

Bereday, George Z. F., and Jaan Pennar, eds. *The Politics of Soviet Education.* New York: Frederick A. Praeger, 1960.

Bereday, George Z. F., William W. Brickman, and Gerald H. Read, eds. *The Changing Soviet School.* Boston: Houghton Mifflin, 1960.

Bowen, James. *Soviet Education. Anton Makarenko and the Years of Experiment.* Madison: The University of Wisconsin Press, 1962.

Deineko, M. *Public Education in the U.S.S.R.* Moscow: Progress Publishers, 1964.

Grant, Nigel. *Soviet Education.* Baltimore: Penguin Books, 1964.

Kassof, Allen. *The Soviet Youth Program: Regimentation and Rebellion.* Cambridge, Mass.: Harvard University Press, 1965.

Möbus, Gerhard. *Unterwerfung durch Erziehung.* Zur Politischen Pädagogik im Sowjetisch Besetzten Deutschland. Mainz: Hase und Koehler, 1965.

Redl, Helen B., ed. *Soviet Educators on Soviet Education.* New York: The Free Press of Glencoe, 1964.

Rosen, S. M. *Significant Aspects of Soviet Education.* Washington, D.C.: U.S. Department of Health, Education and Welfare, 1965.

Roucek, Joseph S., and Kenneth V. Lottich. *Behind the Iron Curtain.* The Soviet Satellite States — East European Nationalisms and Education. Caldwell, Idaho: The Caxton Printers, 1964.

Shapovalenko, S. G., ed. *Polytechnical Education in the USSR.* Paris: UNESCO, 1963.

Index

INDEX

INDEX

INDEX

INDEX

INDEX

INDEX

INDEX